JESUS
the Man and the Myth

£3

JESUS

the Man and the Myth

A Contemporary Christology

JAMES P. MACKEY

SCM PRESS.LTD

334 00772 0

First published 1979
by SCM Press Ltd
58 Bloomsbury Street, London

Photoset by Input Typesetting Ltd
and printed in Great Britain by
Richard Clay Ltd, Bungay, Suffolk

FOR NOELLE
MY WIFE

I should like to acknowledge my debt to Professor Gerard Watson, who read the whole manuscript, and to Professors John H. Elliott and Hamilton Hess, who read parts of it, for their constructive criticism and encouragement.

Contents

viii

Introduction

This book is not written primarily for scholars. The issues concerning the person and the significance of Jesus which recent scholarship has raised are of some importance – and still, I hope, of some interest – to a range of people which extends far beyond the professional historians, exegetes and theologians. I myself imagine that range of people to extend from the pastoral priest through the seminarian, the professed religious and the catechist, to the inquiring lay-person, and I think that my experience of such people justifies me in imagining such a varied and extensive range of relevance. So, the book which I here argue is needed is a book which explains to a range of people reaching far beyond the rather closed ranks of professional scholars, in a language more accessible to these than the technical jargon quite justifiably used by the scholars, the central problems and the tentative solutions which have accrued in recent times to the perennial quest for the spirit of Jesus.

Indeed, at a time when the catalogues of those publishing houses still brave enough to publish works of Christian theology are already saturated with books about Jesus, a fairly persuasive reason for importuning the public interest with yet another one is more than desirable. Studies of a more general religious nature, studies in the philosophy of religion, for instance, or in the history of religions or on the nature of religious experience, nowadays find a more welcoming market. Nor can the writer of still one more book about Jesus use any of the excuses normally at the disposal of writers of other books on almost any other topic. He cannot claim that new evidence has appeared which demands a substantial revision of all past and present interpretations of this historical character. Such an excuse can always be expected from the results of continuing space probes by writers on the prospects of extra-terrestrial life; or from the discoveries of new and intriguing sub-atomic particles by wonderers about the nature of the physical world in which we live; and who knows what Odluvai might not yet disgorge? In fact, not many decades ago, scholarly hearts were set thumping by the discovery of the Dead Sea Scrolls, some in fervent expectation that new data could now be added to the meagre enough information about Jesus in his own time, others in equal trepidation that the prevailing features of our traditional picture of Jesus might be deeply disturbed. Nothing of the kind happened, though the discovery has contributed much to our essential knowledge of the cultural background against which we can best understand the writings of the followers of Jesus, the New Testament. So, if the writer of yet another book about Jesus is at his wit's end for an excuse, he would be a foolish man to wait for an excuse of that particular kind.

Partly because of the fact that it seemed to have little or nothing directly to do with military strategy, political ingenuity, economic expertise, business enterprise, educational theory, international affairs, the arts and crafts, agricultural methods, manual labour, seafaring, athletics, or horse-training ... in a word, partly because of the fact that it seemed to have little or nothing directly to do with any of those things which most commonly occupy people who want to get on in the world, the life of Jesus found very few who reacted favourably to its message, and fewer still who thought any part or aspect of it worth recording in the written word which remains. Religion has ever been of marginal interest to humanity. And even the peripheral attention it receives, it owes primarily to its willingness to play the part of a docile domestic pet, the principal purpose of which is to assure its owner that he is in control of his situation in life. Religious people who tend to disturb the state of a nation are quickly begrudged even such passing notice as they might normally expect; and if they are very good at this their fellow humans will simply rid themselves of their persons and their memories.

No, it is not too likely that new evidence about Jesus is about to turn up in any significant amount.

Still, for all that, Christianity *is* an historical religion. That is an oft-repeated statement. And of all the things it has meant to those who repeat it – when, that is, it has meant anything at all – it must surely sometimes have meant this: that the Christian faith is more closely bound to the person of its founder than any other faith living or dead, or, to put the matter the other way round, that the actual person of Jesus of Nazareth, its historical founder, is more central to the Christian confession of faith than is the founder of any other religion to its formulated confessions. The Buddhist need not confess Gautama Siddartha his Lord, much less his God, and the Parsee proffers no such claims about Zoroaster. Muhammed was the prophet of Allah; he was the one who uttered to the human race the truths of Allah, but he did not think himself, nor was he thought to be, their subject. So whatever else the statement that Christianity is an historical religion may mean, it must certainly mean that the actual person of its founder is infinitely more at the centre of, infinitely more of the essence of the Christian religion than is the case with the actual historical founder of any other of the world's great religions.

Now that scarcely disputable fact would certainly seem to the ordinary person to carry one fairly obvious inference, namely, that the Christian had better be a good historian if he is to present and justify his faith as the following of Jesus and more especially if he is to claim that his faith involves at its very centre belief in Jesus himself. For if Columbus had been not merely the first to discover America (in itself a highly disputable claim: the Irish almost certainly did it first), but the first to define, exemplify and decree what to this day has been known as the American way of life, the American public would have very little patience with scholars who kept on expounding the extreme difficulty of saying anything at all historically reliable about Columbus, and did very little else. They would presumably have even less patience with a scholar who told them that in any case the historical investigation of the sayings and doings of Columbus was quite irrelevant to an attempt to understand the American way of life, and quite irrelevant also to any decision to adhere to it or to continue to adhere to it. And in this example Columbus is not himself the subject of a religious confession, that is to say, he is not identified with the Ground of Being who, in the religious person's view of things, gives ultimate validity to a suggested life-style. Yet the one scholar who straddles, like a Colossus, the world of contemporary Jesus studies, has told us that the quest of the historical Jesus is irrelevant to the faith of Christians. After a lapse of almost two centuries, during which time the scholarship industry proved to be the source of a swelling stream of revisionary material on our traditional image of Jesus, Rudolf Bultmann finally popularized the idea that the faith of the Christian should in no way find itself dependent on the labours of the historian.

However, the perceptive person in the street, if he or she bothers to notice such matters at all, will notice that the increasing scepticism which seemed to accompany the historical quest was and is equalled only by the persistent interest shown in it. The old quest of the historical Jesus, just when it was deemed to have met its most decisive failure, was followed by a new quest – for all that Bultmann could say or do. And the enormous influence which Bultmann has exercised over the contemporary study of Jesus is certainly not due to his making a mistake; one seldom becomes a Colossus, and one more seldom remains one, by making a mistake, even a colossal mistake. There is, as we must see, a kernel of truth in what Bultmann has to say, especially in what he has to say about the content of New Testament documents; and the kernel is always, after all, the heart of the matter. So the historical search for the essential Jesus careers along on its unsteady way. Whenever you see people persist at something while all the time complaining how hopeless it all is, and how unnecessary therefore it ought to be, you know that they are on to something of essential importance to them. So, if the prospective writer of yet another book about Jesus cannot reasonably expect a new piece of historical evidence to turn up in time to justify his project, neither by the nature of the case can he turn purely creative and make himself a Jesus for the times, whatever or whoever Jesus himself may have been in his time.

Because, then, it has felt so bound to the person of Jesus, and because it has felt it has good reason to ignore the possibility of any new data about his person and programme emerging from the mists of history, the Christian tradition has always seen christology – that is, the study of Jesus as the Christ of God – as an exercise in recovery. But recovery, it may be noted, has two meanings. It can mean to re-cover, as one covers the same ground over and over and over again; and Christians have always done this, like a long line of Robinson Crusoes tracing the tracks that lead along the sands of time to Man Friday on a cross. If that, however, were all that Christians had done, and the whole of what they meant by recovery, it would soon have become boring to Christians themselves, and more boring still to the onlookers, even to the most curious of these. But each Robinson Crusoe occupies his own island in time, each with his own mental climate, his own needs (or his own version of the common human need), and his own expectations. And recovery can also be taken in the sense of issuing something into circulation once more, of bringing or coming back into use. The metaphor here is not so much that of covering an old piece of furniture with some new material – as some new theology has simply covered outmoded thoughts in new words in order to make them seem somehow contemporary. The metaphor is rather that of recovering from a period of inactivity, whatever the cause of that inactivity may have been, or recovering something lost, or mislaid, or something from which for some time, again for whatever reason, one had been unable really to benefit.

Each age has set out on the tracks of Jesus of Nazareth with its own concerns uppermost in mind. So far, each age has found, sometimes to its surprise, that the same Jesus, discovered by following exactly the same tracks that every age has followed and that nobody really thinks can be replaced, speaks to its own distinctive form of the deepest human concerns. To recover, then, can also mean to look to Jesus, or for Jesus, while having in mind the distinctive concerns of the contemporary world. In this aspect of the quest, and only in this – but truly in this – the prospect of newness and of the absence of boredom exists. No one, of course, who prescinds for a moment from his or her own commitment to Jesus can give an absolute guarantee that no age will ever outgrow Jesus. Indeed, at a time when some of the more intelligent analysts of the contemporary scene are already talking about a post-Christian era, no one should set out on the quest with an absolute guarantee that the present age has not outgrown him. But the heady prospect that this age might still not be able to declare both buried *and* dead this strange man who was so insignificant to the world into which he was born, but whom successive centuries did not succeed in confining to the tomb of the first century named after him, is more than sufficient to set many a modern person, with all contemporary concern, on the ancient quest once more.

What are the distinctive concerns of contemporary people? One could, I suppose, answer quite simply: humanity itself, or the human. But one would immediately have to anticipate some misunderstandings of this pithy reply. One cannot mean to suggest that the present age is more human, in the sense of more humanitarian, than any previous age, even the most so-called primitive. On the contrary, man's ancient inhumanity to man seems only to have increased with his coming of age. And only someone who knew so little history that he or she had never heard of Protagoras, a Greek Sophist of the fifth century BC, would be tempted to think that it must have been a twentieth-century sage who gave currency to the adage, 'man is the measure of all things'. Yet, just as fifth-century (BC) Athens is not unsimilar to twentieth-century Western civilization, at least in the troubles of its wars and rumours of wars and the burgeoning of its information, so the adage is not altogether inept to express the characteristic mentality of contemporary Western peoples. To an extent undreamt of even by Protagoras, modern people have been inundated with information about their ever-receding origin from species already evolved in this world and about the lengthening odyssey to the present point in time and space. They have been constantly amazed by the variety of life-styles, exhilarated by the succession of growing achievements, and appalled by the tragedies of continuing failures. People nowadays are impressed by an increasingly detailed awareness of the long and varied history of their kind. They are conscious of this history as an irreversible process which has seen the emergence of human nature from the darkness of superstition, the need of magic, the oppression of the preternatural. They talk of the emergence of human nature as the dominant factor within this world and the dominant power for this world's future. The rights of human nature are as prominent in the increasingly democratic political movements of our era as are the ingenuity and adaptability of human nature in science and technology. Political movements and science-technology are the twin areas which have registered our greatest advances; and they have also recorded the greatest tragedies of our modern world. There is something extremely enigmatic about that. But we are more and more convinced that humanity is the key to the future, and in an age the mentality of which is so evolutionarily and historically conditioned, we more and more suspect that its history provides a key to human nature, to what humanity is and can yet be. Humanity and its history: that is the privileged perspective of contemporary people, no matter where or at what they are asked to look; and that is now also their particular form of the human concern.

This fascination with the human and the historical has been totally characteristic of the main tradition of atheistic philosophy, the principal philosophical alternative to Christianity in the modern period. A century has passed since Feuerbach said that religion was nothing other than humanity's consciousness of the infinite possibilities of human nature itself disguised as the worship of a transcedent God. Less than a century has passed since Marx, who also said that religion was humanity's recognition of itself by a kind of detour, took Feuerbach to task on the grounds that human nature is not something abstract to be described in purely conceptual or ideological fashion; it is something concrete, something to be seen in the web of socio-economic relationships, outside which it does not exist and which alone truly define it. Since then Marx has been criticized, even by some Marxists, on the grounds that he held a too deterministic view of the way in which factors of political economy shaped human nature, and in time changed it for the better. Humanity, it is now realized by Marxists like Ernst Bloch, has had a much more hazardous history and has a much more open future than Marx could have understood. Since humanity seems to be at once the disconcertingly unpredictable maker of history and also its product, human nature can only be known from its unique involvement with history, from its continuing story. Christians may not find this Hegelian-Marxist humanism much to their liking, but they would be ill-advised to minimize the attraction for the modern mind of its concentration of humanity's natural prospects within the perspective of humanity's own history.

At their best, modern people do not take the adage, 'man is the measure of all things', to mean that they will accept nothing and wish to know nothing which the human race itself has not produced or discovered – though, of course, they are often not at their best. But they do mean at least this: that whatever is offered to them at this time, they must see to be intrinsically related to humanity and its story, that is to say, to the human and the historical. They cannot be invited to go anywhere, and they will not follow anyone, unless they are allowed to start with humanity and its story, with the human and the historical. They may, of course, be led beyond this but since it is now the underlying theme of all their thoughts and their dominant concern, they will not be led away from it.

Christian leaders and Christian scholars have not ignored the temper of the times. Christians live in the world, like everybody else, and they have never altogether detached themselves from its changing concerns. So one finds quite commonly nowadays, not only a keen Christian interest in problems of justice and peace, not only a general Christian willingness to come to terms at last with prevailing philosophies of life, but also a tendency to channel research on the founder of Christianity towards that

particular form of the human concern already indicated in the
phrase, humanity and history.

A colleague of mine who is a Lutheran priest sometimes
remarks that in his seminary days courses were commonly called 'The History of X' (the Church, Grace, etc.), but when he
joined the theology faculty of our Roman Catholic university he
found that the same courses were now commonly called 'The
Mystery of X' (the Church, Christ, etc.). It is certainly true that
scholars from the main Reformation traditions have long pursued historical research into the origins, the founder, and the
development of Christianity. That is one of their great contributions to contemporary Christianity, and most of the historical
scholarship to which the first chapter and indeed the rest of this
book is indebted is theirs. But Catholics of the Roman persuasion, too, have recently come a little closer to their colleagues
from other Christian traditions, even in christology. They may
be as devoted to mystery as ever, but at least they now approach
this mystery of Christ from an angle which is for them quite
unprecedented: they approach the mystery of Christ through a
growing appreciation of his complete and undiluted humanity.
And this new angle of approach has required of Roman Catholics an intensity in their study of scripture and history which they
have not often before experienced. Lachenschmid wrote in a
survey of modern christology in Volume 3 of *Bilanz der Theologie
im 20. Jahrhundert* (Herder: Freiburg 1970): 'The principal problem of catholic christology in the twentieth century lies in the
endeavour to understand the true human being of Jesus the
Christ. Almost all of the individual questions (in christology
today) are part of this endeavour.'

So there it is again: history and humanity, humanity and its
history.

We are the last (thus far) of a long line of Robinson Crusoes
following always the same footprints back along the sands of
time. There are no new footprints to follow: no new evidence
about Jesus emerges. And we too find the same enigmatic Man
Friday hanging on his cross. But it is our own distinctive form of
the deepest human concern that drives us back along that
ancient trail once more; though it is the same hope that drives
us, the hope that he may still have something to say to our
particular experience of the human predicament, the hope that,
against all odds, he may still be able to do something about it. In
a world divested now of preternatural agents and recurrent
divine intervention we puzzle over the prospects of humanity,

and we puzzle over these prospects primarily in this world and in this history, rather than in some life other than this. In such distinctiveness of the changing forms of the human concern lies the only justification for new books about Jesus of Nazareth.

1

The Problem of the Quest of the Historical Jesus

Humanity and its continuing history. Such is the preferred perspective with which the modern enquirer sets out on the quest of the historical Jesus. And we seem to have identified it. Shall we set off, then?

Perhaps it would be wise to pause for a moment before setting out on that ancient quest once more. We are not the first modern questers to have travelled back along the well-worn trail. And it might be well for us to be aware of some disturbing rumours that have recently begun to circulate amongst practised questers and would-be questers alike. Rumour has it that the quest of the historical Jesus, to be quite blunt about it, is hopeless. And by far the most discouraging feature of this rumour is the fact that it really began to spread only after history had come into its own as a science, only after the quest of the historical Jesus, as a consequence, could at last be called a truly scientific enterprise.

It was just about two centuries ago, as the survey contained in the present chapter will show, that people began to pride themselves on bringing at last to academic christology the scientific methods of the historian. Previous to the eighteenth century, it was felt, people had built their portraits of Jesus from all kinds of unscientific assumptions. Small wonder if false Christs had appeared in Christian devotion and Christian literature. Small wonder if different Christs had appeared at different times and places or in different Christian traditions. The modern questers set out with the calm confidence that by the use of the trusty methods of scientific history the real Jesus could at last be made to stand up. And with the same calm confidence they produced first one portrait of Jesus ... and then another ... and then another, each disturbingly different from the one before, as the following survey will show.

Pessimism spread far beyond the confines of professional scholarship: the 'real' Jesus could not really be found. Sometimes the pessimism found its expression in a misunderstood sentence of Albert Schweitzer, to the effect that there is nothing more negative than the result of the critical study of the life of Jesus. Sometimes it did not seem like pessimism at all, for it took the form of Bultmann's defiant manifesto on faith's independence of the historian's labours. We shall see shortly that no sentence which Schweitzer wrote has been more misunderstood – by me also, I must confess – for though he thought that previous modern questers had gone wrong, he was just as confident as any of them had ever been that he could finally get the story of Jesus right. We shall have to try to come to grips with Bultmann later.

For the moment I wish only to say this: it is obviously of some importance for us to know, before we set out on our own quest, why this modern quest of the historical Jesus, heralded and pursued as it was by expressions and attitudes of such calm confidence, gave rise in the end to such rumours of probable failure.

I think it is true to say that in the popular mind, if not in the minds of many students of the Christian sources themselves, the fault, in this apparent failure, is thought to lie with the sources and not with the students. Consider for a moment the following series of general admissions concerning the state of the sources from which the quest of the historical Jesus must either succeed or fail: that Jesus himself left no written records; that the earliest written account of the movement he started comes from the pen of a man, Paul, who to the best of our knowledge never met him in the flesh, and who begins to write about him some twenty years after his death; that the only writings, the gospels, as they are called, which purport to give any substantial information about his life, are written from about AD 70, about forty years after his death, to the nineties of the first century; that the writers of these four works, though the tradition from an early time named them as apostles (Matthew and John) or close associates of the apostles (Mark and Luke), are really unknown to us apart from their works, and are almost certainly neither apostles nor close associates of known apostles, that apart from the writings of the New Testament, which range in date from about AD 50, to well into the second century, and

which are all written by convinced followers of Jesus to persuade others to follow him, only the barest references to his
existence can be gleaned from other writings of the time.

To all of this add the inconsistencies, of which there is no
shortage even in the synoptic gospels of Mark, Luke and
Matthew, which are supposed to reveal interdependence of a
kind, and the impression seems only to be increased that the
difficulties with the quest of the historical Jesus are after all of a
purely historical nature. By that I mean, they are the kind of
difficulties which a trained historian, fully conscious of the principles and methods of his science and of the source requirements for a confident conclusion, would find rather dismaying if
he or she considered the sources for the quest of the historical
Jesus.

Yet, before we accept this view of the matter and consider, as
a consequence, that any further involvement in the quest would
be rather futile, let us investigate another possibility. I personally believe that much of the present disenchantment with the
modern quest of the historical Jesus is due, not to the kind of
inadequacies which a professional historian might find in the
source of material – for in this case, in spite of the characteristics
just outlined, the source material is adequate to our purpose; the
disenchantment is due, rather, to the persistence of questers in
bringing to this material their own varying expectations and
each seeing a different expectation fulfilled.

Each generation of questers, it has already been observed, sets
out from its own form of the deepest human concern. Now there
lies a hazard which is not always recognized for what it is, partly
because there also lies the prospect of newness and the perennial excitement of the quest. Jesus, whatever else one may say
about him, has to do with the religious dimension of human life,
and that dimension, whether one accepts any or none of the
religions of the race, is where the deepest forms of the human
concern are faced. So, atheist or believer, agnostic or fanatic, we
each of us already have some formed mentality about the deepest human concern and about the way in which it should be
tackled. And this mentality, all the more powerful because it is
usually unconscious, produces those assumptions and expectations, presuppositions and even prejudices, which interfere
with the source material and prevent it from yielding its most
reliable conclusions.

The best way to prevent such preformed mentalities from
abusing our source material, and from producing portraits of

Jesus which owe more to the bias of the student than they do to the source material studied, is to become explicitly aware of them and to make allowances for them. But this, of course, is easier said than done. Bias would scarcely be bias if allowance could so easily be made for it. We have already noticed that fascination with the human and the historical forms the basic mentality of modern questers because it provides the most common bias of modern people. But we will scarcely be able to deal with this mentality effectively if we do no more than speak of it in such general terms; and we can never sense its real power if we dispose of it so briefly in an introductory section.

For 'the human' is a very general category indeed, and what people have considered human and inhuman, sub-human and superhuman, has varied rather consistently with successive centuries and with differing cultures. But biases are deep and pervasive things and need close attention to their specific details. I really see no alternative, therefore, for prospective questers of the historical Jesus, to a preliminary survey of the origins and specific contours of the modern mentality and of the way in which its changing forms have affected the varied portraits of Jesus that have recently emerged. Only the rest of this chapter, and indeed, the rest of this book can show if it is true to say that the subjective prejudices of the students are more responsible for the disturbing differences in the portraits of Jesus than is the condition of the sources. And only a fairly detailed analysis of the history of our modern mentality can alert us prospective questers to its true power and its specific influence upon our chosen task.

So I propose to review in this present chapter the main origins of our modern evolutionary-humanist mentality and the changing forms of its influence on the quest of the historical Jesus. Of course, surveys of the modern history of the quest of the historical Jesus rather commonly preface modern christologies, and particularly they preface those contemporary quests which the hardier scholars still pursue. But it is not always certain that their full preparatory value is understood, especially in alerting us to the presence of the modern bias, whatever form it takes in our own minds. Hence I intend to differ a little in the manner in which I present my own introductory survey. The main difference will be found in the place I give to great modern philosophers in the otherwise well-inspected ranks of professional scholars of the Christian scriptures. For just as it is the philosopher's distinction to be able to give critical expression to the otherwise diffuse mentality of an age, revealing its epistemological structure and charting its furthest logical implications, so it is the philosopher who can best uncover for us those deep mental biases which affect the historical scholars of an era to an extent of which even the latter are seldom aware.

Humanity come of age

It is often said that when Rome conquered the Greek empire, it was itself conquered by Greek culture. It is probably generally true that in such total conflicts, where nothing less than civilization is the bone of contention, nobody walks away complete victor. The Goths and Vandals who actively assisted at the death-throes of one of the finest civilizations the world has known, the Roman, could never themselves be the same again. Such total conflicts can only be compared to an act of piracy on the high seas in which the battle is so bitter and all the goods and lives involved are so much in question that the survivors, themselves now a mixture of attackers and attacked, can manage to leave the scene only by clinging to whatever spars are still afloat after the wreckage of both their structures. Indeed, this metaphor is not at all inept to describe the attitude and behaviour of people of the Middle Ages. For all the dialectical subtlety of their most brilliant minds, there is in these ages a reverence for ancient authorities, and particularly a reverence for the Bible as an accepted depository of revealed truth which would keep people's minds from drowning in doubt and confusion, such as can only remind one of people clinging to spars in an uncertain sea. Even in the thirteenth century, the high point of the Middle Ages, Aquinas, one of the most innovative and powerful minds of Western civilization, still seems to us surprisingly reverential towards ancient authorities, both philosophical and theological.

In the next great period of European culture normally delineated in the text-books, the Renaissance, which can be dated from the fourteenth century to the seventeenth at least, the case is at first little different. Cassirer has summed up the whole programme of the Renaissance in two words, the *studia humanitatis*, human pursuits, and indeed that tiny phrase gives prophetic insight into the future dominant interests of Europeans. But at the beginning of this new cultural movement, people still look to the past. In fact a peculiar ambiguity emerges in the struggle for freedom from one authority, the church, while reverence grows for still more ancient authorities.

The creative art and literature of the early part of this period is in imitation of pagan Greece and Rome. That, however, already introduces an important difference into European affairs. With pre-Christian models to work on, some people are less and less convinced of the necessity of the Christian Bible as revealed truth in order to protect them from the worst effects of their own native ignorance. So, when the human spirit begins to feel able to move forward on its own again, in whatever field, it may well be tempted to think that, just as it fared reasonably before Christianity arrived on the scene, it might fare even better after Christianity has left.

Whether that temptation actually materializes or not, of course, would depend on how official Christianity treated the new confidence and the growing creativity of the human spirit. How official Christianity did treat the new movement, in the case of its most prodigious representative, the scientist, we know only too well from the Galileo incident. Now, the emergence of modern science with men like Galileo and his part-contemporary, Newton, is by no means an optional example of humanity's renewed confidence in itself. Emerging science promised people as their own achievement, apparently limitless knowledge of the natural world. It initiated a new relationship between humanity and the natural world. Furthermore, it seemed to the philosophers, the ones who cultivated reason, and especially in the seventeenth century, to the father of modern philosophy, Descartes, to be the model for all correct reasoning. In the eighteenth century, when Immanuel Kant talks about knowledge and knowing strictly speaking, he will confine its possibility to the world of space and time, the sphere of the scientist.

Just as science is pivotal for Western people's recovery of confidence in themselves, so the meeting of the work of one of the fathers of modern science with the threat of the Inquisition is symptomatic of the stance of official Christianity in this era. The symptom indicates a disease which we may call the revelation complex. The revelation complex is not quite the same thing as a theoretical concept of revelation which theologians, amongst others, use and define in various ways. It is something that could be analysed better, and has been better analysed, by a sociologist like Peter Berger, than by a theologian. Briefly, it makes Christian officials behave as if but recently inherited forms of institution and ritual, creed and code were unchangeable formulations of an immutable God, identical with the content of the Bible. Consequently, it persuades the same officials to resist, with whatever means society places in their power at the particular time, independent probings of the human spirit which seem to touch on any of their very extensive domain.

These are but indications, crude in the extreme, of the kind of survey of European civilization which would make the eighteenth century intelligible, and with it the origins of the quest of the historical Jesus, the nature and history of which we must now trace. Some such survey would alone enable us to understand the power of the preferred adjectives of this century when it deals with religious faith: from the Renaissance, human as distinct from superhuman; from the rise of modern science, natural as opposed to the supernatural; from the philosophers, rational faith as against belief in mysteries. For this century, like those before and those after it, is interested in religious faith – religious faith being as inevitable a dimension of the experience of man as is the aesthetic or the moral. But because of the revelation complex of the official churches with their vested interest in the supernatural, the superman and the super-rational, and because of the power conferred on its preferred adjectives by the newly-awakened self-confidence of Western people, the interest of this age in religion becomes mainly critical of received formulae. Developing culture and ecclesiastical theology were on a collision course, as their different sets of prestige adjectives indicate, and this did not augur well for the prospects of objectivity in the portraits of Jesus produced by either side.

Hegel, who for all the convolutions of his philosophical thought was a very perceptive man, once had this to say about the biblical exegetes. 'The giving of the sense (of Scripture) means, however, the bringing forward of the sense into consciousness, into the region of ideas; and these ideas, which get determinate character elsewhere, then assert their influence in the exposition of the sense supposed to be contained in the words.' He meant that exegesis, the deriving of the sense of the biblical text, is always more eisegesis, or reading sense into a text, than the exegete would care to admit, or is even aware. The determinate character of the exegete's ideas, which inevitably stamps the expression of all his findings, does not come from the Bible, but from 'elsewhere': from the cultural thought-patterns of his time. And the philosopher, since this is his particular vocation and his contribution to the welfare of the race, is best equipped to bring these cultural thought-patterns to critical conscious awareness. We shall therefore begin our history of the modern quest of the historical Jesus, not with an exegete or a historian, but with a philosopher, Immanuel Kant, whose principal publications coincide roughly with the beginnings of the modern quest. There were other philosophers of the eighteenth century who expressed somewhat similar sentiments about reason and revelation, but none of quite his stature, and Hegel's influence belongs to the nineteenth century.

Philosophers and historians

In the preface to the first edition of his first great masterpiece, the *Critique of Pure Reason* (1781), albeit in a footnote, Kant served the summons of his age on religious faith that it could no longer refuse to appear before the court of critical human reason. 'Religion, on the strength of its sanctity, and law, on the strength of its majesty, try to withdraw themselves from it; but by so doing they arouse just suspicions, and cannot claim that sincere respect which reason pays to those only who have been able to stand its free and open examination.'[2] In 1793 Kant himself produced a work entitled *Religion Within the Limits of Reason Alone*, a work which he soon had to defend with uncharacteristic stoutness in a letter to the king, Friedrich Wilhelm II.[3] In the preface to the first edition of that work he declares himself willing to accept the censorship of the biblical theologian, provided only that the latter conduct himself as a university scholar and not as a pastor of souls lest, he says, the Galileo incident recur. He claims, however, that philosophical theology, or rational religion, which his writings represent, is of its nature independent. He holds that it occupies much ground in common with the religion of the Bible; and he even vindicates its right to use biblical texts, provided it uses these as illustrations of its own themes, and not as a means of doing covert biblical exegesis, thereby trespassing on the authority of the biblical theologian.

Some years later, when he was preparing a preface to a second edition of this same work – for the Age of Enlightenment was giving it quite a popular reception – Kant had grown much bolder. Now, in addition to considering revealed or biblical religion as a circular plane which contained within itself the smaller, concentric circle of natural or rational religion, he considered also the possibility of beginning with any given part of revealed religion and seeing if by analysis he could not find some theme of natural religion as its true content, so that, as he puts it, 'reason can be found to be not only compatible with Scripture but also at one with it'.[4] It is obvious that to Kant's mind this identity of revealed with rational religion will turn out to mean that the former is really nothing but the latter in disguise. That is obvious from the very lightly veiled threat to the effect that if such identity of content is not found and admitted, then we shall be in the presence of one religion (true, rational religion) and one cult, as he calls it, and these, when mixed, will be like oil and water, with the former always coming out on top. It is not that Kant, the representative of the rational, is categorically denying the very possibility of the supernatural, of miracle and mystery. What he is denying is that miracle and mystery could belong to the very essence of religion, to the inner nature of man's relationship to God which religion at once describes and attempts to forge. He writes of Jesus:

> The person of the teacher of the one and only religion, valid for all worlds, may indeed be a mystery; his appearance on earth, his translation thence, and his eventful life and his suffering may all be nothing but miracles; nay, the historical record, which is to authenticate the account of all these miracles, may itself be a miracle (a supersensible revelation). We need not call in question any of these miracles and indeed may honour the trappings which have served to bring into public currency a doctrine whose authenticity rests upon a record indelibly registered in every soul and which stands in need of no miracle. But it is essential that, in the use of these historical accounts, we do not make it a tenet of religion that the knowing, believing, and professing of them are themselves means whereby we can render ourselves well-pleasing to God.[5]

The essence of this religion, the authenticity of which rests upon a record indelibly registered in every soul, is morality, and that to Kant means the will to live according to precepts which can be precepts for all rational agents. It means, in Kierkegaard's language, to live in the universal. It means to eschew actions in pursuit of one's individual inclinations and to live only according to those laws which can govern the commonwealth of rational beings. Religion further involves the postulates which this experience of moral living inevitably and invariably arouses in the human spirit, the postulates that there be a supreme moral being, God, who would see to it, in the next life, that man's fate corresponded to his moral seriousness, as in this life too often it does not. This is the essence of a religion of reason, with respect to which miracle and mystery is at best adventitious.

In a sense, only a philosopher could propose such a view and call it Christian, and only someone who could consistently plead that such a view was purely philosophical could maintain a public teaching position in the Europe of the eighteenth century. What I mean by the first part of that sentence is this: only someone as obsessed by such a carefully circumscribed rational analysis of religion as a philosopher might be could possibly treat the supernatural, the miraculous, the revelatory which is woven into every single strand of the biblical tradition, in such a peripheral manner. What I mean by the second part of that sentence is best illustrated by the example of Reimarus.

Reimarus stands at the head of every account of the modern critical approach to the New Testament; he heads, as Peter did the apostles of old, the list of modern apostles who have set out to make known to men the real historical Jesus. What is not as frequently recognized is that he does this in the name of precisely the same understanding of the essence of true, rational religion so ably proposed by Immanuel Kant. Reimarus has the same view of religion as a pursuit of high moral values which will purify the soul (in itself, as reason knows, immortal) for an eternity of happiness with God. Most say he was influenced in this by the British Deists. In any case, in 1754 he wrote, and had published, a book entitled *The Principal Truths of Natural Religion*. To this St George the supernatural and the mysterious, miracles and mysteries of faith, were the dragons, and his favourite weapons were the adjectives 'rational' and 'natural' sharpened by the usually circumscribed definitions which the eighteenth century used on them.

It is this preconceived notion of a natural religion, rather than any objective historical method, which provides Reimarus with the searchlight for his quest and which discovers for him his clearest results. Nevertheless – and here one begins to notice his differences from Kant – he does wish to proceed as a historian. Humanity *and its story* begins to emerge as the preferred vantage point. And because Reimarus took himself to be a historian, as indeed for that age he was, he could not simply, as Kant did, allow that the supernatural occurred, but give it the status of a prop which is necessary sometimes for the beginnings of growth. A rational philosopher is quite a different animal from a rationalist who takes himself to be a historian. The philosopher might not care much for what may have happened in the past; the historian must and does.

This difference from the Kants of this world held two impor-

tant implications for the life and work of Reimarus. First, he has
to impugn the supernatural in all its interventions in the biblical
record. Common or garden variety miracles of loaves and fishes
are easily enough dismissed by a simple appeal to the usually
very self-conscious critical sense of the educated man: 'to discover whether miracles are true requires as much investigation
as the thing they are supposed to prove'.[6] (So miracles are to
prove something, but it is well nigh impossible to prove them.)
The more substantial interventions of the supernatural, though,
must be eradicated more thoroughly. These are the resurrection
of Jesus to the mysterious status of a divine saviour and the
ensuing mystery of the trinitarian nature of God. In order to
remove these he has to define carefully the extent, and the
limits, of the rational, that distinctive element in the definition of
the human being. Nothing which occurs outside these limits, no
matter how often recorded, can be part of the story of humanity.
'Unerring signs of truth and falsehood are clear, distinct consistency and contradiction.'[7] So he writes. Logical consistency,
then, is his criterion of truth. Before paying brief attention to his
application of this criterion, let us simply pause to notice that it
will function as a criterion only for one who, like Kant, has a
philosophy of life (in both moral and physical forms) totally
made up of unalterable universal laws of nature (including
human nature) and perhaps also of postulates which can be
drawn from experience of these, postulates which may concern
immortality and the existence of God. Only one who can presuppose such a philosophy can also regard logical consistency as
the criterion of truth and inconsistency as the indicator of falsehood. Most other people understand readily enough that to be
logically consistent is not necessarily to be true to reality, and
that inconsistency may be just a poor description of fidelity to
changing experience of changing situations. Something like this
is what I meant by referring to the carefully circumscribed
definitions of the rational which characterize this age. When
Europeans did finally regain full confidence in their own rational
resources, they still took too small a view of human nature and
human reason. It is often the case with those who recover from a
trauma that for some time after they have again become independent agents they are still very far from realizing their fullest
possibilities.

In any case, Reimarus has a field day on the inconsistencies
between the various resurrection narratives in the New Testament. This proves to his own manifest satisfaction, since incon-

sistency to him implies falsehood, that the record of this supernatural event is a blatant falsification, and so therefore is the
mystery of the divine saviour status of Jesus which he clearly
sees is connected with the resurrection in the New Testament.
With the supernatural and the mysterious extracted, what
remains of the New Testament record? What was the founder of
Christianity really like? Well, the historical Jesus was really not
the founder of Christianity at all, at least not of the Christianity
of the churches. Jesus anticipated, rather, in a remarkable manner the kind of understanding of religion which the century of
Reimarus most prized. The main intention of the historic mission of Jesus was to deepen and refine man's moral character in
order that man might repent and have his soul god-like. Jesus
accepted as a matter of course the 'essential elements of religion', namely, the doctrines of the salvation and immortality of
the soul. Beyond that, Jesus had absolutely no intention of
introducing new mysteries or additional religious rituals. His
endorsement of baptism and of the meal ritual meant no more to
Jesus himself than the adoption of optional Jewish practices.
Jesus did, however, also think of the result of his mission, the
inauguration of the reign of God, in the more material terms of
prosperity and peace here on earth – as there was ample prophetic precedent for him to do – and he did envisage himself as the
messianic king of this new era in human history. This additional
and more material aspect of his conception of the reign of God
amongst men brought two serious consequences in its wake.
First, it brought him to his death at the hands of the Roman
overlords of the land. Second, together with the disappointment
of his death, it made his closest followers feel so cheated that
they determined to have the prosperity in one way or another.
They therefore stole his body, invented the story of his resurrection, circulated the promise of his return from heaven, where,
they said, he was throned at the right hand of God, and in view
of all this they urged their converts to this falsehood to sell all
their goods and to give the proceeds to themselves, the apostles
of the new religion, a religion now replete with supernatural
interventions and mystifying mysteries.

This, then, is the very first historical Jesus available to us from
what has become known as the modern period of critical study
of the New Testament; although, if the word 'critical' means
more than 'objectionable to established opinion', if it means, as
modern philosophy from Descartes has taken it to mean, the
ability to question one's own concepts and categories as far as

questioning will go, nothing could be more uncritical than Reimarus's quest of the historical Jesus. Before commenting further on this matter, however, let us briefly record the second implication for his life's work of Reimarus's main difference from Kant. Because he had so contradicted the established image of the sacred books of the Judaeo-Christian tradition, and had done so precisely as historian and exegete, Reimarus realized that he could not hope to maintain his teaching position at Hamburg if he published *An Apologia or Defence for the Rational Worshipper of God*. Six years after his death in 1768, the German man of letters, Lessing, began to publish anonymously some fragments of that monumental work until, some four years later, the Duke of Brunswick put a stop to this posthumous promulgation. It is from the fragments which caused such a furore in their time, and specifically, from the sixth and seventh of them, that the above account of the historical Jesus has been drawn.

How to assess Reimarus? It seems important to do so because he has been called, not just the father of Life of Jesus research, but the father of modern biblical criticism even in its most advanced form, in the form of redaction criticism.[8] He has had the latter honour conferred on him because, it is said, in his study of the New Testament he showed the necessity of assuming a creative element in the tradition. That is to say, he brought to our attention the fact that the New Testament writers had concerns other than purely biographical ones in their treatment of Jesus. Perhaps we should accept this assessment of Reimarus and record our gratitude, though I personally feel at this point like a man who is asked to express gratitude to someone who has chopped off his head and thereby taken a major step toward solving his dandruff problem. It may well be that my dandruff problem came to general recognition only when my head rolled on the floor and some of the dandruff came off on the rug, but I still think the original step too drastic by ten for the result achieved, and I fear that expressions of gratitude might only tempt others to equally drastic action in pursuit of even slighter results.

Reimarus, whatever his intentions, is a hatchet-man. He destroys the source material he is trying to treat. Jesus was certainly a moral reformer, though not primarily that. Did he believe in the immortality of the soul in the kind of Platonic sense of Reimarus? Did he see himself as an earthly king? Were his closest followers charlatans, liars and thieves? The answer to all these questions is, no. Reimarus, the 'historian', in pursuit of the philosophical presuppositions of this age, reads all this into his sources. He simply falsifies what is actually in these sources. Is he then the one from whom we can begin to learn, what every historian would wish to know, the precise nature of the documents with which we are dealing? How could he be? Somebody whose method is as atrociously bad as his results indicate can hardly be a guide to the otherwise blind – or could some historian seriously suggest that correct methodological procedures can yet yield the worst results? If this is the father of modern critical historical and exegetical studies, the outlook for such studies must be poor indeed. It is quite possible that the people who thought of the New Testament writings as biographies of Jesus written to evoke faith were far closer to understanding the actual nature of these writings than was Reimarus. It would not have been the first time that conservatives, for all their pigheadedness and their penchant for persecution, were more clear-sighted than progressives.

It cannot seriously be maintained that Reimarsu is the father of modern biblical criticism. Someone who maintains that the New Testament material is the work of charlatans and liars, who still somehow allowed some of the true traits of the historical Jesus to slip through, is as likely to be the father of modern biblical criticism as Hitler is to be the father of the present democratic state of West Germany. It is possible, though, that Reimarus is the father of the modern quest of the historical Jesus – in so far as this can be distinguished, as we shall say it can, from the development of modern biblical criticism – but not, again, in any complimentary sense. The driving and consuming determination to find Jesus (not the Buddha or Zoroaster), and the real historical Jesus at that; the huge, quiet confidence with which his picture is painted when he is found; the wrongheadedness of the conclusions (comparable only to the confidence with which they are reached), which soon becomes obvious; these perhaps are the characteristics which make Reimarus the father of the modern quest of the historical Jesus. These characteristics do not suggest, primarily at least, that there is any distinctively historical difficulty about getting to know the real, historical Jesus. Some obstacle deriving from the researchers, philosophical or theological presuppositions, yes, but some obstacle deriving from the nature of scientific historical research and the nature of the subject it is here asked to treat is not suggested either by Reimarus's procedures or by his results.

Compared with Kant, Hegel extended considerably the understanding of human rationality, and therefore his understanding
of the human being as a rational animal; and nineteenth-century
European thought lay greatly under the influence of that great
philosopher. At first, in his early theological writings, Hegel's
assessment of the essence of Christianity and of the person of its
founder was very Kantian indeed. 'Jesus', he wrote, 'was the
teacher of a purely moral religion, not a positive one.'[9] But in
order to get this moral religion accepted, Jesus was forced to
defend his person and so to draw attention to his own personal
qualities and destiny; he even had to allow some messianic mis-
apprehensions of his mission because public expectation of a
new religious era were cast in such categories; and he even had
to perform as a thaumaturge. So 'just as the Jews made
sacrifices, ceremonies, and a compulsory faith into the essence
of religion, so the Christians made its essence consist in lip
service, external actions, inner feelings and a historical faith'.[10]
In other words, creeds (full of wonders and mysteries of Jesus
himself) and cult, such things as we have to accept from historical records, came to be confused with the essence of the Christian religion, instead of being seen to be, as Kant saw them,
merely adventitious factors which religion could do very well
without.

But Hegel was soon dissatisfied with a theory of the moral and
religious dimensions of man which comprised a morality the
sole criterion of which was the universal applicability of its precepts and then some postulates about God and an immortal
soul, neither of which could really be said to be known. As this
was not the place to give an account of the philosophical system
of Kant, so it is even less possible in a few pages to give even a
summary of the labyrinthine system of Hegel (if such a thing as
a summary of the System is even conceivable). One may simply
remark that Hegel's is a philosophy of Spirit; and that it is best
not to ask whether this is the Spirit of God or the spirit of man. It
seems best to say simply (if one can say anything simply when
Hegel is the subject) that spirit is something which we are all
somehow aware of – for in my very self-consciousness, however
poorly that may be developed, I know that I am more than
matter – and that in and through man spirit will come to full
consciousness of itself, and that will be the Absolute, at once
Absolute Idea or Reality and Pure Personality.

Hegel wants to know God. Kantian postulates do not satisfy
him. But it is important to understand the kind of knowledge of

God that Hegel wants. It is not the knowledge of God as an object, no matter how exalted or infinite an object; that is to say, it is not knowledge of God as something or somebody other than me which I can finally describe quite accurately. He wants knowledge of God as subject,[11] that is, the kind of knowledge which a subject has of itself when it is not any longer alienated or estranged from itself. That is again to say that the goal of Hegel's philosophy is spirit fully conscious of itself as its own self, not as somebody else's self, and certainly not as something which is not a self at all. Since it is spirit which is to reach this goal – indeed only when it does will it be truly spirit – and since this spirit is one, so that it makes no difference whether one calls it God or the spirit of man, its progress toward this goal can be described in religious language.

Already in one of his earliest writings Hegel traces in one pithy paragraph the three great stages through which man's spirit passes. First, in the child it is naively self-centred and at one with itself, but it understands nothing of its true relationship to its world; later, it begins to be, as we say, more objective, as its content is wholly taken up with others and other things and it does not even know its own self any more; finally, it does recognize itself in its world and it is reconciled to the world and to itself. Simply substitute the word 'God' for the mind or self or spirit in man which passes through these 'ages of man', and the analysis comes out in religious language of the most traditional kind, as in the paragraph already mentioned and now quoted:

> Everything lives in the Godhead, every living thing is its child, but the child carries the unity, the connection, the concord with the entire harmony, undisturbed though undeveloped, in itself. It begins with faith in gods outside itself, with fear, until through its actions it has (isolated and) separated itself more and more; but then it returns through associations to the original unity which now is developed, self-produced, and sensed as a unity. The child now knows God, i.e. the spirit of God is present in the child, issues from its restrictions, annuls the modification, and restores the whole. God, the Son, the Holy Spirit.[12]

Hegel was as anxious for the identity of faith with reason as was Kant or any other representative of the Age of Enlightenment; otherwise, he thinks 'religious feeling becomes yearning hypocrisy'.[13] But just as he is convinced that the biblical scholar cannot help but read the ideas of his time into the text he studies, he is equally convinced that the philosophical theologian, à la Kant, can reach nothing better than a concept of

God which is 'hollow, empty and poor'.[14] Just as inevitably as would-be exegetes become eisegetes, philosophers with their purely rational probes, isolated from the positive data of history, end up with an ultimately indefinable infinite something, a poor empty idea. (Indeed such is probably the kind of idea of God they will then read back into the Bible, some hollow Unmoved Mover, or some ultimately unintelligible Necessary Being.) Hegel's own solution to this dilemma is to take into his system fully and boldly the singular mysteries of the Christian faith – Incarnation, Atonement, Trinity ... All shall have their place and none will be omitted. So he can take from the Bible and from the Christian tradition what is actually there, and he need omit nothing that he finds in the historical texts, and his treatment of God will no longer be as hollow and empty and poor as is the God of the philosophers who went before him.

Notice, however, from the fate of the Trinity in the paragraph quoted above, and from the fate of similar mysteries of the faith in other paragraphs scattered throughout Hegel's work, the precise role these mysteries play in the System. The mystery of the Trinity expresses or relates the ages of man in its own way. First, spirit (God) is one with itself, then it immerses (or incarnates) itself in the world (God Incarnate or Son); finally, at the resurrection (for even Paul says that the risen Lord is the Spirit – II Cor. 3.17) the self recognizes itself simultaneously in its world and in itself, and it is truly spirit then, reconciled to its world and to itself, atoned or at-oned. The traditional, historic mysteries of the faith are intellectual symbols,[15] forged to express realities which do actually occur, but which could also be expressed in the adequate concepts of a truly adequate philosophical system (namely, the Hegelian). Understood in this way the mysteries indicate the true content that is in religious thought, and thus they drive one beyond the empty theological ideas of the 'rationalist' philosophers and the eisegete-exegetes who are their camp-followers.

The ages of man, which can be expressed in traditional religious formulae, describe the stages through which human kind passes just as well as they describe the stages through which each individual passes. But even when a particular civilization or culture reaches the highest stage of spirit and is, as it then must be, capable of expressing this in adequate philosophical concepts, such a culture still cannot simply eschew the mysteries of faith. People have imaginative faculties in their make-up as well as pure rational faculties; they are creatures of sentiment as much as they are intelligent. So they apprehend and express the reality of themselves and their world in the forms of art and religion as well as in the highest form of philosophy. Still, the fact that the ages of man describe the stages through which human kind passes means that the good Hegelian has at his fingertips a philosophy of history, and never just a history of philosophy, or a history of art, religion and philosophy. History for him moves through its ages and stages with all the regularity of the most conventional, if most intricate, dance.

Because Hegel is such a dominant figure in the nineteenth century, it is not at all surprising to find surveyors of the critical period of biblical studies refer to some of its nineteenth-century exponents as Hegelians, though I am personally sometimes baffled to know exactly what this appellation is meant to convey. Take, for example, Baur, who reflected for the greater part of his academic life on the contribution of history to the study of the origins and the nature of Christianity, and who is confidently called a Hegelian. Did he approach his task with a fully-fledged Hegelian philosophy of history? No he did not. For if he had, it would be Lutheran Christianity which would have come out as the high point of the development of the human spirit, in its religious mode of expression, and of this Jesus would have represented an earlier stage, a remote and lesser preparation. What, then? Well, there are themes in Baur which find sympathetic echoes in the works of Hegel, and in other works of that culture.

Baur will have nothing to do with supernaturalism, for instance. By this he means to indicate the view that the essence or founding structure of the Christian religion was pre-packaged in heaven for delivery here on earth so that, although some of its outward features can change, as people change on their way through time, it itself does not change and cannot. Supernaturalism means a religion replete with mysteries from heaven recommended by miracles on earth. Baur is equally opposed to rationalism, but on this point his sentences sound more like Hegel's strictures on the exegetes. He notices, quite correctly, that some scholars, like Reimarus, under the guise of telling us what is really revealed in a historical text, are merely revealing the prejudices of their own philosophical positions. History written by such men can never be more than a series of disjointed subjective viewpoints. He tries to steer between the Scylla of supernaturalism and the Charybdis of rationalism, as he calls it, by adopting a Hegelian philosophy of history, in short, by seeing history as the unfolding of Divine Spirit as it moves in and through the (distinct) spirit of man to its own self-realization in and reconciliation with the spirit of man. But, of course, he cannot really do this. The most that he can manage is the use of distinctively Hegelian terminology to clothe a different traditional Christian position.

For example, Baur wants to maintain that Jesus (the historical Jesus, surely) realized in himself the highest point of the development of the human spirit, that perfect unity of the human spirit with knowledge of the divine Spirit reconciled to it. Thus he wants to save the historical concreteness of the Christian faith in the actual and indispensable person of its founder. He is not naively unaware of the historical difficulty of doing this: he understands quite well that the New Testament documents are of a very special kind. 'The content of the New Testament,' he writes, 'cannot merely be made the presupposition of the history of dogma'; and 'the teaching of the apostles – if not also the teaching of Jesus itself, in so far as it is not immediately given – already belongs to the sphere of the historical movement of dogma.'[16] In other words, in the documents of the New Testament we are already dealing with material that has begun to reflect the change and movement through history (according to Hegelian laws) of the Idea of Christianity perfectly realized in Jesus.

The point, however, is this: if Baur pursued his project in fidelity to Hegel's philosophy of history, he would for ever be prevented from maintaining what he clearly wants to maintain, namely, that the historical Jesus realized in his person the goal of Spirit and thus founded the Christian faith. In other words, if Baur were really true to Hegel, his difficulty in making dogmatic texts yield reliable information about the historical Jesus would not ever have arisen. As far as Hegel's philosophy, and philosophy of history, is concerned, we have as little to thank Jesus for the possibility of the absolute goal of Spirit in history as we have to look to Jesus to find out what the goal is.[17] History moves mightily through the ages, but it is Spirit that moves according to its own intrinsic dialectic, and not any historic individual. It therefore seems obvious that Baur, the historian of Christianity, knows some things which the philosophy of history of a Hegel could never discover for him, and he then clothes these as best he can in the language of Hegel's philosophy.

Is it possible to generalize from this instance? Is it possible, once again, to say that when apparently insurmountable

difficulties arise for the attempt to get to know the historical
Jesus, these difficulties will be found to derive from a philosophy of history and not from historical research as such? I think
that it is possible to say this. A philosophy of history, after all, is
nothing other than a formed mentality, a philosophical view of
reality which is superimposed on the data which the record of
the race supplies. If it can aid the historian in discovering or
interpreting some data from the past (principally those which
prove to be anticipations of itself), it can as easily hinder him
from seeing anything else. It is, in any case, no different from
any other type of philosophical presupposition which restricts
one's view of the realities one is prepared to meet either in the
past or in the present.

More recently the suggestion has proved popular that it was
the nineteenth century positive ideal or philosophy of history
which resulted in the agnosticism about the historical Jesus.[18]
(Where is all this agnosticism? Every writer from the critical
period I meet is only too happy to supply me with the most
substantial information about the historical Jesus. Mistaken
identity there may be in abundance, but agnosticism is in very
short supply amongst the actual questers themselves. And the
nineteenth century, we have just seen, had ideals of history
other than the positivist one.) The positivist historian is supposedly interested only in objectively observed and observable
facts in sequence. I suppose if there ever were a practising historian who adhered strictly to such a programme, he would miss
most of what is significant about the historical Jesus, as indeed
he would miss most of what is significant about the story of the
race *tout simple.* But it is no answer to such a stultifying empiri-
cist philosophy in the practice of historical science to propose to
replace it in the practice of the science of history with yet
another philosophy. The proposal is also popular in the circle to
which we here refer that human history contains a series of what
are known as human existential self-understandings which,
when the historian, as is his proper task, brings them into the
light of the present, challenge the self-understanding of contemporary man. Some historical data may, of course, reveal the
self-understandings of some ancients, and some of our contemporaries may find some of these challenging or illuminating. But
in general it must be said that philosophical presuppositions of
an existentialist nature are as likely to be a hindrance to the
general task of the historian as are philosophical presuppositions of an empirical, or a positivist, or any other kind.[19] So I

repeat my conviction, born from my perusal of this material, and which I hope to illustrate even further from this material, that there has not been and there is not now any serious *historical* problem about knowing the historical Jesus. There are plenty of problems in evidence which derive from preconceptions of a philosophical nature, and the point of this last section has been to show that as some of these are philosophical presuppositions about human rationality, humanity's most specific character, some are philosophical presuppositions about history or the structure of the story of humanity, and both can be equally disadvantageous to the quest of the historical Jesus. Both actually were.

History and myth

D. F. Strauss, the stormy petrel of this 'critical' period, the most openly controversial of the life of Jesus questers, is also commonly called a Hegelian. He did not try, as did his teacher, Baur, to press Christian history from its origins into the mould of the Hegelian dialectic. So the reason for calling him Hegelian is the fact that he borrowed from Hegel the realization that religious faith of its nature uses inadequate concepts, intellectual symbols, in short, imaginative representations as embodiments of the truth. His word for these is 'myth', and his insistence on understanding the nature of myth in the documents of religious faith, however defective his own understanding of myth may have been, is his greatest single contribution to the modern quest.

> If religion be defined as the perception of truth, not in the form of an idea, which is the philosophic perception, but invested with imagery; it is easy to see that the mythical element can be wanting only when religion either falls short of, or goes beyond, its peculiar province, and that in the proper religious sphere it must necessarily exist.[20]

Much of Strauss's time and energy is spent in trying to persuade his readers that myth actually does occur in the Bible, no less than it does in the records of more 'primitive' civilizations which Christian Europe had always considered to be its home. And like the powerful persuader that he is, he uses the *argumentum ad hominem*. Christian writers, he argues, had always accepted, almost as a matter of course, the existence of allegory in the sacred sources. But what else does allegorical interpretation do except to treat an apparently historical tale as the outward clothing of an idea or religious conception? Interpretation of parts of the biblical records as mythical, he urges, does exactly the same thing, with this one difference, that the allegorical interpreter considers the idea hidden in the outward clothing of the story to be of divine provenance, whereas the mythic interpreter considers the idea so clothed to be the product of some human community. The principle of interpretation, however, is the same; it involves the search for the idea behind the symbols of the characters and events in the story which at once conceal and contain it; and if that principle is unobjectionable in the one case, it should be equally so in the other. The contention that the idea mythically expressed is of human provenance is normally proven by a simple survey of human cultures.

Strauss defines a biblical or evangelical myth, therefore, as 'a narrative relating directly or indirectly to Jesus, which may be considered not as the expression of a fact, but as the product of an idea of his earliest followers'. 'The mythus,' he adds, 'meets us sometimes in its pure form, constituting the substance of the narrative, and sometimes as an accidental adjunct to the actual history.'[21] The latter cases of impure or historical myths occur when some stories with foundation in fact are embellished to convey a religious conception of the community.

The picture of the historical Jesus which emerges when Strauss has demythologized the New Testament – for that, as we shall see, is what he thinks ought to be done – must be pieced together from scattered statements in this long and detailed book. When this is done, Jesus appears as a disciple of John who pursued his mission first in Galilee, who came to regard himself as the Messiah, called disciples to himself on this understanding, went to Jerusalem intending the recognition of his messiahship, had premonitions there of his violent death, predicted his return as the apocalyptic figure of the Son of Man, and had his colourful career ended by a Roman execution. Again a very substantial picture of the historical Jesus is presented to us, however different it might be this time from the moral philosopher of Reimarus or the Hegelian prototype of Baur.

Let us, in turn, leave aside for the moment this exercise in historical research and its results, with its calm confidence and its by now obvious inadequacy, and concentrate instead on the first topic brought to our attention by Strauss as his major contribution to this subject, myth. However Hegelian one may decide he was in his treatment of this topic (and it is the only topic on which I can see he merits to be described as Hegelian at all), he did not succeed in being fully and exclusively Hegelian even here. Indeed no writer can be a full-blooded follower of Hegel who tries to understand the historical uniqueness of the Christian faith and its founder, and for as long as he tries to do this. It was Hegel's conviction – and in this much he may very well be correct – that, first, religion would always be with us, since man is not pure intellect but sentiment and imagination as well, and, second, that religion by its nature finds expression in those imaginative representations or symbols which the word 'myth' so generally includes. The 'if' of Strauss's hypothetical statement quoted above does not occur to Hegel. Hegel does, of course, believe that there is a function or development of the human spirit which is higher than religion, which is at the level of philosophy and which operates with pure concepts or ideas; and he believes that whatever truth is apprehended in the lower forms of art or religion is here at this highest level apprehended in a purer and higher form; and about this he may be wrong.

But Hegel did not make the mistake – if this is a mistake, as I believe it to be – of thinking that the mythological was a merely transitory stage in the evolution of man, and so he did not make the corresponding mistake of thinking that religion should at some stage shed the mythical. As far as Strauss is concerned, on the contrary, myth belongs to the past and has no place in the scientific age, as he thinks his age to be. He is even a little surprised that myth should turn up in the documents of the age of Roman civilization and from there perpetuate itself in the traditions of Christianity, so he tries to make this point palatable by means of the following metaphor: 'The sun is not visible at the same instant to every place on the same meridian at the same time of year ... (so) the historic age dawns not upon all people at the same period.'[22] Here, in well nigh classic form, is the conviction, so widespread in contemporary thought, that myth belongs to a primitive stage of human development, and that it has no place in a scientific culture. Amongst the criteria which Strauss offers us for the detection of myth in our material are, first, evidence of the presence of an imaginatively embodied idea in the community at the time our material was composed; second, elements in the account which contradict the known and universally valid laws of physics and psychology; third, inconsistencies in the narratives or their later contradiction.

It should be clear enough from this attitude, and especially from the second and third criteria above, that the dominant

philosophical preconception in Strauss's mind is not so much
the Hegelian system as the much more superficial, if also much
more widespread rationalism of his time. He is not much farther
on than Reimarus in the manner in which he obviously thinks
truth to be a matter of universally applicable laws of physis and
psyche, and its criteria logical consistency and absence of contradiction. If Hegel had been the true philosophy of his mind he
would at least have given us a tolerable account of the nature of
myth in the expression of religious faith. In Strauss's case it is
once again true that an hour with Hegel is worth more than a
week with one of the so-called Hegelians, for Hegel at least is a
truly perceptive man and he does face one with a choice of
realistic philosophies of life. And if his advertisement of the
centrality of myth in the founding expression of the Christian
faith is to be called Strauss's great contribution to this critical
period, this must surely be understood in the manner in which a
man who makes a complete hash of something, does it so noisily
that he draws the attention of competent men to the task.

This is not the time or the place to talk at length about the
nature of myth in the expression of religious faith; the time and
place for that will occur more naturally later. But it may be
permissible here to record, simply for purposes of the present
survey of the so-called critical period, some of the anticipated
results of the later discussion of myth. Myth, it may be seen, is
so necessary to the expression of religious faith that although
straight concepts and the literal language which expresses these
can clearly be used in the analysis and expression of religious
faith, these can never replace the myths as full and adequate
substitutes. Second, it is necessary to say, in order to prevent
people from getting the impression that mythical is equivalent to
fanciful or untrue, myth is equally capable of the expression of
any view of life and the world which, though not religious,
moves at the same depth and comprehension as religious views
tend to do. The mythical is simply a constitutionally inevitable
mode of human understanding and human expression. There is
no age which does not have its myths, which does not, indeed,
live in them. The story of a scientific age which has outgrown all
myths is, of course, one of the most comprehensive myths ever
produced by the fertile spirit of man, and it is proving to be one
of the least viable.

There is, then, no possible excuse (except, of course, a basic
mistake about the nature of myth) for contrasting myth and
history or, as Strauss does, for confining myth to the darkness

which he presumes to have preceded the dawn of the 'historic age'. If myth is an inevitable expression of religious faith, and religious faith is, sometimes at least, the source or goal of the most memorable actions, then myth is part of the raw material on which the historian exercises his craft. Furthermore, if myth is the vehicle for the expression of the nature of a particular religious faith, it may also be a necessary vehicle for conveying the manner in which that particular faith entered into history and made its way in history. Then the only material which the historian can use in order to research this religious movement or this aspect of the human odyssey will be mythical material or material which contains mythical elements. In no other way, in this case, could the historian discover and present the facts of human life which are here in question. So myth, I hope it may appear, is material of history and for the history of every age, and it can in no way be contrasted with history. Once again, it is not scientific history in its proper and many-faceted practice which persuades Strauss to demythologize the New Testament and thereby misconceive the historical Jesus; it is, rather, a too narrow view of 'scientific' reason, a closed view of human nature and human faith, a restrictive philosophical preconception, which makes him demythologize in the name of history and thus ruin his history of the origins of Christianity.

History and faith

The quest of the historical Jesus, however, continued to career along on its wavering way, wavering between the different and sometimes opposite certainties which so rapidly replaced each other. Frederick Engels wrote in *Der Sozialdemokrat* (4 May 1882):

> In Berlin on April 13 a man died who once played a role as a philosopher and a theologian but was hardly heard of for years, only attracting the attention of the public from time to time as a 'literary eccentric'. Official theologians, including Renan, wrote him off and therefore maintained a silence of death about him. And yet he was wroth more than them all and did more than all of them in a question which interests us Socialists too: the question of the historical origin of Christianity.[23]

The man so neglected in later life and yet so praised in death was Bruno Bauer. In 1840, five years after Strauss's first *Life of Jesus*; his published work began to appear in the area of New Testament criticism. For, like Strauss, he did decide to have his work published, however unwelcome his results might be to his contemporaries and, like Strauss in this also, he did suffer the consequences in the loss of his university position.

Bauer chooses not to follow up on one of Strauss's major categories, namely, that of myth. The category is too vague, he decides, to be of any real help to the biblical critic. That decision may have been more significant for his results and for his ultimate fall from favour than he himself realized. He decides instead to go the way of literary criticism as such. He begins with the Fourth Gospel and has no difficulty in showing that it is an artistic creation rather than a biography. It appears that he expected to find a higher historical reliability in the synoptics, but when he did turn his critical eye on them he first accepted and defended the view that Mark was the first gospel written and that Matthew and Luke were based on Mark, and then he found himself forced to the conclusion that the gospel of Mark also was a literary creation, not a biography and not even a collection of previous Jesus-traditions, some of which might contain accurate memories of the man. Mark, he felt, was an artist who recorded the experiences of the little community in the form of the life of a single person. Since Matthew and Luke depended on Mark as their source, they could not help to get us behind his creation to the historical Jesus.

It seems that Bauer, even after his first survey of the gospel sources, still thought that he could detect at least the existence of some powerful Personality behind the community experiences now written up by Mark as a life of this Person, though there could be no certainty at all about the features of this historical individual, since it was the community and not the Personality which provided Mark with his material. By the end of his life, however, Bauer had decided that no such Personality existed. He had come to focus instead on Philo of Alexandria, whose allegorizing had fused Jewish religion with Greek philosophy; on Seneca, who tried to make Greek religious philosophy in its Stoic form the spirit of Roman civilization; and on Josephus, the 'new-style Jew', the cosmopolitan, the Roman. From a wedding of such disparate traditions, celebrated by such historical characters as these, Bauer thinks Christianity was ultimately born. It is this conclusion, when adjusted by the necessary sociological commentary, that Engels posthumously applauds. It is on the way to this conclusion that Bauer, quite rightly, loses the respect and even the interest of the most thorough scholars of his age.

Schweitzer, to whose masterful survey of the quest of the historical Jesus[24] I am indebted for this appreciation of the drift of Bauer's voluminous work, thinks that it was Bauer's over-polemical spirit which led him to such excessive conclusions, but that he did bring clearly into critical view the creativity of the New Testament writers and thus raised a problem which could never again be allowed to go unsolved. I have already sufficiently recorded my determination to qualify all expressions of appreciation to men whose methods have led to such blatantly false conclusions. And I think I can justify this determination on the grounds that it can help towards a correction of methods or viewpoints and thus lead to more reliable results.

This latest application to Christian sources of the newly developed critical methods has had the unfortunate result of losing sight of the founder altogether. This unfortunate result was no doubt partly caused by the shock of discovery of the amount of creativity due to the gospel writers. However, as we shall have occasion to note shortly, such creativity on the part of writers is not necessarily contrary to hopes of historical recovery. These hopes will depend on what kind of creativity is in question and on the use to which it has been put. There are more ways of recovering a character from history than finding his diary.

The discovery of the dominance of the mythical element in the New Testament was an important one, for in fact the mythical element is detectable in the accounts of all the major events of Jesus' life, his birth, baptism, public mission, death, and in the statements of his significance. Miracle and mystery, particularly resurrection, atonement and titles of exaltation, are virtually omnipresent in the New Testament, and it is in connection with such material that Strauss quite rightly identifies the category of myth. But to conclude that myth was a form of primitive fancy, rather than a perennial way of telling the truth; and to conclude this on the basis of similarities with images, symbols and myths from surrounding cultures, as if similar symbols could not be as easily used to say distinctively different things as much as similar concepts could be; that was the double mistake of the time, a mistake which deprived the New Testament of a very large body of its most distinctive and telling material. For if myth, as we shall later see, can depict not only a distinctive type of human faith, but its actual emergence in history and even the character through whom it emerged, it is little wonder if those who both misunderstand the nature of a myth and misplace its distinctiveness in cross-cultural generalities should also finally lose sight altogether of the character of the founder.

Those who, under the influence of the rationalist bias, mis-understand myth do not usually go so far as to lose sight entirely of the founder of Christianity, but neither can they ever get much closer to him than the questers we have already passed in review. Ernest Renan, for instance, whose life of Jesus appeared in 1863 – and it is by far the most artistically delightful of all lives of Jesus – prefers the category of legend to that of myth in his attempt to understand the kind of material he is dealing with in the New Testament, and particularly in the gospels. He asks himself the question: 'What kind of historical value do I attribute to the Gospels?', and he answers that 'they are legendary biog-raphies. I should willingly compare them to the legends of the Saints ... in which historical truth and the desire to present models of virtue are combined in various degrees.'[25] So he pro-ceeds on the rationalist assumption most widespread in his age that stories featuring the miraculous should be discounted (with the possible exception of some thaumaturge-type wonders), on the grounds that they can never be proved. The preaching of the resurrection and all related themes is dismissed with the sen-tence: 'For the historian, the life of Jesus finishes with his last sigh.'[26] And for the rest Renan takes as his guides the known and universally valid laws of human psychology. As he puts it in his delicate way,

> There is no great abuse of hypothesis in supposing that a founder of a new religion commences by attaching himself to the moral aphor-isms already in circulation in his time, and to the practices which are in vogue; that, when riper, and in full possession of his idea, he delights in a kind of calm and poetical eloquence, remote from all controversy, sweet and free as pure feeling; that he warms by degrees, becomes animated by opposition, and finishes by polemics and strong invectives.[27]

Accordingly, Renan's historical Jesus preaches the purest, idyllic dependence on God, like the lilies of the field, but soon, without metaphysical pretensions, claims himself nearer to God than any other man and looks forward, in the name of man's true relationship to God which he preaches, to judging the men of this world. Add his animated polemics and his strong invec-tives when opposition to his view arises, and you can under-stand his death. Once again a very substantial picture of the historical Jesus emerges, however different it might be this time from the moral philosopher of Reimarus, the Hegelian pro-totype of Baur, the failure-prone messianic pretender of Strauss (with his apocalyptic visions), or the (substituted) Philo-

Josephus-Seneca hybrid of Bauer. Once again, though it has to be admitted, of course, that all these pictures contain important elements of truth – it would be impossible to conceive of such intelligent men dealing always with the same historical material and missing absolutely everything – Renan's picture, too, is inadequate to the figure of Jesus, and is soon seen to be so by his successors in the quest. And once again this psychological Jesus of Renan, so unique and at the same time so typical, seems to draw from the real Jesus of the ancient records the rebuttal that it is not history as such that need necessarily be nonplussed by his person, but rather that some restricted view of humanity and its story, some philosophical presupposition is preventing him from appearing whole. In the case of Bauer and Renan this philosophical-type presupposition, this cultural blindfold, this restriction on the view, takes the form, partly, of an ignorance of the nature and necessity of myth, a failure to follow up on a major hint that Strauss had thrown out; for myth is at one and the same time a powerful expression of religious faith and therefore indicative of the real depths and the real heights reached by the human spirit in history.

Even Albert Schweitzer who, of all the questers, had the clearest conception of the way in which Jesus, that strange figure behind the exegete's documents, breaks asunder the mummy's bands in which each age tries to bind him, and who gives pride of place to one major myth from the New Testament, the myth of apocalyptic eschatology which centres on the figure of the Son of Man, even he misunderstood the nature of myth in general, and the nature of this myth in particular. He therefore, as must be inevitable from the place he gives this myth in his picture of the historical Jesus, misunderstands the manner in which Jesus, the real historical Jesus, comes to meet every age which searches for him by challenging it. That he misconceived the myth to which he himself gave pride of place is amply argued in recent scholarship.[28] That he then inevitably misunderstood the manner in which Jesus challenges every age must be seen from whatever success can be achieved by books such as this one, and from their whole content.

Schweitzer may well be correct in thinking that the way in which Jesus speaks to each age is to challenge its terms, rather than find himelf forced to endorse them.

There came a Man to rule over the world; He ruled it for good or ill, as history testifies; He destroyed the world into which He was born;

the spiritual life of our own time seems like to perish at His hands, for He leads to battle against our thought a host of dead ideas, a ghostly army upon which death has no power, and Himself destroys again the truth and goodness which His Spirit creates in us, so that it cannot rule the world. That he continues, notwithstanding, to reign as the alone Great and alone True in a world of which He denied the continuance, is the prime example of that antithesis between spiritual and natural truth which underlies all life and all events, and in Him emerges into the field of history.[29]

So Schweitzer introduces his quest through the questers for the real historical Jesus.

Schweitzer takes issue with Wrede's famous theory of the messianic secret in Mark – a theory based on the fact that Jesus, in Mark's gospel, continually tries to silence those who acknowledge him in one way or another as Messiah – and in this instance at least he challenges the view that evangelical creativity obscures the historical figure. He believes that it was Jesus himself for prudential reasons, and not Mark for literary and dogmatic ones, who tried to make a secret of Jesus' messianic stature during his life. For Jesus, according to Schweitzer, had a supernatural conviction of the apocalyptic in-breaking of the eschaton or end-time, and of his own identity as the Son of Man who would at that time judge the world. He tried to hasten the end-time, the great cosmic catastrophe, by sending his disciples out to preach its imminence. When that failed, he turned his own face for Jerusalem. Peter discovered his true identity in a momentary 'transfiguration' or ecstatic trance of Jesus, and told the other apostles. They kept this a secret, as requested by Jesus himself, until Judas betrayed his secret to the Jewish leaders, who promptly had him killed as a messianic pretender of the most dangerous kind. Jesus, in Schweitzer's resounding words,

in the knowledge that He is the coming Son of Man lays hold of the wheel of the world to set it moving on that last revolution which is to bring all ordinary history to a close. It refuses to turn, and He throws Himself upon it. Then it does turn; and crushes Him. Instead of bringing in the eschatological conditions, He has destroyed them. The wheel rolls onward, and the mangled body of the one immeasurably great Man, who was strong enough to think of Himself as the spiritual ruler of mankind and to bend history to His purpose, is hanging on it still. That is His victory and His reign.[30]

Despite the persuasive power of this Moby-Dick-like ending, the pen-picture painted by Schweitzer of the historical Jesus has long been considered quite distorted. That there is an antithesis

between 'spiritual' and 'natural' truth some Christians have
clearly understood and stated, and most have dimly suspected.
That the embodiment of this antithesis in Jesus' clash with his
own and with other times is at once destructive and dynamic is
amply illustrated in the lives of Christian saints, and not least in
the great humanitarian escapades of Schweitzer's own life. But
all this as the result of a Grand Illusion? Scarcely. Men do not
rule history, as Jesus has done, nor do they attract attention
permanently to them, by means of an illusion, not even a grand
illusion. The mistake is Schweitzer's, not Jesus', and it is a mistake about a myth. For the one myth in the New Testament
which Schweitzer took absolutely seriously, he also unfortunately took absolutely literally, as a literal belief quite literally
held by a very literal-minded Jesus. It seems to be the destiny of
men who think they live in a post-mythological age to be unable
to understand men who consciously live in myth. It seems to be
the destiny of people who take such a restricted view of humanity, its spirit and its story, to be over-run by the Jesus they set
out to seek.

It should come as no surprise to those who understand the
intrinsic relationship between myth and religious faith that
some of the writers here under review are already beginning to
sense a clash between faith and history. It is not, I persist in
thinking, that history as such has any inherent difficulty in dealing with Jesus as founder of a faith, or with the myths which
inevitably communicate both faith and founder. Rather is it the
case that people who mistake the nature and necessity of myth
in the presentation of both faith and founder incur difficulties
which the sacred text and the (very existence of the) Christian
tradition will not for long allow to go unnoticed. It is not normally the official, conservative exponents of the tradition who
are capable of pointing out where exactly these difficulties stem
from, any more than these people are capable of seeing what is
valuable in the very spirit of the new proposals. But the difficulties of one author's solutions are revealed by the next author in
the very process of incurring his own, and it is the persistently
revisionary nature of the quest and its solutions which finally
makes some people blame faith, others doubt history (and cling
to faith as the alternative and indeed the only access to the
historical Jesus), and others still finally to work out a theory of
faith and history in which the two, though each can legitimately
reach its own results, can never meet.

Renan, for instance, was not shy about his qualifications as a quester of the historical Jesus, and he expressed them with his customary elegance as follows:

> If the love of a subject can help one to understand it, it will also, I hope, be recognized that I have not been wanting in this condition. To write the history of a religion, it is necessary: firstly, to have believed it (otherwise we should not be able to understand how it has charmed and satisfied the human conscience); in the second place, to believe it no longer in an absolute manner, for absolute faith is incompatible with sincere history. But love is possible without faith.[31]

Questions literally spring to mind about the kind of understanding of faith and love he must have had in order to be able to end the paragraph with such a sentence. But pass this over for a moment in favour of concentration on his main point, which is that faith hinders history. Faith, he does allow, can help by explaining the power a man has exercised over others, but only if it is not absolute, that is, only to the extent that it can be set aside for the occasion or relativized, can the historical task be pursued. I, personally, cannot forget that this paragraph was written by a man who so ignored the presence of myth in his sources that he first substituted the more insubstantial category of legend and then thought of the historical task in terms of distilling the facts from this. In one way, of course, Renan is merely repeating the classical error of the quest up to this point. The miraculous in the life of Jesus (parables and other teachings, meals and other practices could be accepted in so far as they could be interpreted without appeal to their mythological elements), the resurrection kerygma, the atonement, the divine functions and titles, all were dismissed as the lies of charlatans (Reimarus), ciphers for a doctrine of reconciliation (the Hegelian element in Baur), myths, but myths as obsolete forms from a pre-scientific age (Strauss), hybrid creations of merging cultures (Bauer) and, finally, legends. The person and the achievement of Jesus had to be discovered in spite of these, not because of them. Yet all these belong to myth, and if myth, as we have maintained, is essential to the expression of a faith and of the role of a man as the founder of a faith, is it any wonder that Renan not only repeats the mistake of his predecessors, but actually gives it expression in the form of a conflict between faith and history? He thus takes his place amongst the first of those who bequeath to us in explicit form a problem which is based on so many hidden false assumptions that it is proving well-nigh insoluble.

Schweitzer, surprisingly, also opposes an encounter with the spirit of Jesus (though he does not in the context call this faith) to history, and this time to the detriment of history. 'The abiding and eternal in Jesus is absolutely (there goes that word again) independent of historical knowledge and can only be understood by contact with His spirit which is still at work in the world.'[32] I say surprisingly, because Schweitzer seemed to have done a very good job of discovering the spirit of the historical Jesus. One can only suppose that in the sentence just quoted he means by the spirit of Jesus a lived conviction of 'that antithesis between spiritual and natural truth which underlies all life and all events', and which drove him too from his academic chair in Strasbourg and from his seat at the organ of its great cathedral to help the truly needy in the primitive conditions of tribal Africa. But then when he says that history cannot help us to contact this spirit, is he not acknowledging, however obliquely or even unconsciously, that we cannot derive this spirit directly from a man who really thought that he was, or was to be, the Son of Man of the great apocalyptic catastrophe? Is it not the case that this man who gives the myth such an obvious place in his reproduction of the historical Jesus just as obviously mistakes the nature of the myth; for if the myth can only be understood as a literal and fanciful belief of (in this case) Jesus, then, of course, that poor deluded man could be at most the occasion, never the source, of what we have nevertheless managed to call the spirit of Jesus by means of some unexplained later refinement. And if the historical Jesus, reached by history as Schweitzer reached him, can never function as our contact with the spirit of Jesus, what can so function or of what kind could this contact be? Some people will say something absolute and independent which they will be only too happy to call, mistakenly, faith. But Schweitzer does not know. One of his most oft-quoted sentences, in which he seems to give the answer to that question, in effect says that he does not know: 'He comes to us as One unknown, without a name, as of old, by the lakeside, He came to those men who knew Him not.'[33] The sentence has an inspiring sound, and makes no sense. In any case, the odd thing is that the quest of the historical Jesus is resulting in a wedge driven deeper between history and faith (or contact with the spirit of Jesus).

And then came Martin Kähler. Or, to be more accurate about

this matter, Kähler had already come, but he had come as one unknown and had gone unrecognized by the Schweitzers of this world. Already in 1892, fourteen years before Schweitzer's book, was published the first edition of his more recently renowned *The So-Called Historical Jesus and the Historic Biblical Christ*. Kähler it is who truly believes, and who behaves exactly as if he truly believed, that the quest of the historical Jesus is an absolutely hopeless task. He is every bit as cognizant of the fact as was Schweitzer later on, and every bit as anxious to point it out, that the portraits of the historical Jesus painted by the questers are as dogmatic in their way as the most abstruse formulae of the dogmaticians.[34] His own conviction is that we do not have in the New Testament or elsewhere the material for the construction of a biography of Jesus, or even documents of a sufficiently historical nature to enable us to reconstruct his public ministry. So, whereas Schweitzer goes from the conviction that other questers painted prejudiced portraits in pursuit of the philosophical presuppositions of their time to the impression that he can paint a true portrait precisely by finding a historical Jesus whose innermost beliefs oppose him to time (that is, to the world and its history) as such,Kähler, on the contrary, proceeds to the conclusion that the New Testament has quite a different purpose from the furnishing of data about the historical Jesus, and until that simple fact is recognized it will always be misunderstood by scholars, though it will more than likely be well enough understood by the ordinary believers who make up the vast majority of the followers of Jesus.

As far as Kähler is concerned, it is the business of the biblical documents to present us with a portrait of the historic Christ. The adjective 'historic', as distinct from its near-verbal neighbour 'historical', indicates, not any particular data about the actual man in his time, but rather the impact he has had on the history of this world. So indeed does the word Christ for, although in common usage it has become a proper name for the man, it is really a title conferred on him, and it means to say that some have taken him as their Messiah, the anointed of God in their midst, and have at least tried to live accordingly. The portrait, therefore, which the Bible paints is a portrait of One in whom the authors have faith as their saviour and Lord, as God revealed in this world. It is a portrait of which one could well say that it is as much preached in the words as painted, and it is preached for the single purpose of eliciting the same faith in the readers.[35] I personally have some difficulty in understanding

the role of the resurrection in Kähler's view of the biblical portrait; I find it difficult to decide whether he takes the resurrection
to be an event which made possible the faith of the disciples of
Jesus and, indirectly, our faith also, or whether the preaching of
the resurrection of Jesus is just another way of expressing their
faith in him with the usual hope, in all such preaching, of eliciting in us a similar faith in Jesus as our saviour and Lord. But that
confusion affects more talk of the resurrection than Kähler's,
and will have to await a fuller analysis later on. In any case, in
Kähler's view, the sermon-portrait, though it is made up in part
of some fragmentary traditions and half-understood recollections, witnesses to something beyond mere historical actuality,
namely, to salvation and revelation. It may be possible to guess
at some data about the historical Jesus – Kähler suggests that
while alive Jesus could win only a very shaky loyalty from his
followers (which makes one wonder again about the role of the
resurrection) – but the only real result of portrayal by means of
fragmentary recollections is to let us see Man in the saviour and
Lord, not an historical character.[36] That, presumably, allows us
to realize that salvation, though not reducible to mere historical
factuality, is salvation for human beings, and that the revelation,
too, though as little reducible to mere historical factuality, is
through and for the human.

It seems that the tables are turned. Where some scholars had
eschewed faith and its necessary myths in pursuit of the historical figure, and were destined to see their efforts fail, if only
through their propensity for perpetual self-reversal, now Kähler
insists that the documents are faith documents, portraying and
soliciting a faith, that they were never meant to yield historical
data about an historical individual, and that they can never do
so in any worthwhile quantity. The tables are turned, but apparently only with the effect of defiantly establishing a thesis which
was beginning to be dimly perceived in any case, the thesis that
history and faith can find no common ground in research into
the origins of Christianity. The thesis has been maintained more
recently, more thoroughly, and even more defiantly, by the
great Bultmann – as already remarked. Therefore it cannot
properly be treated in an introductory chapter devoted to an
historical survey. This much, however, can be said about this
thesis concerning faith and history: it is not at all obvious. History has not yet had a proper chance. It has been persistently
hindered by preconceptions. And perhaps this new (and old)
idea that faith, at least in its source, is entirely above and beyond

history, and that documents presenting faith are not therefore
amenable to source-research of the normal rational kind,
perhaps this is just another preconception hindering the historical task from achieving any proper success.

For if there can be philosophical-type presuppositions concerning human nature and human reason, and therefore concerning myth and the way in which people tell and understand
the story of the race, there can surely also be presuppositions of
a philosophical nature concerning the nature of faith, and these
too can, like all presuppositions, prevent the researcher from
seeing what is historically true and what is actually expressed in
the historical records.

Kähler clearly considers religious faith to be something that
appears in human lives and human history, but something
independent of human nature and human life, independent of
the stuff of which human history is made. How exactly religious
faith originates according to this theory, on what its existence is
dependent, need not concern us here – perhaps it owes its existence to some totally indescribable but recurring act of God.
What does concern us is that faith so conceived, since it is independent of the ordinary stuff of human life and human history,
need raise no questions at all about the man Jesus, whose name
it nevertheless claims somehow for itself. What concerns us
even more is that there are hidden presuppositions here about
the nature of faith, and that those also involve presuppositions
about ordinary human nature and the ordinary stuff of history,
namely, that human life and human history do not at all provide
any source or support for religious faith. 'History' and 'exegesis'
in the hands of a series of scholars had – despite their objectivity (?) and the objectivity of their presuppositionless methods (?)
– proved unable to arrive at an agreed view of the founder of
Christianity. And now Kähler, approaching the task from his
conception of the nature of Christian faith, has claimed that the
historical quest is both impossible and fortunately irrelevant to
that faith. The wheel of critical and historical effort seems to
have come full circle. We are back again before Reimarus. Or are
we?

More recent theory of faith has shown that there is more than
one way of thinking about the nature of faith and of conceiving
Jesus' role as founder of a faith; so that the quest of the historical
Jesus is not pre-empted by presuppositions about the nature of
faith any more than it is by any other of the presuppositions we
met in the course of this survey. The quest has not in fact been

halted, not even by the great scholarly bulk of Bultmann, and we shall have occasion to notice some of the contemporary questers later.

For the moment it is only necessary to say that Kähler was quite right to insist that the New Testament is written from faith to faith. But it is as little obvious in the case of Kähler as it is in the case of Reimarus that a correct perception – or, to be more precise, a perception which can be expressed in unobjectionable form – can yield correct results when the subject is Jesus. Reimarus, it is said, was aware of the creativity of the New Testament writers, as Kähler was aware of their faith. But if Kähler's understanding of their faith was anywhere near as wrong-headed as Reimarus's concept of their creativity, then the correctness of his perception, too, is more apparent than real, and his contribution to the research into Christian origins is equally questionable. To put the matter another way, there is no reason to suppose that Kähler's restriction of the source and nature of faith to an area beyond historical reach is any more balanced than Reimarus's restriction of religious faith to a Kantian-type moral reason and its postulates. In both cases it may very well be true, indeed it is very likely, that a restricted understanding of human nature (for faith, in one form or another, is always part of human life) gets in the way of an adequate reading of history, and of the truth we could learn from history, particularly the truth we could learn about Jesus and the way in which he introduced a distinctive faith to our world.

In short, the mere fact that modern people prefer to approach Jesus from the point of view of humanity and its history does not automatically guarantee an adequate view of Jesus; nor does it automatically prevent an adequate view. The lesson to be learned from the survey we have just conducted, brief as it has been, is this: we do all set out on the quest of the historical Jesus with our own preconceptions about humanity, its nature and limits, its concerns and prospects. These preconceptions have often in recent times proved rather restrictive in their assessment of the range of human reason, in their over-dependence on a rather narrowly-conceived science, in their attempts to plot the movement of human history, and in their understanding of the source and nature of the religious faith of which human beings have always proved capable. For to insist that religious faith must consist of a Kantian-type morality together with its so-called postulates is potentially as restrictive of the possibilities of human nature in history as, in an obverse fashion, is the insistence that the source and nature of religious faith is exclusively supernatural.

It cannot be concluded from this survey that the quest of the historical Jesus is futile, or that there is any inherent failure in the sources through which the quest must be conducted. It can only be concluded that preconceptions mar whatever prospects of success there may be, and that those who would set out on the quest must do all in their power to bring their own particular preconceptions about nature and faith into focus, and to allow these to be challenged by their sources rather than impose their terms on the one who is sought.

Life of Jesus questers and biblical critics

It would be unhelpful to distinguish in too dichotomous a manner the history of life of Jesus research from the history of biblical criticism in modern times. Too dichotomous a distinction here would simply hide the dogmatic decision that one could learn a lot about the text and its content, but little or nothing about the historical Jesus. Since nothing that we have so far seen can force us to accept such a dogmatic decision, it would not be correct to assume such a distinction in this last brief section of this historical survey. In any case, it soon becomes obvious to those who attempt a survey like this that the life of Jesus research contributed its own impetus – however crudely at times – to the recognition of the necessity of working out the principles and methods of biblical exegesis; and it is also clear that the canons of biblical criticism, as they were gradually worked out, had a kind of see-saw effect on the proposed results of life of Jesus research. Since we have already noted, in however critical a fashion, the manner in which some life-of-Jesus research precipitated a change in people's views about the nature of the New Testament literature, it can do no harm to note briefly now the main developments in the canons of biblical criticism and their wavering effects on the quest of the historical Jesus. The distinction between life-of-Jesus research and development of the canons of biblical criticism is not at all easy to make in the period under survey. Different surveyors will choose different candidates for each title. But there are writers and there is a section of the literature which produce more acceptable results in the direction of the development of the methods and principles of biblical interpretation than they pro-

duce for the quest of the historical Jesus, and however questionable the present author's selection may be, it will be of some
help to end with a brief overview of this kind of material and of
its relevance to our purpose.

So, then, from the mid-nineteenth century, and due to the
work of men like Weisse and Holtzmann, it came to be accepted
that Mark was the first of the gospels to be written, and that
Matthew and Luke made use of it. This result naturally tempted
people to think that Mark was therefore the nearest thing to a
biography in the New Testament. Then in 1901 Wilhelm Wrede
published his book, *The Messianic Secret in the Gospels*, in which
by long and detailed exegesis of the text he showed that the
writer of the gospel of Mark portrayed the historical Jesus as a
messianic figure, which in fact he was only seen to be after the
resurrection, and then attempted to do justice to the true historical facts by having Jesus make a secret of his messianic status
and of the acts in which it was manifest during the whole course
of his earthly life. The portrait of Jesus in Mark then owes more
to this theological bias (*Tendenz*) of Mark's than it does to the
actual facts of the earthly life of Jesus. Did this mean that the
quest of the historical Jesus via the gospel of Mark was now
hopeless, since a theological bias had seriously threatened the
'biographical' status of that work? Some people clearly thought
so, if we can judge from their resistance to Wrede's thesis, but
clearly they were wrong. Wrede's thesis obviously implies that
the historical Jesus was not a messianic figure and, furthermore,
that Mark had good reason to believe that he was not. Otherwise the elaborate paraphernalia of the messianic secret would
not have been necessary at all. Thus Wrede's thesis gives direction to the historical quest instead of blocking it. The thesis did
show, though, and with detailed exegetical evidence, the free
creativity which some have attributed to what they call the
theological conceptions of the gospel writers. But this was not
elaborated, or its full implications seen, until quite recently.

The next major move in the modern development of biblical
criticism was initiated by Julius Wellhausen before the First
World War. He concentrated on the oral tradition about Jesus
and his faith which was elaborated in a variety of ways by the
community of Jesus-followers before the New Testament writers
began to use it. After the war a number of scholars, principally
Dibelius and Bultmann, developed the technique known as
form criticism from this kind of basis. This technique tries to
isolate the various units of the tradition which the New Testa-

ment writers had collected and made part of a larger whole, e.g. a gospel. The technique concentrates on the form of the unit – a parable, miracle story, saying of Jesus – or the collection of units, tries to discover its source in the particular situation of a particular community – in the ritual, polemical or catechetical context – and thus tries to understand its meaning and place in the history of the tradition. Clearly enough this technique is in itself neutral as far as the quest of the historical Jesus is concerned. If it betrays, on the one hand, a heavy emphasis on the free creativity of the early communities in pursuit of their own particular needs, it holds out the hope, on the other hand, that some of these units might contain elements that could be shown by means of the technique to derive from Jesus himself. The study of the parables is perhaps the case in which this type of criticism in a highly refined form has yielded the most spectacular results.

More recently still the hint of Wrede has been followed, and it has been seen that form criticism needs the complement of another technique or another type of criticism, now known as redaction criticism. This type of criticism stems from the view that the writers of what we call the gospels were not simple collectors of units or previously collected units of the tradition, imposing on these at the very most a loose and superficial framework made up mostly of temporal clauses such as 'at that time' or 'when Jesus had said these things'. The redaction critic regards the writers of the gospels as creative artists who worked with a theological concept of their own, and with it worked their material. Therefore, men like Marxsen, Conzelmann and Bornkamm, the pioneers in this field, try to find first the guiding idea or theology of the redactor, the creative writer of each gospel. With this final complement to the critic's method, the presence of free creativity seems to have reached an extreme intensity, and the quest of the historical Jesus might seem to have to back away from whatever hopes the technique of the form critic left still within its grasp: the see-saw effect is noticed again.

Once again, though, the impression conveyed here is more apparent than real. For one thing, a clear understanding of the special viewpoint of the author can facilitate rather than impede the search for the more original forms of the units of tradition he is using. For that reason it was said that the two types of criticism, form criticism and redaction criticism, are complementary rather than competitive. For another, there is no reason to assume that the 'theology' of the writer of a gospel must necessarily be a hindrance rather than a help in the quest of the historical Jesus. If the historical Jesus was founder of a faith, if that is the historical fact about him which makes the historical quest worth the trouble, then, since theology is a formulation of faith, the theology which informs the work of a particular writer could give its own clues to the faith of the historical Jesus. Paul, after all, who did not use the form we call gospel at all, who did not use traditions about the life of Jesus to any extent worth mentioning, gives invaluable information about the faith of the historical Jesus, as we shall see. And if it is Napoleon's statesmanship and military genius that we most want to read about in histories of his life, it is surely the faith of Jesus, the faith he founded, we most want to hear about in results of the quest of the historical Jesus.

The present section of this chapter is the briefest, because amidst all the varied material available to the student of the Jesus-phenomenon I am least capable in the technical methods and principles of biblical hermeneutics. I include the very brief survey of this section, not with the intention of attempting to do any justice to the truly amazing development of modern biblical criticism, but to carry through, with some semblance of completeness, a point which I hope is beginning to come clear through this chapter, the point, namely, that if there are difficulties about getting to know the historical Jesus – as undoubtedly there are – these are not difficulties which are intrinsic either to the science of history as such or to the principles and methods of the various forms of criticism. For the rest, I hope it may be allowed that one who is not at all capable in the techniques of modern biblical criticism can yet avail himself of its more widely acknowledged results. If this is not allowed, then very few of us could talk or write at all about Jesus nowadays, and those who on this criterion could do so, the expert exegetes, might turn out to be the least inclined to talk or write about anything other than particular documents or texts.

Conclusion

The principles and methods of biblical interpretation, honed to such fine instruments by the dedicated professional work of by now some two centuries, in what they are themselves, decide nothing, before actual use, about the prospects of success or failure in the quest of the historical Jesus. But any survey of the same two centuries could quickly show that the quest and its results went through so many radical revisions as to cast serious doubts on whatever prospects of success the early questers had set out to entertain. Early in the second century of this period the apparent discomfiture of the historians and exegetes was turned by some Christian theologians into a dogmatic thesis about the irrelevance to Christian faith of the methods and results of the historian's labours. Yet one factor seems constant throughout the whole period, that is, the determination to look out, in the critical quest for the origins of Christianity, from the vantage point of human nature itself in the concrete conditions of its historical existence. Nothing that we have so far seen precludes the possibility of encountering the real, historical Jesus; provided, of course, that we recognize the modern perspective for what it is and refuse to allow any of its specific forms to turn into dominating preconceptions; provided, in other words, that we are prepared to find that the person and the time to which we now look in human history may reveal as much about the whence and whither of human kind as any presumed contemporary understanding of human nature could tell us. But it was with this hope, as already remarked, that every age set out in quest of Jesus, each with its own assumptions about humanity and its own questions based on these. The historical Jesus may hold some creative surprises for us, too, if we truly set out in search of him and refuse simply to sketch his portrait according to any set of recent or contemporary specifications.

2

The Death of Jesus

The whole direction of the last chapter argued for more confidence than is normally shown nowadays in the quest of the historical Jesus. The suggestion I wish to make at the beginning of this chapter is that the best starting point for the quest is that event in which the historical life of Jesus ended, his death.

It is true that in the last chapter much was made of the claim that so many of the scholars who set out on the search for the historical Jesus in the course of the last two centuries had either ignored the presence of myth in the New Testament or had mistaken its nature, and the complaint was often present implicitly, at the very least, that such ignorance or error did as much as anything else to prevent the quest of the historical Jesus from reaching its attainable goals. It might seem, then, that the logical way to proceed at this point would be first to analyse the nature of myth in an effort to see how it can in fact help or hinder historical quests. There are, however, strong deterrents here. Myth means so many things to so many people that a general analysis of the nature and function of myth at this point would inevitably take up too much of our time and space. It would either turn out too broad for our present purposes, or it could reasonably be suspected of being tailored to our preconceived needs. So it seems best simply to set out without more ado on the historical quest, to let the myth arise in the course of that quest, as it inevitably will, then to seek an understanding of that myth which, though broader than the New Testament material which requires it, is still not so broad as to cover every context in which myth has appeared and been studied, and in this narrower context to analyse the relation of myth to history.

But why start the quest of the historical Jesus with his death? Because, quite simply, the death of Jesus is central in every way. Of those with mainly historical interest in the matter, none but the few extravagant souls who wish altogether to deny the very existence of a character called Jesus of Nazareth doubt the statement that he suffered under Pontius Pilate – a Roman official known to us from historical sources of unquestioned reliability. The death of Jesus at least brings him into contact with a known historical figure and with the great empire he represented. But there is more than the caution of the careful and circumspect historian to recommend that those who wish to know Jesus should start with his death.

The one incident in the life of Jesus on this lean earth which interests Paul, the first great propagandist for the Jesus movement whose writings we possess, is the death of Jesus. Round the dual focus of the death and resurrection of Jesus all Paul's teaching and preaching revolves. And this is surely because the death of Jesus is in fact central to every form of expression and practice of the religion he founded.

For the writer of the Fourth Gospel the death of Jesus is his 'hour', not just his finest hour in some Churchillian sense, though it is undoubtedly that too, but the hour of his exaltation, of his glorification, and of his breathing forth of the spirit. The full implications of these phrases must be gathered, significantly enough as we hope to see later, from the theme of resurrection. For the moment, enter them simply as evidence of the centrality of the death of Jesus in the minds of his followers. 'And I, when I am lifted up from the earth, will draw all men to myself' (John 12.32); 'Father, save me from this hour? No, for this purpose I have come to this hour. Father, glorify thy name' (John 12.27f.; 16.32 – 17.5); and where Mark and Luke describe the moment of his death as breathing his last (after Luke has had him commit his spirit to his Father), and Matthew has him yield up his spirit in a verb that conveys an impression of someone simply letting go, John uses a word for this death-breath of spirit which is normally used to describe the act of handing on something precious to those who come after – *paradosis, traditio*; tradition (Mark 15.37; Matthew 27.50; Luke 23.46; John 19.30). In the synoptic gospels, however, it should be added, though the theology of the death of Jesus is not as substantial as it is in John, the very structure of these gospels can still show its centrality. For it is almost as true of the other synoptic gospels as D. E. Nineham once said of Mark, that they are like tadpoles, with large heads composed of the so-called passion narratives, weaving behind them longer but much thinner tales. So is the death of Jesus the central focus of the New Testament as a whole. Likewise, it is

quite literally at the centre of those other great formal and
authoritative expressions of the essence of Christianity, the oldest and most popular of the creeds.

In addition to all this, if anyone should still remain even
slightly sceptical of its centrality, the death of Jesus is the heart
of the most essential and unique Christian ritual. It is the badge
of discipleship, the most prominent symbol of Christian art and
the beginning and end of Christian prayer.

The Lord's Supper, the eucharist, according to Paul proclaims
the death of Jesus (I Corinthians 11.26), just as our baptism, in
Paul's view also, is a baptism 'into his death' (Romans 6.3). And
anyone who would be a disciple of Jesus needs no more accurate
description than the one who is prepared to take up his cross
daily and follow Jesus (Mark 8.34).[1]

If any single incident or image could stand as sole sign and
summary of Christianity, it would be the crucifixion of Jesus. If
there is a focal point in the characteristic expressions and practices of Christianity on which myth and history converge in full
force, it is Jesus' death. What, then, are the facts about his
death? How and why did he die? Unfortunately, the centrality
of the death of Jesus in all the records and in all the practical and
theoretical implications that have been drawn from the
phenomenon of Jesus does not mean that the exact details of
that tragic occurrence come easily within the historian's grasp.

The facts, just the facts

The investigator into the causes and circumstances of the death
of Jesus must be mainly concerned with the incidents described
in the passion narratives, arrest, trials and execution – leaving
out of account for the moment the descriptions of the Last Supper which usually open these narratives; these will engage our
attention under another heading later on.

The clearest and most certain fact to emerge from these narratives is that Jesus was executed in the Roman manner of crucifixion, after sentence by a Roman tribunal, on a charge which
Romans considered capital. Whether, as the gospel narratives
convey with increasing insistence, Pilate was reluctant to have
Jesus executed on the charges brought, is also a matter which
may be postponed for later consideration.

Now the quest of the causes and circumstances of this historic
execution quickly runs aground in confusion if we do not distinguish at the very outset two different directions it might take –

and here the relation between myth and history, with which we shall have much to do, begins to assume its first concrete form. Answers to the question, 'Why was Jesus executed?', which refer us to decisions allegedly made in heaven for some of heaven's purposes – to have Jesus die for the sins of humanity – belong to the realm of myth. They are true after their own fashion and will be considered in their own place. But for reasons which will, I hope, appear ever more obvious as this quest proceeds, and in order to end with the clearest possible understanding of the relation between myth and history, it seems best to begin by donning the historian's gown and to act on the assumption that a Roman procurator in a troublesome province of the empire is more interested in Caesar's purposes than in God's, if he can adequately distinguish these at all. Even his fellow-countrymen who co-operated in the trial and execution of Jesus were established political as well as religious leaders in the land. In their case also it is legitimate to ask about their political motives, and preferable, according to the line of approach adopted here, to begin with these. In short, the Roman involvement in the trial and execution of Jesus, as well as the political offices held by the hostile leaders of his own people, give us every reason to ask about political motives for his death. And if the theme of our opening chapter is at all correct about the priority accorded to humanity and its history in the contemporary quest for the founder of Christianity, it is obvious that we should ask about the political motives first. In any case, and in any conceivable approach to the matter, it would scarcely ever be possible to understand fully this central act of the drama of Jesus without at least inquiring after the political causes and circumstances which brought about what to any observer, believer or not, appears to be a political execution. Even those who have rested most unreflectively satisfied with the single answer that Jesus died for the sins of the race scarcely conceive of God communicating this intention to Caiaphas and Pilate and having them carry it out. Caiaphas and Pilate had their own reasons, and it is after these that we now inquire.

Unfortunately in a way, the political causes and circumstances of a single incident are not normally available, and they are certainly not very intelligible, apart from the general historical condition of the people amongst whom the incident took place. The details of this background information, in great profusion, can be read in many books published at the present time;[2] it would, in any quantity, be out of place in this book. But since any attempted account of the execution of Jesus requires at least some historical background to the groups, forces and policies from which he might have expected hostility or to which he might reasonably have looked for support, it is well to describe the main examples of these, not indeed in the kind of detail the professional historian would require, but in terms, rather, of the real life-options they offered to the people, life-options of such depth and significance that people would be prepared to die for them – or to kill. Life-options, in any case, tend to recur in recurring political circumstances of human societies, and they are therefore intelligible far beyond the particularities of any one time or place.

Those who have been so unfortunate as to have had any experience of political oppression by overlords foreign or domestic have no difficulty in recognizing the option offered by the Zealots of Jesus' day. They are the IRA, the Ernesto 'Che' Guevaras of the race, romanticized as freedom fighters and liberators by those who agree with their causes and methods, at least after they have won; denounced as terrorists, thugs and brigands (like Barabbas) by those who do not agree with them, and usually when they lose. Their perennial belief is that nothing short of armed force can change a situation of oppression into one where freedom and justice prevail, that those who benefit from oppression are simply not amenable to any other type of persuasion. History has recorded too many victories in their favour to allow any people to dismiss out of hand the attractiveness of their proffered solution which can, in any case, call on all the pent-up frustrations of deprived humanity.

People are most prone to violence when their bellies are threatened, and Palestine of the first Christian century was a poor rural area without much of the usual sources of wealth. The people laboured under a double taxation system. Taxes had to be paid to their Roman overlords. Temple taxes had also to be paid to keep their own native administration, a combined civic and religious authority, in office, and their religious piety as Jews enjoined on them tithing and other incidental expenses. Although there were wealthy Jews in the land, too many lived just above starvation level, and the sight of needed wealth going to Romans, or even to the quisling temple authority in Jerusalem, was enough to make many of them decide to take up the sword. In addition, those who took a radical view of the Law, the religion of the Jews, thought of the land as God's, its fruits belonged to God, the first fruits were given to God, and the rest God gave, as he had given the land, to his chosen people. To take any of the fruits of the land and to pay them in taxes to foreigners, who in any case polluted the place by the very presence of themselves and their gods, was the worst combination of wickedness conceivable, treason and apostasy rolled into one. As far as the Zealots were concerned, the quisling Jewish leadership of the Jerusalem temple, who dealt with the Romans for whatever remnant of native authority they were allowed, were as worthy of the sword as the Romans themselves. Such, then, was the awful option which the Zealots offered their contemporaries, and amongst these, Jesus.

Could Jesus have looked for sympathy in this direction? Was Jesus a Zealot? Serious scholars have discussed this question. Some deny any possible connection, angry that men of blood should still invoke the name of Jesus today. Others are more soberly impressed by the following points: that a Zealot is named amongst Jesus' closest followers (Mark 3.18), that he was executed with Zealots in the usual manner of executing Zealots, that he came into lethal conflict with the temple authority, and that he took a very radical view of the Law, the Jewish religion. Even his advice when asked about taxes, to render to Caesar the things that are Caesar's and to God the things that are God's, could be heard by a Zealot as the advice to give Caesar the sharp end of the sword, and the tithes to Yahweh.[3] This question will inevitably come up again. At the moment it need only be remarked that Jesus, like other non-violent figures in history, like Socrates or Gandhi, probably posed a more radical threat to the powers that be than any armed man could do. This in itself could easily explain why a convinced Zealot might go over to his side, and why Pilate would execute him with others who to him posed a similar threat.

The party which offered the very opposite life-option to that of the Zealots and whose members were, amongst their fellow-countrymen, the most natural enemies of the latter, was the party of the Sadducees. The option they offered their oppressed comrades was one of realistic, if reluctant cooperation with over-lords far too strong to challenge on any military terms. If the Zealots were impressed still by the memory of the last great liberation struggle of the Jews some sixteen decades before Jesus, the so-called Maccabean revolt, the Sadducees were far more impressed by the manner in which great empires passed the civilized world like a football from one to the other, and by the concomitant fact that their little people had been dominated

The Death of Jesus

by such empires for far greater lengths of their history than they had been free. Deal, was their advice, deal with the great power of Rome to gain all you can for yourselves; do not fight and lose all you have. The Sadducees, in short, were conservatives. This is usually taken to mean that they opted for the older Israelite ignorance or agnosticism about an after-life and in general preferred to rest their national and religious identity on the more primitive written form of their religion, the so-called Books of Moses, than on any later writings or interpretations. All this, indeed, they did. Conservatives, however, are conservatives, not so much because they have any more fidelity to the past than the rest of humanity, but because they want at all costs to conserve what they have in the present. The Sadducees' lack of interest in after-life was probably due more to the natural wish of people in power to see rewards and punishments portioned out in this life than to any deep metaphysical speculation, and their insistence on sticking with the simpler and more primitive forms of Jewish religion probably owed more to the dealer's reluctance to distance himself too much from his opposite number than it owes to any romance of the pristine purity of the nation's past.

The Sadducee party drew its membership mainly from the aristocratic families and from the *nouveaux riches*, and exercised its influence principally through the puppet government in Jerusalem. This puppet government was constituted as follows. The head of state was the high priest. He represented all Jews before Yahweh, and in theory he represented all Jews before the emperor; in reality he represented the people of Judaea before the procurator. He presided over the various structures of the puppet government. The principal structure was the high council or the Sanhedrin, made up of seventy-one members. This council had an executive committee, a consistory of priests and laity, sometimes referred to in the New Testament as 'the high priests'. It also numbered scribes amongst its members, many of whom because of their interest and expertise in interpreting the Law, would have been Pharisees. This government was the puppet of Rome, but more immediately the puppet of the personal representative of the Roman emperor, at the time of the death of Jesus a procurator named Pontius Pilate. The procurator could appoint and dismiss high priests; he symbolically kept the high-priestly vestments in the Antonia, a Roman fortress overlooking the Temple, overlooking the seat of the high priest's civil and religious power. Ever since the Roman general,

Pompey, entered Jerusalem in 69 BC, the traditional land of the Jewish people had been ruled by puppets from the House of Hasmon, successors of the once briefly successful leaders of the Maccabean revolt. But because of unusual unrest around Jerusalem the Romans had decided in AD 6 to rule Judaea, together with Samaria and Idumea, by a personal representative of the Roman emperor, under whom was his appointee, the high priest, and the latter's council. Poised in such a delicate position of uncertain power, the Sadducees, the strongest party in this puppet government, recommended as the only reasonable life-option for their subjugated people that they make the best deal they could by political negotiations with superior power. In the conflict stories told about Jesus in the New Testament, the chief priests and the elders, who would have been mostly of the Sadducee party, are named as Jesus' main opponents in the passion narratives, as scribes and Pharisees are mainly his opponents in the earlier parts of the gospels. The reason for this opposition when Jesus brought his cause to Jerusalem must soon be investigated. But first, the Pharisees.

The Pharisees are described as the popular party, not, I suspect, because much is known about the extent of their membership or about the popularity of their views, but to distinguish them from the Temple authority in Jerusalem. It is the nature of their life-option that interests us, in any case, more than the origin of their name or the extent of their numbers. They would not fight like the Zealots, nor would they wheel and deal like the Sadducees. Both these options they regarded as suicidal: the Zealot option literally so, and the Sadducee option of dealing closely with a powerful foreign empire they would only see as courting a cultural and national death-by-inches. Instead they thought they saw a way in which the smallest and most insignificant people can indefinitely maintain their identity in the face of the nearest and greatest Leviathan conceivable. That way was to hold to such unique beliefs and practices and to make these so obvious in every single detail of daily life that a kind of spiritual identity would be formed which political impotence of the worst kind and of the longest duration could never extinguish. It was the way of ideological and behavioural purity reinforcing national identity and distinction. At the turn of this century the oppressed Irish tried it, with less lasting results.

So the Pharisees took the written Law of Moses and interpreted it to apply to every circumstance of life, and by such minute observance of God's will for them they tried to form a people of God uncorrupted by the powerful cultures of foreign nations. Finally, a resurrection-life, they believed, would more than compensate those who followed their life-option for any deprivation incurred because of it in this (a belief which the Pharisee Paul was not slow to put to his own converts; Romans 8.18).

From New Testament times on the Pharisees have been more maligned than any other group, and quite unjustly so. Of course, their life-option was often corrupted by legalistic tendencies and the ensuing hypocrisy of people who cannot bear so much law. But it is no more a crippling objection to Pharisaism that it is the natural home of legalism and hypocrisy than it is a crippling objection to Zealotry that it naturally attracts psychopaths or to Sadduceeism that it appeals to self-seekers hungry for power. The abuse of life-options does not negate their value, and honest men could give their lives with full conviction to each of these while fully cognizant of the misuse which knaves could make of any or all of them.

Besides, on the options mentioned already and on one more to be briefly described below history has already sat in judgment, and has given its verdict in favour of the Pharisees. When the Romans destroyed Jerusalem in AD 70, and with it the native structures of the Jewish nation, the Zealots perished in the conflict they had precipitated (though they did make one more tragic stand about sixty years later), and there was no longer any intermediate place of power for Sadducees, while Jewish identity and the Jewish future has been in the safe hands of scribal or Pharisaic Judaism to this day. It is no coincidence that the gospels were written just when the future of Judaism was falling to the Pharisees. Matthew in particular, who was engaged in writing the new Law, the new religious constitution for the followers of Jesus, saw his closest and most dangerous rivals in the Pharisees who were just then codifying the Mosaic Law, the detailed and distinctive badge of Jewish identity. This is not to say that Jesus was not in conflict with Pharisees also – as he most certainly was – but it is to cast serious doubt on the impression so roundly conveyed by Matthew that so many of them were whited sepulchres and thoroughly deserving of his chapter of woes (Matthew 23).

The last option offered by a contemporary group to the oppressed people into which Jesus was born is of least interest in this context. It is the option of seceding from human society and its ways, from the polis and its politics, an option followed at all times and in all cultures, by the Epicurean philosopher, the Christian contemplative, the twentieth-century drop-outs in the deserts and hills of California. It is the option of seeking far from the madding crowd a perfect life, uncontaminated by contact with the corruptions of human society, and to wait in this state or place for a better world to appear or for this one to come to its senses. The Qumran community and more generally the Essenes favoured this option at the time of Jesus. Aiming at pure observance of the Law where alone they felt it could be achieved, in a monastic setting, and at a pure cult away from the compromised temple at Jerusalem, they lived truly ascetic lives of poverty and obedience and waited for the grand intervention of God. Since such groups are always parasitic on the societies from which they secede – a simple statement of economic or political nature this, not an evaluation of the life-option in question – they normally disappear with the structures of the society to which they opposed themselves. There is no convincing evidence in the records that Jesus came in contact with these groups. They therefore represent an option which his ministry to the people did not consider.

These, then, were the real live options available to the people into which Jesus was born. They are life-options recognizable to most times and places. They are deep enough and broad enough to make people live for them or die for them or, occasionally, to kill for them. They are all designed to allow a people with its own country and its own culture to survive, and survival is the most dominant of all human motives. It is against the background they paint that the death of Jesus must be seen.

When we turn, against this background, to the four passion narratives – and these are all we have, for, with the exception of one or two later and uninformative extra-biblical references, neither the chroniclers of the Jews nor the chroniclers of the Roman Empire thought the death of Jesus, this constitutive event of the Christian tradition, worth recording – we had better recognize immediately some peculiarities of the literature here so that these need not impede our inquiry. I do not mean to refer yet to the myth which is interlaced with all New Testament data, nor to introduce at this point the complex of literary, form and redaction criticism which has attempted over the last two centuries or so to reveal the precise structure of New Testament literature. But there is a peculiarity of the passion narratives which, though connected with the myth of Jesus, deserves special and separate mention. It is a particular case of a general tendency of the New Testament writers toward what Barnabas Lindars calls New Testament apologetic.[4] It was generally important for those who first preached Jesus, since they preached him first to his fellow Jews, to establish his life work as a legitimate development of the Jewish religion, and to use for this purpose the authoritative text of the Old Testament. But the greatest single stumbling-block, to use Paul's phrase, in the path of this process was the execution of the alleged Messiah as a common criminal. The passion narratives, therefore, make more use of the Old Testament than any other part of the gospels; they are in fact a veritable mosaic of implicit reference to familiar psalms and to prophecies familiar and unfamiliar. A reading of Psalm 22, for instance, would give not only the actual words of forsakenness placed on the lips of Jesus on the cross, but also details of the destiny of his garments and of the jeers and attitudes of the onlookers. Psalm 69 talks of a man given vinegar to drink, Psalm 41 has reference to betrayal by a man who ate one's bread, and from the prophecy of Zechariah 9-13 one can glean references to a man being pierced (now taken as a reference to crucifixion), to the sheep being scattered when the shepherd is stricken, and so on.

Obviously even this brief list of examples of implicit Old Testament reference in the passion narratives faces the historical investigator with a rather crucial choice. Are we to take it that the concrete details just mentioned actually took place in the course of the arrest, trial and execution of Jesus, and then it was found that Old Testament passages anticipated them with astounding accuracy? Or are we to take it rather that the followers of Jesus, wishing to show their fellow Jews that Jesus in his passion fully fitted the character of the obedient servant of Yahweh, unjustly persecuted, whom Yahweh would nevertheless not allow utterly to fail, used the techniques of subliminal persuasion and painted the picture of Jesus' passion in terms literally reminiscent of this composite Old Testament character, so that concrete details like those briefly recorded above were carried into the passion narrative by these techniques? There can scarcely be any doubt that in many cases of detail, if not in most, the latter is the less naive explanation. For our present purposes, in any case, it is sufficient to have noticed this peculiarity of the passion narratives, to be prepared to face the choice involved, and then to continue with the quest.

Most of us who have, quite correctly, thought of Jesus always as the founder of our faith have also, and probably as a consequence of this, considered the trial of Jesus before the Jewish authorities as the 'real' trial, conducted on purely religious charges, and the trial before the Roman procurator as a simple subsidiary travesty of justice. And we have mostly failed to see, until recent critical scholarship brings them to our notice, how many difficulties this assumption must meet. For, first, the four gospels show their usual disregard for mutual consistency when describing the circumstances of the Jewish trial (if, in fact, it was a formal trial at all, and not just a hearing before some Jewish officials). Matthew and Mark have a trial of Jesus at night, continued the following morning; Luke has a trial in the morning only, all of these before the full high council; whereas John has Jesus brought first before Annas and then before the reigning high priest, Caiaphas, with no mention of an assembly of the full high council at all. Second, and more seriously, some scholars who are expert in the history of Jewish institutions argue that a trial before the full high council such as our synoptic gospels describe could not have taken place, that Jewish law would not have countenanced such a trial at such a time (at night), in such circumstances (with a capital verdict rendered so quickly afterwards), and on such charges (in Jewish law the charge of blasphemy could not be proved against Jesus from anything brought forward by his accusers).[5] Some scholars argue on more purely exegetical grounds simply that the gospel records we possess do not allow us to conclude that any trial or trials before the high council took place.[6] And though there are still others who argue on both historical and exegetical grounds that a trial before the Sanhedrin could have taken place and did in fact take place,[7] the matter must be open to serious doubt.

There are many minor irritants in this debate. Learned scholars disagree as to whether or not Jewish authorities at the time of Jesus had the right to inflict capital punishment. For if they did not have this right, as John clearly states they did not (John 18.31), that would explain why there would have to be a Roman trial even after full criminal proceedings before the highest Jewish court. But if, as some argue, they did have the right, there would be no explanation for the Roman trial – except that, as a matter of historical fact, it was the 'real' trial after all. Finally, we are reminded by more than one exegete that we dare not ignore the increasing apologetic tendency of the gospel writers to shift the blame for the death of Jesus from the Romans, whose empire the Christians were by this time trying to win for their faith, to the Jews. This apologetic interest, undoubtedly present, would certainly account for the addition, as time went on, of more and more narrative detail to the Jewish involvement in the death of Jesus, and hence to the Jewish trial or hearing.

In the end, it is probably not unfair to remark, this very erudite debate has probably done a good deal more for the academic careers of those involved in it than it has done for clarity and conclusion in the subject in question. For if we search out the commonest and most essential elements of the gospel narratives, we shall no doubt end with a tolerable grasp of all we really need to know about this tragic event.

There is, as Gerard Sloyan says and as we hope to fully illustrate from the life of Jesus, a dependable tradition of antipathy between Jesus and certain Jewish leaders,[8] proponents of other life-options which they felt he threatened. There is therefore no doubt that Jewish leaders had a hand in his death, and little doubt that he was arraigned before some of them in Jerusalem, whatever the more precise circumstances of time and place and tribunal. But what were the charges against Jesus that weighed with the Jerusalem leaders? That poses a more important question than do the precise circumstances of time, place and tribunal; because it is important to know for what a man died, especially if it can then be seen that it was also that for which he lived.

All four gospel accounts have Jesus charged with claiming to be Son of God, in that or an alternative phrase. Three of them – John is the exception here – attach the claim to be Messiah to this first claim, almost as if it were its equivalent. All have the charge uncontested. Two of the accounts, those of Mark and Matthew, have the admission of these charges described as blasphemy, and have the high priest tear his garments, the ritual act enjoined on him when he is witness to a blasphemy. The same two accounts have the further charge brought against Jesus that he threatened the Temple, and though it is said that this was false witness, there are other records in the New Testament of something Jesus said which could certainly be construed by the Temple authority as being against the Temple (Mark 13.2; 15.29 and John 2.19-22).[9]

The problems with these accounts of the charges against Jesus are many. For a start, it is not an offence for a Jew to claim to be Son of God, especially in the hearing of another Jew, and it is certainly not a capital offence, though it might be offensive to those sensitive to the due claims of humility in self-description. From far back in Jewish history the nation of Israel was Son of

God when faithful to Yahweh, and an individual Israelite, if unusually faithful to the will of God in this world, could claim to be Son of God in that sense, and have the claim allowed. In the Judaea royal ritual the King was declared Son of God on his enthronement.

Even if we take this claim outside the Jewish context altogether, and understand it in a sense which in that context would have no place, not, at least, without long explanations, it would still be very difficult to consider it a capital offence. I once met a man in what used to be known unkindly as a lunatic asylum who claimed to be the Holy Ghost incarnate. Knowing that I was a priest, he urged me, as the Holy Ghost might well be expected to do, not to stay in Ireland where there were too many priests, but to go instead 'on the missions'. When we meet such a person we either believe what he says, and then do what he says, or we simply dismiss him and get him some treatment, or we might, as in my case, end up doing what he says though we did not believe his claim at all. In short, the claim itself is of no consequence, and we all realize that very well; it is what is done under the claim that can, if anything, be offensive, and perhaps even capitally so.

Much the same must be said of the claim to be Messiah. In the thirteenth decade of the Christian era, leading up to the last tragic stand of the Jews against the Romans, a man called Bar Kochba claimed to be Messiah, and one of the most renowned rabbis of the age, Rabbi Akiba, endorsed his claim. Now the Jerusalem aristocracy might well want to see dead a messianic pretender with Zealot tendencies, but they would have to use something other than Jewish legal process to accomplish their goal. Once again the claim to be God's Messiah was simply not punishable by Jewish law – unless one expected that the real Messiah when he finally did stand up would then have to stand trial for his life before getting on with his life's work – but what was attempted or accomplished under that claim could conceivably be so punishable.

Strangest of all in these accounts of the Jewish trial of Jesus is the assumption that this combined claim constitutes blasphemy, for from all that we know of Jewish law of the time, it simply did not. Technically speaking, blasphemy was committed by one who uttered the holy name, Yahweh, for only the high priest was permitted to utter it on the Day of Atonement. Neither the claim to be Messiah, nor the claim to be Son of God, nor even the combination of these constituted blasphemy in Jewish law.

And the upshot of all this is that the gospel accounts do not give us any straightforward description of the charges which in the case of Jesus the Jewish authorities thought to be proven and knew to be worthy of death.[10]

The best suggestion here is that we are dealing with a later Christian shorthand which conceals, though not altogether from the eyes of a good historian, the literal charges on which the Jews thought Jesus should be executed. Because it was Jesus' business, as we must see shortly, not to promote himself, but to forge a new relationship between man and God, he may never have claimed the titles Son of God or Messiah, or indeed any other title for himself at all. He said and did certain things, though, which in the view of those who accepted them entitled him to the claim to be Messiah, and Son of God, and saviour, and much more, but to those who could not accept them proved him only to be an enemy of their religion, which was the very cement of the nation, and therefore an enemy of the people. The charge that he threatened the Temple, though it is quickly passed over in our present accounts – for it would not interest writers or readers of the year AD 70 and after, when the Jerusalem temple was destroyed, nearly as much as the claim that he was Messiah and the foundation of the new spiritual temple of God (Ephesians 20.19-22) – might in the end provide us with our best clue. Jeremiah, before Jesus, nearly died for saying that God might move from the Temple.

The Temple was the centre and symbol of the Jewish religion. It was also the situs of the power of the high priest and his council, the acknowledged officers and leaders of this religion. Any attempt to alter radically the religion could be seen as an attack on the leadership – in shorthand again, an attack on the Temple. Observers of the recent Roman Catholic debate about contraception must have noticed how quickly it turned from moral considerations to an argument about power and authority, and those who tried to change the accepted morality of marriage were accused of attacking the Vatican. The precise manner in which Jesus was radical about his inherited religion must wait for the chapter on the life of Jesus. For the moment it need only be noted that religion, being the outward embodiment of religious faith, is an inextricable complex of creed and code, ritual and institution (or office), and that any attempt to alter any part of this always involves the others and inevitably involves the status of the officers. The officers in this case are the duly appointed civic *and* religious leaders in the land. And the

Temple is both physical centre and symbol of their power.

There are clues elsewhere that Jesus' attempt to change radically the religion of his people was what brought about his death. Paul once wrote: 'If justification were through the Law (read 'the Jewish religion'), Christ died to no purpose' (Galatians 2.21). A little reflection will surely show that that passing remark is not entirely true, as passing remarks are simply assumed to be, unless Jesus died precisely because of his challenge to the Law. And Frances Young has drawn from a long line of Jesus-followers persecuted by the Jews, from Stephen (see Acts 6.14) and Paul on, the lesson that Jews prized orthopraxis over orthodoxy, that is to say, that whereas beliefs about the Messiah, for instance, were somewhat optional, challenges to the practices and institutions of Judaism could be counted in the category of treason/apostasy and could reach the point, as in the case of Paul also, where they could be found worthy of death.[11]

It is even probable – and here the otherwise confusing reference to blasphemy provides our final clue – that one good way of describing the radical change Jesus tried to bring to his inherited religion is to say that he tried to bring about a new nearness of God to every human person such that human mediators between God and man would no longer be necessary. This would leave the religion with its officers, of course, but it would radically alter their status. Jesus may even have vindicated the right of every person to utter the holy name of God, though his own preferred form of address was 'Father', and he may even have done this in the hearing of the high priest as a concrete illustration of what his mission was meant to achieve. But whether he did this or not, if the above is at all an accurate description of his mission – and we shall see that it is – he had broken the Law in spirit.

The nucleus of historical fact contained in our present passion narratives can then be expressed as follows. Jesus was very probably arraigned before a group of influential Jewish leaders in Jerusalem, including, no doubt, the high priest. And the best hypothesis about the charges investigated on that occasion – a hypothesis which can be further tested in the chapter on the life of Jesus – is that they concerned a change he was attempting to bring about in the Jewish Law (or religion) of the land, a change which the leaders thought radical and feared or perceived would threaten their own roles and status. Are these charges religious or political? Clearly, they cannot be considered purely religious.

Jesus' life is not being sought by the leaders of his people simply to carry out a divine decision to have him die for the sins of mankind, nor do they want him killed simply because he has arrived at some mistaken view on some important aspect of Jewish theory. On the contrary, the only adequate answer to the above question must be that the charges are inextricably religious *and* political. Jesus was inaugurating in both theory and practice moves that would at one and the same time change the religion and threaten both its institutions and those who manned them – for theory by itself is harmless and practice without theory behind it soon runs out in disarray.

What Jesus achieved, then, made him to some the Christ, the Son of God; and to others it made him merely a threat to the status of the lawful government. Since it is the former who give us the account of the Jewish trial, it is no wonder that the charges are expressed in their kind of language. This is the later Christian shorthand to which I referred, shorthand for that disruptive public mission of his and its effects, which made him Lord to some, and threatened the familiar lordship of others.

Our accounts of the trial before Pilate are, by contrast with the Jewish 'trials', quite clear on the nature of the charges on which Pilate condemned Jesus to death. But why was there a Roman trial at all in addition to the Jewish hearing? There are three basic types of answer to this intriguing question.

(*a*) Jewish leaders conjured up a purely political charge against Jesus in order to have Pilate condemn him because: 1. they could not themselves legally execute a capital sentence; and 2. Pilate would have had no interest in their religious differences.

(*b*) Jesus – no pacifist he – was in fact in the course of his mission inciting the people to revolutionary action against the powers that were in the land, and Pilate, from his experience of, for instance, the Zealots, could recognize Jesus' activity as a crime worthy of death.

(*c*) The substance of the very same charge which persuaded the Jewish leaders to have Jesus put to death would, and did in fact, equally engage Pilate's interest in Jesus' case, though, since the nature of the charge was religio-political, it might well have had its religious aspect stressed before the Jewish leaders and its political side more emphasized before the Roman.

The four gospel accounts of the incident leave us in no possible doubt about the political nature of the charges brought against Jesus as he stood before Pilate. All four have Pilate ask Jesus if he claims to be King of the Jews, a messianic title with

the clearest political implications. The synoptic gospels have
Jesus answer 'you have said so'; John has 'you say that I am a
king', in the course of a theological instruction on the nature of
his kingship. All four gospels have the charge on which Jesus
was condemned and which was customarily fixed to the instrument of execution describe him as a messianic pretender to the
Jewish throne. In the Barabbas incident Mark and John have
Pilate ask if the people would not prefer him to release their
king, Matthew has Jesus referred to as the Christ, and Luke
omits any messianic reference. We may use this incident in evidence here whether the Barabbas story is historical or whether,
as some think, the story was simply inserted in the passion
narrative to point the contrast between Jesus and Barabbas, for
Barabbas is depicted as an armed revolutionary. (Bar-Abbas
means 'son of the Father'; and Jesus called God 'Abba' as God's
son.) Luke expands on the political charge: 'We found this man
perverting our nation, and forbidding us to give tribute to
Caesar, and saying that he himself is Christ a king' (Luke 23.1),
and John has 'the Jews' make clear to Pilate, as if he did not see
them, the literal implications of Jesus' alleged claim and crime:
'everyone who makes himself king sets himself against Caesar'
(John 19.12). Even the Roman soldiery mocks him as a poor,
failed pretender to a throne.[12]

If I were asked to choose between the explanations, enumerated above, of the occurrence of this Roman trial and of its
relation to the Jewish hearing, I must say I would choose (c), the
third. The suggestion that the Jewish leaders trumped up a
charge and then bullied Pilate into finding Jesus guilty of it is
both unlikely and unnecessary; unnecessary in view of better
suggestions available and unlikely from all that we know about
the career and character of Pontius Pilate. Any bullying that was
done during Pilate's ten year procuratorship (and ten years as
procurator then was almost as remarkable as ten years as college
president now), at least while he was protégé of Sejanus, a
Roman politician with imperial ambitions, was done by Pilate,
not to him. Nor are the specific reasons given for this suggestion
at all convincing. It is not certain that the Jewish leaders did not
have the legal power of capital punishment over their subjects;
and we have already argued that the charges against Jesus at the
Jewish hearing were not purely religious. The trouble with suggestions of type (b) above is that they generally put the cart
before the horse. They try first to place Jesus in one of the
contrary categories of pacifist or man of violence and then to

decide whether or not the Roman trial of Jesus was a 'real' trial conducted on its own independent charge, of a purely political nature. But this is surely to tackle the question the wrong way round. The concepts 'pacifist' and 'violent revolutionary' are so elastic that they can be stretched to cover each other's ground. Most people who engage in acts of war or armed insurrection do so in the name of peace and claim with great conviction to be the only true pacifists at heart; while someone, like Jesus perhaps, who never raised as much as a finger in physical assault on another human being could bring about more radical changes in human society, and more seriously threaten more structures, and provoke thereby more violence against himself and his followers, than could the best armed guerrilla force in the world.[13] It seems better, then, to use the accounts of the trials to discover what in his conduct these officials could have considered a charge against Jesus, than to use these vague and elastic categories to find out what actually happened at the trial or trials.

The more positive reason for preferring an explanation of type (c) above is best illustrated by an anecdote. An anti-war film, a classic of its kind, I believe, but the name of which I now cannot recall, had for its subject a group of German officers in an occupied village in Poland. One of the officers tried to persuade his peers to treat the native population, and especially their leading citizens, with some decency and respect, so as to elicit some necessary cooperation from them. His advice was disregarded, and as the inevitable acts of terrorism began on both sides, the human situation in the village rapidly worsened. One night, as the officers sat listening to a triumphant broadcast from the homeland telling of more and vaster areas annexed by the Nazi forces, our officer, with a hollow laugh, made this unforgettable remark. 'The flies,' he mocked, 'have captured more fly-paper.'

No group of people can long maintain any in the least enjoyable control over another group of people without some minimum form of collaboration from the latter. The Romans seem to have realized that more than most imperial forces in history. Today also great world powers like Russia and America, who would, of course, hotly deny any imperial intent, intervene to keep particular governments in power in countries which, quite voluntarily, naturally, belong amongst their allies. It is quite easy to understand, then, that a man whose mission somehow threatened the status of the subordinate officers and offices should be of as much interest to Pilate as he was to the high priest, and that Pilate should be as little reluctant, as little in need of persuasion to kill him, on charges of threatening the security of the state, as he would be to kill a Zealot.

The fact that Jesus' mission was itself of a religious nature would account for his arraignment first before the Jewish leaders, and also for the prominence of these as his accusers before Pilate. The apologetic interest of Christian writers to persuade the people of the Roman empire that the empire never had anything to fear from their leader would then account for the growing insistence in the passion narratives on the reluctance of Pilate to have Jesus executed and for the corresponding increase of blame laid on the part played by the Jewish leaders in his death. But the clearest fact, we may repeat, is that Jesus was executed in the Roman manner of crucifixion, after sentence by a Roman tribunal, on a charge which Romans considered capital and proven. And the best explanation of this fact is that Jesus, it was thought, threatened the status of the officers of the puppet government whose life-option it was to collaborate with the Romans, that he thus threatened the delicate structures of that necessary area of collusion between overlords and oppressed, and could then reasonably be accused of threatening the whole fabric of the two-tiered civil power in the land. Both his Jewish and his Roman accusers saw him as some kind of messianic pretender – once again more detail on possible grounds for this view of him will have to await the chapter on the life of Jesus. This alleged role of his inextricably combined religious and political aspects. It was the political aspect of it, though, that before both tribunals endangered his life, and finally before Pilate made his life forfeit.

All this might almost suggest that Pilate and the high priest were acting within their legal rights, protecting the interests of the state, and that Jesus, consequently, might reasonably have been considered guilty. The belief that Jesus was guilty, of course, has sometimes been held by life-of-Jesus researchers who like to think of him as a rabid apocalyptic doing his damnedest to usher in the great cosmic catastrophe. But even when these fanciful reconstructions are set firmly aside, the suggestion of Jesus' guilt comes back in more subtle forms. In the course of Albert Camus's *The Fall*, the Ancient Mariner-type subject of that novel thinks aloud the following thought:

Say, do you know why he was crucified – the one you are perhaps thinking of at the moment? Well, there were heaps of reasons for that. There are always reasons for murdering a man. On the contrary, it is impossible to justify his living. That's why crime always finds lawyers, and innocence only rarely. But, besides the reasons that have been very well explained to us for the past two thousand years, there was a major one for that terrible agony, and I don't know why it has been so carefully hidden. The real reason is that he knew he was not altogether innocent.[14]

What can one say to that? It would not be sufficient to say that the enemies of a man can often see him more clearly than can his friends, and can have a sharper view of the further implications of what he is about – though that is undoubtedly true. It would be necessary to add that the innocence we attribute to Jesus when we say that he was like to us in all things, sin alone excepted, is an innocence above and beyond legal innocence. Legal innocence is a relative thing, relative to the structures and constitutions of the countries in which it is judged. And on that relative understanding of legal innocence, Jesus may not have been altogether innocent.

It is a primary concern of all governments, both ancient and modern, to protect their own power. It is a primary concern of all systems of law to protect the authority of the properly designated leaders of a people. There are always special powers which can be legally evoked by the leaders to protect, as they say, the security of the state. The British put all suspected Irish Republican Army members in prison camps in Northern Ireland in the early 1970s; the Americans put Japanese living in America in prison camps after Pearl Harbour. Legal innocence is indeed a shifting substance. It appears that John, for all the alleged historical unreliability of his gospel, was well aware of both the area of collusion between Romans and puppet Jewish government and of the threat which Jesus posed to the security of the state, that is, to the status of lordship and authority which one group of human beings wields over another. John describes a meeting of the council called by high priests and Pharisees at which it is decided: 'if we let him go on thus everyone will believe in him, and the Romans will come and destroy both our holy place and our nation.' Caiaphas then declares: 'It is expedient for you that one man should die for the people, and that the whole nation should not perish.' To which John adds rather laconically that the man was a prophet without knowing it. It was indeed necessary that this man should die, not only for that nation, but for all the nations of the earth (John 11.48-53). All are held in the same human servitude, and all are fashioners of their own chains.

There is one further thought worth thinking at this point. Every tragedy contains its own comment on the human condition, and it is always a comment worth dwelling upon. But not every tragedy has the same revelatory force, or the same power to raise human consciousness or to move the human will and emotions to a finer state. The great poetic tragedies from Oedipus to Hamlet or King Lear do not, after all, take as their subjects the killing of a man by thugs who act with malice aforethought and with nothing but their own self-interest at stake. They raise, rather, to historic heights those conflicts which seem endemic to their characters' very relationships within the family and the social structure. Because they do this, they are great tragedies and their poetic effect can amount to catharsis.[15] So too the tragedy of Jesus' death is all the more significant for the understanding of the human condition, and perhaps for its betterment, if it is seen to result from one of those deep clashes between human personalities who, given the roles they had to play, could seemingly do no different than they did. Any further consideration of this point, however, takes us into the next section, and into the rest of the book. But it takes us first to the topic of myth, to the search for those deeply resonating symbols in which people have always tried to capture and to express to themselves the deepest significance of their world, of the human condition, and of the persons and events which have most shaped their historic state.

The myth that grew around the facts

Already in one of the earliest written references to the death of Jesus – itself a solemn and received formula – we find the concrete historical details of tribunal, charge and other circumstance replaced by phrases that indicate, for the followers of Jesus at least, the fuller implications and the broader significance of that tragic event. 'I delivered to you as of first importance what I also received,' Paul wrote to his Corinthian converts (I Corinthians 15.3), 'That Christ died for our sins in accordance with the scriptures.' So the death of Jesus, whenever and however it was engineered, has some effect on the sinfulness of the human race, and some place in the projections of the sacred writings of the Jews, themselves descriptive of the relationships between God and humanity. In actual fact, those writings sacred to the

followers of Jesus and known as the New Testament make use
of quite a variety of symbolism in order to search out and present the deepest significance for human kind of the death of
Jesus.

In general this symbolism tries to come to grips with what the
followers of Jesus sense as a new or renewed relationship between humanity and God. But when it comes to particulars,
those of us at least who have not had our sensitivity to symbol
altogether dulled by frequent and mindless repetition must be
astounded first at the variety of symbols produced by the fertile
imaginations of the early writers.

Sometimes the writers depict the death of Jesus as effecting a
new or renewed access to God, simply that (Romans 5.2;
Ephesians 2.18). The symbol here is the opening of a road after
an avalanche, or the discovery of the Northwest Passage. Sometimes the symbol is taken from our experience of the law courts,
particularly from the decree of acquittal read to one unfortunate
enough to have been arraigned on some charge before them,
and the death of Jesus is described as our justification, as having
brought about a declaration of our 'righteousness' before God
(Romans 5.9, passim). On yet other occasions the symbolism is
drawn from yet another common area of human experience, the
market-place, and in particular, in those earlier days, the
slave-market. Now the death of Jesus is our redemption or our
ransom, the act of buying us back or the price paid (Romans
3.24; Mark 10.45). The experience of being reconciled with a
friend after a period of estrangement provides, at other times,
the symbolism in which we can sense the effect of the death of
Jesus (II Corinthians 5.17-21); or our more positive or fortunate
encounters with members of the medical profession are evoked
in symbol, and the death of Jesus becomes our healing or 'salvation' (Romans 5.9; 2.16). In some contexts the symbolism is
drawn more directly from the ritual experiences of the religion to
which readers and writers belong. The death of Jesus is
described as the spilling or sprinkling of blood which, in ancient
times, sealed a covenant between God and his people (Mark
14.24); or the priestly sacrifice offered on the great Day of
Atonement provides the imagery in which the implications of
the death of Jesus for our relationship to God are depicted (Hebrews 9.11-14). Finally, the common and precious sense of liberation, experienced on all kinds of occasions, from getting out of
tight trousers to getting out of death row in a state penitentiary,
is evoked in an attempt to let us know what the death of Jesus

means to us (Galatians 1.4).

Perhaps the worst mistake that could be made here would be to take any of these, or all of them, literally. To do so would be to mistake the nature of symbolism in a very elementary way, and to mistake, consequently, the true significance of the death of Jesus which these writers are trying by means of these rich images to bring to our notice and appreciation. Since the history of Christian theology has shown some regrettable tendencies to deal literally with some of the examples given above, and particularly the ones drawn from Jewish ritual, it might be wise to choose this point for a reflective pause, to consider more closely the nature of image and symbol, and the nature of that very comprehensive form which weaves image and symbol into a story, that is to say, myth.

The nature of myth

Colours shade into each other, and myth is difficult to delimit clearly. But as certain strong and simple shades clearly belong to blue, so let it be with myth. It even seems as if there is no single context to which myth belongs and in which it is invariably found. It used to be fashionable to say that myth had its unique origin in religious ritual or, more generally, that its place was in the area of the sacred rather than the profane, but even this does not appear to be quite true.[16]

For those who attempt a brief and rather general definition of myth perhaps the best thing to say is that myth finds its place somewhere on the broad spectrum of human perception and expression, and to try to discover where that place may be. The spectrum of perception and expression ranges, on the most elementary account of it, from the concrete, where the medium of expression, the word or image used, is nearest to individual things or elements, to the abstract, where it is furthest from these because it represents them by the smallest number (one) of their actual characteristics. Garden and desert, for instance, are concrete words and images, order and chaos are abstract. 'Unity of opposites and centred wholeness' is abstract, a mandala is concrete.

This distinction, it should perhaps be said, has nothing to do with depth or universality of significance; it has to do merely with the medium of perception and expression, with the nature of this, with the question whether we are dealing with an image-word or an abstract concept-word. It is too easy to think that abstract concepts, together with the words which acquire and express them, are capable of universal significance and application precisely because they leave out of account most of what is concretely characteristic of the things they talk about, and because they therefore move on what can only be considered a superficial level. It is just as easy to think that concrete images, together with the words which acquire and express these, achieve a greater depth of significance because they stay closer to the detailed contours of the things and characters with which they deal,[17] but that they are correspondingly localized and lacking in universality of significance. Neither of these positions, however, is anywhere near as easy to defend as it is to assume.

Universality of significance is, of course, almost the natural inheritance of the abstract concept, but one has only to watch the manipulation of such a concept by a great philosopher to realize that he can reach by means of it whatever depths of reality there are. The pursuit of the final meaning of substance (the Greek *ousia* can also be translated 'being'), for instance, carries Aristotle all the way to God.[18] Modern science, too, in its own realm, penetrates quite deeply into the nature and structure of our empirical world by means of the most abstract words and signs conceivable. (Science and philosophy, significantly enough, have the same cultural origins.)

It is inevitably more difficult to explain how the concrete image which in the hands of a great artist, we are made to sense, plumbs the depths of our experience of the world, can also attain universal significance, since the very explanation uses abstract, analytic concepts and is thereby automatically placed outside the phenomenon it is trying to explain. And it is scarcely enough simply to state that the concrete image in the hands of a great artist does in fact achieve universal meaning and significance – though that is undoubtedly true. I once read somewhere a theory of the theatre which maintained that the less localized and particularized the props, the greater the number of cultural and geographical areas the message of the play could reach. But it was found, on the contrary, that people in California who had never been to the West of Ireland could resonate more deeply to a West of Ireland kitchen scene in a Synge play than they could to a series of abstract patterns of colour and lighting specially designed to accompany Synge's dialogue.

The 'in' thing at the moment, of course, is to explain the

universality of appeal of a great variety of concrete images in Jungian terms. This type of explanation postulates that there are in the unconscious certain forms, or patterns, or structures, something like the forms and categories which Kant postulated in the conscious mind.[19] These archetypes in turn so mould the fund of images available in any particular culture or environment that the resulting representations reveal a striking similarity and achieve a resonance across all human boundaries of time and space.

There is probably a good deal to be said for this type of explanation. The only thing I really have against it is that it can sometimes, in the hands of its more enthusiastic exponents, convey the impression that a thorough scientific analysis of the structures of the human consciousness will tell us all we ever need to know about ourselves, our world and our history.[20] It therefore allots too much of the current scientific omniscience to the psychologist. I harbour the suspicion that the reason why a great variety of images resonates across the barriers of time and space is simpler still and still more profound. There are indeed recurring patterns, but they are patterns which derive from the vital ties that bind all of us to our earth and to our fellow earthlings, and that are literally a matter of life and death to us at every level of our psycho-physical existence.

Like the disturbance caused by a stone thrown into a pool, the recurrence of these patterns is in two different directions simultaneously; it is at once widespread and deep. We all need to breathe, and to eat and drink, and to practise some form of hygiene, no matter how elementary, and to breed, and to maintain some form of regularity in the internal relationships of mind and body and in the external relationships that exist between ourselves and our fellow humans and the good earth we all share. We need, as we say, to behave ourselves in a whole series of contexts that are similar in all human societies.

A great variety of images originates in these vital ties that bind us internally and to the larger world around us, and because of recurring patterns that are so widespread, these images acquire a certain universality of meaning despite the particularity of their concrete details. Every one knows about eating, no matter how much the stuff they like to eat may differ.

But in addition to this widespread recurrence in the patterns of our human experience, there is also a recurrence of patterns at different levels or depths of our experience. I need to eat, but I also know I need deeper forms of sustenance, that I cannot live by bread alone. Starvation may occur at different levels of my being. My stomach may be full, and I may still waste away.

Because patterns in our experience also recur at different depths of that experience images which derive from the vital ties that bind us to our world acquire, in addition to their universality of meaning, a power to evoke different depths of meaning, a power to refer, anywhere in the world, to levels of human experience far deeper than the superficial level to which they literally apply. Every human being knows what it is to be short of breath, but the image of suffocation can evoke for any human being levels of distress and of the desire to breathe freely again, deeper than the malfunctioning and renewed functioning of physical lungs. An image in itself is simply an imaginative or concrete pictorial representation of something or other. But an image which is derived from the vital ties that bind us to our world and which, because of the two-way recurring patterns of all our human experience, can evoke deeper and deeper levels of that experience across the barriers of time and space, such an image is what is known as a symbol. The artist is drawn to such images, or by them, and is capable of giving them such form as can guarantee their deep and universal significance.

Images, then, which evoke a certain depth and universality of human experience may be called symbols. It is often said of symbols that they point beyond themselves to a depth of reality not independently accessible[21] – by conceptual analysis, I presume – and that in this feature they differ from metaphor and allegory. But if our contentions above about a basic parity of concrete image and abstract concept is at all correct, then, whatever preferences for one or the other we may later discover, the relevant difference between symbol and metaphor or allegory at this point is that the former stands and operates on its own whereas the latter function as an illustratory adjunct to perceptions already achieved and expressed through the medium of abstract thought.

Myth, finally, is a symbol or a series of symbols developed in the form of a story. Let us accept Paul Ricoeur's suggestion to this effect; though it does not seem at all necessary to accept his further suggestion that these stories must be 'articulated in a space and time that cannot be co-ordinated with the time and space of history and geography according to the critical method'.[22] We are, after all, about to deal with the myth of Jesus, and we shall shortly see that myth can attach itself to historical characters and events as much as to those that are fabulous. We need only insist again at this point on the same parity of myth and abstract thought where depth and universality of significance are concerned. There are myths, for instance, in many of Plato's published dialogues. And of the many critical assessments of the role and status of these myths in such a context – that they express mere wishful thinking about cosmic harmonies and gods and other worlds when all the realizable successes of responsible thought have been reported,[23] or that they reach realms of truth inaccessible to the more dialectical methods of philosophy[24] – I prefer the attitude that harps on Plato's realization of the limits of all forms of human expression, because all of it, mythic and otherwise, points ultimately beyond itself to depths the human mind cannot finally fathom; all of it butts against the boundaries of human finitude, and in the hands of an expert craftsman like Plato can be the very instrument by which he tries to realize some degree of immortality.[25]

Very many questions about myth, of course, remain. Is myth, for instance, the only adequate way to deal with what is called the religious dimension of experience or the corresponding depth of reality? The answer, continuing the line of thought above, would appear to be, no.[26] But are there some symbols or myths which are more apt than others to put us in touch with the religious dimension? The answer here would appear to be a qualified yes. Karl Jaspers' contention that any thing or event, experience or expression thereof can be transparent to transcendence – unless we deliberately or by simple omission stop short at some previous level of dealing with it, as we normally do – is surely correct.[27] But two qualifications need to be added. Some experiences bring us more quickly than others face to face with the question-mark which is at the very heart of our empirical existence. These are usually experiences of things which are more critically matters of life or death for us, and they therefore bring home to us more effectively the sense of our contingency, the sense of the simultaneous preciousness and fragility of life in which, we shall see, the possibility of religious faith is given. Secondly, there is the problem of directing and sustaining attention, if anything at all is to be transparent of transcendence. So particular religious traditions bracket some key experiences – such as breathing, eating, drinking, washing – in a particular way and repeat them ritually and so concentrate attention that transcendence can more easily shine through.

But now to return to the myth of Jesus' death, and to come down from this highly abstract analysis to more concrete and relevant examples: the symbols which are used to express the significance of Jesus' death, and which are woven into the story of that tragic event, are all powerfully evocative of the fragile and decaying side of our experience of life. The experience of being accused, for instance, reaches manageable dimensions in the context of the court room, and most civilized systems of law try to confine it to that barely tolerable place. But the image of accusation escapes from the court room where it applies literally, and it becomes a symbol for that floating sense of guilt in everyone's experience of life, so ably depicted in Kafka's *The Trial*, and so stubbornly persistent despite Camus's defiant declarations of human innocence in *The Myth of Sisyphus*. Here i an image that takes its detail from any given tribunal of human justice, but quickly broadens out to conjure a recurrent pattern at other levels of human experience and across all human borders.

The image of sickness, too, is most literally verified in the malfunctioning of some organ. But this image also can evoke a recurring pattern at different levels in our lives and in the history of the race in which the whole organism, in its place in nature and society, and the whole race even in its relationship to its empirical world and in its internal harmony, can seem to be malfunctioning. When we say we are sick, we often refer to more than the medical practitioner would care to handle.

Our sense of having sold ourselves, or of being sold out, did not disappear with the slave-market, though there once again the image of selling and being sold, the image of slavery, found its literal application. Too many of us are old enough to remember the ideals of our youth, the patience with which it was explained to us, that we should not pursue them too hastily lest we disturb too many people, the small compromises growing more numerous and, first gradually, then rapidly proving irreversible, the final nostalgia which is the emotional dirge for lost visions, the sense of having sold out for small comforts that now seem indispensable; sold into slavery long after the slave-market has disappeared; and the price that we know would have to be paid to regain our freedom seems impossible now to pay.

Reconciliation, we know, names a felt need that goes beyond all our numbered and broken friendships, where once again the image finds literal application; and freedom is a symbol of such extraordinary evocative powers that it scarcely has a literal reference any more.

These images, then, are symbols because they are derived from those vital ties which bind us to our world and to our fellows – ties of responsibility, harmony and proper functioning, of true appreciation of ourselves and our world (true 'pricing'), of union with all things great and small – and because, too, they live in the recurrent patterns of our lives in which these ties are either enhanced or threatened. Woven into the story of the death of Jesus, these same symbols become its myth.

One final question: is there any advantage to the concrete, the symbolic, the mythic manner of perception and expression, over the abstract? The answer here must surely be, yes. For, first, there is a priority in perception of the concrete over the abstract which is as obvious as it is difficult to define. When Engels, in giving the panegyric at the grave of Marx, and in order to show that Marx had discovered the social laws of evolution as Darwin had discovered the biological, said that before we can philosophize we must first see how to feed, clothe and shelter ourselves, he was probably putting the priority in its most elementary form. Art, which deals in image and symbol, must, of course, maintain a certain distance and a certain objectivity *vis-à-vis* its subject matter.[28] An ill-informed and undisciplined immediate response is no more art than it could be science or philosophy. But the worker in images still stays closer to the concrete contours of reality than does the particular type of abstraction used by the scientist or the philosopher, and it is significant how often in the history of epistemology the advice is offered that the speculative intellect had better stay close to the images formed by those senses more directly stimulated by the empirical world. Aquinas talked of the agent intellect's return to the phantasm, and Kant's schemata were meant to provide the necessary affinity between the categories of the understanding and the forms of sense perception. It seems necessary for both life and wisdom to stay close to the detailed particularities of nature and society, the very matrix of our empirical existence.

As a consequence of this, the imaginative or symbolic form of expression appeals more to the whole person, reaching more directly those elements of emotion and will which are the very springs of action. Myth is as powerful in its effect as it is concrete in its manner of comprehension. In the myth of the death of Jesus our attention has no sooner been drawn to the threatened and decaying aspect of our experience of life, and we no sooner feel the need for someone to make the sacrifice to be the mediator to restore the lost unity and wholeness, than we are told that, if we can only take it, we are already acquitted, healed, ransomed, reconciled, freed, and we feel that we can move out again.[29]

Myth, then, is a perfectly valid way of apprehending and expressing reality in all its breadth and depth, and at probing whatever person, thing, or event is thought to be of deep significance in our world. It is therefore a perfectly valid way in all ages of apprehending the reality of God or of giving expression to faith, which one world religion at least regards as *the term* for man's contact with God; provided, of course, that its symbols move our awareness to that depth where the vital ties that bind us to our world and to our fellows, where matters of life and death, where the awful ambiguity, the contingency of existence, come into focus, for it is at this depth of experience that religious faith (or, alternatively, true atheism) finds its home. So if the New Testament is myth to its very core, that tells us something about the point on the spectrum of human perception and expression at which it operates; not whether it is right or wrong, but how to interpret what it has to say. And the problem we have to face at this point is not the problem of justifying the presence of myth in a context such as the one with which we are now dealing,[30] but the problem, rather, of explaining how *this* myth attached itself to *the death of this man*.

Why this myth of the death of this man?

The myth of the death of Jesus, then, declares that by this event we have been redeemed from the bondages of our lives, at least in principle, healed of the ensuing sickness in being, acquitted of the charges of failure in our responsibilities to our world, reconciled in an existence which is the gift of God, the creator of all things and the author of life in all its fullness – in short, freed for a new and true access in and through our empirical existence to the true God. Before we inquire more closely into the meaning of this myth, the precise meaning of this alienation from God and the new reconciliation which is talked about here, we need to ask how any such deep significance could ever have been seen in the kind of facts which the best historical research presents as the most likely causes and circumstances of the death of Jesus. Even though myth simply occupies one end of the spectrum of human perception and expression, and can therefore have the question, 'True or false?', asked of it as much as can any other type of human perception and expression at any other point on the spectrum, we can still be puzzled, from what we know of this event, that anyone should have thought of weaving a myth about it at all.

The problem here does not seem to be that myths are not normally attached to persons and events known to the myth-makers as actual historical characters at particular places and times. Myth and symbol, since they are habitual media of insight and communication, can of course, and very frequently do concern themselves with the significance of actual persons, events, times and places. This is true of great philosophers, like Plato, for instance, who was quasi-divinized in the course of the long Platonic tradition; it is true of military leaders, of founders of states, as well as of religious leaders and founders of new faiths.

The problem is, and was apparently seen from the very beginning of the spread of the message about Jesus, that the event in question, the common cruel death of a convicted man, is not of the type normally selected for interpretation by myth, and certainly not by myth of such existential and religious depth as the one with which we now have to deal. Jews, after all, have hanged from every gibbet which the ingenious cruelty of man could devise. Perhaps such treatment of a member of some other nation might occasion some comment – though hardly, since man's inhumanity to man is legendary in all human traditions – but this could scarcely happen in the case of a Jew. Jesus, the objective historian might well say, is just another Jew on another gibbet. His fate was regrettable, perhaps, but unfortunately not unusual. Why then the myth, and why this myth, of the execution of this Jew?

Many types of justification can be offered, and many have been. Perhaps the one most implied, if not explicitly put forward, is that the religious significance of the cross of Jesus was itself a matter of special divine revelation. But that will scarcely do; not, at least, in any literal sense. For, first, this answer raises more problems than it solves. When and where did this revelation occur? How do we know that it was not just Jesus' own view of his death, or Paul's, attributed by these to God, though God had not in fact revealed anything on the subject? The problem of justifying the myth of the death of Jesus is just pushed back some steps further by this type of explanation.

Secondly, the tendency of revelation theology nowadays is to see divine revelation, not as the dictation of sentences, or a divine infusion of truths, but as the religious meaning contained in historical events. So let us take this hint and examine the type of attempted justification of the myth of the cross which leads directly to our next topic, the resurrection of Jesus.

It is fairly commonplace both for those who write on the resurrection and for those who write on the faith of the followers of Jesus to claim that the latter could not have originated in anything other than the former. As R. H. Fuller writes:

> Even the most sceptical historian has to postulate an 'x', as M. Dibelius put it, to account for the complete change in the behaviour of the disciples, who at Jesus' arrest had fled and scattered to their own homes, but who in a few weeks were found boldly preaching their message to the very people who had sought to crush the movement launched by Jesus by disposing of its leader.[31]

And 'x', of course, equals the resurrection of Jesus. 'If Jesus has been raised,' Pannenberg put the same point more positively, 'this for a Jew can only mean that God himself has confirmed the pre-Easter activity of Jesus.'[32] The argument here is simple and seemingly cogent. The faith of the followers of Jesus was faith in Jesus, that is to say, it posited the religious significance of Jesus' life and, above all, of his death. But that faith was only made possible by the resurrection of Jesus.

So the solution to the problem of the justification of the myth of the cross is obvious. Perhaps those who witnessed the last days of Jesus in and around Jerusalem might not have been able to see, in these alone, any significance other than the generally tragic human significance of men who act at cross purposes and reach a deadly impasse. And perhaps if things had ended there, nothing further could ever have been concluded about the death of Jesus; no one would have suspected that it ushered in a new relationship between God and humanity. No deep religious significance of the death, to be expressed either in symbol-narrative or in conceptual structure, would ever have been justified. On the contrary, the assessment of the characters in Luke's story about the road to Emmaus would have been the correct one: 'But we had hoped that he was the one to redeem Israel. Yes, and besides all this, it is now the third day since this happened' (the crucifixion of their hope, that is).[33]

But ... something further did happen and was witnessed: 'This Jesus ... you crucified and killed by the hands of lawless men ... God raised him up' (Acts 2.23f.). The resurrection shows that the death of Jesus revealed more than the misunderstandings and machinations of men, that it signified a new relationship between God and humanity, 'according to the definite plan and foreknowledge of God' (ibid.). The resurrection of Jesus, in short, justifies the myth that was told about his death.

There is no way of assessing the plausibility of this explanation of the myth of the death of Jesus other than an analysis of the New Testament data on the resurrection.

3

The Resurrection

'There never was a time,' wrote Barnabas Lindars, 'when Christianity existed as an interpretation of Judaism without the Resurrection as the fundamental belief.'[1] This is undoubtedly true, and it might well lead us to expect unanimity amongst Christians on a topic so clearly essential to their cause. When we find, on the contrary, that few topics at the present time reveal such deep disagreement, not just on the general nature and prospect of resurrection from the dead, where such disagreement might be expected, but on what the New Testament has to say to the subject, a matter in which exegetical studies should by now have reported some acknowledged success, we feel the need to ask after the causes of this rather unexpected confusion. The causes, it seems to me, are mainly two.

First, and perhaps the cruder of the two causes of the current confusion, people have preconceived notions on the nature of resurrection, and preconceived notions are notorious for their ability to prevent us from seeing what is actually written on the pages we read. The sources of these preconceived notions on the nature of resurrection are, no doubt, as varied as the cultural and educational backgrounds of the people who are their victims. The notions themselves vary from the rather elementary and uncritical image of a person emerging from a tomb or grave some time after his or her death, shaking off grave-clothes and clay, to the more refined and unusual, though no less misleading example I am now about to give. I once heard the Cambridge physicist, Fred Hoyle, predict that physical science could in the not-too-distant future code all the particles and their precise combination which make up an individual person and, with due technological advance, reproduce that precise formula, that same individual, at some future date. The New Testament preaching about resurrection, he claimed, was thus blatantly false for its age, but still oddly prophetic of ours! Such notions on the nature of resurrection from the extremes of physical simplicity and physical subtlety are clearly unhelpful in approaching the New Testament; but I use them to illustrate the point that preconceived notions of any description are better done without.

Role-requirements for the resurrection

The second cause of contemporary confusion about the New Testament understanding of resurrection is cousin to the first. Scholars who would abjure any preconceived notions on the nature of the resurrection preached in the New Testament, who would smile a small, superior smile at the two examples offered above, still approach the New Testament data on resurrection, I am convinced, with the expectation that it must play a certain part in the argument of the New Testament as a whole. These requirements of the role the resurrection must play in the theology of the New Testament can be just as preconceived, just as uncritical, and in the end just as detrimental to our prospects of seeing what the New Testament is actually saying as can the crudest assumptions about the nature of resurrection itself. One of these role-requirements actually ended the last chapter, though it was not there described in these terms. The resurrection was there required to justify the issuing of a myth, a symbolic expression of the significance of Jesus' death, with no reflection as to whether the New Testament writers themselves required the resurrection they wrote about to do such a thing, or whether resurrection, on any conceivable understanding of it, could do any such thing. It is necessary, unfortunately, to look at some of the roles which modern authors apparently require the resurrection in the New Testament to play, in order to notice and avoid the subtler kinds of preconception here involved.

First, then, at the end of the last chapter we saw the resurrection in a faith-creating or re-creating role. It was the resurrection of Jesus, was it not, that put the disciples in possession of a faith which his death would have prevented or indefinitely suspended, or which neither his life nor his death would otherwise have produced. This faith, which has its source in the resurrection, is expressed, as religious faith tends to be, in myth, partly in the myth of the death of Jesus, partly in myths scattered elsewhere in the New Testament. So, to say that the resurrection creates the faith, and to say that it justifies the myth, are one and the same thing.

Another claim is quite common amongst writers on the New Testament in general and it reveals expectations of another, perhaps quite similar role for the resurrection. The gospels in particular, this claim goes, are written in the light of the resurrection.[2] This is the light-shedding or illuminating role of the resurrection. It means that something about Jesus' life and death came to light in the resurrection or with the resurrection which would not otherwise have come to light.

In both cases the question can be asked concerning whatever is now seen or believed about Jesus, as a result of the resurrection: was it true of Jesus before the resurrection, or was it visible or credible before the resurrection? Most often, in answer to this question, the suggestion seems to be that whatever could be seen as significant about Jesus, whatever could be believed about him, was both visible and credible before his resurrection as after, but that the blindness and stubbornness of people, aggravated perhaps by the shock of his criminal execution, prevented them from seeing and believing. Sometimes, however, the suggestion seems to be that certain features of Jesus' status and significance simply were not manifest before the resurrection, and could not have been seen or believed by the best-willed people in the world. Raymond Brown, for instance, gives the impression that the divine status of Jesus, the most substantial myth about him which we will have to consider, simply could not be seen or believed before his resurrection.[3]

Much more infrequently still, a writer may suggest that certain things were not even true of Jesus before his resurrection, much less manifest or ignored by the blind and the stubborn. Bruce Vawter, for example, thinks that Jesus became truly Son of God at his resurrection, though he was that always by that peculiar process known as retroactivity.[4] I must confess I do not know what retroactivity could mean in this context, since I always thought it to be a legal or economic fiction. But there are some passages in the New Testament which strongly suggest that the resurrection had some constitutive role *vis-à-vis* the functions or status of Jesus. The Epistle to the Romans (1.4), for instance, says that Jesus was 'designated Son of God in power according to the Spirit of holiness by his resurrection from the dead', and the Revised Standard Version, in a footnote to this verse, expands on the word 'designated' with the phrase 'manifested and installed in his true status'. And there are other places and themes in the New Testament which seem to imply, at the very least, that Jesus was constituted in some function or status at his resurrection which before that he did not enjoy. Paul again, in a chapter on the resurrection, says that 'the last Adam (Jesus) became a life-giving spirit' (I Corinthians 15.45), and the general themes of exaltation and enthronement, found frequently in the New Testament in connection with the resurrection, contain seemingly a similar suggestion (Acts 3.32, 36; 5.31; 13.33).

Varied though these foregoing views of the role of the resurrection in the argument of the New Testament as a whole may be, they still may be said to be contrary as a group to another and quite different view. On this contrary view, preaching the resurrection of Jesus is simply a way of saying that faith in Jesus or the faith of Jesus did survive his death. The preaching about Jesus, the kerygma as it is called, did succeed in bringing about faith, it did succeed in gaining followers for him, even after his execution. So Jesus lived on in his followers, or – a more exotic way of putting the same viewpoint – Jesus rose in the kerygma. The role of resurrection preaching, then, the role of stories about the resurrection, is to record, in 'mythological' terms, this known fact of the continuing preaching and the continuing faith of his followers. (Here 'mythological' does mean a fanciful, imaginative way of putting over something that can be, and had better sooner or later be put more properly in more literal terms.)[5]

Just as previous views of the resurrection, then, saw it in one way or another as enabling the faith of Jesus' followers to be all that it was, this last view, on the contrary, sees resurrection kerygma as a way of announcing that the faith of Jesus' followers continued to be whatever it was. Hence Moule's question, 'Was resurrection meant by the New Testament writers to be an expression of the continuance of faith, or its cause?'[6]

Since this matter of the resurrection is so unfortunately complicated in contemporary theological writing, it might be well, before going on to analyse the preconceptions involved in these various role-requirements, to tabulate and summarize them as follows. The resurrection of Jesus, as presented in the New Testament:

(*a*) enabled people to have faith which the life and death of Jesus could never have given them;

(*b*) enabled people to have faith which the life and death of Jesus could have given them but, because of the stubbornness which makes people stick to their familiar ways, did not give them;

(c) enabled people to have faith which the life of Jesus had perhaps begun to give them, but which the criminal execution of Jesus destroyed;[7]

(d) lighted aspects of Jesus' person and mission which witnesses to his public life and death had, because of their blindness, been unable to see;

(e) lighted aspects of Jesus' person and mission which previous to it had not been in any way perceptible;

(f) constituted certain features of Jesus' personal status and function which previous to it had not existed;

(g) is simply a powerful imaginative way of expressing the fact that the preaching of Jesus continued, and continued to effect the response of faith.

When first I became a homeowner and things began to go wrong with lights and fires and sinks and stoves, and I began to learn the great cost of labour and parts, I found myself practically forced to function as a handyman about the house. My first outing in my new role brought me to a hardware store, face to face with a kindly and experienced salesman. I described to him as accurately as I could in layman's language the job I wished to do, and then asked him if he would show me the tools and parts I would need to do it. He explained in his kindly and experienced way that if I did succeed in doing what I had in mind, the plumbing in my house would probably never work properly again and, if he might make a general suggestion, it would be better for me first of all to acquaint myself with the tools and parts available for house plumbing and from these learn what jobs it might be feasible to do. The lesson was not lost on me, and I gradually realized that it applied to more than plumbing. My excursion to the hardware store was not at all unlike the procedure of people who first of all decide that a certain logical job of apologetics or of propaganda must be done in Christian theology, and then go to the New Testament to find the kind of resurrection that would do it. The New Testament store just may not contain the kind of resurrection-tool they need, for the simple reason that its writers never envisaged that particular kind of apologia or that kind of propaganda. They may never have envisaged the resurrection at all in these particular roles.

The preconceptions behind the role-requirements

If we take the first five roles ((a) to (e)) which the resurrection, as preached in the New Testament, has been required to play, it is fairly obvious from the contexts in which these are found that the resurrection of Jesus is conceived as a single and singular event of which Jesus himself is object. Furthermore, as this event is surely conceived, however vastly different it may be thought to be from other events of life, like birth, baptism, and death, it is an event in the sense in which all of these are events, standing in some conceivable relationship of time and place (on the third day, for instance, and in the environs of Jerusalem) to these others. It may not itself have been directly witnessed. The only early documents which claim that it was are, significantly, judged apocryphal. In fact, being an act of God himself,[8] it may have been so vastly different from all other events which we witness that it could not have been witnessed by human beings at all. But if it can be shown by circumstantial evidence, such as an empty tomb or appearances of Jesus after his execution, to have occurred, as many other events in our experience have to be proved by circumstantial evidence, then it can still be classified in that general category which we label 'events'.

For the sake of brevity of future reference and, I hope, for the sake of some clarity in this confused subject, we may refer to the conception so far outlined as that of the personal resurrection of Jesus himself.

Now in the first five roles above ((a) to (e)), either the event of the personal resurrection of Jesus itself or some of those events, such as the appearances, which form the circumstantial evidence for its occurrence, must be conceived to have been revelatory in the literal sense of that word; events, in short, which conveyed to those who witnessed them whatever was to be believed or believed anew. At the very least, they would have to have been the kind of revelatory events which conveyed in some explicit fashion *that* something was to be believed or believed anew.[9] The message conveyed as to what was to be believed, and the manner of its conveyance, we would then expect to be preserved carefully in the course of the resurrection narratives of the New Testament.

Further, in order to be an event which founded faith or founded faith anew, the resurrection, or any of those events which formed its circumstantial evidence, would have to be conceived as the kind of event which did not itself require faith in its occurrence. It would have to be the kind of event which imposed itself on its witnesses by the force of its own objective evidence. To suggest that an event which grounds faith had itself to be believed – as if I had a vision of one recently dead, a vision seen only by me, and then had to decide whether to believe she was really alive again or not – that is clearly circular. Nor would the number of visions help here, since it is their quality, not their quantity that counts. The problem is, of course, that precisely the kind of evidence which would count most in favour of the objectivity of the alleged act of witness, would also count most against its being witness of a resurrection. Lazarus, if the story about him is to be believed, was seen alive after his death. He was not only visible, but palpable, audible, and perhaps slightly odoriferous. Yet the raising of Lazarus is not presented as resurrection; merely as his (temporary) re-introduction to the known conditions of our present existence. We are not concerned at the moment, however, with difficulties about the preconceptions – these will concern us later – but merely with the preconceptions themselves which underlie the roles enumerated above and required of the resurrection proclaimed in the New Testament.

It is truly difficult to decide what kind of event could at one and the same time be witnessed as the personal resurrection of Jesus and still fulfil the sixth role requirement (*f*) above, could constitute, that is, certain features of Jesus' status and function which previous to it had not existed. If there is truth in that particular role-requirement at all – and it does seem to have good scriptural backing – then, at the very least, it suggests that the resurrection witnessed was much more than the revival of a man who had certainly died. Take again, for example, the story of the raising of Lazarus. Whether that story is to be taken as literally true or symbolic of something else, at least it is clear that the writer who tells the story does not even consider that he has involved himself in the kinds of claim to status and function in the case of Lazarus which are present in the case of the risen Jesus. Yet, and here is the question which must cause difficulty for the sixth role-requirement, what could a witness to a raising from the dead see that would constitute a claim to have witnessed more than the revival of a dead man? An upward motion of the revived body and a certain seating-arrangement in the heavens would scarcely constitute evidence of the kind of change in Jesus' personal status or function which is now envisaged.[10] Could a revived man be seen to do any more than a living one could be seen to do, to constitute a claim to new status or function? In short, it is almost impossible to say what kind of personal resurrection of Jesus would have to be witnessed to justify the role-requirement now under consideration. It is therefore difficult to say what kind of preconception about the nature of Jesus' personal resurrection underlies this particular role-requirement. Further, as in the case of the first five role-requirements, it is also true here that if the perception or acceptance of this new status or function of Jesus depends on faith, then it is no longer the resurrection itself that constitutes the status or function, and the new role-requirement is not fulfilled.

In the case of the last role-requirement tabulated above, the one which regards the resurrection stories in the New Testament simply as ways of expressing the fact that the preaching of Jesus was continued and continued to effect the response of faith, there is no such problem. Holders of this view do not have to submit to examination to see what preconception about the personal resurrection of Jesus they are hiding from us and, perhaps from themselves, for the simple reason that they do not believe the New Testament writers to be talking at all about a personal resurrection of Jesus, a singular event which happened to Jesus after his death, which was witnessed by certain distinct individuals amongst his followers, and not by other believers. When the New Testament, on this view, pictures Jesus in various ways as the Risen One, it does indeed present him as Lord of history and as judge of the living and the dead, it does attribute to him such function and status, but in this aspect of its preaching also it is still referring really to the continuation of the preaching of Jesus and to the power of this preaching to inspire faith by which, as Paul would have it, we are saved. Here we have no preconception about the personal resurrection of Jesus, but we do have a preconception about the nature of New Testament resurrection preaching in general. And this preconception, particularly in its pure form where it virtually excludes any essential reference to the personal resurrection of Jesus himself, may be just as misleading to the prospective reader of the New Testament as any of the preconceptions found underlying the other role-requirements above.

These, then, in so far as they can be detected at all by the critical eye, are the kinds of preconception generally harboured by those who look to the New Testament to see the resurrection of Jesus cast in one of the propagandist or apologetic roles tabulated above. As we have already hinted earlier, they are here tabulated and analysed in some detail for one purpose and one purpose only, namely, so that we may do our very best to rid our minds entirely of them before approaching the pages in which the New Testament preaches and depicts the resurrection of Jesus. If we can manage to see the contents of these pages with clear and unblinkered eyes, we shall be in a good position to return to these role-requirements and preconceptions to see what, if any, truth is contained in any of them.

The complex and comprehensive resurrection-preaching of the New Testament

It seems best to begin with Paul. He is the only one whose own word we have for it that he himself was privileged to have witnessed what was known as an appearance of the risen Lord. The claim is made about others in the extant New Testament literature, but not by them. Furthermore, Paul's letters are the earliest New Testament documents on the resurrection. Undoubtedly, both in his letters and in other New Testament documents earlier testimonies on the resurrection are preserved; in the sermons attributed to Peter, for instance, in the Acts of the Apostles. But it is difficult now to determine the exact meaning of these testimonies in their original contexts, or even to say what the original contexts were. We shall be looking almost immediately at Fuller's book, which is one attempt to trace the history of the tradition of testimony about the resurrection. But it seems best for our purposes to begin with the testimony of a self-proclaimed witness of the resurrection, a testimony clearly embedded in its original context: and that means beginning with Paul.

Fuller begins with Paul. But he concentrates mainly on the fifteenth chapter of Paul's first letter to the Corinthians (with the help of one or two other references to Paul's own witness to an appearance: Galatians 1.11-17 (?), and I Corinthians 9.1. This is an important Pauline text on resurrection, though not the only one. But, then, within this chapter, Fuller concentrates mainly on the list of appearances of the risen Jesus found near the opening of the chapter: 'He appeared to Cephas, then to the twelve. Then he appeared to more than five hundred .... Then he appeared to James, then to all the apostles. Last of all, as to one untimely born, he appeared also to me (I Corinthians 15.5-8). And from this point onwards Fuller is engaged in the quest of the original event or events, the appearances of the risen Jesus or the discoveries of an empty tomb, pertaining to the resurrection of Jesus and witnessed by particular individuals or distinctive groups within the general body of Jesus-followers. Having provided the best information available on such individual events as these, the whole purpose of his work thereafter is to trace the development of the long and varied tradition of these events from simple proclamation of the resurrection of Jesus, to which not even a list of witnessed appearances is added, through simple lists of appearances (with no narrative details attached), through empty tomb stories, to the very detailed narratives about appearances of Jesus found in the later writings of the New Testament.

Now the quest of original events such as the personal resurrection of Jesus, himself, or the 'non-hallucinatory' visions and discoveries of a tomb emptied which provided the circumstantial evidence for this, is undoubtedly a legitimate enterprise. It is even legitimate when pursued in isolation from the larger understandings of resurrection which the New Testament, as we shall soon see, has to offer. It is legitimate if only because, in tracing, as Fuller does, the developing traditions about these 'original' events, one learns along the way in any case a good deal about the wider context of New Testament thought on the resurrection of Jesus. Perhaps, indeed, most of us are most inclined to think that this particular priority in the search for the New Testament understanding of the resurrection of Jesus – first the quest of the original event or events and then the tracing of the developing traditions about them – is the only one that seriously recommends itself to serious scholarship.

It is important, nevertheless, at least to raise the suspicion that this priority may owe more to the insidious influence of the types of role-requirement and their preconceptions already tabulated and analysed above, than it corresponds to the priorities of any New Testament writer. It is just possible that none of the New Testament writers were interested, as a matter of isolated or even primary concern, in establishing for posterity the historical details and actual occurrence of events such as the personal resurrection of Jesus, the 'non-hallucinatory' visions and the discoveries of an empty tomb. It is quite possible that larger conceptions of the resurrection of Jesus had priority in their minds, to which the matters of concern just named were tributary, and not the other way round.[11]

Take Paul for example. Even the list of appearances and their witnesses given in the fifteenth chapter of I Corinthians must be assessed for their contribution to Paul's argument in the context of at least the whole chapter, not taken out and used in isolation in the quest of some other writer's preconceived goal. When one does broaden one's attention to the argument of the whole chapter, it soon becomes obvious that Paul does not need a list of witnesses to a proof-miracle, for the simple reason that he does not wish to prove anything by means of a miracle. (It is surely true in the experience of most of us that the beliefs we hold dear and which move us most effectively are not dependent on miracles either experienced or recorded.) In particular Paul did not need witnesses to a proof-miracle to prove that the dead would be raised. He held that belief before he ever heard of Jesus; it is the central belief of his Pharisaic philosophy that shines like a bright thread of continuity through his broken life. 'But if there is no resurrection of the dead,' he can argue, in the chapter under consideration, 'then Christ has not been raised.' But he always believed there would be resurrection of the dead; therefore he is not deluded in preaching Jesus raised. No, Paul's experience of an appearance of the risen Lord and his list of other appearances did not put him in possession of a belief in resurrection from the dead, for he was already in possession of such belief.

Perhaps Paul wishes to establish the resurrection of Jesus himself as a strong priority, and for this reason produces his list of witnesses, because he means to argue from this that the personal raising of individuals from the dead had now begun and would soon culminate in a general resurrection? Paul probably did hold a belief in the early advent of a general resurrection and the belief is likely to be contained in our chapter (I Corinthians 15.51). But if he did, it was a mistaken expectation; and if the main point of our chapter had been to establish it, we should not be reading the chapter so avidly today in our attempt to understand the New Testament teaching on resurrection.

What, then? Perhaps the suggestion behind some of the role-requirements we have seen is true; perhaps Paul is proving the personal resurrection of Jesus himself by this list of witnessed appearances so that he can then prove some faith to be valid; if not faith in resurrection, then faith in Jesus as Christ, Lord, Son of God; or perhaps he wishes to prove valid the faith of Jesus, that is, the faith that Jesus himself tried to recommend to people. Perhaps, but a close reading of chapter 15 makes this suggestion also highly unlikely. Support for this suggestion is sometimes sought in Paul's statements to the effect that if Christ has not been raised, then his readers' faith is vain (or void) and futile (I Corinthians 15.14, 17). But it is precisely these statements which, on more thorough analysis, makes the suggestion they are meant to support highly improbable.

The absence of whatever proof might be provided for the personal resurrection of Jesus himself would not make our Christian faith either void or futile. For if the resurrection of Jesus is thought to be primarily a proof-miracle, then we should have to say, as already hinted in passing, that it is the rule and not the exception that faith is found worthwhile and survives without proof-miracles; and if the resurrection of Jesus were thought to be one article of faith amongst others, then failure to establish it might deprive the faith of one of its articles (perhaps a most important one), but that does not amount to making the faith utterly void and futile.

It is highly unlikely, then, that Paul in this chapter understands the resurrection of Jesus primarily as an event of Jesus' own personal destiny which, when established by circumstantial evidence, can then establish some or all of the Christian faith. It is much more likely, from both the wording and the logic of his argument here, that he understands by the resurrection of Jesus primarily the Christian experience of Jesus as Spirit or Lord in the lives of his followers. Now *that* experience is substantially identical with the lived experience known as the Christian faith, so that it would make perfect sense to say, on this understanding of the matter, that those who denied the resurrection of Jesus *voided* their faith and rendered it totally futile. Consider a key passage in our chapter in which Paul is trying to explain the very nature of resurrection (I Corinthians 15.42-50, 'So it is with the resurrection of the dead ....'), and uses for this purpose one of his Adam-Christ contrasts.

The first Adam became a living being, he writes, and we are so in his image. Now 'Adam' in Hebrew simply means 'man' or humanity; so Paul is saying here that without Jesus we are alive, but just barely alive, conscious of all the fragility of our finite existence, of its vulnerability to both the enemy within and the enemies without. But the last Adam, he adds, became a life-giving spirit, and we shall be so in his image. Jesus, the risen Jesus of Paul's experience, about whom he writes and preaches, is life-giving spirit. The words are almost synonymous. Spirit in Paul's vocabulary means the ultimate source and power of life and more abundant life. So, to understand this in terms that could be cashed in ordinary human experience, one would need to range rather widely over those many contexts in his writings where Paul expands on what this spirit does in our lives; that it enables us to have faith, for example, that it enables us to overcome the destructive forces of human evil (sin), that it equips us with those practical gifts of wisdom and prophecy (that is, the ability to speak to the current human situation), and healing and, above all, love which infinitely enrich human life for ourselves and for others. It should be noted by readers of I Corinthians 15 that the three chapters preceding it are all devoted to the effects or 'charisms' of the Spirit in the communal lives of Jesus' followers (see also texts like Galatians 5.22-26). In such experiential terms, then, one identifies the life-giving spirit who is, for Paul, the last Adam, the perfect man, Jesus raised.

To say that Jesus is raised, then, means for Paul that Jesus is a life-giving spirit palpable in these ways in our lives. Admittedly, in the chapter which now most immediately concerns us, he is most interested in a further power of this spirit, over and above its power to give us faith and love and prophetic wisdom, the power, namely, to overcome for us even the last enemy, the death we must all of us one day die. So he writes: 'If for this life only we have hoped in Christ, we are of all men most to be pitied' (I Corinthians 15.19). Paul uses the primordial symbol of the seed dying in order to give new life, because literal description of victory over biological death inevitably escapes our grasp, and in traditional imagery he paints the magnificent picture of the great general resurrection, immortalized in the trumpet obbligato of Handel's *Messiah*.

It would be a mistake, however, to think that the resurrection of Jesus means to Paul an event of Jesus' personal raising from the dead (victory for Jesus himself over 'the last enemy') which took place some time past, to be followed in the uncertain future, but hopefully soon, by a similar raising from the dead of the rest of us; that and nothing more, an event which was the first recorded of its kind to be followed soon by others of its kind. It is not the personal resurrection of Jesus which is 'the first fruits of those who have fallen asleep (died)'; as if this event which happened to Jesus himself after the death he one day died gave some statistical probability that we too would experience a similar event after the deaths we must some day die, as if the effects of Jesus' resurrection and therefore its meaning for us were postponed to such future times,[12] as if 'first-fruits' meant anything like statistical probability and not, rather, first instalment of something received here and now in this life and the assurance of hope consequent on this. The risen Jesus himself is first-fruits, and he is so precisely as life-giving spirit. Paul can talk equally easily of the first-fruits of spirit (Romans 8.23), which give us the hope, the saving hope, of that glorious future beyond the death we must one day die.

The resurrection of Jesus, therefore, means to Paul that Jesus is a life-giving spirit, palpable experientially in those capacities for faith and love which overcome the destructive forces in our lives and enhance human life itself, not least by germinating a healing hope which cannot be stunted even by the death we must all of us one day die. 'Now the Lord is the Spirit,' as Paul himself put it, 'and where the Spirit of the Lord is, there is freedom. And we all, with unveiled face, beholding the glory of the Lord, are being changed into his likeness from one degree of glory to another; for this comes from the Lord who is the Spirit' (II Corinthians 3.17f.). The attentive reader of the New Testament must have noticed at this point that terms familiar from the myth of Jesus' death are being repeated in Paul's understanding of his resurrection – freeing, saving. But it is not that which most immediately concerns us now. What concerns us now is Paul's understanding of the resurrection of Jesus. And he understands the resurrection of Jesus to mean, not primarily an event in the personal destiny of Jesus himself, not primarily what we have called the personal resurrection of Jesus, but that Jesus is a power or spirit in our lives, enabling us to overcome destructive evil, enhancing our lives with faith and love and a hope that defies death. Now that, in a nutshell, is the faith of Jesus-followers. And if to deny the resurrection of Jesus is to deny that, as in Paul's view of the resurrection it clearly is, then those who deny the resurrection are in fact literally voiding their faith, as he quite soberly tells them they are. And finally, the witnesses called at the beginning of the chapter to give evidence of the resurrection of Jesus are all, as almost all commentators agree, founders and leaders, at home and on the missions of the groups of Jesus-followers who live by this faith, because each of them, like Paul, had such deep and infectious experience of that which can be called either the resurrection of Jesus or the faith - experience of a Jesus-follower.

Whether, in addition to the experience of the spirit of Jesus in their lives which is known as the living faith-experience of Jesus-followers, Paul, or any of the others whose company he claims at the beginning of the chapter, also experienced or did not experience something else that could count as evidence of the resurrection of Jesus, is a question that may later concern us. For the moment we may rest satisfied with the result that there can be little doubt in any case about the meaning of the resurrection of Jesus to which Paul is calling on this list of eminent leaders to be co-witnesses with himself.

In order to fill out and substantiate more fully this view of what Paul understands by the resurrection of Jesus, it would be necessary to embark on a fairly complete analysis of the whole Pauline corpus. For such adequate analysis of a man's literary production the tape-and-scissors method is usually a very poor substitute. The tape-and-scissors method involves cutting out all the explicit references made by an author to the topic in his writings that immediately interests one, ignoring all the rest, and then taping all these together to get a total view of the author's understanding of the topic in question. Inadequate as this method admittedly is, the need for brevity in the present context may excuse us in using it merely to see if it corroborates a contention already based on a more careful analysis of a more individual text.[13] Now, when one tabulates according to their dominant themes the explicit Pauline texts on the resurrection of Jesus in which Paul conveys his understanding of it, the following table emerges:

1. In some texts the phrase 'the resurrection of Jesus' or 'Jesus is raised' is aligned with Paul's experience of his own call to and practice of apostleship. In other words, Paul's vocation and drive to apostleship and the resurrection of Jesus refer to the same experience in his life. 'Am I not an apostle,' he asks the Corinthians, 'Have I not seen Jesus our Lord?' (I Corinthians 9.1). And in other scattered texts he expands on this theme when he conveys to his readers the impression that the power or spirit which works through him and constitutes his apostleship is, in fact, the power or life-giving spirit that is identical with the risen Jesus. 'You desire proof,' he writes again to the Corinthians, 'that Christ is speaking in me. He is not weak in dealing with you, but is powerful in you. For he was crucified in weakness but lives by the power of God. For we are weak in him, but in dealing with you we shall live with him by the power of God.' (II Corinthians 13.4; consult also Galatians 1.1; Romans 1.3-5; Philippians 3.10).

2. In other texts, the conviction of Jesus' resurrection coincides with a sense of new power and new life in ourselves. For Paul, as the last quotation above indicates, is merely the channel

through which the spirit or power, which the risen Jesus *is*, reaches and affects our lives. 'If to others I am not an apostle,' he told the Corinthians, 'at least I am to you; for you are the seal of my apostleship in the Lord.' Are not you my workmanship in the Lord?' (II Corinthians 9.1f.).

This new life which we are empowered to live, which to us means both that Paul is an apostle and that Jesus is raised, is variously described as a life free from evil-doing or sin (Romans 6.4-11), a life of faith or grace (Philippians 3.9; Galatians 2.20; Romans 1.5), a life of glory (II Corinthians 3.17f.; Philippians 3.21), a justified or saved life (Romans 4.24f.; 10.9), a life in the spirit (I Corinthians 15.45-50) or power (II Corinthians 13.4), the life of Christ himself (II Corinthians 4.7–5.15).

3. In still other texts of Paul the resurrection of Jesus means that we too can hope to be raised again after the total destruction of death has lowered us to the bottom of the pit of nothingness: consult I Thessalonians 4.14; Philippians 3.11; I Corinthians 6.13f.; II Corinthians 4.13f. The meaning here is clear enough, and needs no comment, if only because it corresponds to what we all rather uncritically thought was the primary implication of the resurrection of Jesus, the primary human experience (of hope) in which the term could be interpreted. It may be of interest to note, though, that in the case of two of the texts just enumerated the context is explicit about the faith or life of Jesus which is in the follower of Jesus and on which the hope of final victory over death seems immediately to depend. In Philippians, for instance, Paul is talking about having that rightness which is through the faith of Christ (the Greek has the genitive here in 3.9), that he may know Jesus and the power of his resurrection, and may share his sufferings, becoming like him in death, that if possible he may attain the resurrection from the dead.

4. Finally, and particularly in some texts from his earlier letters, Paul thinks that the resurrection of Jesus implies that Jesus can be expected to return to himself and his readers: 'You turned to God from idols, to serve a living and true God, and to wait for his Son from heaven, whom he raised from the dead' (I Thessalonians 1.9f.; also Philippians 3.20).

By far the most frequently recurring theme, of course, in all of these texts and contexts, is the theme of the personal resurrection of Jesus, the theme of Jesus himself, as part of his own

personal destiny, experiencing that act of God described as raising from the dead (I Thessalonians 1.9f.; 4.14; I Corinthians 6.14;
I Corinthians 15; II Corinthians 4.13f.; 5.15; Galatians 1.1;
Romans 1.3-5; 4.24f.; 6.4-11; 7.4; 10.9; 14.7-9). So why has not
this theme been given an entry of its own in the tabulation, and
indeed the largest entry of all? For the simple reason that the
personal resurrection of Jesus, though naturally attracting the
most numerous references of all, is still, in by far the greater
number of instances, mentioned precisely in the course of presenting or expanding on some of the other themes just tabulated. One inevitably gets the impression, then, that were it not
for these other themes, these other ways of really understanding
(because they are ways of experiencing) the resurrection of
Jesus, the personal resurrection of Jesus, as we have called it,
that is, the resurrection as an occurrence in Jesus' own destiny,
might not be known at all or, if somehow known (e.g., from lists
of more 'individual' appearances to select people), might be of
little enough interest to either Paul or his readers. A little further
analysis should be sufficient to corroborate that impression and,
correspondingly, to justify the tabulation by theme offered
above of the Pauline texts which explicitly mention the resurrection of Jesus.

Let the eye rest for a moment on the entries in the table above,
and on the number of references in each. It soon becomes obvious that the resurrection preaching of Paul concentrates most
heavily on the theme of the second entry above, the resurrection
of Jesus as the presence of his power and his life in ourselves,
and that it then tapers off at either end. This implicit graph
suggests, to me at least, that the resurrection of Jesus, in Paul's
understanding of it, is like a meteor that comes into the range of
our vision from places too remote for the eye to detect in any
detail (some act of God on or in Jesus which finally resulted in
the personal resurrection of Jesus himself by God), overwhelms
us with its brightness and colour while still within our earthly
purview, and then gradually fades from us again into regions
we still cannot penetrate with our human powers of perception
(our own hoped-for raising, after biological death, in likeness of
his).

For Paul, Jesus' resurrection really comes into view simultaneously with his own apostolate. This is clear, not only from
those texts in which he explicitly bases his claim to apostolic
dignity on his privilege of having witnessed an appearance of
the risen Lord, but also from those other texts in entry 1. above

in which he understands his apostolate in terms of the presence in and through him of the power of the life-giving spirit, Jesus. But what does this mean? What actually happened on the road to Damascus?

The only detailed descriptions of Paul's experience on the road to Damascus are those given in Luke's three accounts of that incident in chapters 9, 22 and 26 of the Acts of the Apostles. The details of the three accounts, as we might by now expect from the New Testament, do not agree, and they are in any case fairly obviously taken from Old Testament descriptions of epiphanies and calls to prophetic office. The details, in short, represent literary conventions rather than records of eye-witness testimony. Significantly enough, Paul himself, the only first-hand witness to an appearance of the risen Lord that we hear from, gives no details whatever of that pivotal incident in his life which was at once his conversion and his call to apostolate.

Now Paul was never noticeably short of words or images or ideas when something of importance needed to be said and insisted upon. If it had been important to Paul to provide evidence, from Jesus' special appearance to Paul, of the personal resurrection of Jesus, as proof of the faith which Jesus, on this view and presumably on that occasion, told him was the true one, and as prelude to the explicit call to apostolate which on that same occasion he would presumably have received, we may be very sure that Paul would not leave us without a detailed description of the one who appeared and of how he made himself known, of the circumstances of the appearances, and of what, in particular, was said or otherwise communicated. Yet Paul gives no details of the 'appearance' at all, any more than he gives details of the other appearances which he lists with his own in I Corinthians 15. The only thing he wants us to understand about this pivotal experience in his life, but the thing he really wants us to understand about it, is that it was his conversion to the one and only gospel that came from Jesus himself, the one good news which, when we allow it to form in us the faith that guides our lives, is the very power of God himself to save us (Galatians 1; Romans 1.16). No matter how one reads Paul, and no matter how often one reads him, the appearance of the risen Jesus to him comes down to his reception of the gospel, of the faith of Jesus which is the palpable spirit of Jesus himself in his life and the very power of God. One will search the writings of Paul absolutely in vain for a single detail of the appear-

ance of Jesus to him over and above this description of a conversion to this faith which was deep and powerful enough to make
him an apostle, and to require his life in its service.

If one is unkind enough to question Paul's contention that he
is truly an apostle of Jesus – and we may gather from his extant
writings that many were unkind enough to question this contention in a most trenchant manner – he will still not produce any
details of a numinous-looking Galilean with a recordable message. What will he do? He will point quite simply to his own
converts and to the lives they now live. That the faith he lives
and preaches to others has the spirit of Jesus and the power of
God behind it, that he is therefore a true apostle of Jesus, the
lives of his converts will prove, and only they can prove it. 'You
yourselves,' he warmly tells his Corinthian converts, 'are our
letter of recommendation, written on your hearts, to be known
and read by all men; and you show that you are a letter from
Christ delivered by us, written not with ink but with the Spirit of
the living God, not on tablets of stone but on tablets of human
hearts' (II Corinthians 3.2f.). No recordable message written in
ink will prove Paul an apostle; nothing but the lives of those he
has fashioned in the faith of Jesus could be adequate to that task.

The lives of those converted to the following of Jesus, then,
are the next palpable, experiential effects of the life-giving spirit
who is the risen Jesus, and the next source of our understanding
of what the resurrection of Jesus means to Paul. The kind of lives
these are is variously described, as we have already implied.
They are lives which exhibit the life or faith of Jesus lived by
others (and what that involves must be explained more fully in
the chapter on the life and faith of Jesus); life in the Spirit, which
Paul has described in great detail in all those passages of his on
the gifts and charisms of the Spirit, the greatest of which is love;
life freed from evil and its destructiveness; life healed and
acquitted; life lived upright in the eyes of God our Father, and
already revealing something of his glory. (See the texts under
entry 2. of the table above, and notice again how terms from the
myth of Jesus' death are reappearing in these accounts of the
meaning of his resurrection.)

So, for Paul, to say that Jesus is risen is to say that Jesus is the
Lord or the Spirit in his life and in the lives of his converts; and
that statement can be interpreted in terms of the new life they
lead. Finally, those who feel this power can anticipate that, as it
overcomes all other destructive forces in life, it will also overcome the last enemy, the death we all have to die on some

particular day (entry 3. above; entry 4. is a mistake of Paul's; if it were not, we would not be here to discuss this problem). But though the experienced power of the risen Jesus in our present lives blesses us with the hope that we will live again beyond death, as Jesus did, we can be given no details whatever of a literal kind of what that other life may be like. The meteor is again disappearing from view. That we do in fact experience it is our surety that it came from somewhere and that it is going somewhere. The personal resurrection of Jesus is as explicitly presupposed and as clearly implied by all that we can experience and therefore really understand of Jesus as a spirit or power in our present lives, as our own personal resurrections can be firmly hoped for, on he basis of the same experience, some time after the end of those lives. But since the conditions of our present existence alone fall within our powers of description, we do not have, nor have we ever had, any details of the personal resurrection of Jesus or on the final resurrection we may hope for in the likeness of his. The resurrection of Jesus, as understood by Paul, is an experiential meteor that comes into our earthly life-range, from a place we could not know, and which disappears again to a far, far better place (presumably) than we have ever known.

Another route to this same conclusion about Paul's understanding of the resurrection of Jesus could be followed through Ingo Hermann's masterly work, *Kyrios und Pneuma*.[14] It is the thesis of that book, and one as ably argued as any I have seen, that there is, for Paul, a functional identity between the Spirit and the risen Lord Jesus, a functional identity given in the life-experience of Christians. In other words, Jesus-followers experience Jesus precisely as the Spirit of God in their lives, and this is how he is experienced as risen, raised by God to Lordship. So, whether Paul is talking about his apostolate, his converts' life of faith, their freedom from sin, law, death, or their final resurrection, it is always the Lord Jesus as Spirit in their lives, palpable now and so full of promise for an indefinite future, that he has in mind. The resurrection of Jesus means primarily that Jesus, the Lord, is the Spirit, palpable in apostolate, in the new life and in the hope of defeating even biological death, the last enemy;[15] and inextricably bound to this is the conviction of the personal resurrection of Jesus himself which finally resulted from some act of God on Jesus that is not only unwitnessed but incapable of independent proof.

Approach now the descriptions of the resurrection which

occur at the ends of the four gospels and it will seem, at first
sight at least, that they are much more interested than Paul
appeared to be in putting us in some contact with what we have
called the personal resurrection of Jesus himself, the resurrection, that is, as an event in Jesus' own destiny which occurred to
him shortly after his death. All four gospels have stories of
women finding a tomb empty on Sunday morning. And, beginning with Matthew at least – Mark is in dispute here, since many
influential manuscripts and many responsible scholars have the
'original' gospel ending at 16.8, immediately after the finding of
the empty tomb[16] – appearances of the risen Jesus are not
merely listed but also narrated; that is, concrete and, in some
cases, most elaborate details of these alleged occurrences are
supplied. These range from the rather brief details of Matthew's
first appearance scene, where Jesus greets the women who have
just discovered his tomb empty and they worship him, to the
highly developed scenarios of Luke's road to Emmaus story, to
John's doubting Thomas and the lakeside drama of John 21. It
certainly does seem at first sight as if the writers of these gospel
endings are very interested indeed in supplying quite sufficient
circumstantial evidence for the personal resurrection of Jesus, as
much as any unconvinced reader could reasonably require. Are
we here, then, faced with a very different set of priorities in the
understanding of the resurrection of Jesus from those evident in
the writings of Paul?

It is customary by now to treat separately the stories about the
finding of the tomb empty in which the body of Jesus had been
seen to be laid, despite the fact that, in the gospels of Matthew
and John, these stories are part and parcel of accounts of
appearances of the risen Jesus. Around these empty tomb
stories scholarly storms have raged, and they continue to rage
unabated.[17] The basic disagreement emerges in answer to the
question, Are these empty tomb stories early and authentic or
late, derivative and apologetic? That is to say, do the stories
actually come down from witnesses who did discover empty the
tomb in which Jesus had been buried, or are they later fabrica-
tions, deriving their existence and details from the apologetic
need to stress the reality of the resurrection of Jesus in face of
growing denials that it had ever occurred? On the one hand, a
sentence from the Acts of the Apostles 13.29 – 'They (the
Jerusalem crowd, that is, and their leaders) took him down from
a tree and laid him in a tomb' – may retain the memory of a fate
of the body of Jesus similar to that which befalls many an

executed criminal, hasty burial in an unmarked place as a last act of hostility and rejection by the body politic; and the whole story of Joseph's tomb placed at the disciples' disposal may be a later fabrication to sweeten somewhat that last bitter memory. On the other hand, the figure of Magdalen coming to the place where she saw him buried and finding the body gone has a curious persistence through all the erratic details of these resurrection narratives.

The historical facts will probably always be more in dispute here than in any other part of the New Testament. Yet, one noticeable feature of the empty tomb stories should help lessen our frustration. With the single exception of that elusive 'other disciple' of John 20.8, the New Testament never suggests that the discovery of the empty tomb in itself did anything to initiate the belief that Jesus was raised from the dead. Even in the case of that 'other disciple' it is simply stated that he saw and believed, without any indication as to how he made the leap from the empty tomb to his new-found faith. Magdalen, when she found the tomb empty, simply assumed that the gardener had removed the body, and this was, surely, by far the most natural kind of assumption to make in the circumstances. It would take most of us no time at all to persuade ourselves that emptied tombs do not as a matter of course indicate resurrection from the dead.[18]

Therefore, though it would scarcely be possible to prove that all these early authors understood them in this way, it seems clear that empty tomb stories are better fitted to form part of the imagery or symbolism of resurrection, than part of its supporting evidence, and that, in the former role, we could reasonably expect their increasing elaboration, mainly by adding more vivid detail, as the need grows against growing denials to insist on the truth of the resurrection of Jesus. For, first, the apologetic interest in countering Jewish propaganda is already massively present in Matthew and, second, just as surely as going down into the grave stands as a symbol for death, so rising up out of the tomb is a naturally symbolic way of referring to life beginning anew. To the Corinthians who tried Paul's patience so sorely by their questioning of the resurrection and who wondered, presumably amongst other things, what kind of bodies (i.e. selves) were raised, Paul stressed the vast difference between the bodies we are now and the bodies that resurrection, we may hope, finally brings. 'What is sown,' he wrote, in obvious reference to the time-honoured image of the seed that stays in the ground to disintegrate in order that new life might come, 'is perishable, what is raised is imperishable' (I Corinthians 15.35-44). And the first is as necessary to the second as a piece of old cloth to a new garment.

Taking a hint, then, from the total inadequacy of a story of a revived corpse escaping from a tomb to express the New Testament understanding of the resurrection of Jesus, let us look briefly at the gospel narratives of the appearances of Jesus to chosen disciples. There seems even less prospect of arriving at a concordant account of the details of the appearances of Jesus than there is in the case of the empty tomb stories, where at least Mary Magdalen is consistently a principal character. That has to be recognized at the very outset. Apart from the major discrepancy amongst the gospels as to whether the appearances of Jesus took place in Galilee or in and around Jerusalem, all the appearances stories have different settings, details and messages. As Reumann, I think it was, pointed out, there is not even, as there is in the case of the passion narratives, an agreed framework for the appearance narratives, within which discrepancies of detail occur and by comparison to which they could reasonably be counted negligible. But once again, one noticeable feature emerges from the most cursory perusal of the four gospel ends: the more elaborate the detail of the appearance narrative, the more obvious it becomes that the writer's interest has gone far beyond any simple intention of providing, what seems at first sight his aim, physical 'proof' of the presence of a living body identifiable as that of the late Jesus of Nazareth.

In Matthew (28.16-20), the narrative of the appearance of the risen Jesus on a mountain in Galilee is all about the great commission to his close followers to make disciples of all nations. In Luke (24.13-32), it is sometimes said, the details of the appearance to the disciples on the road to Emmaus and in the town of that name suggest that some of the appearances may have occurred in a eucharistic setting.[19] But it is not as often noticed, perhaps, that the features of the narrative which suggest this conclusion could as easily suggest another. 'They recognised him in the breaking of bread,' is surely the punch-line of the Emmaus story, and it could easily tell the readers whom Luke was addressing that they will not meet Jesus along any road, but they will meet him in the eucharist, and really know him there, where he is really present to them.[20]

On returning to Jerusalem, the Emmaus disciples are told of an appearance to Peter, of which no details are given, and then, the narrative continues, Jesus appears before the whole assembly of disciples somewhere in Jerusalem. This appearance is characterized by an 'eating-proof' of his real presence to them (Luke 24.36-43 – they are not hallucinating or 'seeing ghosts'), but its main purpose in the context seems to be to give them the scripture evidence for the divine source of the significance of his death and destiny (which has already been given to the disciples on the road to Emmaus and is now repeated), to commission them to preach repentance, and to promise them the Spirit for this task (Luke 24.44-49). This, to the clean eye, must surely look like the expression in narrative form of the traditional conviction, handed on by Paul, 'that Christ died for our sins in accordance with the scriptures, that he was buried, that he was raised on the third day in accordance with the scriptures' (I Corinthians 15.3f.), that his resurrection means a changed life (repentance) to his followers, and the power or Spirit to bring that about.

In the Fourth Gospel, Jesus appears to his assembled disciples in a room, presumably somewhere in Jerusalem, and straightaway confers the Spirit on them, so that they can forgive sin. And then follows what appears to be the greatest physical proof-text of them all. It is the story of Doubting Thomas – a man unlikely named, for from his few appearances in the gospel narrative he seems always to have been absolutely sure of himself, especially when, as usual, he was wrong, and never to have harboured an honest doubt in his life. Now surely, once again, the punch-line of this story indicates its main thrust, and surely the punch-line of the story is, 'Have you believed because you have seen me? Blessed are those who have not seen and yet believe.' (John 20.29). One cannot but get the impression that the author here wishes to place the emphasis on meeting the risen Jesus in faith or in the Spirit, and not any more in the wounded flesh. Mary Magdalen too is told in the same gospel not to try to hold on to the physical body of Jesus (John 20.17), presumably because if she did, the Spirit would not come (John 16.7).

In the last chapter of the Fourth Gospel, added, it is believed by responsible scholars, by another hand, the scene abruptly changes from Jerusalem to the Sea of Tiberias. Here, after a miraculous catch of fishes and a breakfast of bread and fish, some pastoral instructions are given to Peter and a puzzle about that elusive 'other disciple' is solved (not, however, the puzzle about his identity!). One does not need to be an exegete to know how significant for the missionary activity of Jesus' first disciples are the images of fishing and feeding and how expertly woven, therefore, from familiar symbolism is this latest of the appearance 'narratives' in the gospels.

If one keeps in mind the seeming impossibility of forming any coherent pattern out of these appearance narratives, and if one agrees that some coherent pattern is necessary to the view that they represent literal recorded memories of actual occurrences, the following interpretation would seem justified. The writers here are just as convinced as was Paul that the Jesus who preached along the dusty roads of Galilee and Judaea lives after his death on the cross. To emphasize that it was the same individual they dealt with after his death as before they use the normal language of human encounter – seeing, hearing, touching, dining with. But this is the conventional language of encounter, and it was not intended to convey, nor could it in fact convey what these writers mainly understand by the resurrection of Jesus, (any more than details of an empty tomb could convey this). For, like Paul, they mainly experience and understand the resurrection of Jesus as the gift of the Spirit, and the missionary activity which ensued from this, as new life, the experience of forgiveness and the act of changing one's ways known as repentance, as new faith, and as eucharistic presence. This is surely the understanding of the resurrection of Jesus which these writers convey in the dominant details of their appearance narratives. So, once again, as in the case of Paul, if one considers carefully, comprehensively and without presuppositions all that the gospels have to say about the resurrection of Jesus, it seems preferable to conclude that Jesus is experienced as source of Spirit, new life, faith and in this way known to be alive with God, rather than conclude that Jesus was known to have been revived after death, because certain people saw, felt, dined with him, and therefore we are entitled to believe such and such a claim made by or about him. The first preference has a strength which can be appreciated more and more as the analysis of the Jesus-phenomenon proceeds; the second has a weakness that is only too well known to anyone who ever tried to prove anything by means of a miracle.

In effect, then, the understanding of the resurrection of Jesus in the gospels and in the Acts of the Apostles is no different from that which we find in Paul. It is again a meteor, originating in a place or act of God on Jesus which we cannot know, entering our earthly experience in describable form and movement, and fading from sight again into the future – although, at this third stage, there is a noticeable difference between Paul and the gospel writers in that the latter are progressively more anxious to prevent their readers from speculating on where the future path of the meteor might lead, and correspondingly anxious to keep our eyes fixed on the new possibilities of life opened for us here and now in the world we know. In Luke's ascension scene in the Acts of the Apostles the message comes from the messengers (as one might expect): 'Men of Galilee, why do you stand looking into heaven?' (Acts 1.11).

One final feature of the New Testament treatment of the resurrection might be mentioned in order to clinch the argument for the preferred priority stated in the last paragraph but one. Just as the New Testament has a number of phrases with which to refer to a post-Calvary encounter with Jesus – God revealed his Son to X (Galatians 1.16), or X saw the Lord Jesus (I Corinthians 9.1), or the risen Jesus appeared to X (I Corinthians 15.5-8) – so it has a number of words or phrases in which to refer to that total occurrence that happened in and around Jesus and his followers and those who became his followers when Jesus died. The normal phrase for this, of course, is the one we have been using all along, and which the New Testament uses most frequently, in these words or their equivalent, viz., the resurrection of Jesus. But there are other words and phrases which can equally well describe the same comprehensive occurrence: the exaltation of Jesus, for instance, to Lordship; or his ascension to, or his session at the right hand of the Father; or his breathing or sending of Spirit.[21] The complex and comprehensive understanding of the resurrection in the New Testament can be conveyed in that phrase itself and/or in any or all of these other phrases. From this feature of the New Testament treatment of our topic two types of conclusion immediately emerge.

First, the principal experience and understanding of the resurrection of Jesus which the New Testament writers wish to convey to those who would be followers of Jesus is the experience and consequent understanding of Jesus as an exalted power or spirit in our lives. To this experience circumstantial evidence of the revivification of a corpse, no matter how vivid and persuasive, is totally inadequate. For this reason we need express no surprise that Paul gives us no details at all which could serve as such circumstantial evidence. For this reason also it is better not to try to separate out from the dominant details of the gospel presentations of the resurrection of Jesus those rather erratic

details which could serve as circumstantial evidence of the
revivification of a dead man, and force them, as a matter of
strong priority, to do so. It is far wiser to take these details of
hearing and touching and dining with as images expanded in
narrative form, expansions of the images of seeing, appearing
to, being revealed to. It is wiser to understand them as the
imaginative, narrative form of the conviction, which the gospel
writers shared with Paul, that the Jesus they now experienced as
power in their lives was the same Jesus who preached and died
on the cross, that he, therefore, still lived and reigned. Whether
they had, over and above the experience of the risen Jesus as an
effective power in their lives, other evidence that Jesus was still
alive, the state of our documents will never allow us now to
decide. And it is far better for us that they should not do so. For
we will not be made followers of Jesus – the sole purpose for
which these documents were written – by any physical seeing or
touching of the bodily Jesus on any road or in any room, but by
the experience of his power in our lives which these writers so
vividly described so long ago, and which can alone convince us
today that Jesus lives and reigns.

Secondly, in all the New Testament treatment of the resurrection of Jesus, it is necessary to recognize that we are dealing
once more in the language of image and symbol. Some of these
images and symbols, as Lindars' chapter on resurrection in *New
Testament Apologetic* illustrates, are borrowed from the Old Testament, and for the same reason as the passion narratives borrowed from there. Indeed, if one read just one text and a few
psalms which contain some features of the enthronement ritual
for Judaean kings (II Samuel 7; Psalms 2, 110, and 89), one
would find the same enthronement symbolized as resurrection,
or raising up (II Samuel 7.12), as exaltation, as session at the
right hand of God, so that the one so raised, exalted and seated
can be called Son of God, Lord and Christ. Such contexts (and
others like Joel's prophecy that in the end-time God would pour
his spirit on all flesh: 2.28-32) should be sufficient to warn us
that in the New Testament texts on resurrection, ascension or
exaltation, session at the right hand and spirit-breathing, we are
dealing with symbols fashioned for ancient institutions of king
and prophet, and not with literal description of newly witnessed
events.

But we do not have to be scholars of the Old Testament to
recognize the images or to feel their power. Being exalted or
asked to go up higher, until one is at the very elbow and ear of

the person at the top, and shares most fully in that person's influence, that is an experience known and quite concrete in all cultures. And having air or wind at one's command, that is one of the most primitive and still powerful images of life itself and of the power to enhance or deplete it.

The two Greek words which underlie our word 'resurrection' in the New Testament refer respectively to waking up and standing or rising up, both natural symbols for new beginning, new involvement, new life. Even the most mundane experiences of seeing, touching, travelling, eating, belong to the most basic relationships that bind us to our world and our fellows; and because they are so basic, they are capable of invoking recurring patterns of our experience from the most superficially physical to the most deeply spiritual – we see eye-to-eye with someone, are touched by what someone does, travel the same road towards the same goal in life. These images, therefore, as the last chapter argued, and as is also true of the other images just mentioned above, are capable of functioning as symbols, and in the resurrection kerygma that is what all of them do.

We see Jesus, we walk with him, we break bread with him, because to us he is raised, exalted, powerful, and he breathes new life into us all the time. Someone has said that the only way to prevent another from taking a metaphor of yours too literally is to put beside it another metaphor for the same thing. Perhaps the same is true of symbols. So, even if those who concentrate exclusively on the resurrection image, with its concomitant images of seeing, touching, travelling and eating with, could be excused for taking it all too literally and thinking they were dealing with a case of circumstantial evidence for revival of a dead man, their excuse would soon be taken away by the simple addition of the symbols of exaltation, ascension to power, session at the right hand of power, and spirit-breathing. Nor is narrative form really an excuse for the too literal minded. For the only thing that narrative form does for symbol is to make it into myth.

The complex nature of the resurrection of Jesus and its role in the New Testament

There are three basic elements in the New Testament understanding of the resurrection of Jesus. First, there is what we have called the personal resurrection of Jesus himself, that is to say, an occurrence which personally affected, and precisely in so far as it affected, the person known as Jesus of Nazareth, and which has to be 'placed' or 'timed' after his death on the cross. Second, there is the raising, ascension, or exaltation of Jesus to a position of power from which he can infuse new spirit into the lives of his followers. This is variously described in the symbols of resurrection, ascension and exaltation, session at the right hand and spirit-breathing, and also in the titles conferred on Jesus, titles such as Messiah (in the New Testament concept of messianic dignity), Lord, Son of God in power, titles which we shall deal with separately in their own place. Further, this second element in the resurrection of Jesus as the New Testament understands this, has its experiential counterpart in our changed ways, our new faith, our new lives. Third, there is the hope, sometimes expressed by Paul with a vividness that brings it almost too near, of personal resurrection for each individual, somewhat similar to the personal resurrection of Jesus.

The New Testament writers seem unwilling or unable to offer us any reliable details bearing directly on the first element or the last, on the personal survival of death by Jesus or by anyone else. But details of the second element, of the power or spirit by which Jesus still reigns in our lives, details by which that reign can be experienced and its meaning understood, the New Testament writers offer us in almost embarrassing abundance. It seems, therefore, wise to conclude that the first and third elements in the New Testament presentation of the resurrection of Jesus, namely, the personal resurrection of Jesus and the 'first-fruits of those who have fallen asleep', are, respectively, a conviction and a hope firmly based on the second element, the experienced lordship of Jesus in the lives of his followers. To try to take the first and third elements in isolation, to try to 'prove' them by means of evidence, circumstantial or otherwise, directly bearing on them – much less, to try to 'prove' anything else by means of them – would seem to be, not only an exercise in futility, but a serious misunderstanding of the innate priorities, the inherent logic of the resurrection of Jesus as presented by the New Testament.

Having arrived at this summary statement, it might be interesting now to look back at some of the role-requirements outlined earlier to see what, if any, truth there is in any of them.

First, then, the resurrection of Jesus is not simply a way of expressing the fact that the preaching of Jesus continued and continued to effect faith (role-requirement (g) above). Of course, the preaching of Jesus did continue, and so did the distinctive faith, though not exclusively due to the preaching (as every preacher knows). The living faith of the followers of Jesus is indeed the experiential counterpart of the centrepiece of the resurrection triptych presented by the New Testament, not the centrepiece itself and not the whole triptych. The New Testament says that Jesus is Lord, that this is palpable in our lives of faith, that Jesus lives after death and that we may hope to do so too. The New Testament may be wrong about all this, but there seems little point in pretending that it does not say all this, that all it says is that preaching continues, and continues to effect faith.

Nor does the New Testament really allow us to say that the resurrection of Jesus either enabled people to have faith which the life and death of Jesus could never have given them, or lighted aspects of Jesus' person and mission which previous to it had not been in any way perceptible (role-requirements (*a*) and (*e*) above). By the time these writers are producing the documents we now read in the New Testament, Jesus has already, they are convinced, experienced his personal resurrection from the dead; and it is this Jesus who inspires that faith in them which lights the way ahead. But this merely chronological factor does not entitle us to conclude that the Jesus who walked the roads of Galilee could not and did not inspire the same faith and shed the same light. In fact, the oft-noted penchant of these writers to emphasize the identity of the risen Lord with the man Jesus who walked amongst them should act as a deterrent to prevent us from reaching this conclusion.

Somewhat similar remarks must be made about three other role-requirements tabulated above. To say that the stubbornness of people, or their blindness, or the shock of the criminal execution of Jesus, deprived people of the possibility of the faith of Jesus or stunted it (role-requirements (*b*), (*c*), and (*d*) above), is to hazard some rather questionable historical guesses about the psychological development of these people, whoever or however few or many they are supposed to have been. But it does not entitle us to claim anything about the nature or role of the resurrection of Jesus. We are all surely familiar with the way in which faith can edge through our blindness or stubborness, or recover again after a shock, with nothing more than a period of quiet reflection to facilitate such enrichment of our lives. Many of us indeed can think of an example of how the tragic death of a good man in pursuit of a good cause first shocked us into near despair, but then, without the help of any subsequent event, itself overcame the shock it had caused and ended by proving even more inspiring to us than was the man's life. We have already seen how some New Testament stories, which seem at first sight anxious to show how a specific personal-resurrection-connected event changed doubters into believers, could reasonably be interpreted to mean that scripture or eucharist did this, or that faith could very well, if not better, survive without such 'proofs'.[22]

That leaves us with one last role-requirement (*f*) tabulated above, the one which claimed for the personal resurrection of Jesus himself the role of constituting certain features of his personal status and function which previous to it had not existed. Now this, it must be said, is the least likely of all the role-requirements imposed upon the New Testament texts on the resurrection of Jesus, despite the fact that some of these texts, if interpreted rather simplistically, would seem to suggest it.

For, first, as we have already hinted, a person can achieve a status in death which no other event before or after death could confer. We are no strangers to the experience of a person's stature increasing with his or her death. A person can sometimes achieve more for a cause by dying for it than by living for it, can effect more influence on others, more of a power in their lives, in death than during life. This may be partly explained by saying that death for one's cause or mission is the final emptying (in the negative sense of voiding) of any last vestige of self-interest that might otherwise blight one's harvest of influence for good, and consequently the final emptying out (in the positive sense of pouring) of one's spirit on one's contemporaries. Whatever the explanation, the experience is not completely strange to any of us.

Secondly, we have established that the language used in resurrection-kerygma is symbolic language, and cannot therefore be taken literally as description of an event of Jesus' own personal destiny witnessed (at least in the form of circumstantial evidence) by a specific number of Jesus' followers and not by others. No more than the raising by God, or exaltation by God, or seating by God at God's right hand, when said of the Judaic kings can be taken as a literal description of the translation of the kings to a physical place of immortal power in the heavens, but was rather the symbolic statement of the king's leadership, as God's representative, of God's people on earth, no more can these symbols, when applied to a new leader of God's people, be taken as literal description of an actual heavenly enthronement of Jesus which was somehow witnessed to have taken place after his death.

Third, and again a point which has been hinted already on a number of occasions and which can draw the two previous points together, so many of the symbols which made up the myth of Jesus' death turn up again in the resurrection preaching. In fact, as we already noted, the Fourth Gospel uses the most substantial symbols of that preaching – the raising or exaltation of Jesus, his glorification, his spirit-breathing – of the death of Jesus. All of which suggests that if there is any single event at which Jesus achieved an exalted status or function, it was at his death, and not at or during any event after that.

In short, the resurrection preaching seems to be *the* myth of the death of Jesus. That conclusion should not be surprising to thoughtful Christians. It cannot be without significance that Paul, for instance, regards the eucharist, the central and essential Christian ritual, as the memorial, not of the resurrection of Jesus, but of his death (I Corinthians 11. 26). And it will yet be found to be of more than passing interest to the substance of this study of the faith of Jesus to note that it is precisely by dying that one lives.

There are three basic elements in the New Testament preaching on the resurrection of Jesus: a part of Jesus' own personal destiny after his death which primarily concerned Jesus himself; a status of Jesus as exalted Lord which concerns us and which has its experiential counterpart in the lives we can now live; a hope, derived from this, that we too can survive the death we must one day die. The central and principal element of this resurrection preaching, I am now saying, is *the* myth of the death of Jesus. It is *the* statement, in the form of narrated symbols, of the deep significance for human kind of the death of this man.

Perhaps that conclusion needs qualification. Perhaps it should read: the central and principal part of the resurrection preaching is the myth of the man Jesus, the myth of the man who died.[23] For the central and principal element of the resurrection preaching seems to convey the significance of the man and not just the significance of his death, even though his death, as we shall have cause to notice again, is itself of central importance for understanding the significance of the man.

Of course, it would probably be impossible to distinguish in the New Testament material a myth of the death of Jesus from the more comprehensive myth of the man. Probably all that one would find if one conducted a detailed enumeration and analysis of the major symbols is this: that wherever the death of Jesus is explicitly the subject of the preaching or teaching, the significance for us would for the most part be described in terms of overcoming the negative features of our existence in which we experience ourselves as trapped, bound, sold-out, sick. On balance that is what our own slight investigations into the myth of the death of Jesus in the last chapter would suggest. We did indeed find John depicting the death of Jesus as his exaltation to spirit-breathing glory, but for the most part we saw the death described as our reconciliation, acquittal, ransom, cure and freedom, thereby drawing attention to the negative features of our estranged and guilty lives. And that is not surprising.

That feature of our most existential experience of life which the philosophers call its contingency has been already observed, in the course of inquiring after the nature of myth, and it will no doubt occupy us again later. It points to that ambivalence of life whereby we know it, either in moments of crisis or at times of deep reflection, to be at one and the same time positive, affirmative, full of wonder, bursting with promise, and fragile, uncertain, subject to decline and decay, threatened, negative. Those people or events seen to have most significance for human existence do something to overcome the negative aspects and to enhance the positive, and usually their significance can be described in either way, or preferably in both. But death, especially death at the hands of one's fellows, who are thus accomplices of the very evil that destroys the quality of human existence, will tend to have its significance described more in terms of overcoming the negative features of human existence than in terms of enhancing the positive.

But the overcoming of the negative features of human existence is but one side of the coin, enhancing the positive is the other. The full resurrection myth does repeat the symbols specifically associated with the death of Jesus; it does depict Jesus as the one in whom God heals and frees and gains acquittal for us. But it also claims that in Jesus God enhances our most positive experiences in life, and thus answers the question, for what are we freed and acquitted and healed? Jesus, in this myth, is by God's action a high power inspiring us (that is, breathing spirit into us) to change our lives, breathing new lives into us, lives of faith and hope, lives like the life of Jesus himself, gracious lives, glorious lives – and if one wished to follow the clue of these spirit-filled lives further, particularly through Paul's descriptions of the graces and fruits of the spirit, one would see them also as lives of love and service, from each according to his or her ability, to each according to his or her need. So does the full resurrection myth bring out in strong relief the more positive features of the significance of Jesus.

In any case, it does not really make much sense to talk about the significance of a man's death until one knows something of the significance of the man who died. Now the resurrection of Jesus, as preached in the New Testament, is the first complex and comprehensive myth of this man who died. In its principal and central element, as we have seen, the resurrection preaching presents Jesus as one possessed of the power and spirit to renew the lives of his followers. We have argued already that the fact that the writers who paint this picture probably did not have the experience which guarantees its truth until after the death of Jesus does not warrant us in assuming that Jesus could not be so described until after his death. One writer, we saw, applied this description to Jesus at the time of his death. Other writers, like Paul, can use composite names such as 'Jesus Christ, our Lord', which clearly convey the conviction that it is the same individual who was known as Jesus of Nazareth who was, is and will be the one anointed by God to be Lord of our lives. We might add here that New Testament writers have no difficulty about using the terms 'dying' and 'living anew' within the perimeters of life on this earth.[24] We are dealing, in the central element of the resurrection preaching, with myth, that is, with a narrative arrangement of symbols which tells us of the significance for our lives of the man who died on Calvary: we are not dealing with a literal description of yet another event. As it is possible for us to live or die every day, and not just on the date of our biological deaths, so it was possible for Jesus to be author of life every day he lived, and perhaps particularly on the day he died, but not just on the day after his execution, or three days after it.

The resurrection theme in the New Testament, then, is the myth of the man Jesus. Its constitutive symbols present him as a man of ultimate significance for the basic ambivalence of life. He is an exalted one, a Lord, possessed of a powerful spirit, victorious over the destructive powers of death, increasing and enriching life. The resurrection of Jesus in the New Testament is not primarily an event like birth, baptism, or biological death, and no light shines from it back into the life of Jesus, no light which did not shine already in that life – except perhaps the light that is generated by our growing awareness of the effects of that life in the lengthening course of the centuries. The resurrection in the New Testament is primarily the myth of the man Jesus in his life and death. It is a myth the truth of which can be tested by any follower of Jesus, from the follower so powerfully inspired as to become a missionary, to the one who has barely touched its energy field.

Because the principal and central element in the resurrection preaching depicts Jesus as being, by God's act, author of life (Acts 3.15), it carries the conviction that he lives to God (Romans 6.10), that he did in fact survive his death on the cross, and it carries the hope that we too will survive the deaths we must one day die. But we have no details of that conviction or that hope for, unlike the central element in the resurrection preaching, these other elements have no experiential counterparts. They represent the points at which our best images and concepts which carry us through most dimensions of our existence finally fail for want of applicable content. That conviction about Jesus' own personal destiny, as distinct from his relationship to us, and that hope for our own lives after death, both lives therefore, and live well, from the strength of the principal and central element of the resurrection preaching, once it takes effect in our lives, not it from them.

The resurrection of Jesus in the New Testament is the myth of the man Jesus. It is the first comprehensive christology from which all others, as we shall see, develop. Because it is the myth of the man Jesus who died at the hands of Pontius Pilate, it cannot answer the question with which we ended the last chapter, and which some people expect it to answer: why this myth of the death of this man? All it can do is replace that with a broader question; why this myth of the man who died in this way? What could possibly justify the application to this man who died as a common criminal of these mighty symbols of victory, lordship, and inspiration?

Once again, as this broader question is urged upon us in this way, a hint is also given as to the direction in which we might look for an answer. There has been much talk in the myth of the spirit of Jesus and of the life it enables us to live. This surely suggests that we might look to the life of Jesus for an answer to our question. There is, in any case, no other direction left in which to look. Who is this man? What is the spirit of this man? What is the life which was consummated in such a death and which is said to be of ultimate significance for all of us?

4

The Life of Jesus

The quest for the man within the myth

Myth is a way of telling the truth about the world we live in. If it can tell the truth about human kind, there appears to be no reason why it cannot tell the truth about an individual person; if it can tell the truth about the world of space and time, there is no reason why it cannot tell the truth about a particular life lived at a particular place and a particular time: provided, of course, that the individual whose life is in question had some profound significance for human kind in the world of space and time. There are more ways of living in the memory of posterity than ensuring that one's diaries are found, more ways of being remembered than writing diaries, more ways of being faithful to the memory of someone than writing straight biographies and making sure that they are read. Myth, we shall maintain for the moment, until the point is clarified as we go on, is no more of a hindrance than it can be a help in the quest of a historic character.

We shall not devote any space at the opening of this chapter to the technical problem of the different types of literature found in the New Testament, much less to the different kinds of criticism – from textual criticism to redaction criticism – perfected over the last two centuries to deal with these. We have already recorded our opinion that the various kinds of criticism, similar in this respect to the mythical material they deal with, are in themselves neutral toward the prospects of the quest of the historical Jesus. We shall therefore continue the attitude of the chapter on the death of Jesus, use the best results which the different kinds of criticism have reported, and make reference to the type of literature or criticism involved only if the occasion particularly demands it. In this way we shall see more quickly what the best of contemporary scholarship has to say on the subject of the life of the historical Jesus.

Finally, we shall not devote any space at the outset to any of those even broader generalizations often made about the subject-matter through which we must now pursue our quest and about the literature in which it is contained, such as, for instance, that we are dealing with faith documents, written by those who already had a certain faith in Jesus in order to initiate, inspire, preserve or perfect the same faith in others. If Jesus' very life was an attempt to inspire faith of a particular kind in others, then, quite clearly, provided they got right the particular kind of faith he tried to inspire, no documents could be truer to his memory than faith documents.[1] In general, then, it is best to set out on the quest, and to let the questions about the different types of material we have to deal with arise naturally in the course of it, rather than first discuss in a vacuum such literary and philosophical issues as those just mentioned, and then approach our material with the vacuous generalizations in mind which alone result from issues discussed in a vacuum.

One set of preliminary remarks might, however, be in order. The title of this chapter would be seriously misleading if it did lead people to expect that a fairly full account of the life of Jesus from infancy to death could now be reconstructed. Nothing could be further from the truth. And if this is what scepticism about life of Jesus questing is meant to suggest, the scepticism is justified.

First, the narratives about the conception, birth and infancy of Jesus found at the beginnings of the gospels of Matthew and Luke are of extremely doubtful historical value if taken at all literally.[2] They are, however, as true as any other part of the New Testament if taken symbolically or mythically.[3] In fact, before what is known as his public ministry, a period which is commonly thought to have lasted for as little as a year and a quarter or, at most, for something just over three years, little or nothing can be said with historical certainty about Jesus of Nazareth. (Well, it is most likely that he was from Galilee, anyway, even if not from Nazareth.) There is no evidence strong enough to suggest with any force that he was part of an Essene community. He did, apparently, have some connections with a reformer called John the Baptist, but that connection is now so overlaid by New Testament apologetic, intended to show Jesus superior to John the Baptist, whose followers were still apparently strong at the time of writing, and, furthermore, the connection with John is put to such ulterior usage by various New Testament 'redactors'[4] that it would be impossible to reconstruct its precise lines with any accuracy. So, the life of Jesus before what is known as his public ministry must be left to the artistic imaginations of the Nikos Kazantzakis's of this world,[5] or to all our childhood memories of the little boy who made mud birds and bade them fly away. (Though that childish story, too, it would not be right to pass without saying, contained its own memorial, tempered to the mind of the young, of the man who gave wings of faith and hope and love to those who were made of clay.)

For our purposes, then, the life of Jesus means the cause he lived and died for, and it refers to that brief period during which he put that cause to his people, and which ended with his dying for it. That is all of his personal life that his most faithful followers cared to remember and to record. But it was, as we shall see, more than enough. That his cause should have seen such historic, world-wide success despite such a short exposure to a public presumably as indifferent as publics before and since have been known to be, is sufficient indication that it struck a note of profound significance for human kind. That cause was his life and, however or whenever he may have prepared for it, he truly began to live it when he took his first public stance. What, then, was the cause for which he lived and died? How does one depict his life?

Even of the few public years, not many purely factual data can be discovered. The journey is one of the great symbols for a human life, and since it is so used by the New Testament writers, as the redaction critics point out, it would be difficult indeed to trace Jesus' itinerary in any detail. It is widely accepted that he came from Galilee, highly probable that he began his public mission there, and certain that he ended that same mission in Jerusalem. Of his more particular deeds and words recorded in the New Testament it is difficult now to be certain of the authenticity, much less the more specific occasions of time and place and other circumstance. Miracles and meals are by far the most prominent of the deeds attributed to Jesus, and we shall have much to say about these. The difficulty of finding some authentic words of his in the New Testament is compounded by the tendency of prophets amongst his followers to put words in the mouth of him who was now their Lord, as the prophets of the Old Testament had prefaced their statements with the solemn formula: 'Thus saith the Lord.' But the parables of Jesus most scholars recognize to be in a class by themselves, and even the non-scholar can think of many of them that are strictly unforgettable. His prayer also, though much less detail on its original wording is available than in the case of the parables, is in a class apart as far as reliable authenticity is concerned. And there is one phrase of which there can be very little doubt that he used it and, further, that it was his favourite phrase for what his whole mission was all about: the kingdom of God. We shall be on ground as solid, then, as the best of scholarly research can provide if, in searching for the cause of Jesus for which he lived and died, in searching for the only life of Jesus that mattered to him or to us, we look for the meaning that he gave to that phrase 'the kingdom of God' in his parables, his prayer, and his practical ministry of 'miracle' and meal.

The kingdom of God

'Now after John was arrested, Jesus came into Galilee, preaching the gospel of God and saying: "The time is fulfilled, and the kingdom of God is at hand; repent, and believe in the gospel" ' (Mark 1.14f.).

The phrase 'kingdom of God' is not used in the writings of early Christianity, and it is not found in the Old Testament, with the possible exception of Yahweh being made to refer to his kingdom in I Chronicles 17.14. Some writers suggest that we substitute the phrase 'Reign of God' in order that we might not even be tempted to think of a territory, and might think instead, as the original Aramaic or Greek would make us think, of the actual ruling or reigning of God in this world. We should certainly accept this suggestion for change in the translation and understanding of the phrase, yet resist the thought of God's reign as a private effect on the individual. The thought of a territory may seldom be part of the phrase, but the social connotations are never lacking; the phrase never endorses private pietism. Though the phrase itself might be strange, the thought is there from the time when Israel first borrowed from surrounding cultures the institution of monarchy and, with that, another symbol for divinity. Yahweh, then, ruled as a king over the world and its nations, governing the mighty forces of nature and bringing nations to fulfilment or disaster as they deserved. In particular he ruled over his chosen people, Israel, which he had brought out of slavery, given rest from its wandering, and made into a nation special to himself. Sometimes, indeed, the human king seems more than a symbol, the kingdom and rule seem to be his, though given to him by Yahweh for the benefit of the people, and the thought of a territory is not far off at all. 'Your house and your kingdom shall be made sure for ever before me,' Yahweh is made to say to David in II Samuel 7.16, 'your throne shall be established for ever.'

Inevitably this theme of God ruling the world, and particularly Israel, as a king might do, rang the changes of the tenses. It was all very well for Israel's solemn ritual to recall Yahweh's mighty deeds for his people in the past – though this same solemn ritual was supposed to spread their effectiveness to the present – but in times of national misery, more assurance of Yahweh's reign seemed necessary. It was then that the prophets assured the people that God was with them, if only to chastise them for their wrongdoing, and that he would save them and bring them to their happy destiny in the future. As the tradition of the so-called writing prophets developed, these assurances of a glorious future gained in length and magnificence, until Second Isaiah, for instance, is one sustained poem of future peace and prosperity for the world. Thus enters eschatology, the expectation of a future reign of God in a final era more glorious than anything experienced before.

National misery, of course, comes in many grades. At times of savage persecution, such as that perpetrated by Antiochus IV in the seventeenth decade before Christ, the pastoral verses of Second Isaiah could hardly be heard. More powerful imagery was needed to rescue some hope from such horrible times, like that provided by the Book of Daniel, the first fully-fledged apocalyptic work of Jewish history. Apocalyptic is a form of eschatology in that it, too, looks forward to a final time when God's goal for his people and his world will be achieved. It makes much use of one technique familiar from prophetic eschatology, the technique of dating the work some time before it was actually written, so that the writer, by seeming to 'predict' accurately the circumstances of the present, might gain more credibility for the promises which he issues in the name of God for the future. But in other ways it differs substantially from prophetic eschatology. The horrors of the present with which it tries immediately to deal are so destructive that it is driven, in order to describe them, beyond the category of chastisement. It is driven to cosmic categories, at once so primitive and so powerful, of great conflagrations, for instance, purifying the world as fire purifies precious metal, and these symbols then become the symbols in which God's intervention to bring about the final time is described. Awesome destruction and incredible triumph come together in the inflated imagery of apocalyptic. 'Old endgame,' as Beckett put it in his play *Endgame*, 'Old endgame, lost of old / Play and lose, and have done with losing.'

Apocalyptic always holds a certain morbid interest for the human mind. It easily outlives the circumstances which give it birth, and always finds groups to predict the end of the world over the graves of all former predictions. Symbols are always vulnerable to over-literal minds, and the inflated images of apocalyptic seem more prone than most to be taken too literally. But the tendency to take apocalyptic too literally is due to a disease of the human mind rather than to any inherent fault in apocalyptic itself. It is due to a failure of nerve, to the hypochondriac's penchant for exaggerating the evils of the age, to the coward's anxious search for an escape clause in humanity's contract with history. In its own way and for its own peculiar circumstances apocalyptic tries to do what all eschatology does; it presents in powerful symbol the religious person's deepest conviction that God has destined this world for good and that, in spite of the most fearful indications to the contrary, good will finally triumph.[6]

So in Old Testament times the theme of God's reign in the world rang the changes of the tenses of past, present and future. In what is known as the inter-testamental period, that is, the time between the ending of the composition of the books of the Old Testament and the beginning of the New, the very phrase itself, 'the reign of God', did apparently gain much currency. From what we have already seen in this section, and from what we have seen also, in the section on the factions at the time of Jesus, it is quite obvious that this phrase would have given rise to different expectations in different Jewish minds. Nationalists, like the Zealots, in literal memory of David, would naturally understand the phrase to refer to a temporal kingdom free from foreign oppression, and their faith would lead them to hope and fight for that. Pharisees, and rabbinic types in general, would rather think that the reign of God referred to moral and ritual purity and to the full observance of God's law by his people, and from this they would expect God's choicest blessings. Apocalyptic imagery for the coming of the reign of God was very common in the literature of the period, and of the various factions mentioned it probably corresponded most closely to the mentality of the Essenes who withdrew altogether from 'the world' in order to await God's good pleasure. Sadducees, it is almost certain, would have little use for the phrase at all, and probably for the same reason which restricted its use by those Christian missionaries and writers most concerned to convert the Roman world, the reason, namely, that it would not have sounded right in the ears of Romans who ruled the greatest kingdom on earth and brooked no rival kingdom within their wide imperium. Finally, a comparison of the treatment of the theme of the reign of God in the main inter-testamental writings with that of the New Testament would reveal that many of the details of its coming are common to both: it will see victory over Satan, for instance, forgiveness of sins, great healing, instruction for the poor; it will be comparable to harvest time or to a wedding feast.[7]

The reign of God, then, is something of a master-symbol which had deep roots in the historical consciousness of the Jew. It was a master-symbol for his faith that this world of his deepest and daily experience was ultimately in the hands of God and that it was, or would be, or could be made to be the very source of the most abundant life conceivable. As a master-symbol it could mould many subordinate images to its use, depending on the mentality of the user or the temper of the times. It could, therefore, and did, branch out into those many patterns in which people try to believe in a better life. The phrase itself was in common currency at the time of Jesus, and it had a common fund of imaginative detail at its disposal.

In view of all this, it would obviously be quite wrong to decide first what the phrase 'the reign of God' means, so to arrive at a quick conclusion on what Jesus thought he was announcing or inaugurating. The reign of God means what its users make it to mean; it does not have a set meaning by which all users are expected to abide. It would be equally, though not perhaps quite as obviously, wrong to try to arrive first at some general, if abstract features of the reign of God in the teaching of Jesus, and to fill in the concrete details later. There was a time when nothing seemed so important in christology as to decide at the very outset whether Jesus thought of the reign of God as something which would break in suddenly in the future (consistent eschatology), or as something which arrived with his mission (realized eschatology).[8] Attempts to answer such general questions in the inevitably abstract terms in which their answers are cast only tempt the modern mind, already too prone to literal interpretation, to mistake the very nature of symbolism, especially by taking it too literally. Symbol and myth will only yield their full meaning if we attend first to all their concrete detail, and allow ourselves to be totally absorbed in it. Then, and only then, we can translate that meaning into any language we like, and answer any questions that arise about it. So let us study, in all its concrete details, Jesus' own presentation of the reign of God. That means immersing ourselves in the world of his parables, his prayer, his 'miracles' and his meals.

The parables of the kingdom

They are called the parables of the kingdom because the kingdom or reign of God, the single goal of Jesus' life, is their subject, and some of them are actually introduced in the New Testament with a phrase such as, 'The kingdom of God may be likened to ...'

Much has been written on the nature of parable, and probably much needs to be said. Perhaps the commonest cause of misunderstanding is the failure of would-be communicators to take note of the precise form of communication that is being used. And the parable form has often, no doubt, been mistaken for some other. Nevertheless, if we are ever to get to the heart of the matter, even the most important of preliminary remarks must be kept to manageable proportions. So let the following few remarks on the nature of parable suffice.

The most commonplace warning issued to prospective readers of parables is that they should not confuse these with allegory. The same warning, significantly enough, is sometimes issued to readers about to sample myth[9] or poetic imagery and symbol.[10] Now this warning must not be taken to mean that the message conveyed by parable could not be communicated in any other form; for if that were the case, all the erudite books written on the parables could be accused of ignoring their own warning and misleading the general public.

The distinction between parable and allegory may be expressed as follows. One may first analyse and present a subject through the medium of abstract concept, and then illustrate this analysis along the way by use of certain imagery. The imagery is then easily translated back into the conceptual analysis which it is its sole function to illustrate. But it is quite another thing first to probe and present a subject through the use of those images that live in the basic relationships that bind us to our world and our fellows, that evoke the recurring patterns of our experience, and that make a very comprehensive appeal to our total persons. It is quite another thing to probe and present purely through the evocative power of such symbols. Later, of course, if one wishes, one can also communicate the insight thus gained in the more abstract forms of conceptual analysis. This is what books on the parables do. But in the former case, of allegory, the imagery is used in a purely subordinate and supportive role. In the latter case, of parable, image and symbol are themselves the primary means of gaining insight, and only after insight is gained through total attention to their evocative power may the attempt be made to present that same insight in more abstract terms.

Some of the parables of Jesus have already been allegorized in the New Testament. In the case of the parable of the sower in Matthew 13, the evangelist has already fairly obviously in mind four categories of believers, or at least of those to whom the word was preached. The image of the seed and its varied fate, though it precedes these categories, is simply used to illustrate them. The problem with allegorizing old parables, in itself quite a legitimate preaching technique, is that it tends to obscure the messages of the originals, if only by over-extending them. So, the ability to recognize the true nature of parable contributed, with a great many other contextual considerations, to the remarkable form-critical success in uncovering the original, authentic parables of Jesus and, thus, his original message. Parables had been put to other uses, too, by the time the gospels were written, besides being used as allegories. They had been turned into that familiar form, the story-with-a-moral – not only in New Testament times, but in the mainly moralizing sermons preached from most pulpits down to the present day. The parable of the unjust steward, for instance, in Luke 16, has at least four distinguishable 'morals' attached to the end of it, like four consecutive tails pinned by the blindfolded to an original donkey. The most familiar of these 'morals' is to the effect that we cannot serve God and mammon, and it was almost certainly no part of the immediate message which the original parable was meant to convey.

Parables, then, are neither allegories nor stories-with-morals. But they deal in those images which can be made to evoke recurring patterns of our experience, and which therefore function as symbols. Since they are stories, or clusters of stories, they are of the nature of myth. So we may end these preliminary remarks by saying something which we hope will be amply illustrated as we proceed: the parables of Jesus are Jesus' own myth of the reign of God, as meal and prayer are its ritual, and service its life-style. Occupying, as all myth does, the concrete end of the spectrum of human communication, the parables do not analytically dissect and then synthetically compose the experience known as the reign of God, using abstract concept and term. They are rather like a slow saunter round that singular, yet very complex experience, lighting up its concrete facets, sometimes several at a time, as the circle is completed.

When the speculative mind tries to wrest their message from the parables, it tries first to fit their great number and variety into a few clear categories. It is probably of some importance to note that such categorization owes its existence to the systematic requirements of abstract thought. It makes no claim to represent the order in which the parables were originally spoken. It is done differently by different writers.[11] It is always to some extent arbitrary. Images and symbols, no doubt, produce their own dynamic order as they mature into words, but the following categories do not claim to represent even this. Their solitary *raison d'être* is the initial help they provide in bringing the inquisitive mind into contact with the individual power and cumulative impression of the parables of Jesus.

The reign of God, then, is an experience that is or can be available to us in this world: it is, as Jesus said (according to Mark),'at hand' since his own arrival on the scene. What we seek from the parables is the nature and meaning of this experience in the case of Jesus. Mathematicians sometimes begin to solve their problems by making the quantity they are seeking equal to 'x'. If we remember that the parables are of the nature of symbol or myth, and that symbol is the use of an image which has literal application at one level of experience, but is capable of evoking recurring patterns of experience at different levels (and myth is the same use of image in the context of a story), then what we have to do is: first, immerse our minds in the imagery of the parables at its most accessible and literal level; then, allow this imagery to evoke the recurring patterns of experience down to the deepest level possible; or, begin like mathematicians by making the experience known as the reign of God equal to 'x', and then let the evocative power of the imagery gradually reveal to us what 'x' really is.

The first category of parables comprises the story of the treasure which a man found buried in a field, then joyfully sells all he has and buys the field; the story of the precious pearl a man found and again sold all that he had to buy it (Matthew 13.44-46); the story of the joy at finding a lost sheep, or a lost coin (Luke 15.3-10). In these stories, if one simply attends to their unimpeded impact, it is surely the joy that first communicates itself, joy at the discovery of what is already there, but was buried, or somehow hidden from view, or lost, or lost sight of; but joy at a discovery that will yet cost one all that one has, or, at the very least, the lavishness of a shared celebration. That last and, at first sight, rather enigmatic element – of which there is still no hint that it mutes in the least the dominant note of joy – will be developed, no doubt, in succeeding parables.

Next, there is the parable of the great feast to which various people were invited, but were prevented by one concern or another from deciding to accept the invitation (Luke 14.14-16; we do not give here all the references to different versions of these parables, nor do we intend to refer to all the parables in the New Testament; we choose, rather, significant samples), and the parable of the unjust steward, to which reference has already been made, in which a steward about to be dismissed for dishonesty or inefficiency, promptly decides to do favours for his master's debtors, so that they will show favour to him when he needs it. The dominant note here is surely one of decisiveness, of the need for quick and correct decision. Add the impact of this imagery to that of the last group of parables, and the impression begins to grow that even the joyful discovery will be useless unless it is accompanied by quick and correct decision, that procrastination, on whatever excuse, is already a decision against the invitation proffered or implied. Here, too, an enigmatic note enters, in the filling of the banquet seats with the rabble from the highways and byways, and in the direction of praise to such an obviously unworthy character as our friend, the steward. Undoubtedly that enigma also will be resolved as we proceed.

But first we had better notice the insistence of the parables on the cost of possessing or accepting that which is already there for us to possess or offered to us to accept. (The need for decisiveness many of us would find costly enough, but apparently the cost is higher still.) There are stories that can only invite our derision for the king who went to war against an enemy without taking the trouble to assess the relative strength of their forces, for the man who started to build a tall tower without so much as a single calculation to see if he could muster the financial resources to complete it (Luke 14.28-32). Kings fallen in battle and men embarrassed by half-built monuments to their own imprudence are our sombre warnings that the final cost of this strange enterprise may be much higher than we first thought.

The parable of the prodigal son is the almost too well known story of the younger son who wasted his share of the inheritance, then hired himself out as a swineherd to a Gentile and even ate the swine's food; only to be received back into his father's arms and his father's house to the music and laughter of a great banquet. If we can only resist the temptation of this, the easiest of all parables to allegorize, we must surely see that its most profound impact is one of total offence. This young man had committed a complex of crimes, any one of which would probably have been sufficient to excommunicate him from Jewish society, the chosen area of God's saving grace. There were certain types of conduct which, if Jews engaged in them, they made themselves as Gentiles, as the phrase went. Shepherding for hire was one of these.[12] And shepherding swine for a Gentile? And eating swine-food? And living riotously? There are three kinds of people in the world. There are those who share our way of life and its philosophy. These we accept. Then there are those who do not share our way of life, but since they have never really experienced it there is still hope for them. Finally, there are those who have shared our way of life and have rejected it. They are the most offensive, the most unforgivable people conceivable, as we all can verify from our own national experience. They have seen the light and have sinned against it. To celebrate the return of one of these without awaiting a word of repentance from his lips, and to offer him the best that we have, is as offensive as any gesture could be (Luke 15.11-32).

The parable of the Pharisee and the tax-collector (Luke 18.9-14) is equally offensive. But again we can only see that if we stop reading into the story what is not there. The Pharisee is the good, pious man who fasts and prays and gives away one tenth of all he owns. The publican on the other hand exhibits in his otherwise undistinguished person the combustible combination of thievery and treason, and all he does in the story is ask God for mercy. To conclude, as the story does, that he, rather than the Pharisee, stood right before God, is about as inoffensive as stating, as Jesus is said also to have done, that prostitutes (practising prostitutes, presumably) are nearer to the experience of the reign of God than the most pious religious people of the land.

If we let the simple imagery of these parables work its immediate effect on us, then, we should begin to realize that the discovery of this precious thing, the acceptance for what it is of what is there and offered, is equally accessible to all; we should, if we are honest, feel our anger rising at this blatant disregard for our cherished distinctions between types of people, our most institutionalized priorities; and we should gradually begin to realize how the cost of this strange experience might yet increase.

The offence, if we continue to hear the parables of Jesus, is only deepened. The story of the labourers in the vineyard has the laggards who lazed for most of the day and only worked for a fraction of it paid just as much as those who, in our most righteous phrase, had given a good day's work for a good day's wages; and the latter come away with no more consolation than to be told that the man could do what he liked with his own money and that they should not begrudge his generosity (Matthew 20.1-16). Even if we were prepared to set aside those judgments by which we place some people over others in our moral ratings, we should still almost certainly resist such an assault on that iron principle of justice, the principle, namely, that a man shall receive only what he earns, and that free and uncalculated giving (and receiving) must always be kept to the very occasional exception that only proves the rule.

Then there is the parable of the unmerciful servant (Matthew 18.23-35) who, when his master had been so generous as to cancel all his debts, refused a lesser generosity to one of his fellow servants and persecuted the latter until he was paid all that he was owed: he was duly punished as befitted his failure. Enrichment, we get the impression, gratuitous enrichment, treasure, requires of its very nature that we enrich in turn even the most apparently undeserving. That, too, is part of the cost, though there is still no hint that the cost diminishes the original joy or dampens in any way the celebration.

And once again the offence is repeated. Our inbred preferences would naturally lead us to expect that generosity to the unfortunate would first be forthcoming from the recognized custodians of religion, morality and decency in the land, on the grounds that they, surely, were in the best position possible to appreciate the blessings conferred on the fortunate. Yet, in the familiar parable of the good Samaritan (Luke 10.29-37), it is not the priest or the levite who comes to the aid of the unfortunate man who fell foul of brigands, but a native of neighbouring

Samaria, a man as hated as only provincial hatred can hate a close neighbour who has married outside the tribe and has gone his own way.

The point is unrelentingly pressed home, then, in the homely imagery of these parables, that this joyful discovery, this precious thing offered for our decision to accept it for the precious thing it is, especially when we realize that it is equally accessible to all, without respect of persons and with no reference whatever to conventional scales of human deserts, will prove offensive to our most cherished presuppositions and priorities, and vulnerable to the prejudices of ourselves and of others, that it will therefore cost us more than we might at first suspect, not least in demanding from us a generosity similar to that with which we have been treated, and even this reciprocating generosity may well come from quarters from which we would least expect it.

If at this point the picture painted by the complex and concrete imagery of the parables seems dismal, one final group of parables, liberally interspersed with the rest, seems specifically designed to convey the impression that the picture is not dismal at all, but simply realistic and actually full of hope. These are the parables of the seed sown (one of which we have already seen so heavily allegorized), even a tiny mustard seed, or of leaven placed in dough, things small and apparently insignificant, buried from view or hidden in great masses of other material, yet destined to bring fruit and to expand in time, as surely as the seasons roll or bread rises in an oven.

Now let the evocative power of the imagery draw us out beyond the literal details of the pictures it presents. What is the pattern of experience it evokes at the very deepest level it can reach? What is it, at this deepest level, that we can yet discover with great joy to be the most precious thing we know, but that will then claim from us all that we have to give? It is life, obviously, it is existence itself, the very life and existence of ourselves and of everything around us. To discover or to rediscover life and existence, all life and all existence, as the most precious thing we know, always already there and offered for our acceptance, is to see life as a gift to us or, in the original meaning of the word, as grace. And nothing so much as a precious gift can claim our total responsibility, to cherish it infinitely, to do all in our power to maintain and enhance it, to be generous even as we ourselves have been so unstintingly enriched.

As I typed these words my two-year-old daughter invaded

my study. At first I thought, a distraction. But perhaps, after all, more of an illustration, for nowhere else on my visual horizon at the moment is gift so precious, and my responsibility simultaneously so awesome. One begins to understand about receiving with great joy what costs all that one can give. One begins to catch the first fleeting glimpses, perhaps, of what Jesus truly experienced as the Fatherhood of God.

But – the 'but' always falls somehow between the thought and the deed, and here something of that ambiguity in our experience of life and existence which we have elsewhere called the sense of contingency begins to emerge again – we are prevented by all kinds of concerns from making that radical decision to discover all life and existence as something precious to be treasured, the decision to accept the invitation to celebrate the feast of life, to accept all life and existence as gift that inspires at once responsibility and generosity. Most of all in the case of people, our peers on the scale of life, our ability to accept as precious gift is least obvious and most vulnerable, vulnerable to our institutionalized priorities, our prejudices and our presuppositions. We simply find it impossible to accept that all people have equal access to the precious gift of life and existence, that all people *are* part of the precious gift of life and existence to us. Instead, we accept only some, and these not so much as gifts, but more as securities, and the others we keep at their distance. The barriers go up, on grounds of colour, nationality, creed and even social or professional status, and they are at once our outer defences and our prisons, patrolled at first by indifference and ignorance, and later by suspicion and hostility. ('You know,' Annabelle said, 'there are two doctors living on our avenue.')

Of course, as any good Marxist could easily enough show us, a good deal of this divisiveness which so diminishes the quality of life is due more directly to our relationship with the material world, with the rest of life and existence which is the immediate support of human life, than it is simply an endemic and unexplained part of our relationship to our human peers. To put this point in the language of Jesus rather than that of Marx (though there may be something in common between Jesus and Marx at this point): We are incapable of accepting the whole material world as gift. Instead, care-ridden, anxious and full of concern, we grab some of it as property, proper to us individually, our own, something we grasp on to for our security in existence, something to covet, about which to boast (anticipating here some terms of Paul for the opposite of faith). We gather into barns, insure the barns and their contents, buy a German Shepherd or hire a security guard, and try to see to it that Blacks do not build barns in the same area.[13]

A good deal of racial or national cohesion, then, we can see, owes its strength and exclusiveness to the land and the material wealth which it appropriates to some to the exclusion of others ('*pro patria*', twisted a little, would give 'appropriate'). And it becomes less difficult to understand how even religious denominations can come to name ethnic or national interest groups rather than alternative and (potentially at least) mutually enriching modes of relating to the ultimate ground of being. Catholics and Protestants fight over the bloody remains of Northern Ireland; Christians and Muslims fight over the bloody remains of Lebanon. Religious affiliation itself shrinks to a group name, and the *raison d'être* of the group is soon seen to be the conquest, control, or defence of a certain slice of the world-cake. Professions, too, even religious professions like priesthood, can really 'mean' material security and advancement to those who pursue them, rather than development of one's actual talents for the benefit of one's fellow human beings. ('I couldn't leave off priesting and get married to Dolores,' said Father Doyle, 'I'd end up working on some factory floor.')

There are, of course, many other causes of man's inhumanity to man, but grasping for material possessions in anxious quest of security must be amongst the chief of these, not least because it breeds an attitude to others which sees them also as commodities to be used and dispensed as commodities are usable and dispensable. ('Thank you for coming to the interview,' said the personnel manager with professional kindness, 'but we're sorry to say we cannot use you at the present time.') I once leafed through some children's exercise books in a Roman Catholic school in South Africa. They contained the children's geography lessons reproduced verbatim, one after the other. With that awesome matter-of-factness that could only reflect the children's text-book itself they listed the conditions for successful sugar-cane growing in Natal as 1. certain seasonal temperatures; 2. a certain amount of moisture (I cannot remember the quantities involved); 3. a certain richness in the soil; and 4. cheap Bantu labour. This, of course, is just an extreme example of a common attitude, shocking only because it is so explicit and discriminatory, and because it is found in a Christian child's school-book.

So the contingency of existence appears in the parables of

Jesus. We can discover all life and existence, especially our fellow humans, as precious gift. We can realize, however much it costs us to do so, that the discovery of all life and existence as precious gift is equally accessible to all. We can then discover how cherished and consequently how precious are all our fellow humans. We can accept all and enrich others as we have been enriched. And then life is positive, full, enhanced with hope, of limitless possibilities. Sometimes, to some extent, all this is true of ourselves and our lives.

But we can also try to tear life and existence free from the hands of the giver, try to appropriate it, to draw it entirely under our own dominion (a risk that is involved in being lords of creation with knowledge of good and evil).[14] We will then divide ourselves against ourselves, as we divide spoils; the barriers will go up, at once our defences and our prisons; suspicion and hostility will breed fear and further insecurity. And then life will be diminished in quality, fragile in our consciousness of it, threatened.[15] Only too often, to a great extent, all this is true of ourselves and our lives.

This is where we feel unreconciled to our fellows and our world, sold to the very things we think we own,[16] on trial for our lives, suffering from some increasing sickness in our spirits – in need of reconciliation, ransom, acquittal, healing.

So the parables of Jesus bring us to the sense of our contingency, and they shape that sense or experience in their own particular way. They are called parables of the kingdom, parables of the reign of God, parables which try after their manner to give us a certain experience of God in our world because, first, it is in fact in and through the sense of contingency that God becomes a reality in our lives and, second, depending on the precise form of the sense of contingency that we have or can be made to have will depend whether the reality of God is affirmed in our lives, or rejected there, or some substitute of our own creation put in his place. We cannot afford to enter here into the broader reaches of theology in search of the original sources of atheism, idolatry and the various types of religious faith.[17] We can only afford the time to say, and to explain a little, that there is no human perception uncomplicated by human evaluation, that evaluation probably precedes, certainly accompanies, and often succeeds every perception of which we are conscious; that as we obviously differ from one another in the ways in which we perceive ourselves and our world, we equally, if not more so, differ in the evaluations of ourselves and our world which are so much part of all our perceptions; that the sense of contingency, therefore, which is perhaps our most basic and elementary perception-evaluation of ourselves and our world, and though it is truly the sense of contingency in each one, can differ from one to another, and is subject to argument and adjustment in the same way as other perception-evaluations are.

The sense of contingency, then, because of the differing kinds of perception and evaluation which it comprises, is the source of the different kinds of religious faith, as it is also the source of true theism and true idolatry, the twin extremes to which religious faith, like an Aristotelian virtue, is mean. And the way in which Jesus formed or adjusted our sense of our contingency accounted for the precise experience of the reign of God, the precise kind of religious faith for which he was thus responsible.

The difference between atheism, religious faith and idolatry is that the first so emphasizes in its evaluation the negative or threatened aspect perceived in life and existence, that it can see only nothingness as the alternative and end of the empirical existence we now know;[18] the last so emphasizes the positive and promising aspects especially of human life that it sees humanity rapidly coming in to complete control of the destiny of the universe, progressively drawing all life entirely under its dominion, responsible to no higher being.[19] The religious person, holding middle ground between, sees life and existence as positive and promising, yet never to be fully appropriated as altogether one's own, and not at one's command alone. Of course, even in the middle ground there can be substantial variations in perception and evaluation. At one extreme here, there stands the religious person who is convinced, as is every religious person, that life is ultimately positive and promising, who sees, however, that decay and destruction must win in the present conditions of human existence, and who therefore hopes for abundance of life, not here, but hereafter. To this extreme of tolerable variation within religious faith belong strong dualists like the Manichees,[20] apocalyptic types who take their own imagery too literally, and some mainstream themes from the great Eastern religions.[21]

At the other extreme of this same variation stands the religious person, the Jew and, above all, Jesus, who sees both the promise and the threat to abundance of life to be fully involved, and to be dealt with fully, in the present conditions of existence, who insists that only if we see our present life and existence to be infinitely precious and full of promise, as a treasure offered is

precious and full of promise, can we fight the threatening elements of life, which stem mainly from ourselves, maintain and
enhance the positive and thus generate hope for unlimited
fulfilment in a future as yet largely inconceivable. So Jesus' way
of illustrating the contingency of existence in his parables is his
particular way of presenting his version of religious faith, his
version of our contact with God, of God's reign in our lives.

But if we cannot afford to enter further here into the broad
reaches of theology in search of the details of the original source
of the human race's varied and fluctuating religious faith, we
can at least compare and contrast Jesus' parables with other
types of religious mythology, with the aim of illustrating that
they are indeed myth and yet that they present their own
unique form of religious faith.

At the origins of the Israelite tradition people thought of air or
breath, its plenitude or shortage, as the image of life in its fullness and threatenedness. The sky was expansive with air, moving air. So the great sky-God, approached on mountain-tops,
breathed his air (spirit, in Hebrew *ruach*) into all living things,
and while he did they lived.[22] Here the image become symbol is
the very elementary one of breath which maintains and strengthens life, and absence of which threatens and destroys life: in
mythologized form, in the creation myths which open Genesis,
the spirit moves over the formless abyss, or life is breathed into
moulded clay. Other ancient Near Eastern sources characterized
the contingency of existence in terms of the precariousness of
cosmic order faced with threatening chaos. Order and its breakdown are the images become symbol here for life in its positive
and negative aspects, and they are powerful to this present day,
for we know instinctively that order in nature and society
enhances the possibilities of life and that breakdown in the order
of nature or society threatens our very survival: nothing brings
such quick and sometimes such savage reaction from us as the
prospect of a breakdown in law and order. In the old Akkadian
Enuma Elis, this symbolism is mythologized when Tiamat is
identified as the 'god who seized evil', the force that stirs up
conflict and disorder in nature and society, threatening even the
rule of Anu, the great Father-Sky-God himself, and Marduk is
elected in heaven to kill Tiamat and to carve an orderly cosmos
out of Tiamat's dead body.[23] For those inclined to take myth too
literally, of course, this epic was repeated ritually every year,
since the battle for order over chaos continues.

In Platonic mythology, that is, in the ancient myths of the

Orphics and others as they appear in Plato's dialogues, the contingency of existence is portrayed quite differently. In the Platonic dialogues one's mind is concentrated on the life-enhancing ideals of virtue in general, on Truth and Beauty and Justice, and the perfection they bring; as opposed to life-destroying vices and the decay to which they are aligned. The myths then portray the perfect Earth (*Phaedo* 107c-114c) where judgment is given (*Republic* 613e-621d), that is, where virtue does prevail and vice cannot, by any subterfuge of rank or raiment, as too often on this earth, succeed (*Gorgias* 523a-527c). They explain how the one who aspires best to true love, like the charioteer of a winged chariot, ascends to the perfect life of the gods, while those who do not do so effectively, fall (*Phaedrus* 246a-257a), how love (*Eros*) aims at immortality (*Symposium* 202d-212a). They tell how Prometheus by stealth equipped humans with 'the cunning workman's wisdom of Hephaestus and Athena, and with fire' (*Protagoras* 320c-323a). They soar higher still and say that it is the cosmic order, created by God, that must be reproduced in the perfect society and the perfect person (*Timaeus* 29d-92d), that when God has his hand to the wheel of the world the movement is from death to life; when he takes his hand away, from life to death (*Politicus* 268e-274e).

In all this, as many times the myth-tellers in Plato explicitly make plain, we are first and foremost being urged to opt for virtue and wisdom, harmony and love in this life, in which the only hope of life, life more abundant, and perhaps life without end, resides. So here too, as in the case of all myth, we must resist the impression that we are given pictures in literal detail of another·world or another life or another being called God. No, the myth-maker is doing what he always does. He is putting together in narrative form the symbols (or, as is sometimes the case with Plato, the ideals or hypostasized virtues) which in his view best characterize the ambivalence of existence; he is suggesting by means of these same symbols how best to perceive, evaluate and live life in these empirical conditions; he is – since symbol allows one to probe a pattern of experience to its ultimate depth – equivalently claiming that those who perceive, evaluate and live life as he suggests can thus come into contact with the most ultimate reality there is, conventionally known as God; and he is describing God in terms of the symbols which best indicate where and how his presence can be felt, since he has in fact no other way of talking about God at all.

So Jesus, instead of talking about air, or order, or virtue, or even love perhaps, depicted by means of the most ordinary situations of life how we can discover the treasure really hidden under the trodden paths of all our busy travelling, in the bric-à-brac of the pawn-shops of our lives, the invitation that is always given, how we can all discover it and discover it in all, how decisive we must be in possessing and accepting with great joy, in scattering our riches as prodigally as they were showered on us. He used to this end what might be called situation imagery. With surprising economy of vivid detail he paints pictures of familiar situations from the ordinary conduct of human affairs. And by so doing he weaves a complex pattern of experience which can evoke a similar pattern down to any depth we care to plumb. By the same method he let his hearers feel that such unrestricted discovery and possession and sharing would offend, not only against their anxious, grasping, excluding and hostile instincts, but against the most insistently rationalized and the most solemnly institutionalized prejudices and presuppositions of their culture. Thus he gave to understand, to those who had eyes to see it, that they would persecute rather than change their ways, or that they could expect to be persecuted if they did change.

The ancient Near-Eastern myth-maker talked of air and order, and he recommended, because in these he saw the best prospects for life, whatever, like breaths of fresh air, refreshed and strengthened; or he recommended the order of the earth and the heavens, the order of the seasons, and the ordered ranks of society. These, he equivalently or explicitly claimed, characterized the deepest reaches of his universe and therefore its source. (The belief is common to the laboratory of the cancer researcher and the ivory tower of the metaphysician that if one can find the source of something one will understand it or at least know how to deal with it; and that the way to find the source of it is to observe it meticulously in all its moods and moves.) So the myth-maker described God, the name of the source of all life and existence, in terms of the life-enhancing characteristics revealed in his analysis of the very structure of the world he knew. At this point analysis, recommendation and description of divinity became one; to accept this analysis as true, and to follow the recommendations, was to be like God, to be servant or Son of God, to have God as one's goal and destiny.[24]

Plato talked of virtue and vice and judgment, and order too. He recommended virtue and true judgment. He envisaged an ideal order for the individual and for the social group, in which each part of the individual acted according to its place, and each member of society exhibited the virtues of its state; he saw this order stemming from the divine source of the world itself. Those who contemplated this ideal order, this justice, and those who realized it in life, were in the likeness of God, and the greatest hopes for life without limit belonged to them.

Jesus evoked the experience of all living and existing things as gracious gift to us, an experience pregnant with generosity, vulnerable and yet entitled to all our confidence in its final success. This experience, and it alone, enabled us to describe God, the source of this universe, as our father.[25] This, then, is the myth which Jesus himself evolved from his own Genesis myth that God made everything, and it was all good, and it was all good for humanity, and men and women were good for each other. Significantly enough, the opening phrase of the prayer which has become known as the Lord's Prayer is 'Our Father'.

Prayer, meals and miracles

The prayer of Jesus was probably as instructive on the nature of the reign of God as his parables, but Luke is the only New Testament writer who makes Jesus as a man of prayer to be emulated by his followers a dominant theme. John places long prayers on the lips of Jesus, but like much else of the direct speech in his gospel this is undoubtedly John's own composition – though no less true for that to the actual spirit of the historical Jesus. Our investigation of the prayer of Jesus, therefore, can be more or less confined to the Lord's Prayer. This occurs in two versions in the New Testament, of which Matthew's (6.9-13) is thought to be the more original in wording, perhaps, though lengthened and liturgized a little, and Luke's (11.2-4) corresponds more to the original length.

Prayer, in comparison to parable, is like a probe of the dark side of the moon, or like stepping through the looking glass, so that one can see the ultimate depths of reality, no longer as in a glass, darkly, but as it really is itself. It seeks the impossible, it seeks direct converse with God. Borne aloft on the conviction that myth or parable brings, it seeks to increase that conviction, wanting the assurance of God that things are as we think they are, and will be as we hope. It is, therefore, and has always been an inextricable mixture of praise and petition. Prayer turns the normal logic of myth and parable on its head. Instead of saying: I perceive all life and existence as gift, and so God is my Father, it says: God is my Father and so everything and everybody, including myself, is his gift, which he values and cherishes and therefore gives, and will give, isn't that so, Father?

'Our Father', then, or 'Abba' in the more intimate word of old Aramaic (Mark 14.36; Galatians 4.6; Romans 8.15), at once gives expression to the lived conviction and appeals for its continuance, the lived conviction, namely, that God cherishes all things great and small, and all people, good, bad and indifferent, as a father cherishes his children. Like so much taught by Jesus, it is so disappointingly simple to say, and all but impossible to live. To be able to call God father, truly, and to hallow or bless that name for God, requires a great deal from people, as the parables have already pointed out, and as the rest of this prayer will confirm. ('Who art in heaven' is Matthew's additional liturgical solemnity.)

'Thy kingdom come' makes this a prayer of the kingdom, as surely as the parables are parables of the kingdom. And as the parables evoke the kind of experience which is that of the reign of God, so the prayer has already indicated what this experience is, and will continue to expand on it. God's rule is like a father's rule over his children, a rule that is exercised by means of grace and love. (Matthew's 'Thy will be done, on earth as it is in heaven' is one of these poetic doublets so characteristic of Hebrew and so well fashioned for liturgical recital.)

'Give us each day our daily bread' (Matthew has 'this day') has caused some trouble to translators, but through all the subtle suggestions of the experts the impression still comes clear that the one who says this prayer is asking for continuance of the gift of the staff of life, that is, of life itself. So the one who can say this 'petition' accepts all life as God's gracious gift, and is asking for its continuance.

'Forgive us our sins (Matthew 'debts'), for we ourselves forgive everyone who is indebted to us' (Matthew has 'as we also have forgiven our debtors') causes, in Matthew's version, difficulties much more serious than any which concern translators. But first let us concentrate on the experience which this petition intends to convey. When first there is invoked in us the experience of being valued and cherished as a gift is valued, we are already in complicity with the destruction and decay which form the ambivalence of existence. We have already grasped at possessions or power for our security, thrown up the barriers, and sown the seeds of hatred, if we have not actually deprived others of the means of subsistence, or maimed or killed. We are

always already guilty, and to the guilty the sense of being valued and cherished and accepted comes across necessarily as a
sense of being forgiven. Now the forgiveness which Jesus went
round pronouncing so liberally, to the pious horror of the religious leaders in the land, was of this kind. It had nothing to do
with previous acts of contrition or promises of penance, much
less with penance actually performed or sacrifices already made.
It was the sense of our acceptance by God, not despite what we
were, or because of what we were, but as we were.[26]

The sequence of events, then, as the parables make clear, and
as many other places in the New Testament confirm, was this:
having experienced the generosity of God, we should be
inspired to be generous in turn, discounting the damage others
had done us, if that is what was called for, serving their needs, if
it was that, or undoing the damage we had done to others, and
then being more generous still.[27] To put the matter as Matthew
does would seem to suggest a different sequence of events,
namely that we are first generous to our enemies, and then
deserve to be treated in a similar manner by God.

Though the difficulty is not purely one of translation, it can be
solved by translation, for Matthew's sentence can also be translated: 'as we herewith (intend to) forgive our debtors'. In this
way the experience of the reign of God as Jesus depicted it, an
experience of being graced and cherished which inspires us to
generosity in turn, remains intact in the prayer of the kingdom.

'And lead us not into temptation' (to which Matthew adds
another of his doublets, a line of different words with the same
meaning: 'but deliver us from evil'). This last petition has
nothing to do with temptation as the moralists normally understand it: a seductive nude of the opposite sex, or a glass of
whisky to an alcoholic, or unguarded money to a gambler down
on his luck. No, the meaning here is better conveyed by the
word 'test', in the sense of trial. That the attempt to live out the
experience of the reign of God in our lives will involve offence
and persecution has already been sufficiently hinted in the parables, and it will be further emphasized in the history and the
ritual of the meal fellowship. Here in the prayer it is simply
taken for granted that for such a one the trial in the form of
persecution will come – the great persecution which the
apocalyptic writers in their inflated imagery predicted would
precede the coming of the reign of God, persecution, at any rate,
as strong as people thought necessary to put an end to this
apparently senseless and indiscriminate life-style – and the last

petition of the prayer is simply the request that the persecution may not come or, if it does, that we may come out of it with integrity, still faithful to our lived conviction that everyone is of equal value to God and intended to be equally graced with his gifts.

The Lord's Prayer, then, is the prayer of the kingdom, as the parables are parables of the kingdom, the prayer in which we seek God's own assurance for our stability in the experience known as the reign of God. And as such it should be always said. It has one near-counterpart in the New Testament, the prayer which Mark places on the lips of Jesus during his agony in Gethsemane: 'Abba, all things are possible to thee; remove this cup from me; yet not what I will, but what thou wilt' (Mark 14.36). This prayer, too, begins with Jesus addressing God as father; it asks that he be spared from the coming trial; and ends with his prayerful intent to remain true to the experience of the reign or will of God which his whole public ministry had tried to convey and fidelity to which was now, presumably, bringing this terrible trial upon him. It is but a short step from Gethsemane to the meal which the gospels record as having taken place just before that, and that short step takes us from the prayer of the kingdom to its ritual.

When Jesus is the subject and mention is made of meals, the Last Supper naturally comes first to mind, the meal, the New Testament declares, he so desired to eat with his faithful followers before his trial and almost certain death, the one meal on which the same New Testament gives the most substantial detail. Since the New Testament accounts of the Last Supper are so intimately involved with the central Christian ritual, the eucharist, being looked on traditionally as accounts of Jesus' actual institution of that sacrament, they have naturally been subject to a great deal of discussion and, as can be expected whenever religious people engage in long discussion, they have given rise recently to much controversy. Most of this controversy the present context, because of its specific interest, would wish to avoid. There is much agreement that the present accounts of the Last Supper, and particularly of the 'institution' of the eucharist at that meal, accounts which occur just before the story of the arrest of Jesus in the Synoptic Gospels and in chapter eleven of Paul's first letter to the Corinthians, owe their present structure and wording to liturgical practice in the early Christian communities. (John does not have any reference to the 'institution' of the eucharist in his description of the Last Supper; instead, we find a ceremony of the washing of the disciples' feet, though he does treat of the eucharist in its own specific symbolic terms in chapter six of his gospel.)

After that much has been said, agreement thins quickly to vanishing point. Some express doubts about the occurrence of any solemn last meal celebrated by Jesus and his close followers immediately preceding his arrest and trial.[28] Others feel that accounts of such a meal represent a true memory of some of Jesus' disciples, though by the time of the final composition of our documents a highly formalized memory (formalized, again, by the necessities of solemn liturgical practice), and that this memory was at the origin of only one of two main kinds of eucharistic ritual in the scattered communities of early Christianity.[29] Others still feel that the memory of an actual Last Supper is preserved with sufficient accuracy to allow us to hazard a good guess at the actual words used by Jesus in reference to the bread and wine.[30] These last would then hold, obviously, that one could reconstruct the whole scene of the Last Supper with acceptable accuracy.

Further controversy centres on the actual time and form of the Last Supper. Was it a paschal meal, celebrated on the only evening on which that meal could be celebrated, or as John suggests (and Mark in 14.1 gives perhaps a residual hint when he says: 'It was now *two* days before the Passover'), a meal celebrated the evening before the paschal meal was due? Jeremias argues that it was a paschal meal, Lietzmann argues equally eloquently that it was not, and other experts suggest other types of Jewish solemn meal as the proper analogues.

We should naturally wish to avoid as much of this controversy as possible here. That the historical Jesus inaugurated a table-fellowship which lasted beyond his death, that he did so with solemn effect, in a way that was as memorable to his friends as it was offensive to his enemies, that at least can scarcely be doubted. Perrin, who is sceptical about the historical facticity of that particular meal known now as the Last Supper, thinks this practice of table-fellowship the main, even if not alone the sufficient cause of the killing of Jesus – so much is it an integral part of the picture of the historical Jesus presented in the gospels.[31] So, since our interest here is really confined to the part played by the table-fellowship practised by Jesus in furthering amongst his followers that experience known as the reign of God in their lives, we may be permitted to take a middle and potentially neutral road on the problem of the Last Supper, and more particularly on the problem of the relationship between the Last Supper and the meals celebrated both before and after it in solemn or ritual fashion by Jesus and his followers. After all, Jeremias is most insistent that the Last Supper in fact took place nearly enough to its descriptions in the New Testament and, further, that our eucharist stems directly from this Last Supper, and yet I heard Jeremias in a lecture compare the Last Supper to the fellowship meals which preceded it, as proper is compared to common in the Mass. The usual or common, he said, is always the setting in which to try to understand the unusual or proper. If Jeremias can say this, why cannot someone (Perrin perhaps) who likes to tie the common meal-fellowship of Jesus to the cross and thus see the origin of the eucharist without more ado, without in particular envisaging any additional role for the Last Supper, why cannot such a person concede that a certain meal celebrated in the shadow of almost certain death could have intensified the significance of Jesus' table-fellowship to a point both unavoidable and unforgettable, and had that intensified significance expressed in the symbolic and ritual manner which the very context of a meal suggests? It is on this assumption we shall proceed, this middle road we shall follow when analysing the nature and role of the symbolic meals of Jesus in making real for his followers the experience of the reign of God.[32] This will mean taking into account, in search of the historical truth, all that the New Testament has to say about the meals of Jesus, but with the same kind of caution, particularly in the case of the Last Supper, which we had to adopt with the descriptions of the trials of Jesus.

Apart from the Last Supper, as already remarked, there is not much detail in the New Testament on Jesus' practice of table-fellowship. Yet already at the beginning of Mark's gospel the complaint is on the lips of his critics that he eats with tax-collectors and sinners (Mark 2.15).[33] Perhaps because the liturgical details of the Last Supper grew so much in importance so rapidly for the early community, there are now only scattered hints of Jesus' previous practice of table-fellowship and of the animosity it caused. But there is enough to allow one question. We recall the offensiveness of parables which preferred the outcasts of this extremely religious society to the most pious practitioners of all its precepts. Why does the invitation of such people to a meal or, rather, the acceptance of an invitation to dine with such people, cause such open and vehement expression of a similar offence?

First, because every meal is a sacrament, because a meal is the most common and natural sacrament of all. In order to understand what a sacrament is, simply recall all that has been said about image and symbol and add the further involvement that action contributes to our most concrete relationship with our world and our fellows. An action becomes ritual or sacramental in the same way as an image becomes symbolic. Just as an image has literal reference to one level of experience, but can evoke recurring patterns of that experience – as the ancient mariner's ship surges forward again under a fair wind after being so long becalmed, so the creative mind stirs and moves after a period in the spiritual doldrums – an action may have practical relevance at one level of life and yet be capable of evoking similar fulfilment of similar needs at deeper levels. Getting dirty and washing have superficial relevance to certain physical states and actions, but they can also evoke a deeper sense of being soiled and the need for a deeper cleansing. Actions, then, when ritualized, that is to say, when performed in a context which because of special circumstance of time or place or words spoken, release their powers of evocation, can 'symbolize', make real to us, bring us into contact with deeper experiences, deeper realities of our world and of our relationships there, and they can do this with an involvement of the whole person, and with an impact and effect greater than the most imaginative words or the most concrete representations. The one who talks, especially if he talks to God, can effect a great deal, but the one who acts really means business and has more claim on our attention. If you want to know what a man really believes, Blondel said somewhere, don't listen to what he says, but watch what he does.

In order to appreciate how every meal is a sacrament, it is only necessary to consider the actual need to replenish our physical resources with nourishment and the most expeditious way in which this need could be fulfilled (think of an astronaut in space). Even the simplest and most hurried of meals is, by comparison, a most elaborate ritual. The meal has its time and place, its preparation, its seating and service. Every meal fulfils the basic biological need, but it also advertises and realizes the fact of life that at a deeper level life depends on our being together, serving each other and sharing, not like animals who happened to converge on the same morsels of food to fight over them. Man does not live by bread alone. A friend, to a Jew, is 'one who breaks bread with me', and a feast is as obvious a celebration of the joys and successes of life as fasting is a symbol of sorrow.

Even in the abuse of the meal its sacramental power is clearly acknowledged. The social climbers in every society spend an inordinate amount of their time either trying to decide whom to invite to eat and drink in their houses or anxiously waiting to see if certain houses are ever going to invite them. The meal is the natural ritual of life, as growing things are its natural symbol: the seed, the branch of evergreen, the flowers we place on a grave. It naturally evokes, makes real, brings us into contact with those experiences and realities in which life is maintained and enhanced, not just with the physical food but with the fellowship sitting together in peace and harmony, serving each other and sharing the good things provided. The social climber makes no mistake about the power of the ritual: what he or she does mistake is the tendency of status-seeking and exclusiveness to diminish life rather than enhance it.

The meal is, of course, ready-made for religious ritual, since it is such a natural sacrament. No other ritual could half as effectively convey to human beings the experience of God as the author of life. There has not been a religion in the history of human kind, nor will there be, to the ritual of which the meal is not of central importance. The case was no different with the Jews at the time of Jesus. They had long been accustomed to the symbols of the fruit of the tree of life, the manna and water in the desert, as symbols of God's support and favour in their lives. In Exodus 24.9-11 it is the meal which seals the covenant, the most basic relationship between God and his people. And when the prophets look forward to the time when the promises of life will finally be fulfilled, when God's presence will at last be fully effective amongst his people, when, that is, they look forward to the true reign of God, their most natural symbol for that event is the symbol of the joyful feast. Isaiah looks to the future when a feast of fat things will be prepared on the mountain of the Lord, when there will be salvation and death will be swallowed up, when the reproach of his people and their tears will be taken away (25.6-11); he looks to a covenant when the sure love of God for David will be experienced by all his people, and he depicts that experience as a feast to which those who are hungry and thirsty but who have no money can come and be filled (55.1-5). The hope of the experience of a new presence of God is very prominent in inter-testamental literature, particularly of apocalyptic style, and the symbol of the banquet is commoner still for this happy experience. Small wonder, then, that to Jesus, who was trying to convey to his contemporaries the experience of the reign of God in their lives, as he understood this, the ritual of the meal should have presented itself as one of his most powerful means to this end, and that neither his friends nor his enemies should have laboured under the slightest misapprehension as to what was being signified and effected.

Both by reason of its intrinsic nature, then, and by reason of the convention of his culture, the table-fellowship practised by Jesus proved a most effective symbol of the experience of the reign of God which he was trying to share with those who could open themselves to it. It provided an invitation, joyfully accepted, to the good life, an example of generosity from those who felt themselves well-off and, especially when the social, moral, religious or ethnic outcasts were also present, it provided a powerfully effective illustration of the fact that the good things of life, the treasures of life, were equally available to all, and that each was equally acceptable to all. In place of the barriers formed by greed and hostility, on social, moral, religious, and ethnic grounds, it effected a change of ways (repentance) toward reconciliation, peace and harmony. No one who had the slightest inkling of what Jesus' public ministry was about could for one moment miss the point that Jesus was presenting ritually an experience of God as the father who cherished all and graced all equally, and in this way inspired all to cherish and grace each other. Nobody in Jesus' own culture who was in the least familiar with the conventional symbolism for the coming of the reign of God (and who was not?) could fail to be offended deeply by his ritual interpretation of that symbolism. Of course the reign of God would mean almost inconceivable enrichment of life, but for the prostitutes and the tax-collectors as much and as immediately as for anyone else?

The common table-fellowship of Jesus during his public ministry was eucharist. The name eucharist is taken from a Greek verb meaning to give thanks, and these meals were grateful celebrations of God's gift of life, celebrated in the shared food and the joyful fellowship, whatever name they might be given. They were the sacrament of the reign of God, for sacrament, according to the theology text-books, is a ritual which effects what it symbolizes. The vast majority of eucharistic celebrations to-day, of course, achieve only half, if they do achieve that, of what Jesus effected in his table fellowship, for the vast majority of eucharistic communities follow exactly the lines of social, religious and ethnic divisions, and they tend therefore to shore up rather than to tear down the barriers that divide the people and diminish the quality of life.

And the Last Supper, with its special sacrificial imagery? On that subject, even in this context, something can be said, without yet entering into the detailed controversy about one particular meal held, as Paul put it, on the night before he suffered.

There is a sense in which the experience of the reign of God, in Jesus' version, is an experience of giving up life. To experience life truly as a treasure to be discovered, a banquet to which one is invited, is, as already remarked, to experience life as gift, to experience life as one's own and yet not one's own, not to be wrested from the hands of the giver, not to be appropriated as if it could ever be under one's own dominion. To be able to experience life truly as God's gift is to be able to live without anxiety for it; to try to treat it as one's own property, since one is unable really to appropriate and maintain it, is, on the contrary, to live in apprehension of death. To experience life truly as God's gift is to be able to give and, if necessary, to give up.

When might it be necessary to give up one's life? In general, when death approaches and the gift is about to be withdrawn. But more particularly in this context when fidelity to the very experience of life as gift, not as one's own property demands such sacrifice. Life in fidelity to the experience of the reign of God, in Jesus' version of it, as is by now quite clear, can offend people deeply and can draw upon one's head both anger and hostility. In face of such persecution, if one is to remain faithful to the experience of God who graces and cherishes all, one must be prepared to give up rather than grasp, to die rather than kill. Out of such ability to give and to give up, since the ability itself is part of the lived conviction that all life is the treasured gift of the Father God, comes the hope that the author of life can give life again, the hope that robs death of its sting and its victory. Such a death, in turn, undergone in fidelity to the experience of the reign of God, is not only incapable of depriving life of its most substantial hope, it is in effect the very seal and consummation of the experience which grounds that hope.

Those, on the contrary, who try to treat life as their own property and to maintain it out of their own resources, are, again in a phrase of Paul's, without God and without hope in this world, for they must live in daily fear of death, the last enemy of all that we are and have and love, an enemy which no mortal being can resist. The incapacitating and debilitating effect of fear robs life of 'life', or else, in reaction, it turns people into allies of the very destructive forces that threaten the quality of life, for nothing else has quite the same power as fear has to drive people to injurious action. In a very real sense, then, those who try to maintain life out of their own resources experience death in life; whereas those who truly accept life as gift can experience the hope of life in death itself. This is presumably the thought behind the rather paradoxical statement attributed to Jesus, that to try to save one's life is already to lose it, and to be able to lose or let go of one's life is in fact to save it.

Now the meal is an admirable ritual, an admirable symbolic gesture for the holding of life as gift, holding gently in open hands, not grasping or tearing loose or trying to appropriate totally to oneself, but holding in willingness to give and to give up. For in each meal the matter of the sacrament is, after all, the staff of life, food and drink. But each meal consists, not in grabbing as much from the table for oneself as one can, but in offering first to others that which one knows to be necessary for one's own life, and in receiving the staff of one's own life from them. Nowhere outside the meal is it more obvious that to receive life and existence and all the supports of life truly as gift is identical with giving, giving oneself, giving one's life. In any meal it is finally clear, and in that powerful way in which ritual alone can make something clear to the participants, that the cost, the sacrifice, does not diminish the joy of discovering the treasure-gift of life; on the contrary, the ability to receive as gift and to give, as every meal symbolizes, are two parts of the same open-handed gesture, and two modes of the same joy.

All that happens, then, in the meal described in the New Testament and known now as the Last Supper, is that the self-sacrificing symbolism which is inherent in the ritual of every meal, is here, by certain words and special gestures, brought to even more explicit notice. For it is a tragic fact of life that those who show themselves willing to accept all and to serve all will thereby threaten the self-made securities of the appropriators and will have their own conviction that life is grace put to its most crucial test. We may hazard the guess that Jesus gave his followers a new sacrament, not by further specifying the symbolism of special ritual meals already celebrated in his time, but rather by recovering for his followers the natural religious symbolism of all meals.

Jesus' practice of table-fellowship caused hostile comment from the very outset. And it must have been obvious to those who broke bread with him and so formed one body and one spirit with him that real persecution could not be far off. As the prospect of persecution came closer, as enmity increased and death itself loomed ominously near, it must have seemed to those who sat round the sacramental table with Jesus that fidelity to their experience of the reign of God could well demand suffering of them, that it could well demand sacrifice, and perhaps the ultimate sacrifice of their lives. They celebrated at the meals, as always, the reign of God in their lives, the nearness of God in all things and to all people, and if this, as it now seemed, meant death, then they would celebrate it to death itself, they would give up everything for it. It is not possible, of course, to be sure that this is actually how the table-fellowship developed, but neither is there any major difficulty in understanding how a meal could ritually symbolize fellowship in the nearness of God through death itself, or that Jesus did just that with his faithful followers before he died. (No wonder that John could see in Jesus' death the victory of true life, life really lived as God's gift, the experience, in short, of resurrection.)

The bread they shared was, after all, bread broken, apt symbol, if the need arose, for the body broken in death; the wine was wine poured out, sufficiently symbolic of red blood shed in martyrdom. Yet this was the same food and drink which symbolized life, the precious gift of God to all without respect of persons, the precious gift which was to be yet further enriched in a manner almost inconceivable when God did finally reign. In this way the ritual celebrated and effectively symbolized life through death, or death as the very seal on the life for which one had lived and to which one had witnessed as to the greatest cause on earth.[34] As the cross loomed darkly over the brief public career of Jesus, those who still sat round the table with him and in the meal formed one body with him, faithful still to the experience of the reign of God thus ritualized, now celebrated this same gift of life through the very jaws of death. So, whether the accounts of the Last Supper in the New Testament can ever reconstruct the details of a single meal or not, they certainly bear witness to a heightening and sharpening of the common meal ritual without which it would have been incapable of transmitting the full range of the experience of the reign of God as it was available to Jesus, and in the only way it can be available, apparently, in our broken world.

The Last Supper in the New Testament is like the last petition in the Lord's Prayer. In the last petition the great trial suddenly comes into view; in the New Testament's Last Supper the sacrificial symbolism dominates the ritual of the reign of God and the ritual calmly incorporates it. The Last Supper is therefore historical, at least to the extent that the sacrificial element became prominent in the experience of the reign of God, and in all manners, mythic, ritual and otherwise, of realizing that reign, and it is still prominent to this day. It is because our eucharists ritually make us one body with the man who celebrated life in death, who made death itself stamp with the seal of its awful finality the authenticity of his lived conviction that all life was God's gift and not human property, it is because of this that these eucharists are memorials of the death of Jesus – not because sacrament has some magic by which, in defiance of finite time-systems, it can make present today an ancient tragedy which took place on a hill outside Jerusalem.

Still, for all the prominence of the trial and sacrifice elements in this world's experience of the reign of God, it is the experience of life as grace inspiring us to accept and share and serve that is the most basic experience of all. For it is this which brings on the trial and makes the sacrifice fruitful – and so to this we turn again in the analysis of the last of four general areas in which the New Testament writers present the experience of the reign of God of the historical Jesus, the area of miracle stories.

Miracles have been under attack, someone said, from Celsus to Hume. The general tenor of that attack has already been hinted in the course of the survey of the critical quest in our first chapter. As Reimarus, the Peter of that period, put it: 'to discover whether miracles are true requires as much investigation as the thing they are supposed to prove.'[35] 'They are supposed to prove' – there is the clue to a critical attack on the miracle stories of the New Testament almost as old as Christianity itself. Astounding events, attributable apparently to no agency of this natural universe, occurring through a particular person or in connection with his or her work, are supposed to establish that person's credibility and to set God's own seal on his or her mission. And indeed, in that apologetic role, as it is called, they are very vulnerable to Reimarus and his kind. Even where no historical or philosophical prejudice prevents a fair assessment of their case,[36] it is notoriously true that, on historical grounds, coercive evidence of their occurrence can seldom, if ever, be provided, and on philosophical grounds it is difficult to see that any event which happens in this universe could be more indicative of the presence of divinity than the universe itself.[37] If we cannot have religious faith, then, from our native experience of nature and humanity, it would be difficult to see that miracles could provide us with it.

The fact of the matter seems to be that the so-called miracle stories, so plentiful in the four gospels, have been abused in much the same way as the resurrection kerygma was abused, when resurrection was regarded as the greatest proof-miracle of them all. Undoubtedly, some of the types of event represented in the so-called miracle stories of the New Testament are, like the resurrection, essential to the true understanding of the mission of Jesus, necessary to its true identity, part and parcel of its authenticity, so that without them, as without resurrection, it would not be itself. In that sense they 'prove' it is itself, like the voice of an alleged hostage over the telephone 'proves' to those from whom ransom is demanded that the hostage is really their child. But to try to establish first that New Testament 'miracles' really happened, and that they can be attributed to no conceivable natural agency, and then to use them to prove that Jesus' mission, completely describable in itself without reference to them, is true or authentic or all that is claimed for it – that is precisely the abuse of the miracle stories of the New Testament which lays them open to all the devastating criticisms levelled against them both early and late in Christian history. The New Testament writers, it can plausibly be argued, do not understand the 'miracle stories' mainly in this way, and so most of the criticism from Celsus to Hume is wide of the mark.

But how do the New Testament writers mainly understand what we call the miracles recorded in their pages? The problem about giving any simple, straightforward answer to that question is caused by their great variety, a variety certainly great enough to prevent any single generalization, or even a clear distinction into kinds on which a very few generalizations could be based. In his fine book, *The Founder of Christianity*,[38] Dodd suggests that we should not go far wrong if we read the miracle stories of the gospels as pictorial symbols of the power of spiritual renewal which had its source in the historical Jesus. Teilhard de Chardin has said that the modern view of the miracle stories has changed, quite rightly, from seeing them as 'prodigies of detail', to seeing them as means of expressing the vital general success of an evolutionary process which, in his view, is christocentric.[39] There is no doubt that such generalizations have proved invaluable in weaning the Christian mind away from the apologetic use of the so-called miracle stories which tried, we have seen, to make them prove the authenticity of a mission describable without them. And there is no doubt that this effect of such generalizations is quite in line with the repeated warnings of the New Testament writers themselves that those who look for signs and wonders to persuade them to follow Jesus have already gone astray.[40] For all that, these generalizations are still too broad to do justice either to the variety or to the more central purpose of these stories in the New Testament.

It is sometimes suggested that the New Testament miracle stories should be divided into two categories, nature miracles and healing miracles; that the first be seen as a conventional way of drawing attention to a great man (even natural forces like wind and sea recognize him), somewhat in line with Dodd's formula, and that the second, which may possibly have some basis in historical fact, be seen to point to the beneficial effects of Jesus' programme, in a manner somewhat similar to Teilhard's theory. The value of the suggestions will be acknowledged, at least implicitly, in what follows. The trouble with the distinction is that the New Testament writers themselves seem quite unaware of it.[41]

Perhaps the most defensible statement about the miracle stories in the New Testament is that, taken as a body and without distinction of kind or category, they fulfil at least three converging purposes simultaneously. First, they function in the conventional role of such stories in religious literature both ancient and modern: they recount wonders of various kinds performed by their main character as an accepted way, not so much of proving anything, as of drawing attention to his person and achievement. Second, they form a symbolic narrative, or a series of narrated symbols, of the conflict between the forces of life and the forces of death, and they depict the victory in this conflict of the author of life, Jesus. Functioning at this level they resemble the death-resurrection myth. In the gospels they announce in anticipation the final outcome of the great conflict at the centre of which is Jesus. They thus function as symbol and myth to tell the truth about the true significance of Jesus for human existence. Third, they preserve the memory of an actual aspect of the historical ministry of Jesus which is of central importance to our more detailed understanding of his experience of the reign of God. It is because of this third and most important function of theirs that they have been referred to as the so-called miracle stories. For they are not the proofs that many of their users and critics alike took them to be; they do not *simply* fulfil the function of the conventional miracle story in religious literature; nor are they *merely* another part of the myth of Jesus. They also transmit an emphasis in the experience of the reign of God that is essential for its full comprehension. The following features of these New Testament stories should show what that emphasis is.

First, the memory that some extraordinary healings, often termed exorcisms, occurred during the ministry of Jesus is so embedded in all strata of the early tradition, and even in some references to Jesus in Jewish literature, as to give the highest likelihood of the historicity of some such events. Second, healing stories are but a part, even if a major part, of the miracle stories as a whole, remembered now in general, but no longer, most probably, in any particular detail. Yet there is a certain interpretation which the New Testament writers in varied ways place on these stories in general, and if we attend to that interpretation, in connection with the likelihood of healings, we shall undoubtedly discover the necessary emphasis in the experience of the reign of God which these contexts are meant to convey. Consider the following clues.

First, there is a saying of Jesus which has a strong claim to authenticity on any criteria for such a claim,[43] and it places the healing that Jesus practised, under the rubric of exorcism, squarely within the anticipated experience of the reign of God: 'If it is by the finger of God that I cast out demons, then the kingdom of God has come upon you' (Luke 11.20; Matthew 12.28 has spirit of God for finger of God).

Second, there are two occasions on which the gospels picture Jesus having to give a public account of the purpose of his ministry, two occasions on which it would be necessary to be both clear and convincing or, as the saying has it, to the point; once when he faced a home town audience, before whom no one is a prophet, and once in conversation with some disciples of John the Baptist, who would incline to consider him a rival. On both occasions the New Testament writers have him answer in much the same terms, in terms of reversing the misfortunes and ills to which human kind is prey, as Matthew quotes Isaiah, 'he took our infirmities and bore our diseases' (Matthew 8.17). Freedom for the oppressed, release of captives, sight for the blind, hearing for the deaf, cure for the lame, resurrection for the dead and good news for the poor (Luke 7.18-22; 4.16-21; Matthew 11.2-6), these are the terms in which the effect of his ministry is stated.

Thirdly, the section of Matthew's gospel which contains Jesus'

most substantial teaching on the nature of the kingdom of God
contains almost as much healing narrative, and it is marked off
as a unified section with Matthew's characteristic clarity, this
time by repeating, antiphon-like, at the beginning and end of
the section the statement: 'And he went about all Galilee, teaching in their synagogues and preaching the gospel of the kingdom and healing every disease and every infirmity among the
people' (Matthew 4.23-9.34).

Finally, and perhaps most significant of all, the commonest
word in the New Testament for these deeds of Jesus (apart from
John's 'signs') is not miracle, with all its connotations of interference with the laws of nature and apologetic proof, but rather
'dynamis' of deed or power, the very word which is used for the
gospel itself (which is the power of God in Romans 1.16), the
same power or spirit which is at the heart of the experience of
resurrection, as already explained in the chapter on resurrection
(and see Romans 1.4).

If we follow with any fidelity these clues scattered so liberally
throughout the New Testament it must become clear to us that
the so-called miracle stories, as well as their conventional function, and in addition to their function as symbol and myth, have
also the more important purpose of emphasizing that the
experience of the reign of God is, in one most essential aspect,
an experience of a power or spirit in our lives that makes us heal
the ills of our fellows and see to their needs (it is not only Jesus
who heals, any more than it is only Jesus who experiences the
reign of God; see Luke 10.17; 9.50). What is important at this
level is not that the feeding or healing is miraculous: the real
'miracle' when people are hungry is that anyone should feel
favoured enough to feed them. What is important at this level is
not that many of the healings are described as exorcisms. The
power or spirit inherent in the experience of the reign of God
was clearly conceived by the New Testament writers, and probably by Jesus, as overcoming a contrary spirit, the demonic spirit
which maimed and crushed our kind. But it is not as important
at this level to decide whether or not this demonic power has
real personal existence as it is to feel the emphasis on the experience of the reign of God, already an experience of the gift of God
in all things great and small, an experience of the acceptance of
all people good and bad, as an experience of a power or spirit to
answer to human need wherever it is encountered and to overcome the real ills to which all flesh is heir. Beneath the miraculous circumstance and the demonic personnel which are so much

part of their conventional function, this is the emphasis which the so-called miracle stories of the New Testament contribute to the rounding out of our understanding of the experience known as the reign of God. Thus the so-called miracle stories, as treated in the New Testament, heighten in dramatic form the lesson so often repeated in other ways in the New Testament (John's washing of the feet of his disciples by Jesus at the Last Supper, for instance),[44] that unstinting service, not lordship, is the only life compatible with the experience of the reign of God.

The faith of the historical Jesus

The parables of Jesus, then, form the myth in which he conveys the experience known as the reign of God, just as prayer and eucharist are its ritual, and service its life; and between them they no doubt convey a very rounded impression of what the experience of the reign of God is like. Is there a shorter way of conveying an understanding of this experience, at once so complex to the analyst and apparently so singular to the one who enjoys it? Probably not, if any adequacy is expected, but perhaps if the experience itself could find words to summarize its impact in a short space, it would say something like this.

That life is grace to us, our own lives and the lives of all those we encounter, that all things great and small are gift, the treasure we can at any moment discover, the banquet to which all are equally invited.

That delay must not mar this discovery, nor decline the invitation, for such ingratitude instantly ungraces us; that life is more than bread, more than accumulated possessions; that to realize the true value of someone or something and to discover treasure are one and the same imperative act.

That the true value of all that exists is discovered in the unique way in which one values a gift; that we should therefore not crush by grasping, or tear by trying to pull away. The gift has its roots in the giver; like a flower with roots hidden that breaks ground to brighten a common day, grasp and pull it loose and its brightness is already blighted by impending decay. The gift is the bird in the hand, held in a gesture that is more one of holding dear, as the saying goes, than one of grasping and appropriating, a gesture that embodies the ability and willingness to let go, a gesture of trust equal to the sense of having been trusted and entrusted. That we should know how to enjoy without hoarding life with its supports and enrichments, its root and flower, its flesh and flight, as a loved one is possessed but cannot be owned. That we should look again at the birds of the air and the lilies of the field. The naked ape, the territorial principle, Hitler's old adage of a strong, free Germany in a free Europe, America's new adage of a strong America in a peaceful world, is all idiocy, crass idiocy, all grasping and crushing, all pulling and tearing.

As any who truly value them for what they are know, gifts are really priceless. To value something, anything, in the unique way in which one values a gift, is to know that it is priceless. Most of us are lucky enough to have something that cannot be bought, no matter how little the market analysts tell us it is worth. But this means, of course, that in one sense gifts are very costly, that they can cost us all we have. For usually, before we are graced, all that we have is our own anxious ownership of things and control over people, and the illusory peace and security which this brings, our pride and our prejudice, our lack of generosity despite our amazing grace, our greed, our divisions and exclusions, and the latent fear, born of all this, that refuses to die, that feeds, in fact, on death. The experience of the reign of God derived from the parables tells us that the priceless gift of life, valued as such, can cost us all that. That grace has its own logic, and its own economics.

The prayer, then, bids those who can pray it to break through the thin membrane that closes off the limits of our common perception, to penetrate to the promising darkness beyond, to sow there the seeds of confidence already gained, and wait for them to fructify there in growth of similar confidence and consummate joy. Utter the seminal word, it invites them, to the giver hidden in the gift, the source tangible only in the grace. Say 'Father' and feel the acceptance like forgiveness, the strengthened sense of security, fulfilment and peace. Ask for nothing that is not always already discovered, only for continuance of the discovery and the discovered, and of the generosity that discovery and discovered inspire. And add one thing. Having achieved that emotional distance from that first complex experience that first suggested a Father God, having entered the darkness beyond common experience and from it looked back to the light of ordinary earth, now be realistic about the offence that will be caused to common prejudice, about the cost that will be incurred by fidelity to the discovery and the grace, about the trial to come, and ask specifically for deliverance.

And the ritual meal will celebrate. For though the parables hint at offence, the prayer expects trial, and the meal itself symbolizes sacrifice, the joy of the original discovery of grace never diminishes. So celebrate the banquet of life with a banquet, grace with gratitude, or as the Latin has it more accurately, *gratia* with *gratias agere*, grace with doing grace. Eucharist, thanksgiving, giving, thanks, giving.

The meal invites all to share in ritual joy the staff of life, the food and drink, to share a table, be one with, one body and one spirit, with Jesus and his other followers in this living philosophy of life-grace, to partake of, take part in the body of Jesus the Christ, a joyful company without division, at peace, ritually celebrating the goodness of life, sharing and serving, sensing a new spirit amongst them, the awakening of new life.

They must then, of course, live out the life so ritually experienced. Give. Food to the hungry, health to the sick, deliverance to the imprisoned and oppressed, love to the stunted, vision to the frustrated, faith to the hopeless, self to the selfish, life itself to the hope of the future. Break the bread and give it and pour out the wine. Grace is never so much grace as when it is given again. God the giver of life is never so near, life is never so much his gift, as when one ceases to hold on, to grasp and pull at it, and lets go, for greater love than this no one has. Witness to life-grace in face of great persecution at times requires this, and all the other giving and not grasping prepares one to do it, for the hope of the future.

Such, in summary, is the experience of the reign of God which Jesus tried to share with those who could open themselves to it.

Is there any word, of more contemporary currency, other than the phrase 'the reign of God', which could indicate the same experience? Probably none that has the same comprehensive range of reference as that given to the phrase 'the kingdom of God' by the public ministry of Jesus. But there is a word which, like the genetic centre of an organism, can indicate the heart of that experience from which all its limbs and features derive. It is the word 'faith', not in the sense of a faith, like a particular world religion, for instance, but faith as an active quality of a human person. It is in the course of the so-called miracle stories, in terms of which, as we saw, and apparently solely in terms of which, the experience of the reign of God could be peremptorily described, that the suggestive references to this word 'faith' are most frequently found in the gospels. A number of writers have noticed how prevalent is the theme of faith in the healing stories in particular: 'He saw their faith,' 'Your faith has healed you'.[46] There is even that odd incident in Jesus' home town when it is said that he could do no deed of power there, and he marvelled at their lack of faith – and a causal connection between failure and lack is clearly suggested in the context (Mark 6.5f.). On the contrary, where such faith is present, even in quantity as tiny as mustard seed, it can move mountains or uproot the broad-rooted sycamine tree (Matthew 17.20; Luke 17.6). The same writers who notice the frequency of this theme in the healing stories, usually notice also that there seems no need in the context to say faith in whom or in what. So faith is an essential element in that experience of the spirit or power of service in terms of which the reign of God can itself be described. That is our clue. What to make of it?

If we could rid our minds for a moment of all the definitions of faith in terms of accepting certain truths about God and ourselves as coming from God himself, definitions with which most of us have grown up and which have caused most of us more trouble than they were ever worth, then we could perhaps follow this clue. For the lived experience/evaluation/acceptance of all life and existence as gift or grace, which is one particular version of the sense of contingency, is faith. At least the word 'faith' can sensibly be used for that experience/evaluation/ acceptance. And it corresponds to the central element in the experience known as the reign of God in two significant ways. First, that experience/evaluation/acceptance is itself our acknowledgment of God, as acceptance of the gift is acknowledgment of the giver: we have no other way of knowing about God, no independent access to God; God is the name we have for the being at once hidden and revealed in the appreciation of empirical existence as gift. Second, truly to experience/evaluate/accept all life and existence as gift is, as must be already clear, to involve ourselves in that mixture of joy and gratitude, responsibility and generosity, which fill out the rest of that experience known as the reign of God in the ministry of Jesus.

Faith, then, provided we do not misunderstand its nature in this particular Jesus-tradition, can stand for the experience of the reign of God, since it is a perfectly acceptable term for the heart of that experience. Gospel usage already hints that the word can function in this way, and the first great theologian of the Jesus-movement whose writings we have, Paul, uses 'faith' as perhaps his key term for the life-experience which Jesus designated by means of the phrase 'the kingdom of God'.

One final question: was this experience which he called the reign of God an actual, personal experience of Jesus himself, or was it simply one which he recommended in various ways to others? The question will no doubt seem more pointed if we use in framing it our recently-found substitute word, faith. Was the faith described in the course of this chapter the personal faith of Jesus himself, or was it, rather, a faith which he recommended to others, but of which he himself had no need?

If one had a smattering of Greek, one would quickly realize that in many places where the New Testament talks in English about having faith in Jesus, the original Greek could just as easily, and even more literally, be read as recommending the faith of Jesus. For instance, the literal translation of Galatians 2.16 reads: 'We ... who know that a man is not justified by works of the law but through the faith of Jesus Christ, even we have believed in Jesus Christ, in order to be justified by the faith of Christ.'[47] Can we take it, then, that in this and other similar contexts we are being referred to the personal faith of Jesus himself (the faith which was a quality of Jesus as personal subject, not the faith of which Jesus is object), as a way of recommending that we have the same mentality which was that of Jesus (Philippians 2.5)? Are we being urged, as the more literal translation of Paul's sentence suggests, to believe in Jesus so that we may imitate the personal faith of Jesus? Is the New Testament giving us warrant for describing Jesus as himself a man of faith, of the kind of faith we have just been discovering in the course of the present chapter?

There are two kinds of deterrent to our acceptance of this conclusion. First, and much less seriously, even the phrase 'the faith of Jesus' could, with a little mental adjustment to the circumstances, be taken to mean the faith that Jesus recommended to others but had no need of himself. But why make this mental adjustment to what is surely the more obvious meaning of the phrase, the personal faith of Jesus himself? Now we meet the second and more serious deterrent, and we face a problem, in answering our final question, that has wide-ranging consequences for our understanding of the development of the myth of Jesus, the development of christology. It is, in fact, because of these consequences for our understanding of the way in which the myth of Jesus, or christology, developed that this final question is worth some careful consideration at this point.

Both early and late in the course of the Christian tradition, representatives of different branches of that tradition are found issuing decrees which forbid any discussion of Jesus as himself a man of faith. Thomas Aquinas re-affirmed the belief that Jesus from the very first moment of his conception, from the first moment, that is, of his human existence, enjoyed the direct vision of divinity. Now, in Thomas's view, seeing and believing were simply incompatible: if one saw divinity, one could not have religious faith.[48] Jesus, therefore, was not a man of faith.

Much later, Bultmann warned one of the so-called post-Bultmannians, Ernst Fuchs, in peremptory fashion: 'the kerygma does not permit any inquiry into the personal faith of the preacher' (that is, Jesus).[49] There is a good deal of Bultmann behind this warning. He is both heir and defiant defender of a long century of growing scepticism about the ability of the New Testament text to tell us anything at all certain about the historical Jesus. He is an equally staunch opponent of what in the Reformation tradition was known as psychologism, that is, the attempt to describe the inner mental states of Jesus, as if the Christian life consisted in imitating these, as if the Christian faith could be substantiated, and should be substantiated, by discovery of the historical facts about Jesus' inner mental states. In his view, then, to try to find out if Jesus was himself a man of faith was a task both idle and possibly pernicious. The true kerygma, the true preaching of Jesus as Lord, simply forbade it.[50] Faith in Jesus, to put the point in terms of our question, rules out any talk about the faith of Jesus.

Different as are the directions from which these two decrees of prohibition seem to come, they nevertheless reveal, on closer inspection, a common attitude. What is really at stake in the distinction which Aquinas applies to Jesus between seeing and believing is the divinity which the tradition has long confessed of Jesus. Now it does seem to be the case that the common Christian mind finds it easier (not easy, just easier) to harmonize the traditional belief in the divinity of Jesus with a conception of his humanity endowed with every conceivable quality, such as foreknowledge, incomparable grace, and especially direct vision or knowledge of divinity. The Christian mind finds great difficulty indeed in harmonizing the same belief in Jesus' divinity with a conception of his humanity afflicted, as is our common humanity, with ignorance in the present, with the growing-pains of trying to discover oneself and one's world by projecting into an uncertain future, and with all the real temptations to which all flesh is heir.[51] But if to this list of all too human attributes one then added the human quality of religious faith? If one remembered that faith in this tradition means encounter with divinity solely through the perception/evaluation/ acceptance of all life and existence as gift? How could confession of Jesus' divinity ever originate; how could it ever be justified, if Jesus himself is thought to have been a man of such faith?[52]

Bultmann does not hold the same view of the divinity of Jesus as did Aquinas. Yet he is equally convinced that in the preaching of Jesus as Lord, if we are only open to it, God himself encounters us and enables us to make the faith-decision described at some length already. Speculation about the personal faith of the historical Jesus is at best unhelpful to such an encounter with God in the preaching of Jesus as Lord. At best it will mislead us into thinking that Christian faith is merely a matter of imitating some mental states of Jesus presented to us now by some reliable historian.

Both men, though coming from very different theological directions, are equally convinced that if we talk about the personal faith of the historical Jesus we shall never understand, and we cannot justify, what in this book (though, obviously with no pejorative intent) we shall call the myth of the man Jesus, and which in the tradition that we shall shortly inspect reached its most substantial form in the confession of the lordship and divinity of Jesus. What can be said about this double decree of prohibition?

Two things. First, a point that can be made immediately. The New Testament gives more warrant than we have yet seen for speaking of the historical Jesus as himself a man of faith. Second, and a point that will have to wait until later for proper development, both theologians mentioned above are convinced that in Jesus as our Lord we directly encounter the one, true God, but that any discussion of the personal faith of the historical Jesus will threaten or destroy that encounter. We shall certainly agree with them on the first part of their contention, which is their major concern, but we hope to show that the conception of the historical Jesus as himself a man of faith can help rather than hinder our understanding of the conviction, expressed in the myth of Jesus, that in him we do indeed encounter the one, true God, that, as Paul put it, in him God was reconciling the world to himself.

The New Testament, of course, we realize by now, does not provide us with a full biography of Jesus which would allow us to answer almost any substantial question we might care to ask about his life. Much less does it provide us with the kind of post-Joycean stream-of-consciousness treatment of its subject which would allow us to see into his inner mind. Nevertheless, if we range outside the contexts in which the word 'faith' itself is specifically used, to others which use an equivalent phrase, we shall see that the New Testament writers frequently and insistently present Jesus as a man of faith, and we shall then have all the warrant we could expect for doing so ourselves. Let us take one example here of an equivalent phrase for faith which would broaden our New Testament research in this topic, since we do not have space for more.

One of those images-become-symbol which the Hebrew used to evoke patterns of experience at all levels of existence was the image of hearing-speaking. This symbol was all the more comprehensive because his word for hearing was also his word for heeding or obeying. So when he talked at the deepest level of hearing what life or existence was saying and heeding it, he was already using religious language, language at the level of religious faith; he was symbolizing God as the one who talked to him through existence, through creation. It has been pointed out on more than one occasion that Hebrew-Jewish religion is a religion of the word.[53]

In the beginning was the *Word* ... (So opens the Fourth Gospel).

In the beginning God created the heavens and the earth ...
God *said*, 'Let there be ...'
And there was ...
And God said, 'Let there be ...'
And it was so   (The opening of the book of Genesis).

If the lost word is lost, if the spent word is spent
If the unheard, unspoken
Word is unspoken, unheard;
Still is the unspoken word, the Word unheard,
The Word without a word, the Word within
The world and for the world;
And the light shone in darkness and
Against the Word the unstilled world still whirled
About the centre of the silent Word (T. S. Eliot, 'Ash Wednesday').[54]

Sheᵉma Israel: Hear, O Israel. The word of God to be heard and heeded here, at the most basic level of all, is the creation itself, the divine 'word' which is now uttered as creation, our whole empirical world acknowledged as God's creation. The obedience in question is depicted in the myths of Genesis, where all the earth is given to us to have dominion over it, a garden to its husbandman, a challenge and a promise. We must hear God's world (for God saw that it was all good), hear its hints of ultimate creative source to which we are responsible for it, hear its hazardous promises, and obey by struggling with and through it towards a distant goal, towards that limitless life and total knowledge which will make us most like God.[55] To hear, then, to heed, to obey, are mythic symbols for the faith of this people at its very root.

In New Testament Greek, the verb to hear can also mean to heed or to obey, and with people of the same Hebrew tradition it is still synonymous with basic religious faith, so that Paul is waxing tautologous when he writes of the obedience of faith (Romans 1.5; 16.26), or else he is elaborating a little on the symbolism of his tradition. To hear, to heed, the word or will of God, is to see all life and existence as God's good gift to us, to be attentive to its demands and its promises. Of course, a tradition as old as that of Jesus and Paul had already verbalized this perception and evaluation of the world many times over, and had tried over long centuries in the Law and the Prophets to give verbal expression to the demands and promises implied in it. The temptation there, as in all traditions, was to take these words, quite literally, as the word of God, to literalize the myth and symbol in this particular way, to make faith a mindless parrot's assent to past formulae. Many a Sadducee made this mistake about the words of the distant past, and many a Pharisee carried the mistake to the interpretative words of more recent times. But the one who was capable of understanding that all such words were but memorable human ways of capturing the vision of creation as gift and outlining its implications, such a one could live in the original symbol, the original myth of the word of God, could see that the original word of God was really life and existence itself, such a one could be a person who truly heard, a person of true faith.

Again, the necessary brevity of the treatment of this topic in the present context excuses us from the obligation of providing an inclusive list of New Testament references to Jesus as one who heard and obeyed the word or will of God, though all of these, in this tradition, were equivalently describing him as a man of faith. We shall be satisfied with one major context in the New Testament where Jesus, in the terms just outlined, is described as a man of faith and the implications drawn there are near enough to the analysis of his distinctive faith already proposed in this chapter: the Epistle to the Hebrews, especially chapters 2; 5 and 11.

In Hebrews the insistence is strong and explicit that Jesus was like us in all things, sin alone excepted: 'for he who sanctifies and those who are sanctified have all one origin. That is why he is not ashamed to call them brethren' (2.11). And the common human condition of Jesus and his followers is described so: they are 'all those who through fear of death were subject to lifelong bondage' (2.15). Bondage to anxiety, slavery to the fear of death, such is the human condition of all before faith. It was fitting then, so the argument proceeds, that God should fashion the pioneer of human liberation by suffering (2.10). For Jesus is described as one who fully shared our basic fear of death, and the bondage which that involves threatened him also: 'In the days of his flesh, Jesus offered up prayers and supplications, with loud cries and tears, to him who was able to save him from death' (5.7). We were to be liberated, in the only way we could be liberated, from the condition we and Jesus all shared. In Hebrews 5 the parallel is carefully drawn between Jesus and the high priest. So Jesus did not call himself to his high function. So Jesus shared all our weaknesses in the flesh. So Jesus was called, perfected as pioneer, made high priest/Son through suffering. Put more passively, 'As Son,[56] he learned obedience through what he suffered' (5.8). He is, therefore, 'the pioneer and perfecter of our faith' (12.2), a faith which has just been described in Hebrews 11 as that by which Abraham 'went out, not knowing where he was to go' and his successors conquered kingdoms, enforced justice, received promises, won strength out of weakness, and suffered without losing hope. And we shall learn to be sons also as Jesus did if we follow the pioneer (5.7; compare chapters 5 and 12), which we can do because he so fully shared the human condition.

The categories in this context are as old and as quaint as the thought is familiar to those who plumb the depths of human experience. For life is ambivalent. It is a wonderful datum, a given to be cherished. In saying that, though, one says that it points beyond its empirical dimensions, to something which it indicates but hides from us. We are to take it, then, gladly in both hands, but if, as we inevitably do, we seek our security and our goals in the collapsible dimensions of its empirical presence, if, as Kierkegaard puts it, we grasp at finiteness to sustain ourselves, we taste death as an experience of living, we know the full destructiveness of things breaking up, failing, dying. We suffer. And even if we do not do this; even if we refuse to treat any finite thing as an absolute, whether power, or money, or land, or church, or state; even if we look on all of them as gifts and promises of better things ahead and ultimately of the one absolute God, we shall be persecuted by those who do treat such things as ultimates. Either way, it seems, we *learn* faith or obedience through what we suffer. So Jesus did by God's design, so his faith was perfected, and he was freed from the fear of death which makes us slaves, and he thus became the pioneer and perfecter of faith, the one we follow when we have faith like his. To those who fully appreciate life as God's gift or grace, death's sting is drawn. But those who put any of life's offerings in God's place are in bondage to the fear of death all their lives long. In such magnificent sweeps of human vision the writer of Hebrews describes the personal faith of Jesus, and wishes it were ours.[57]

There is one final reason which makes it more than plausible to think of the historical Jesus as himself a man of faith. This kind of faith, it seems, can only spread by contagion. Only carriers can truly give it to others.

Strictly speaking, it cannot be taught, if by teaching is meant some academic exercise such as the writing of this book or lecturing on its contents might illustrate. To say this is not to decry theology or the academic profession in general, and if I thought I would end by decrying this book, I would not have bothered to begin to write it. The kind of abstract analysis and synthesis by which most academic work proceeds provides, at its best, some clarity in one's choice of life-options; at the very least, it prevents the richness of imagery from becoming vague and misleading, and it prevents the enthusiasm of action from running to a destructive fanaticism. It is always well to take thought.

And Jesus taught, of course, though he seems to have preferred, to the abstract conceptuality beloved of academia, the concrete image of the mythmaker. He preferred, in other words, that form of human communication which engages the whole person in closest experience with the uneven contours of the ordinary world from which his specific faith emerges. But words were not enough. Without the experience of sharing and service in meal and 'miracle', abstract thought is all too easily felt to be irrelevant, the pastime of impractical fellows, like philosophers and other inhabitants of ivory towers, and even parables can turn out to be both picturesque and interesting, but ultimately ineffective.

In the end the only way to give people the experience of all life and existence as enabling and inspiring grace, the only way to give them the experience of being themselves grace and treasure, is to treat them as treasure and to be gracious to them. Human kind as a class, of all species of object on this earth, is very class conscious. The sun may indeed rise on the evil and the good, and the same rain refresh the just and the unjust (Matthew 5.45), but the lesson will likely enough be lost on me unless the warmth of another human being envelop me, unless some other human person refresh the weariness of my defeated days. I simply will not feel my own life, my own self, as grace or gift of God, unless someone values me. That is presumably why the gospels can make Jesus describe the whole experience of the reign of God, which it was his whole mission in life to give us, in terms of serving the needs of others. It may seem, at first blush, to stand the whole logic of the experience of the reign of God on its head, putting the effect before the cause. The logic should surely read: first feel all life and existence as gift or grace, then feeling the grace of God, be gracious to others. Not, first feel the grace of some human presence, feel forgiven, accepted, served, then begin to feel all life and existence as grace, and then feel inspired to be gracious to others. But it is really a universal human idiosyncracy that is operative here, not a matter of logic. It may well be that some rare individual, perhaps Jesus himself, followed the former logic, having a power of perception and evaluation and acceptance far beyond the ordinary. Indeed in the case of Jesus, it is very likely that his power to value went far beyond anyone's ability to value him. But for the rest of us, we can only sense ourselves and our world valued and cherished by God when we feel valued and cherished by others.

And there is really no possibility of dissimulation here. We are all only too well aware that a life seemingly dedicated to service can be just another path to power; people making themselves out to be indispensable to us simply to gain whatever advantage can be had from manipulating our lives for us. There are too many examples of that in all social institutions, and too many plays written about it, like Pinter's *The Servant*. But power-seeking in service, like condescension in giving, or cowardly envy in forgiving, is too easily perceptible, if sometimes, unfortunately perceived too late, and no good comes of it, no sense of life and existence as grace, no faith or love, no hope.

So Jesus cherished all life and existence, and especially other people, as God's precious gift, and so, without ulterior motive, he accepted all and served their needs, and so enabled and

inspired them to discover the treasure hidden in their lives. And
that is faith. The only alternative here is to see the human personality of Jesus as a purely passive mask for the dramatic
speeches of divinity. And that neither the scriptures nor the
great tradition allows to do.

Such, then, is the life of Jesus, the only life of Jesus of any
interest to the world. Such is the historical Jesus, who can be
discovered at the end of any quest, old or new. A man of faith, a
life of faith, the very specific faith just described, inspiring to
similar faith those with whom he came in contact, so that they in
turn could inspire others. That was his life. That was the faith
for which he lived and died.

It was a faith that had its deepest roots in the most ordinary
experience of everyday life. The man Jesus – apart from his
tradition, of course, which had already tried to verbalize this
faith – had no more 'information' about God than could be
gleaned from the birds of the air, the farmers in their fields,
kings in their castles, and merchants in the market-place. For
this very reason, because it had its roots in the most ordinary
experience of everyday life, his faith was extraordinarily radical.
Most faiths, most religions, have some places more sacred than
others, some days holier than others, some actions more religious than others, some vocations in life more perfect than others,
some meats, even, cleaner than others. Religious faith, then, has
to do principally with these and it is, in consequence, too easily
restricted to these. As far as Jesus was concerned, though, the
Sabbath was made for man, man was not made for the Sabbath
(Mark 2.27). The holiday, with its special buildings and personnel, its special ritual and food, is there simply to symbolize and
thus to serve the faith which is itself a *lived* conviction that all
times and places, all people and practices, and all things great
and small, are equally close to God as his cherished gift to all of
us.[58] Thus religion would be left with all its panoply intact, but
the status and function of this would be properly adjusted. This
was a radical faith indeed, to live out and, very likely, to die for.

The authority of the historical Jesus

There is a kind of authority that goes with titles. I am Sir Oracle,
and when I open my lips, let no dog bark. First one establishes
one's status and dignity, and then one expects that weight be
given to one's words. Very many titles are applied to Jesus in the
New Testament – Son of Man, Messiah, Lord, etc. – and he is
sometimes made to claim some of them for himself. But though

there is growing agreement now on the meaning of these titles
in their different cultural milieux, no agreement can be reached
on the question of which, if any of them, Jesus claimed for
himself. From the nature of the faith he took it upon himself to
inspire in others, and from the means he chose to do this, it
seems safer to conclude that he did not use the authority of titles
at all – he was amongst us as one who served – and to treat the
titles later as part of the Jesus myth, the myth that developed
about the person of Jesus.

Nor can the question of his authority be settled on the ground
of statements allegedly made about him by contemporaries, and
overheard, passed on, and recorded; that he spoke with authority, for instance, and not as the scribes and Pharisees. Such
hearsay about the manner or effect of his speech is far too flimsy
for historical purposes.

Almost equally slight for historical purposes, though service-
able, no doubt, in its own way, is his alleged independence of
proof-texts; where other teachers felt the need to back up their
religious recommendations with texts from the Old Testament,
it is said, he did not, and so his unique claim to authority was
implicitly presented to his hearers.[59]

Too slight in itself also is his alleged habit of prefixing a solemn 'Amen, Amen' – a traditional formula for assent to God's
word – to his own more important statements.[60] In both these
latter cases, both the practice and its alleged implications,
though perhaps probable, are too difficult to establish.

We are on far safer ground if we take the much more reliable
historical suggestion that his enemies did ask some question
like, 'Why does he eat with publicans and sinners?' For undoubtedly behind that complaining query the true figure of the historical Jesus is visible, the figure of a man who took it upon himself
to give all people without distinction or qualification the experience of being cherished and graced by God, and so motivating
them to cherish and grace others, equally without distinction or
qualification. Because he took it upon himself to do this, with all
its far-reaching implications for the conduct of human affairs,
the question, 'Who do you say that I am?' even if he never asked
it himself in so many words, could not long remain without
some attempt to answer it. For in this essential conduct of his
mission his one, true claim to be the author of new life, his real
authority, resided. In answering that question the myth of the
man Jesus grew, which it is christology's proper task to study.
To this we now turn.

5

The Myth that Jesus developed and the Myth that developed about Jesus

In the famous hymn in Paul's letter to his converts at Philippi (Philippians 2.6-11), the claim is made that because Jesus was obedient unto death, because, in other words, he was a true man of faith through death itself, he had conferred on him the name which is above every name, the title 'Lord'. There is scarcely in the whole of the New Testament a clearer statement of the real reason why Jesus himself became subject of our confession of faith. It was because of the distinctive faith which Jesus inspired in others, because of the distinctive experience, as he would say, of the reign of God which he had himself and conveyed to others who became his followers, because, in short, of the myth in which he himself lived and invited others to live, it was because of this that Jesus himself acquired a name, a title which related him directly to God, the ground of being. He himself, that is, became the subject of a confession of faith. He became the subject of a myth by which and in which his followers lived, and in terms of which their confession was cast.

It is the precise task of this present chapter to analyse that step, taken at the very beginning of the Christian tradition, which carried the followers of Jesus from Jesus' own myth of the kingdom of God to the developing myth of Jesus himself. The step may sometimes seem more like an athlete's long jump – with a kick or two for longer length in the middle – than a common pedestrian step. But careful analysis alone, and not just superficial impression, can reveal its true nature and its real extent. And such analysis, in order to be adequate, normally requires two parts, the historical and the logical. The historical part of the analysis tries simply to describe the sequence of names, titles, images or symbols that made up the developing myth about Jesus. The logical part, as its name implies, asks what logic, if any, connects such a rapidly developing myth about this man to the man with his myth; what reasons can be given to explain this step, how can it be justified, if it can be justified at all? These two questions, and the attempts to answer them, will be intertwined in the account which follows, but it is well to notice the two separate parts of the problem before setting out in search of a solution.

Paul: replacing the kingdom of God myth

The earliest documents we now possess from the Jesus-followers of the first Christian century come from a man called Paul. Our search for the New Testament understanding of the resurrection of Jesus began with Paul. And the resurrection of Jesus (as presented in the New Testament), that third chapter concluded, was his followers' first full myth of the man, Jesus.

It seems to be clearly indicated, then, that when we set out to understand the relationship between Jesus' own myth and the myth that grew around the person of Jesus, we should begin once again with Paul. That there were earlier formulations by his followers of the myth of Jesus the form critics have amply illustrated, and we may nod in their direction before the present chapter is ended. But Paul is the first familiar figure who comes before us with his own distinctive myth of the man, Jesus, and his myth has as its central symbolism the symbolism of resurrection.

In fact, there appear to be even more cogent reasons for the contention that it is best to begin with Paul. The modern mind, with its centuries-old suspicion of myth, is only too prone to assume that a myth can only grow around an actual historical figure when most of the actual historical facts about the figure have already been forgotten. This particular piece of cultural chauvinism, this penchant for opposing myth to history, seems justified for once in the case of Jesus and Paul.

For Paul, to the best of our knowledge, never encountered Jesus at all during the latter's life on this earth. For which reason Luke, who counts familiarity with Jesus during the latter's public ministry as an essential part of the job-description of a true apostle within the supreme consistory of the Twelve, consistently refuses to regard Paul as an apostle on a level with the Twelve; and he even suggests in his subtle way that Paul's resurrection experience was a vision of the risen Lord rather than an appearance of the risen Lord, thereby further disqualifying Paul from the highest rank of apostleship (Acts of the Apostles 1.21f.).

In fact, on his own admission, when Paul first met the Jesus-movement, it was in the role of hostility and harassment, trying to have Jesus-followers excommunicated and penalized by the synagogue penalty of flogging (punishment which he himself was later to suffer for the same cause). More disconcertingly still, perhaps, Paul in his letters shows scant interest in the events of the life of Jesus. That Jesus died and is raised seems sufficient factual reference for the preaching of Paul's gospel. He retells no parable of Jesus and he narrates no miracle story or other significant incident from the latter's life. Paul's references to receiving from the Lord, or to a word of the Lord, are themselves so fluid in their meaning that it is often difficult to know whether he is referring to an actual saying of Jesus, appealing to an authoritative tradition in the community, or prophesying himself, as others had done before him, in the name of the Lord who was now the risen Jesus.[1] All in all, it would take quite an elaborate argument to show that Paul was acquainted with a few actual sayings of the historical Jesus, or, in their original form, with some events of Jesus' life prior to the latter's execution. And, of course, the very fact that such arguments must be so elaborate provides its own proof that Paul was not interested in recording as such some sayings or events from the life of the historical Jesus. So, to make a long story short, we have a man whose self-professed life-purpose it is to preach Jesus the Christ, who never met Jesus in the flesh, and who shows scant interest in the events of Jesus' life. Perfect soil for myth-growing, the modern scientific chauvinist concludes with barely concealed sense of triumph.

Before we are tempted to assent to such a facile conclusion, however, with its clearly pejorative impression of the nature of myth and, certainly, before we are tempted to draw some deep theological implications from it concerning the very nature of the Christian faith, let us consider another approach, one which may prove to be less superficial in the end. It should by now be clear enough that the only life of the historical Jesus worth recovering is the life that he literally poured into his public mission of inaugurating the kingdom of God. It was a life of preaching in parables, of prayer to God the Father, of ritual celebration in sacrament, particularly the sacrament of meal, and of service to all who had been accepted without respect of persons as children of the one Father.

It becomes equally clear, on the most cursory perusal of Paul's extant letters, that these essential features of the public ministry of Jesus are also central to Paul's missionary activity, if only because we see him declare them essential in the lives of his converts. The beginning of prayer for Paul, the source from which all prayer flows, is the address to God as Abba, Father. This conviction-petition which is constitutive of children of God, and which makes us co-heirs with Jesus to all that is thereby promised, is the work of the Spirit in us. And it is by speaking of the Spirit, as we already saw, that Paul depicts the risen Lord Jesus effective in our lives. The essential prayer of Jesus, then, continues, and its continuance is both compared to Jesus' own experience of God and attributed to Jesus (Romans 8.15-17, 26-27, 34).

In his first letter to the Corinthians (11.17-34), Paul introduces the eucharist with the same solemn formula as he uses shortly afterwards to introduce another essential tradition of the Jesus-communities, the resurrection, and he draws out some important implications of its proper celebration, in terms of remembering what Jesus died for, in terms of discerning the body of the Lord and ending the divisiveness that was emptying the Lord's Supper of its symbolism and its effect.

The central significance of the miracle stories in the gospels, we have already seen, was that they made it clear that the service of the needs of one's fellow human beings is a primary feature of the experience of the reign of God, a primary apprehension and effect of the power or spirit which characterizes that reign. For those who might be tempted to see miracles, in the sense of defiances of the so-called laws of nature, as the major theme of the gospels, and service as the minor theme running through the same stories, Paul puts the priorities right. He seldom mentions miracle-working – though he does mention it – and his major effort is to develop as fully as possible his converts' appreciation of the necessity and nature of mutual service in the lives of Jesus' followers. He does this in a number of ways. First, he reminds his readers that the body, though a unity, is made up of different organs, each with its own specific and essential contribution to the welfare of the others and to the health and growth of the whole body. Then, he specifies the different gifts (charisms), services, or activities, such as healing, consoling, teaching, speaking a prophetic word to the times, administering, preaching, providing for the hungry and deprived, and, above all, loving in the most practical and individual manner possible. Finally, he asks his readers to desire to be gifted in the ways that will best help build up the one body of Jesus-followers, the one body of Christ in the world; and he reminds them insistently that all these gifts and services and activities come from the one God, the one Lord, the self-same Spirit (Romans 12.4-21; I Corinthians 12;13).

So much for prayers, meals and 'miracles'. In all cases it seems that central elements in the public ministry of Jesus are continued by Paul in his effort to convert the whole civilized world to Jesus – for that, no less, Paul took to be his mission in life.

What element, then, of the public life of Jesus could Paul be said to have ignored or neglected? Only Jesus' verbalization of the experience which he called the reign of God, a verbalization which we now possess principally in the parables. It seems that Paul replaced Jesus' verbal myth of the kingdom with a literary construction largely of Paul's own making. Does it follow, then, that Paul also changed the meaning of that event or experience known to Jesus as the reign of God? As Paul replaced the parables, did he also replace Jesus' original understanding of the reign of God? And is it really true that the myth about Jesus could only grow when Jesus' own understanding of the reign of God which he had tried to inaugurate was changed or dropped in favour of some substitute?

It may be well to pause briefly to answer the question: did Paul, in substituting his own construction for Jesus' myth of the reign of God, still convey the same sense of that unique experience? This is the kind of question that must be asked many times in the course of the Christian tradition. It must be asked whenever a new construction is substituted for previous ways of communicating the experience of the reign of God. And an answer to that first question is always preliminary to the answer to the second question: how did the myth about Jesus in its many forms derive from Jesus' myth of the reign of God and from the many constructions which later replaced this? It is sufficient for us to ask the first question once, if only because with Paul it occurs in its most crucial form. In the case of Paul we have the problem of comparing one man's written construction of the experience of the reign of God with a myth (Jesus' myth) which has itself to be reconstructed from the writings of men other than its maker. In all later cases it is more simply a matter of comparing different constructions of Jesus' myth in the written forms in which their makers left them to us. So we ask the first question once, but the second question, concerning the origin of the myth about Jesus from various forms of Jesus' myth, will lead us to direct consideration of a number of developing forms of the myth about Jesus.[2]

To Jesus' own symbolic terms for the experience which Jesus introduced to the world, 'the kingdom of God', Paul prefers other terms for that experience and event, and predominant amongst these is the term 'faith'. This is a substantial change in the principal terminology for the distinctive experience which Jesus wished to convey. And it is in fact indicative of even more wide-ranging changes in Paul's way of receiving, understanding and transmitting that same experience.

For Paul was a Pharisee, and though born and raised in the diaspora, in the city of Tarsus, he appears to have been as stringent in his adherence to that particular way of life as were any of his homeland counterparts who challenged Jesus on almost every important aspect of the latter's proclamation.[3] Even before his conversion to Jesus, Paul may have been engaged in some missionary activity on behalf of Pharisaic or scribal Judaism; he certainly engaged in active persecution of Jesus' followers, hounding them out of the synagogue and having them flogged.[4] Therefore, the experience which Jesus described as the in-breaking reign of God came to Paul himself, in that mysterious conversion episode of his life, not so much as a new way of life, but as a contrary way of life. It is naturally in terms of contrast, then, that Paul perceives the new experience in his own life, and in terms of contrast he naturally presents it to his fellow Jews. Contrast to what? Contrast to the way of life which had found it so contrary, contrast to the Pharisaic philosophy of minute adherence to the Law (read, the religion) of the Jews, as the cement of the nation, the unmistakable badge of identity, and the source of security for the future before God and man. If Paul had been as convinced a Zealot, or a Sadducee, or an Essene, he might still have written and talked in terms of contrast, but then, in each case the actual terms of the contrast would have been different. Under such specific conditions, then, Paul the Pharisee evolves that characteristic combination of theological analysis and mythic or semi-mythic imagery, from which to this day his understanding of the achievement of Jesus has to be distilled.

The contrast in which Paul presents his shattering perception of Jesus' way of life is stark indeed. On one side of the contrast is life under the Law, and the Law for Paul the Pharisee means that up-to-date development and detailed interpretation of the Jewish faith and Jewish ethics which makes a Jew distinctive in all that a Jew is and does. On the same side of the contrast, for reasons to be explained shortly, is life or existence which is subject to the destructive force of sin (Romans 7.11), existence according to the flesh (Romans 8.4), existence under the implacable reign of death (Romans 5.12-14). On the other side of the contrast is the option of living by faith (Galatians 2.20), living under grace (Romans 6.14), living by the Spirit (Galatians 5.25), living, simply, in contrast to dying (Romans 8.13).

Place these characteristics in parallel columns, and the contrast is balanced:

Law	faith
sin	grace
flesh	spirit
death	life.

Read some of Paul's shorter, thesis-like statements and it becomes clear that the contrast is complete: 'You are not under the Law, but under grace' (Romans 6.14).

If one takes the trouble, with the help of some responsible scholarship, to come to grips with these by now rather strange Pauline categories, in the contexts in which they occur,[5] then Paul's understanding of the achievement of Jesus, and of what it means to follow Jesus, comes across somewhat as follows.

The formulated tradition of a people, containing the best they know and the best they think they ought to achieve, the tradition enshrined in institution and constitution, in custom and convention, in a word, in a Jewish term, the Law, is itself, in Paul's language, holy and spiritual. That is to say, it puts people in contact with the wholly other God, from whom it all ultimately derives, and it mediates the power or spirit of God in human life.[6] But, as Paul perceives, law – and this applies to the best formulated traditions of all people – is doubly vulnerable to our human proneness for perversion. First, it advertises the very wrongs it wishes to prohibit. There is no need to go into the psychology of forbidden fruit here. Paul's point seems to be a simpler one: that the more we can codify goodness and the more we know about it, the less we can keep up with our developing standards and the more our guilt becomes apparent. The full extent of our covetousness becomes clear, to use one of Paul's own examples, when the law forbids covetousness in some detail. But the law itself is impotent to prevent the evil it describes – or, you cannot make man virtuous by act of parliament.

Second, and more seriously, there is the evil that people do, not in contravention of the best they know, but in pursuit of it. *Corruptio optimi pessima*, as the old adage has it. Second only to the penchant for contravention is the temptation to rigid adherence and imposition, to complacency, to boasting, in Paul's terminology. The formulated tradition carries to us the call of a goodness and a truth and a beauty which obliges us beyond any limit we have yet reached. But we idolize the formulations already achieved, we rest on our laurels instead of placing them on our poets' heads, and we persecute our present prophets in the name of the prophetic past.

To treat the law in these two diametrically opposite ways is to sin, to sin against the light and the good, against the ultimate source of all light and good whose call echoes, still not adequately answered, in the best of our visions and the most exalted of our ideals. This is also the work of the flesh; for flesh to Paul, at least in the contexts which concern us here, means human nature characterized by its propensity for treating its present possessions and achievements as its own securities in existence, tearing them free from the hands of the Giver, the earnest of whose creative goodness it is their sole privilege to be, putting them in the place of God, and, as a consequence, feeling sooner or later the full brunt of our common mortality. Flesh, in this meaning of the word, whether grabbing for some passing power or pleasure in contravention of the law or placing the law itself on a cosmic pedestal which only God could occupy, is sin in Paul's view, and the wages of sin is death.

We have already noticed that death to Paul does not refer exclusively to the singular event of the biological death we each of us must one day die. Death, rather, can be an experience of everyday life. To grasp at the things or the projects that make up our daily experience and to try to sustain ourselves totally by means of them is to sense the fragility of all things finite, to be afraid of their inevitable disintegration, to be slaves all our lives long to the fear of death, to live under the implacable reign of death.

It is not that the Law, the Pharisees' life-option for the survival of religious and national identity as a boon to all humankind, has itself become destructive instead of life-enhancing as a result of the mission of Jesus; and it is certainly not true, nor is it in any sense Paul's view, that the Law itself had always had, as its primary effect, to prove people sinful, to excite their pride and bring about their fall. The Law in itself, the traditional formulation of a people's vision, always carries to our human consciousness the claim of the Absolute upon us and, further, when it is interpreted for contemporary usage by scribes, and purged by prophets of its obsolete literalism, it makes the claim of the Absolute concrete and therefore practical in the best terms available for any particular time.

What Paul really intends to convey, then, and what he does in fact convey, is that the Law when taken advantage of by people's natural proclivity for grasping at finite things to sustain their spirits (which is the original sin of all people, the sin of idolatry), works in their daily lives the experience of going the way of all flesh, the experience of death. In short, the experience of Law which is described by Paul in the familiar imagery of the experience of slavery, is precisely an experience of the Law robbed by our own life-decision of the enabling and enhancing experience of grace. To this radical perversion of Law or religion itself the mission of Jesus finally alerted Paul. And this, then, is the viewpoint which his own shattering conversion, in debate with the stubborn resistance of his fellow Jews to his overtures on behalf of Jesus, makes him propose sometimes in such stark contrasts as his sentence: 'you are not under the Law, but under grace'. For the rest, it is scarcely necessary to remark, such brief and unadorned statements of contrast should be understood in the light of Paul's more nuanced and expansive thought on the complex role of law in human life (so barely outlined above), and not taken as thesis-headings to be developed independently by less subtle minds. [7]

On the other side of Paul's contrast is the option of living by faith. Paul can write about faith in the same unqualified way as can some of the gospel writers who allow us our insights into the life of the historical Jesus, that is, he can talk about faith without seeming to need to say faith in what or in whom. Take now the opportunity which, we already noticed, Paul's Greek affords us to translate in terms of salvation by the faith of Jesus, rather than salvation by faith in Jesus. [8] Return to the conviction that Jesus was himself a man of faith. It will then seem reasonable to conclude that the alternative which Paul is offering us, the alternative to a life lived under a Law made destructive by sin and, as such, hurrying us along the way of all flesh to death, is a life lived by the same faith by which Jesus lived and which he tried to inspire in all who would follow him.

The parables of Jesus, his myth of the event and experience which he called the reign of God in our world, depicted life itself as a gracious gift to be discovered and accepted joyfully – and this is the experience known as grace, in its most basic and foundational form. To sense all life and existence, including one's own life and self, as God's cherished gift, irrespective of achievements (the 'works of the law' or the Law itself as an achievement and possession), that is the experience of grace which coincides with the faith-experience of Jesus and his followers; for the faith of Jesus is precisely the acknowledgment of God as Father and giver of self, others, world. So Paul can say: 'I live by the faith of the Son of God who loved me and gave himself for me, I do not nullify the grace of God; for if justification were through the Law, then Christ died to no purpose' (Galatians 2.20f.).

For Paul this grace experience, as already noted, resulted in these personal qualifications for and dedication to the services to the needs of our fellows which can be called either charismata (itself a derivative of the Greek word for grace), or gifts of the Spirit. This corresponds to that aspect of Jesus' parable-myth of the kingdom in which joyful acceptance inspires responsibility and generosity to others. In Pauline terminology, to live in faith is to live under grace, to live by the Spirit, to wager in our daily existence for life and more abundant life, against the permanent prospect of death.

> the just man justices;
> Keeps grace: that keeps all his goings graces;
> Acts in God's eye what in God's eye he is –
> Christ – for Christ plays in ten thousand places,
> Lovely in limbs, and lovely in eyes not his
> To the Father through the features of men's faces.[9]

It goes almost without saying that those who live in the faith of Jesus, under grace and by the spirit or power of God, are not without law. They are never without normative formulations of their tradition. Law in the broadest sense, as the body of formulated precepts and ideals of a people, is not abolished. Rather, for those who live the experience of faith or grace, law is truly spiritual, a true vehicle of the sensed power or spirit of God in their graced lives (Romans 7.14). Our lived conviction that God's gracious acceptance of us as his own gift constitutes our primordial relationship to him, prevents our pride (flesh) from so 'weakening' the law that it cannot achieve its end (Romans

8.3f.). In short, the Law is now the Law of Christ (Galatians 6.2). Its precepts and provisions are open to reinterpretation and revision by his prophetic spirit. But even more essentially, the true status of law or religion is now established. It is no longer the formula for all that entitles us to God's favour. It is rather the formulation of the best response we can now make to the experience of a gracious God, and always inadequate to that experience.

It is fairly obvious, then, even from this brief perusal of Paul's central contrast between the life of faith and life under the Law that he is in fact, in his own distinctive categories, conveying the substance of precisely that same sense of contingency, and thus the possibility of the same type of religious faith, as Jesus conveyed by means of his parable-myth. It is the same sense of God's radical grace in life, the same sense of all life and existence as God's gift. It is an experience pregnant with generosity, vulnerable not only to our anxious, grasping, excluding and hostile instincts, but to the most solemnly institutionalized prejudices and presuppositions of our culture of which these instincts take advantage. And it is, after all, an experience entitled to all our confidence in its power to grow and expand and to change the world for the better.

Though it is true, then, that Paul replaces Jesus' parable-myth with his own analysis of the event and experience known to Jesus as the reign of God, he did not mistake to the least extent the nature of that event which Jesus inaugurated, of that experience which Jesus himself had and which he conveyed to others. And it is already clear that Paul faithfully continued these other elements in the mission of Jesus – prayer, meal fellowship, and service – in which the essence of the experience of the reign of God was contained and contagious.

There will be many more substitutions for Jesus' own myth in the on-going communication of the meaning of the rule of God as the tradition grows older and the centuries grind along. And again and again the question will have to be raised, if these changing formulations, whether symbolic or conceptual, still convey the same event, the same experience. We cannot afford to pursue that question any further in the present context. We have just assured ourselves from the case of Paul that fidelity to the self-same rule of God is perfectly possible in forms of expression quite different from those which Jesus used. And from Paul's time onward, we can be sure, that same question is in principle easier to answer, for, from that time onward, we have the check of these first written formulations of the rule of God on all subsequent attempts to reformulate – this is the normative rule of scripture – in judging all later traditional expressions of the Christian faith.

And so we can pass to our second question: what is the logic which connects the developing myth about the man, Jesus, to Jesus' own myth? What is the logic which binds increasing faith in Jesus to the faith which Jesus' own myth embodied? This is *the* christological question, this is the question concerning the very origin of christology as such, and though our attempt to answer it must of necessity carry us well beyond Paul, it is well to begin here also with Paul.

Paul: building the Jesus myth

The logic which carried his earlier followers from the myth which Jesus himself lived to the myth about Jesus is actually quite simple and perfectly cogent; only the great variety of ways in which this development took place, only the rich early growth of concept and symbol, makes it seem at first sight quite complex.[10] So it may be permissible to open this section with a straightforward statement of the logical formula, followed by a brief invoice of the principal types of construction in which the formula is carried out.

Briefly, then, whether Paul is writing about those features which were characteristic of the life-task of Jesus himself, and which he wishes to continue in his scattered communities – I mean prayer, the meal-fellowship, and the service – or whether he is writing in terms of his own conceptual symbols[11] for the new existence of the followers of Jesus – life, grace, faith, spirit – Paul, in either case, gives us clearly to understand that these features were introduced to our lives by Jesus, that they were features of Jesus' own existence and were caught by us in the contagion of his life-service to our human destiny. Jesus, the historical Jesus, is the one responsible for our ability to live this distinctive faith, this distinctive perception-evaluation of, and behaviour in, our world. He is the one who is responsible for our ability to say his prayer, to join in his meal and to serve as he served. Jesus himself, therefore, and not just the faith and fellowship he inspired, is of the deepest possible significance to our destiny. And it is precisely to tell of such deep significance that myth is required. Hence, the myth of the man Jesus is an absolute necessity if the full historical truth is ever to be told by his followers.

The logic of this development from Jesus' own lived myth to the myth about Jesus is carried through by the early Christians in three principal ways: first, in the earliest comprehensive myth of Jesus, the resurrection preaching; second, in the titles conferred on Jesus by his followers; and, third, in the more abstract conceptual analysis of his role and status which achieved, substantially in the first five Christian centuries, its most definitive form thus far.

So much for the brief statement of the logical formula for the development of the myth about Jesus, and an invoice of the principal types of literary construction in which the formula was carried through. And now for some details of both the logical formula and its concrete implementations.

The logical formula we seek, the logic, that is to say, that allows Jesus' followers to proceed from their acceptance of Jesus' own lived myth to their myth about Jesus, is found in collapsed form in simple phrases like 'the Lord's Supper' (I Corinthians 11.20). By this I mean that this small phrase has folded or collapsed into it (like a collapsible ladder) a sequence of logical steps which, if fully unfolded, would read somewhat as follows:

There is a supper, a ritual, sacramental meal in which we are now able to participate – at least if we are united and considerate, rather than divisive and selfish (I Corinthians 11.20-22). 'We have an altar from which those who serve the tent have no right to eat' (Hebrews 13.10). It is a meal in which we ritualize both the conviction that all life and existence is gift freely offered to all, and the sacrificial intent to give of ourselves in response. Jesus is the one responsible for such meals, for our ability to celebrate such meals, in so far as we can at all claim such ability. He is therefore our Lord, the Lord of our new lives. This is the explicit logic which is collapsed into the single phrase 'the Lord's Supper'.

The same logic which is found in Paul's reference to the meal is found also in his references to the other two means of access to that experience which Jesus called the reign of God: I mean, the prayer and the life of service.

The Abba prayer of Paul's converts is obviously the prayer of Jesus. It can make us in our lives what we are in our truest reality, sons of God and co-heirs with Jesus who, it is implied in the word 'co-heirs', is the son of God (Romans 8.15-17). Jesus is Son of God to those who are inspired by him to say his prayer;

and he inspired them to do this, not just by teaching them a verbal formula, but by treating them in every way as cherished children of the God he called Father. Their sonship, in other words, is derivative of his sonship and in this way it implies his original and originative sonship. Their experience requires this myth of the man in order to tell the full story of its source. To those whom Jesus enabled to pray and live and hope as sons of God, Jesus is Son of God *par excellence*.

The gifts and charismata, the services and activities, by which we care for and share with each other and build up the community of the race, are effected by the one spirit of the body of Christ (I Corinthians 12). To unfold once again the collapsed logic of this context: we make up the body, the tightly-knit, interdependent and mutually supportive body of those who live and experience the life of Jesus, because the spirit of Jesus empowers us for such service; and so for us Jesus is the Christ.

It seems clear enough here that Jesus is Christ, Son of God, Lord – the main titles conferred on him by Paul, and indeed the principal titles in the traditional myth of Jesus – because Jesus introduced into history and still brings to human life the prayer, ritual and life-style that enhances human existence with the experienced event of the reign of God, an event of truly awesome significance for human destiny.

Turn now to the conceptual symbols in which Paul depicts the achievement of Jesus, and the same logic of the development of the myth of Jesus shows through Paul's writing just as clearly.

'It is no longer I who live, but Christ who lives in me' (Galatians 2.20), so Paul puts it in one of his more mystical sentences. Again we can detect easily a kind of collapsed logic-sequence, shorthand for the argument that his new life is owed to Jesus and, therefore, Jesus to him is God's anointed, the Christ. That this is indeed the intrinsic logic of his confessions becomes even clearer in the case of Paul's other conceptual symbols.

The grace of which Paul speaks to his converts is the grace of Jesus, 'the grace of the one man Jesus Christ' (Romans 5.15), 'the grace of the Lord Jesus Christ' (II Corinthians 13.14). There are times in fact when Paul speaks as if the grace in question were specifically the grace of Jesus' death, or as if the grace of which he speaks were somehow equivalent to the death of Jesus, as if Jesus' dying were the grace: 'All are justified by his grace as a gift, through the redemption which is in Christ Jesus, whom God put forward as an expiation by his blood to be received by faith' (Romans 3.24f.), or, 'I live by the faith of the Son of God, who loved me and gave himself for me. I do not nullify the grace of God; for if justification were through the Law, then Christ died to no purpose' (Galatians 2.20f.).

The logical formula which we now pursue may not be so clear in the latter passages, partly because of the specific connection between grace and the death of Jesus, partly because of bad habits we have contracted in thinking of grace as some kind of quantified substance, partly because of a combination of these factors which allowed us loosely to imagine that Jesus merited a certain quantity of grace by letting himself be killed, and that this is distributed amongst us through various channels to this day.[12]

Grace, of course, does not name something that can be quantified and transported. The word grace, rather, in its Christian usage, refers to the fact that all life and existence is God's good and free gift to us, and that we, at least in our more uncalculating moments, are God's gift in openness and service to others; in short, that God is gracious Father. Grace recalls the fact that we are all God's gift, and precious therefore to God and to each other, just as we are. Grace becomes experiential in that lived conviction known as faith, specifically in the faith of Jesus.

The grace of Jesus means, then, first that basic feature of all life and existence in which it is revealed as the precious gift of a gracious Father God, a feature of reality which came to consciousness in the distinctive faith-conviction of Jesus and which was realized or made real in his life-mission. That basic feature of all our existence was realized or made real supremely in the death of Jesus – and that is why Paul can speak of the grace and of the self-sacrificing death of Jesus in parallel phrases. For, as already remarked, to sense life as the gift of the gracious God is to hold it in a gesture that is less a grasping or tearing than a holding in trust, ready to give and to give up: gift is never so much gift as when it enables one to give. Grace was never more realized in the life of Jesus than it was in his death. He had lived out in his life the faith-conviction that all was grace and God was gracious to all; he had given his life in witness to this conviction and in the openness and service to others which that conviction required for its own realization. When that lived conviction threatened the power-structures of his society to the point where those who manned these structures, in full conviction that they were necessary for the people's peace, decided that he should therefore be executed, then he gave his life in that final and complete gesture of witness to his faith-conviction and so consummated his lived conviction of grace. He thus gave it the greatest power, the supreme inspirational potential, the most effective spirit, that any lived conviction can be given on this earth.

The grace of which Paul speaks, then, is the grace of Jesus because Jesus so brought to consciousness in his faith and made so real in his life that feature of existence which is called the givenness of creation or the Fatherhood of God, that the conviction and the reality were inspirational, contagious. According to the priorities already outlined, he first gave to others, by his openness and service to them, and supremely by giving up life itself for the sake of the coming to them of the reign of God, a concrete experience of being graced by him, and in this way he opened up for others the possibility of the conviction, the faith that all was grace, and each was grace to all, that God was Father.

So Paul can speak of grace without qualification, or of the grace of God, or of the grace of Jesus, and say that it is the saving of us. To be truly graced by the world in its greatness and smallness, its joy and suffering, to live in this state of grace, this overcomes the grasping and coveting, the tearing away and boasting, with all their life-destroying implications. It does this when we can 'receive it' in faith, that is to say, when the faith of Jesus, inspired in us by him, enables us to see all life and existence as grace, enables all life and existence to grace us, and simultaneously empowers us to grace others. This is the conviction of grace, the experience and power of grace, the reality of grace that Jesus brought into our history, particularly by his death, and because of that, to Paul, he is Christ, Son of God and Lord.

The self-same logic works through Paul's treatment of faith – perhaps his major concept for the achievement, effect and significance of Jesus in his own life and in the lives of his converts. The faith of which Paul speaks is the faith of Jesus. 'We have believed in Christ Jesus', he reminds his converts in Galatia, 'in order to be justified by the faith of Christ' (Galatians 2.16), that is to say, we make Jesus the object of our faith and trust because his faith alone allows us to stand right before God and each other in this world. One way of expressing this faith of ours in Jesus is to call him our Lord, the Lord of our lives and destinies. And this brings us back again to the thought behind the hymn in Paul's Epistle to the Philippians (2.6-11). Because Jesus proved himself a man of faith through death itself, and so

inspired a similar faith in us, a version of his own distinctive
life-enhancing faith (so that we 'live by the faith of the Son of
God'), he is our Lord; that is now his name or title. The faith
which justifies us, in Paul's symbolism, is the faith of Jesus. It is
ours because it was his and is of his inspiration; and because of
this he is our Christ and Lord, and Son of God to us.

Finally, the spirit of which Paul speaks – the last of the four
main concepts and symbols which form Paul's substitute
analysis of what Jesus called the reign of God – is the spirit of
Jesus. In fact, just as he can speak of grace, without
qualification, or of the grace of God, or of the grace of Jesus,
which, when it becomes grace to us, makes Jesus our Christ and
our Lord, so Paul can speak of the Spirit without qualification,
or of the Spirit of God, or of the Spirit of Jesus who is the Christ
(I Corinthians 8.9-11). Spirit, as we already noted, is one of
those primordial symbols; it is taken from the image of the air
which is breathed. As a mythic symbol it refers to that in us
which makes us live and live more fully, to the source of life in
us, to the source of life itself, to the very power that makes
existing things be, to the power of life over threatening death. In
Paul's tradition, as indeed in Paul's own letters, the word can
refer to human beings in so far as they are truly sustained by
God, or to God's sustaining power, or to God himself as the
power of being. So to say that the spirit which is in us now,
enhancing our lives and giving us unlimited hope for the future,
is the spirit of Jesus, is tantamount to saying that Jesus himself
plays some role in fashioning God's relationship to us.

The spirit of which Paul speaks is the spirit of Jesus. Jesus
lived by the spirit of God. The very spirit that breathed the
powerful breath through his whole mission was the spirit of the
one, true God. Those whom he inspired, those whom he
inspires still, live by the power of the spirit of God, because they
live the graced life, the life of Jesus' distinctive faith with all its
practical implications for openness and service and all its
engendered hope; and this they now know as the spirit of Jesus
– because, simply, it was the spirit of Jesus, and it is precisely
because it was the spirit which animated Jesus' own public mission that it is now the spirit which animates their lives. Jesus, to
those who can live such lives, or at least try to, is God's
anointed, the Christ.

The logic by which the myth of Jesus developed from Jesus'
own lived myth of the rule of God is by now transparent. Jesus,
because of the life he lived and enabled others to live, because of

the grace he knew and allowed others to know, because of the faith he had and inspired others to have, because of the spirit he breathed into a dying world, in his verbal myth, his prayer, his table-fellowship, his practical ministry ... Jesus, because of all this, proved significant, to put the matter mildly, in humanity's struggle for life over death; and people who prove significant in this way are the material of which myths are made, for which myths are needed. Myth, it is hardly necessary to repeat, is an imaginative or symbolic way of plumbing these depths of human experience in the world at which ultimate questions are asked and attempts are made to come to grips with them.

So much for the logic which justified those who lived Jesus' own myth of the Fatherhood of God in their formulation of the myth about Jesus. This same logic, incidentally, when applied specifically to the first comprehensive formulation of the myth about Jesus, contained in the resurrection preaching, is the only possible answer to the question which ended Chapter 2: why this myth of the death of this man? and also to the question which ended Chapter 3 (an extension of the former question): why this myth of the man who died on the cross?

If we now turn our attention from the logic which justifies the myth to some details of the main stages through which this myth about Jesus developed, we shall first have to recall some conclusions already reached about the resurrection, then consider in more detail such titles as Christ, Son of God, and Lord, from which the myth is further woven, and finally move into the great christological definitions of the early tradition.

The resurrection of Jesus is primarily a symbolic way of expressing the fact that Jesus is a life-giving spirit. So concluded our study of the main texts. Resurrection, we noticed then, is a symbol. The two Greek words which lie behind 'resurrection' in the New Testament refer literally to waking up and to rising or getting up. Just as going to sleep or going down (e.g. into a grave) are symbols of death, waking or rising is a symbol of new life. And like all images that become symbols by invoking different levels of experience, the image of waking or rising becomes a symbol by invoking different levels at which the word 'life' applies to our existence. Jesus, those who follow his way know, is a life-giving spirit. He inspires in his followers that lived conviction of the Fatherhood of God which enhances and enriches life for us all, and enables a limitless hope to germinate. Other symbols, corresponding to resurrection, which are woven into this first comprehensive myth of the man Jesus, are those of exaltation, ascension, session at the right hand of power, spirit breathing. None of these, since they belong to the realm of symbol and myth, can be taken literally. None describes in literal detail an actual event in the history of the man Jesus which can be situated in a particular moment of time (on the third, fortieth, or fiftieth day after his death), or at a particular place (outside Jerusalem, over the Mount of Olives, in the heavens, in an upper room, in Jerusalem). The resurrection of Jesus as the single symbol which amongst all these has achieved such dominance in use as to in fact represent all the others is the first comprehensive, narrated symbol, the first myth of the man Jesus.

The truth which this first comprehensive myth tells about Jesus did not somehow become true of him after his death, though some people – and Paul in particular – may have come upon the truth about him only after his death, and though his death may have played a unique role in bringing the truth about him to light. The truth which this narrated symbol, this myth, tells about the man Jesus has already been outlined in the treatment of Paul's contribution to the chapter on resurrection.[13]

It tells that Jesus is, was and will be life-giving spirit, that is to say, that Jesus introduced into our world, and that he still introduces into our world a power or spirit – for it is palpable in our world still and will continue to be so – a power or spirit which can be alternately described as faith, a lived conviction that all life and existence comes to us as cherished gift from the hands of God, our Father, a persuasion of grace persuading us to be gracious, a sense of the richness of life motivating us to enrich life for all, and allowing us to hope, out of the depth of our conviction and the intensity of our commitment, that life will triumph over the harbingers of death, and finally triumph over the last enemy, death itself.

The resurrection myth also tells that Jesus, as life-giving spirit, experienced as such in the effects just mentioned, overcomes those features of our existence which form the negative side of our ambivalent sense of contingency. For the opposite to the faith of Jesus is the practice of grasping at finite things and finite achievements in a futile effort to sustain our spirits. This is orginal sin, idolatry. It is the very contrary to the experience of grace. It makes us slaves to the fear of death which reigns over all things finite. We sell ourselves to the wealth or position or power which we have set before us as our goal in life. A sickness enters the very heart of our existence. Our lives are impoverished and we threaten the life-prospects of those around us, making them our rivals, foils to our personal successes, part of our expense account in life, and as easily expendable. A pervasive sense of guilt invades our very sub-conscious, because some basic biological awareness tells us we have been unfaithful to the deepest dignity of our common humanity. We need some power or spirit to free us, to heal us, to make us repent, change our ways, stand us upright again, righteous or justified, as Paul would put it, before God and man.

The resurrection of Jesus as presented in the New Testament is, in its central element, the first comprehensive myth of Jesus. It is therefore the first comprehensive myth of the death of Jesus, the myth, above all else, of the man who died on Calvary, because the death of Jesus gave consummate significance to his life. So emerges the centrality of the death of Jesus in the assessment of his significance to his followers, and in all the ways in which they confess and celebrate that significance, in the writings they hold sacred, in the creeds they profess, in their distinctive ritual, in prayer, and in the practice of discipleship. So also it becomes understandable that the first comprehensive myth of the man Jesus should crystallize in particular round his death.

The faith of the historical Jesus by which he lived his life was his lived conviction that all things great and small, and particularly all people, were treasure, given us by our Father to be treasured as he, who gave them, treasured them. Jesus' achievement was to accept all those with whom he came in contact, as God accepted his children, especially those whom society decreed outcasts, to seat them at the ritual banquet, and to serve their real needs. Like the rest of us, the man Jesus came from nothing and he had nothing except what was given to him. His very life and everything which came to him in life was gift. Out of the bounty freely given he freely gave. Life itself, and everything that became part of that life, he held as a grace, as one holds a precious gift, gently, as one holds a soft, delicate thread which, as it is drawn back will, if one does not pull at it and break it, draw one to its very source. With this lived conviction, this faith that is made real only in act, he inspired some, and as deeply offended the deepest convictions of others. When force was brought to bear on him, inevitably, in order to make him divide and grasp like the rest, then, in final witness to the faith by which he lived and by which alone life is served, he refused to do so. He held the thread as gently as ever, as it was drawn back, and in doing so he deprived death of its sting, robbed it of its only victory. Death's victory over us is to enslave us in fear, to make us grasp more eagerly and tear more savagely at the things we think can give us the life we want, and, as we do so, feel more utterly the futility, and fear more persistently the hopelessness of it all. Jesus denied death that victory.

In denying death that victory, Jesus recorded the only victory over death, but also the one real victory over death, which it is given to mortals to achieve. The Prince of Life was victorious over death in the act of dying. The one whose conviction of grace had wagered for life in life, whose living faith had overcome in life the agents of death, the grasping, tearing divisions of human kind, now consummated the victory of life over death by still treating life as grace at the one moment in which the conviction that life is gift is subjected to the ultimate test, the final trial, the moment when the gift is withdrawn. His death was the supreme act of faith in God the Father, the giver of the grace of life, and so it was the supreme act of hope.

The death of Jesus, of course, is seen from two very different angles by the New Testament writers, as well it ought to be. He died; he was killed. He went to his death; he was arrested, tried, found guilty and duly executed. Looked at from the second and more negative angle, his death was a refusal to join the death-dealing forces in human life, the people who placed their religion, morality, power, national identity in God's own place and killed in the name of these. It was a victory over the death-dealers. By refusing to join them even in the face of death, Jesus consummated his life-long refusal to join the forces of death, to deal death by opting for the philosophies and factions whose real goal, however they themselves might like to conceive it, is always death. His death was the supreme witness to his life mission, the supreme act of passive resistance to all that opposed that mission. In both cases his death was the ultimate inspiration of those who would follow him. If salvation is through the Law, as Paul put it, then Christ died to no purpose.

The resurrection myth says that Jesus breathes the spirit or power into our world which liberates and heals us and stands us upright again before God and man. The resurrection myth is a most comprehensive myth of the man Jesus because it tells the truth about Jesus who not only identified the positive features of existence and enhanced them, but also identified the negative features and overcame them. [14]

Unquestionably, the myth known as the resurrection (exalta-

tion, ascension, session at the right hand, spirit-breathing) of
Jesus contained within itself as an essential part of it the belief
that the individual Jesus himself lives beyond his death, that
Jesus of Nazareth lives with God, that the tomb did not see the
end of that particular person (here the imagery of the emptied
tomb finds its full force). Only that is not what our New Testament writers are primarily concerned to preach to us when they
preach the resurrection of Jesus. Therefore they do not provide
for us in any detail the kind of clear and cogent circumstantial
evidence which would first allow us to conclude that what we
have called the personal resurrection of Jesus himself took place,
so that we could then argue from that established fact to some
further conclusions about the faith of Jesus (that is, if such a fact
allows any logical steps to be taken to any such conclusion –
which is questionable). On the contrary, both Paul and the writers of the gospels and Acts clearly press their treatment of the
resurrection in the direction of the experience we may have of
Jesus in our lives – an experience so potentially powerful that it
made of some, and still makes of some, as a total life-vocation,
apostles or preachers or teachers or purveyors of other types of
service to humanity – an experience without which evidence for
the personal resurrection of Jesus himself would presumably be
of little enough interest or import for the majority of human
kind. So, for those who make the New Testament their sacred
book, the personal resurrection of Jesus, like the prospect of
their own personal resurrection, is entailed in the living logic of
their faith experience, and is not susceptible of independent
evidence of its occurrence or independent detail about its
nature.

Another way of making the same point is to say that the New
Testament writers on resurrection are not so much interested in
the fact that Jesus of Nazareth lived again by God's act after he
had died, and not so much interested in the fact that he was
individually translated to a new form of existence, as they are
interested in depicting a new, dynamic role which he plays in
what they believe to be the divine direction of our history in this
universe. Now it is precisely this role which can be experienced
in our lives, if it is to be verified at all, in the manner explained
by the New Testament authors whenever they write about the
resurrection of Jesus. And it is precisely this role that calls for the
myth-maker's art. For, as we already remarked, myths which
move at that depth of human experience where ultimate questions are asked and attempts are made to deal with them do not

convey any literal information about worlds other than this one or about beings other than those we meet in this empirical world of ours. Rather, they identify those features of existence which hold out most promise for the continuity and increase of life – and they also identify those which threaten both – and they speak of the ultimate ground and guarantor of being in terms of the former. So the myth of the man Jesus identifies his spirit, his faith, as these have been described, as the life-enhancing elements which can give us life and life more abundant; and it identifies Jesus himself as the source of this spirit and faith. For that reason, and because it moves at this depth, the myth inevitably considers the role of Jesus *vis-à-vis* the very source of life and existence in our universe. And so the resurrection myth, the first comprehensive myth of the man Jesus, forms a natural context for, and has as its natural complement, the titles conferred on Jesus in the New Testament and afterwards, titles like those we have already met, Christ, Son of God, Lord. For the resurrection of Jesus in the New Testament is never preached simply in terms of God's revival of a corpse, but rather in terms of God's raising, exalting Jesus to the status of Christ, Son of God, Lord. 'What God promised to the fathers, this he has fulfilled to us their children by raising Jesus; as also it is written in the second psalm, "Thou art my Son, today I have begotten thee" ' (Acts 13.32). 'God has made him both Lord and Christ, this Jesus whom you crucified' (Acts 2.36), 'designated Son of God in power according to the Spirit of holiness by his resurrection from the dead, Jesus Christ our Lord' (Romans 1.4).

Such titles conferred on Jesus comprise the second principal way in which the development of the myth about Jesus is carried through by his early followers. Hence a brief survey of these titles provides the best illustration of the development of the myth of Jesus in the early Christian centuries.

The titles: building the Jesus myth

The second and more scattered form of the myth of Jesus – growing out of the resurrection kerygma – is composed of the titles conferred on Jesus in scripture and tradition by those who from the beginning sensed and stated the significance and power of the Prince of Life in their living and dying.

The most important question to be asked about titles, then, concerns their place in forming the myth of Jesus, their contribution as internal images or symbols in the development of the myth of Jesus, their role in explaining the deep significance of Jesus for human destiny. Inquiry into the contribution of the titles to the evolution of the myth of Jesus, however, has often been distracted from this, its major concern, by two other types of question asked about the titles.

The first question asks whether Jesus made use of any of the New Testament titles in forming his own self-understanding during his mission or in communicating this to others. Affirmative answers to this question vary with the authors consulted. The most recent Christology of Walter Kasper argues that Jesus made use of the title 'the Son (of God)', that he accepted the title 'Messiah' at least at the trial, and that he spoke of the Son of Man at least in the third person. Cullmann believed that Jesus himself forged a unique unity between the hitherto disparate titles of Messiah and Suffering Servant. Fuller who, like Cullmann, bases a whole New Testament christology on a study of the titles, thinks that Jesus understood himself in terms of eschatological prophet. Tödt is convinced that Jesus used the title Son of Man to pass judgment on those who would not accept him. And so on. [15] The solution to this question of Jesus' own use or non-use of the New Testament titles probably leads us beyond the bounds of what our source material could reasonably decide for us. We already outlined the life of Jesus as a life of faith, a very distinctive faith, and a living out of this faith's practical implications in prayer, ritual and service, and we presented an account of his death. Not much more can be said with certainty about his life – or needs to be said. The way he spoke in parables and prayer, the way he acted in ritual and service, this was more than sufficient to inspire dedicated disciples and to create implacable enemies, more than sufficient to win for him all the significance for human kind which myth attempts to communicate. It would probably have been unwise for him to adopt any of the New Testament titles for purposes of personal designation, and this for two reasons.

First, the distinctive faith of Jesus can only be conveyed by contagion – as we saw – not imposed by claims to any alleged positions of authority. There are significant differences between claiming titles for oneself and having them conferred by others. For one thing, claiming titles for oneself in the course of recommending one's proposals certainly implies a decision to go the way of power and authority, rather than the way of service. For another, such claims either leave one open to one's hearers' version of the expectations contained in the title (think only of someone claiming the title Messiah amongst the warring factions of Galilee and Judaea), or they impose on one the necessity of appending detailed interpretations of the precise meaning in which one wishes one's claims to be understood. That last consideration is even more relevant to the next point.

Second, as we shall see in the very next paragraph, each of the New Testament titles was already formed in a particular cultural milieu, and use of it by Jesus would therefore have invited the listener to understand Jesus on his or her terms rather than have his or her life changed on Jesus' terms. In that case, the figure of Jesus would have been fragmented into as many titles as it is thought he used and the Bauers of this world would be right after all – that the Jesus we can now know is simply a montage of different philosophies and myths, and not a unique person whose unique spirit changed the shape of human destiny.

The second question asked about the titles inquires after the cultural origin of each title used in the New Testament, for none is original to the New Testament, all are borrowed. This inquiry is not only legitimate in itself, but it can be of considerable help in trying to arrive at an historical account of the development of the traditions about Jesus. Three broad cultural milieux have been identified through which the preaching of Jesus and the tradition about him passed and from which titles for Jesus are known to have been drawn.

Palestinian Jews sometimes envisaged a better future in messianic terms (Messiah, Son of David); sometimes in apocalyptic terms (the Son of Man theme from Daniel); and sometimes in less specific terms of a prophet, perhaps a prophet who would finally usher in God's own age, the eschaton. Hellenistic Jews, the Jews who had gone abroad into an empire that was Greek in culture, though by the time of Jesus Roman in administration, had naturally less interest in messianic or apocalyptic hopes, so they favoured more titles such as Lord, a title which could be conferred on anyone from a freeman, through a Roman Emperor, to a divine saviour of one of the mystery religions, and which was often used in Greek translation of Jewish scriptures for Yahweh himself. Hellenistic Jews would also be familiarized by their Greek scriptures – Proverbs, Qoheleth, and the apocryphal Wisdom of Solomon – with the personification of Wisdom as a kind of intermediary between God and this world. Philo, a part contemporary of Jesus and a very philosophical Jew of Alexandria, had personified the Word or Logos of God and even referred to it as the elder son of God. Finally, in purely

Graeco-Roman cultural circles, the conventions of emperor worship, adopted somewhat unevenly by Roman emperors, had
some of these emperors proclaimed Lords, Gods, Sons of God (if
only by apotheosis after death) and Saviours, the gospels or
good news of whose coming were heralded by annunciations.
There was more, much more; but this gives some idea of the
variety of titles which lay ready to hand for preachers of Jesus as
they spread out from Palestine to convert the known world to
his cause.

It would clearly be outside the scope of this present study to
trace the origin of all the New Testament titles for Jesus, to
categorize the rich variety of their meanings or contents, to
show in each case how they were each and all adapted to form
the myth of Jesus, and much more so to try to plot in this way
the detailed historical development of that myth. The matter is
extremely complicated, the scholarly literature rather extensive,
and the range of scholarly opinion even broader than that
encountered on the question of Jesus' own use of titles. A few
brief examples may indicate the complexity of the task. Some
titles migrate with the Jesus tradition from one cultural milieu to
another and, in doing so, they change or even lose their original
meanings. The title Messiah or Christ, for instance, soon loses
all meaning and begins to function as part of Jesus' proper
name. He is no longer Jesus, the Christ, in a cultural milieu
which entertains no messianic expectations; he is simply Jesus
Christ, and other titles take over the task of drawing attention to
his historic significance; Jesus Christ our Lord, Jesus Christ
Superstar.

Some titles could acquire quite a variety of expectational content even in the same cultural milieu. Norman Perrin seems to
me to have demonstrated quite clearly that the apocalyptic title,
Son of Man, did not have any settled content which imposed
itself on all who used the title, but that the basic imagery of this
mysterious figure was flexible enough to lend itself to different
writers – the Jesus-people, the writers of the Similitudes of
Enoch, the writers of IV Ezra, and the composers of some of the
Talmudic and Midrashic traditions – in each case moulded by
these in order to express their own distinctive views of the
future which was to come and of the agents, real or symbolic,
who would bring it into being.[16]

Some titles sound as if they were adapted in a mood of
defiance. One way of making a prospective audience sit up and
pay attention is to use personified symbols which this particular

audience either does not want to hear at all, or has already reserved for its own chosen leaders and liberators. The intriguing suggestion has been made that it was his enemies' application of the title Christ to Jesus – he was, after all, executed as a messianic pretender of sorts – in addition to their derisive references to his followers as Christians or Messiah-freaks that really persuaded the latter to use and bear such titles proudly. And there is no doubt that Domitian, a Roman emperor of the last decade of the first century (about the time that John's gospel was written), claimed for himself the title of Lord and God, and presumably had his claim allowed ... by all except those who applied the title to Jesus. In such cases the very polemics involved in the use of these titles would force followers of Jesus either to keep refining their meaning in order to bring out the precise point of applying them to Jesus, or to suffer for them – or, as happened, to do both, for even developments and refinements of the symbolic contents do not always mollify those who can see that their chosen saviours of the human race are about to be upstaged.

Finally, in the gospels of the New Testament, even in the synoptics, from which people have long expected the more reliable historical data on Jesus, redaction critics in particular have shown how the meanings of the individual titles are often so fully subordinated to the over-riding christology of the gospel writer that the distinctive, original meanings of some of the titles have virtually disappeared from the text. According to Conzelmann's classical redaction critique of Luke, for instance, the latter's favourite titles for Jesus are Lord and Christ. All the original apocalyptic perculiarities of the title Son of Man have been lost and other titles used by Luke have virtually the same meaning as his favourite pair.[17] The meaning Luke attributes to Lord and Christ, in turn, must be gleaned from the over-riding christology of Luke's history, and not decided from some other sources and then read back into Luke. Luke's scenario places Jesus at the centre of time. While he was on earth, the Spirit of God through him held undisputed sway over a small area of our world and people knew what God's own reign was like. To this period all previous ages looked forward, and it is normative for all future time, its character made present to us still by the community in which the Spirit still breathes, by the message of the original witnesses, and by the commemorative meal. In such terms as these one understands what Luke means by calling Jesus Lord and Christ.

Matthew's book is quite clearly designed as a new Pentateuch, so that his over-riding view of Jesus casts the latter in the character of a new Moses, prophet *par excellence*, purveyor without equal of the Law of God, the new verbal revelation, the new religion which truly binds men to God and to each other.

Mark's gospel is now generally considered to be an apocalypse. But it is also a sustained criticism of the more naive realism of apocalyptic expectation which looks for dazzling sons of God to bring miraculous victories out of our tragic situation. Instead, Mark's Son of Man is one who suffers at the hands of his fellow men for the healing faith he spread amongst them and the grace he showed even to the lawless.[18] And Mark's message to the followers of Jesus is that they had better prepare for similar sacrifice and suffering before any success for their cause could even be envisaged.

Such in brief is the complexity of the task of tracing the titles of Jesus in the New Testament from their varied cultural origins, through their successive adaptations to the person and achievement of Jesus, until they reach the final meaning they acquired in the final redaction of the New Testament documents as we now have them. Such, too, is the reason for saying that it would be quite beyond the scope of the present book even to attempt this complicated task of tracing the early development of the myth of Jesus through the titles conferred on him. Some titles, of course, went on to inspire the great speculative christologies of the first five Christian centuries – and these we must meet again shortly.

Undoubtedly there was a real development in the myth of Jesus; there were different and successive christologies in vogue amongst the early followers of Jesus. Indeed, the fact that some of these outlived the stages of development in his followers' perception of the significance of Jesus to which they were originally adequate itself leads to much of what later came to be called heresy. For though the adoption of such personified symbols was, of course, an obvious ploy for those who wished to interest people from these different cultural milieux in the existential significance of Jesus, the danger they incurred in such adoption was similar to, if lesser than, that which we have argued might well have deterred Jesus himself from using these titles. That is to say, the title, with its fixed symbolic content in the mind of the user and hearer alike, might have worked to confine the person and achievement of Jesus to its terms, and might have quite unconsciously bred a resistance in the mind to any attempt to stretch its meaning sufficiently to accommodate the new and unique significance of this man.

It would have been natural enough for his earlier Palestinian followers to see and present Jesus as a divinely inspired prophet – perhaps a rival to Moses himself, in terms of Deuteronomy 18. 15-19 – and evidence can be excavated from the tradition by means of form-critical techniques to show that they did so. But such acclamation might just as easily have prevented people from seeing more and more clearly the truly radical achievement of Jesus, one which would so extend the traditional lineaments of the prophet's role as to make it in the end inadequate as a descriptive symbol for this man. Similarly, Son of God, either in its native Palestinian symbolism of the one obedient to God's (traditionally Jewish) will, or in its more Hellenistic symbolism of the one through whom divine power flowed to perform astounding physical and intellectual wonders, might also have prevented people from seeing how much Jesus radically challenged all conventional religion and how little he depended on literal miracle to do so (though this title, as we shall see, proved capable of greater conceptual expansion as time passed).

Scholarly research, then, into the titles of Jesus in the New Testament, with the aim of revealing something at least of the precise historical details of the complex development of the myth of Jesus, is as legitimate in itself as it is clearly outside the scope of the present work, which can afford only the following few closing remarks on this intriguing subject.

First, the symbolism of practically all those titles is very remote from contemporary minds. The symbolism of a messianic figure fleshed out on the skeletal memory of King David is no longer generally available to us Gentiles. The distance which separates a powerful president whose very subjects can call him Jimmy from a quasi-divine first-century emperor is just too great for the untrained mind to traverse. Prophets have been replaced by economic advisers, military strategists, social planners, consciousness raisers, and an incredible proliferation of counsellors; and we only know of masters and slaves – though we are thankful for this – from series syndicated from the BBC. UFOs are all that come with the clouds of heaven these days, and their inhabitants are said to be not at all like the sons of men. The Word of God, far from being capable of symbolic personification, has yielded to the arid linguistic analysis of God-talk, and the eternal wisdom of God on which our universe was once said to be founded was finally dismissed by Laplace, who is reputed to have said, in the name of science, 'I no longer need that hypothesis'. The whole Greek pantheon of gods, with their semi-earthly sons and daughters, has receded into the diminishing halls of departments of ancient classics; and initiation into mystical union with the saviours of the mystery religions has given way to the adolescent's first great drinking spree. In short, scarcely one of the titles is now capable of telling the significance of Jesus for human destiny – at least not without a long exegetical explanation, which could just as well replace it. In addition to old titles losing their meaning, and as if to corroborate the thesis that these have lost their meaning, new titles have emerged on the contemporary scene. Some of these are quite harmless: Jesus Christ Superstar. Some are lethal: Jesus Christ Guerrilla Fighter.

So, next, if we cannot use the New Testament titles nowadays, as once they could be used, without long interpretative derivations of their origins, and we cannot afford the time or space to try to trace the stages of their development in the myth of Jesus, and yet we need to know what to do about titles in general, what is left to do or say?

Well, we can at least insist on the general interpretative principle that it is the needs of the developing myth of Jesus which dictate the adaptation of the various titles; it is not the acquisition of the titles which dictates the direction in which the myth develops. And the logic by which the titles are adapted to flesh out the myth of Jesus is precisely the same logic which we discovered at work in our general analysis, in the writings of Paul, of the process by which the myth of Jesus developed from Jesus' own myth of the reign of God, from embodiments of the experience of the reign of God similar to those which Jesus used – prayer, table-fellowship, and service – or from expressions of the reign of God which were substituted for Jesus' own particular myth without any loss of its distinctive character. In short, it is precisely Jesus the pioneer and perfecter of that distinctive faith, Jesus the conveyor of that distinctive conviction of grace, Jesus the source of mutual service in the new fellowship of love and hope, *this* Jesus of deepest existential significance for human kind that all these titles are tailored to fit, and to present him to others, and thus they form part of the true myth of Jesus.[19]

Though we cannot pursue the early hazardous, though commendable, steps of the adaptation of the titles of Jesus, we have actually seen at least one important example of such adaptation in the theology of Paul. This was his particular adaptation of the title Lord, a title which, as we already noticed, could address anyone from a freeman to an emperor, from a cultic deity to Yahweh himself. (A Bantu lady – in itself, to a Boer, a contradiction in terms – from whom I once asked directions on the streets of Port Elizabeth, addressed me as 'master', a term of address used by an inferior person, as she had been led to believe she was, to a superior. That was one modern counterpart to the New Testament title Lord.)

For Paul to say that Jesus is Lord means to say that he is Spirit. He is a spirit or power in our lives, inspiring us with that distinctive and foundational faith which changes all our lives, keeping grace with us so that we should sense the grace of God in the world, arousing in us those latent qualities that enable us to serve the best interest of our fellow humans, and blessing us with unlimited hope. As Paul himself puts it, it is the Spirit that enables us to say that Jesus is Lord (I Corinthians 12.3). Paul adapts the current range of meaning of the title Lord, therefore, to refer to the person and presence of this particular powerful Spirit. Or, to put the matter the other way round, it is precisely because we know Jesus as the spirit who introduces us to that distinctive faith and love and hope that we call him Lord.

Second, though we do not have the data, the space or the expertise to trace all the early requisitions and adaptations of the New Testament titles for Jesus, we can take two of those titles and trace their paths, however sketchily, through much longer periods of time in which they wielded unusual influence on the development of the full myth of Jesus. We shall thus enter on an era in which the literature is much more abundant and the lines of the logic which has occupied our attention in this chapter much more clear. We shall, we hope, see the final development of the myth of the man, Jesus, and the full cogency of the logic which binds this developing myth to the myth in which Jesus himself lived and which he inspired others to live.

The two titles we choose are Word of God and Son of God, the latter quite frequent in the New Testament, the former very infrequent, deriving most of its familiarity from the Prologue to the Fourth Gospel. Both are symbols drawn from the most natural of our experiences and carrying, therefore, the promise of the most powerful impact. Probably since the origin of language people have sensed in the word the most effective means of making their presence felt, of communicating their understanding of things, of ordering affairs according to their wishes. Obviously a symbol drawn from such natural imagery could not long escape the interest of religious artists. And in fact some of the earliest records of religious faith show God's effective presence in the world, drawing people's attention to him, making people 'hear' and heed, depicted as God's word.[20] To procreate, to bear, or to be a son, is also a powerful natural image that, as we saw, can symbolize love and allegiance, fidelity and cooperation, on one side; love and trust and pride, and extension of one's influence and presence, on the other. This symbol, too, was used from time immemorial in the cultures from which Jesus' culture developed. The king, in particular, who was principal agent of peace and prosperity, order and justice in the land, and who was arbiter of life and death, could be called Son of God, and was so titled. More generally, anyone thought to know the mind of God or to do God's will or to possess some of God's attributes in exceptional degree could be called Son of God, and sometimes was so called (Wisdom of Solomon 2. 13-18).

These two titles, then, have long ages of tenure and broad ranges of cross-cultural relevance in religious usage. They attracted the attention of philosophers as well as myth-makers. They are largely responsible for carrying the development of the myth of Jesus far beyond the spatial, temporal, and cultural limits of the New Testament writings, into different forms of the perception and expression of the significance of Jesus, to the point where Christians engage in abstract conceptual terms with the divinity incarnate in Jesus.

6

Faith in the Founder: the Question of Divinity in Human Form

Acknowledging founders of faiths

The myth of Jesus relates him to divinity. There is nothing odd about that. It is clear, in the case of myth in general, that when images evoke the deepest levels of experience possible, they sift the life-supporting from the life-destroying forces and from the former they name or describe or 'reveal' the divinity as the ultimate source and support of life.

Now when it is an actual individual who puts us in active touch with the most fundamental life-supporting force, and who identifies for us the ultimate life-destroying elements as he or she sees them, and empowers us to meet and overcome them, then we must extend to such a one the myth in which this vision of life's final prospects is expressed. And so we inevitably relate such a one to divinity.

For it is seldom a disembodied vision, a purely theoretical conviction, that enables us to come to grips with the most crucial forces in existence, and so relates us to the furthest ground of being which we conventionally call God. No, it is a vision embodied at some point of human history, a conviction lived out in the life of some particular human being, that inspires us and empowers us so. As a consequence, the myth which expresses to us such high vision and such deep conviction naturally extends itself to embrace the one who brought us both vision and conviction in the first place, and as the myth at this depth, as part of its natural evocation, furnishes our images of God, so it naturally conveys some special relationship between God and this one who brought the experience of God into our lives by means of this very vision, this lived conviction, this particular form of human faith.

Myths which move at a certain depth of human experience in the world are religious myths. This is because they make us acutely conscious of those conditions of existence – elsewhere referred to as the contingency of existence – which are, in Tillich's phrase, of ultimate concern to us; and they try to equip us with those qualities of conviction, courage and commitment, they offer us the light, the sense of direction, and the inspiration which enable us to deal with these conditions. Those great ones from our past, whether real or imaginary, well remembered or half legendary, whose religious myths enable us to come to creative terms with our existential contingency are the founders of faiths, and as historical truthfulness requires, they are acknowledged as such in the confessions of those in whose spirits they managed to found their faith.[1] They are acknowledged precisely by being drawn into the myth in which they lived and enabled others to live.

For if I find that I can relate to divinity as revealed by one of these founders, I must confess, as a matter of plain historical fact, that I could not have related so to divinity were it not for this founder. Such dependence of followers on founders for actual access to divinity is an actual and historical fact of the faith founded and, consequently, in the verbal and other symbolic elements of the confession of this faith the founder's particular mediation of divinity to disciples must be symbolized and confessed. The founder's own original and originating relationship to divinity must become part of the myth told by the disciples.

The self-same logic, therefore, which drew the myth about Jesus from the myth which Jesus lived, once it is recognized that the myth in question here is a religious myth, explains how Jesus must be related to divinity in the confession of faith of his followers. So, to return for a moment to Paul's terminology, it makes no difference to Paul whether he talks of faith simply, or of the faith of Jesus, whether he talks of life simply or the life of Jesus, for this can be our faith and our life precisely because it was the life and faith of Jesus and he is its author in our history; and more significantly still in the present context, it makes no difference to Paul whether he writes of the spirit simply, or the spirit of Jesus, or the spirit of God, and he can equally interchange references to grace, the grace of Jesus, and the grace of God.

For this distinctive faith, this particular conviction of grace, this powerful spirit, which Jesus mediates to others, puts them in living, experiential contact with the one in whom they live

and move and have their being. This makes Jesus mediator between God and those who are capable of this faith, and so they
must draw him into their confession of faith if they are to tell the
whole truth about this faith. For those, on the contrary, who
have not caught the spirit of Jesus, no confession is justified
which would involve his person. He does not relate them to any
divinity, and so for them he stands in no particular relation to
divinity. He is at most another interesting historical figure
whom they see perhaps as the proponent of a theory about the
human condition, and even that theory they may not accept just
because he proposed it, or at least they may say that they do not
accept it because he proposed it. At most they might do him the
honour of saying that he anticipated some of their finest
thoughts: acknowledgment of a kind, yes, but one which falls
far short of the acknowledgment to which founders of faiths at
least are entitled and which in the case of Jesus we must
examine in detail.

The point, however, of the present chapter is this. The sacred
books or solemn formulae of all the world's faiths relate their
founders to the absolute as, we have just seen, they must. But
for the most part they each do so differently from the others. Is
there a logic by which the differences can be justified? Is there a
way of understanding, not just the fact that the members of a
faith relate their founder to God or the absolute, but the particular manner in which they forge that relationship within their
particular religious tradition? In terms more immediate to our
purpose, is there a way of justifying the particularly Christian
confession about Jesus?

A painstaking analysis of the myths of the founders of the
world's living faiths – an analysis more extensive than this book
or its writer has either the space or the data to provide – would
surely show some distinctive pattern by which is revealed the
further logic of each myth's refinement to the point where it
forges its own peculiar relationship between the founder and
the absolute which he sought in human fashion to reveal. But,
even if we cannot provide such a detailed survey from the history of religions, we can take some brief samples from that
extensive field, and see if suggestions of a pattern emerge.

The founder of Buddhism was a young man called Siddhartha, of the Gautama family, who lived in the sixth century
BC. The highest title which the myth of this man conferred on
him was the title Buddha, from which the faith he founded took
its name, just as Christianity took its name from one of Jesus'

earliest titles, the Christ. Now Buddha can be translated, 'the enlightened one', because Siddhartha was accredited by those who followed him with having mapped out the paths which led the way to human enlightenment about the absolute reality which is hidden behind the illusory reality of this empirical world.[2] Enlightenment here is a dominant symbol. Narrated in the account of Siddhartha's life and achievement, it becomes the myth of the man. It is the centre and essence of this faith, then, which determines the precise way in which the founder is described *vis-à-vis* the absolute; and it is this which determines the exact way in which the myth when fully refined relates the founder to the absolute. The absolute in the faith founded by Siddhartha is a hidden depth of reality the way to which must be lighted, revealed. Hence Siddhartha is related to the absolute (Nirvana) as the one who lights the way. He is the enlightened one, the Buddha, to whom the way has been revealed.

The quest of the historical Zoroaster, the founder of one of the great ancient religions of the world who also lived in the sixth century BC, is even more complicated than the quest of the historical Jesus. But it appears that he was considered by his followers to have been a visionary who had 'seen' the one good God, and above all to have been a prophet who heard, or heeded, or obeyed[3] the word spoken to him and in turn spoke it to his people.[4] The dominant myth of this founder, probably created and propagated by the man himself, and accepted by those who followed him, described him as a confidant, a 'friend' of Ahura Mazdah, the one, true, holy and bountiful God. The centre and essence of this faith, this ethical monotheism so like the Jewish religion in many ways, was the hearing and obeying of the detailed verbal revelation of what people were to believe and to do, and of what they were to avoid, in the hope that they would one day be companions of Ahura Mazdah, as their founder already was. Hence the dominant myth of the Zoroaster, founder of this faith, related the latter to the divinity precisely as visionary and prophet of Ahura Mazdah.

Early in the sixth century AD Muhammad founded the faith known as Islam. The myth of this man makes use of the purest form of the prophet image to be found in religious literature. Orthodox Islam presents its founder as one purely passive to the verbal revelations of the one, true God, Allah. Later development of the myth did have Muhammad ascend to heaven where he enjoyed briefly the vision of God, and a mystical offshoot of Islam talked of the Light of Muhammad existing from before creation and enlightening the other prophets.[5] But these are adventitious and somewhat peripheral factors in the myth. The centre and essence of Islam (a word which means commitment to God's will) is the belief in a verbal revelation of the prescriptions of the Koran, prescriptions which, once again, govern all that the followers of Muhammad, the first one fully to commit himself to the express will of Allah, must believe and do and avoid. Since this is the centre and essence of this faith, the dominant myth naturally relates its founder to God as the one who passively received God's verbal revelations, and committed himself to them and faithfully transmitted them to the people. The verbal-prescriptive essence of this faith is confirmed by the myth of the last judgment when all will be judged by their adherence to the Koran. And it is consistent with Muhammad's role that he will then play the advocate for his people at this final judicial hearing.

This is brief and hasty sampling indeed of the manner in which the myth developed by the members of a particular faith finds the proper symbols for the precise relationship of the founder to the object of that particular faith, the one conventionally known as God in most faiths, but differently conceived in each of them. But even from such brief and hasty sampling, suggestions of a logical pattern already begin to emerge, and that logic can be tested in the case of the Christian confession of faith.

The logic is this: it is the specific nature of the faith or religion founded which dictates to the believer the exact relationship in which the founder stands to the divinity. In other words, the specific nature of the faith or religion founded will decide what titles, what final form of the myth of the founder is necessary in order to tell the whole truth. If the specific nature or essence of the faith consists in enlightenment, then the founder will be mythically presented in the symbols of enlightened and enlightener and his or her relation to the absolute will be that of one who lights the path to the absolute for others. If the essence of the religion is thought to be obedience, commitment to the verbal revelation of the will of God, then the founder must be mythically presented in the symbolism of hearing God's word and speaking this to his or her followers, and his or her relationship to the absolute must be seen by those who accept this faith as that of prophet of the Most High, that is to say, literally, the one who speaks for the Most High its specific will for the rest of humanity.

In each case, to repeat the logic briefly, the nature of the faith experience which relates the disciple to God dictates how the one who made this faith possible for the disciple stands between the disciple and God. The final myth of the founder, then, in every case tells how the founder brings the believer to God, and God to the believer, and so situates the founder for the believer in his or her precise relationship to God. It follows, then, quite logically that the final myth of the founder must still tell of the precise kind of faith by which the founder brought the believer to God and God to the believer. The nature of the original faith-experience, and not any additional information, shows the believer how the founder has brought God close and so how the founder must be envisaged in relationship to God. Thus it is the nature of the faith-experience by which the founder makes one a believer which develops in the believer's mind the final myth of the founder or, alternatively, the final set of symbols or concepts in which the believer tells the whole truth about faith and founder alike.

The full-grown myth: the defeat of Arius

Within three centuries of the death of Jesus it was being said officially by the leaders of his followers that the Word or Son of God incarnate in him was 'one in being with the Father', probably the most substantial literal claim ever made about a known historical founder of a religion.

As well as answering the question, why a myth of this man? some attempt must also be made to answer the question, why *this* myth of this man? And, as in the case of justifying the myth of Jesus in general both an historical and a logical part were required, these same parts are also required in any attempt to justify the furthest refinements of this myth, if, once again, these can be justified at all. For there are, of course, peculiar problems which arise when the myth of the man Jesus makes such clear and enormous claims about him. The question arises, for example, as to whether we are any longer dealing in mythic terms. The statement that the Word or Son of God incarnate in Jesus is 'one in being with the Father' seems to represent a conceptual construct, and as such must be meant to be taken quite literally, it would seem. Even so, the problem of justification remains basically the same.

A more serious question, then, would be this one: does it not change the nature of the faith of Jesus when the faith of his followers becomes faith in Jesus in such an absolute way? After all, from everything we have seen, it would seem that the faith which Jesus tried to elicit in his followers was that radical perception, evaluation, and lived conviction that all things were God's grace, and that God, correspondingly, was Father. If now we are to confess the divinity of Jesus, in the precise form of considering him Son or Word of God incarnate, and as such equal to the Father, has not the whole focus of faith changed for us and with it faith's very nature? For what could strange supernatural incarnation events of a Son or Word of God, who is one in being with the Father, have to do with the radically human, down-to-earth creation faith of the book of Genesis and the parables of Jesus?

Or, to put the matter another way, surely by the time the Christian tradition evolves such a literal acknowledgment of its founder, the logic which we thought we discovered in the preceding section has long ago broken down. This is the logic according to which the precise kind of acknowledgment which a founder receives is dictated by the kind of religious faith he or she founds. How could it possibly be true in the case of Jesus that the faith which Jesus founded should dictate faith in Jesus as the incarnate Son or Word of God? Let us proceed patiently here, since painstaking procedure is necessary at this point, and begin by enquiring about the development of these furthest reaches of the myth of Jesus. As we trace this development we may simultaneously test the logic and we may hope to arrive at some sort of satisfactory answer to the questions just posed.

One often gets the impression from the writings of experts in the period now under review that no substantial development in the myth of Jesus took place at all between the late first and the early fourth centuries – at least if we mean by development, not simply change in the ways things are said, but actual increase or decrease in the substance of what is said. There is a debate, for instance, on whether or not Jesus is called God in set terms in the New Testament itself. To the extent that this debate goes in favour of proponents of the thesis that Jesus is called God in set terms in the New Testament,[6] the impression would certainly be conveyed that no more substantial claim could be made for Jesus in the course of the tradition.

Now the assertion may well be true that there is no significant development in the substance of the claims made about Jesus between the first century and the fourth – however much the terms in which the claims were made may have changed – but it is still doubtful that to say Jesus was called God in set terms in the New Testament is the proper way to make that point. For, first, as already remarked, every instance in the New Testament in which it is said that Jesus is called God in set terms is strenuously debated, and can therefore be called in doubt by honest and scrupulous scholars. But, second, and far more important for the solution to our present problem, the statement 'Jesus is God', together with kindred references to the divinity of Jesus, is a kind of popular shorthand by which a very subtle relationship indeed between Jesus and the God he called Father is commonly indicated. Such popular shorthand is inevitable where a deep and cherished conviction, complex and subtle in communicable terms, requires that constant reference which deep and cherished convictions tend to require.

Consequently, if in the literature of the early Christian centuries there are many repetitions of the blunt statement that Jesus is God, these must surely be understood in the context of the elaborate explanations of that conviction to which that same literature devotes a considerable amount of its space.[7] Which, in turn, means that we still have to pursue our quest of the history and logic of the development of the myth of Jesus through the many evocations of symbol and the nice adjustments of concept at least until we reach the 'one in being' of Nicaea, for there, as we already remarked, we find what is perhaps the most substantial *literal* claim ever made about a known historical founder of a religion. After that claim is established there is nothing left to christology but the admittedly tortuous task of explaining how one in whom the Son or Word of God was declared incarnate could still be fully and truly human, and but one individual person despite all that. (The fact that the tradition has said 'Jesus is man' as clearly as it has said 'Jesus is God' should be adequate enough warning to people that the latter of these statements would have to be interpreted and explained.)

Now it is clear that all the titles used of Jesus in the New Testament relate him to God – and the logic which justifies this relationship has already been investigated and found cogent. Even the title Son of Man which is sometimes used in the New Testament to bring into strong relief the human condition of Jesus and his distinctive contribution to that condition trails behind it the threads that link it to religious contexts, and to the figures of those who do God's work in the world. It has also been said that there is evidence in the New Testament of titles becoming obsolete – 'prophet' seems to have been dropped early on, and Messiah becomes part of his proper name – and so there is evidence, at the beginning of the tradition at least, of some substantial development in the myth of Jesus. It is probable that the full implications of the faith that Jesus tried to foster did not dawn at once, especially on his fellow Jews – to whom the titles of prophet and Messiah would have been natural options – hence they were largely unable to appreciate the revolutionary character of his role in changing the religious allegiance of those who would fully become his followers.

But long before the writings which comprise our New Testament are completed, it is being said that Jesus breathes or sends the spirit, indeed that he is himself the spirit, a spirit which turns us from evil, gives life and the qualities which make life more abundant. Now spirit is the oldest and most impressive symbol for divinity in this tradition. At the opening of the book of Genesis the spirit of God hovers over the primeval waters and creation and life are under way. 'God is spirit,' as John puts it, 'and those who worship him must worship in spirit and truth' (John 4.24). What was long attributed to and expected from God is now attributed to and expected from Jesus; that he is our saviour as God was *go'el* of Israel, for instance, and that he will be our judge. Only the direct act of creation is denied Jesus as Lord, though, precisely in so far as he is the image of God, he is naturally professed to have a role in God's creative activity (for God creates in accordance with his own image)[8], and he does directly affect the renewal of creation which the prophets expected. It is therefore commonplace for New Testament scholars to observe, as Hermann has done, that there is a functional identity between Jesus, experienced now in the community as Lord, and the divine spirit,[9] or, more generally, that Jesus is functionally related to God, if not functionally identical with God in the New Testament.

Finally, to press home a point already made about the titles of Jesus in the New Testament: a title like Lord, which can range in meaning anywhere from the polite 'sir' to a substitute name for Yahweh, or a title like Son of God, which can range anywhere from reference to Israel's more faithful and graceful moments to a divine or semi-divine individual, such titles are finally designed to express just that functional identity between Jesus and God which Christian experience suggests. Jesus introduces to the lives of his followers just that power or spirit which they always expected from God. Functional is the operative word; it is sometimes distinguished from ontological, and sometimes, too, the distinction is meant to prepare us for the assertion that functional terms for this relationship between Jesus and God are preferable.

This distinction between function and nature, as Cullmann would put it,[10] amongst the terms which try to define Jesus in relationship to God, with its accompanying suggestion of the superiority of the former, is nowadays part of a much more widespread discrimination against the conceptual, the philosophical, the Greek, and in favour of the concrete, the biblical, the Jewish.[11] One is sometimes at a loss to know precisely what is being suggested by such distinctions and discriminations. Perhaps the intention is to suggest that the biblical writers, being more inspired than their later counterparts, told the truth about Jesus in purer form and that later constructions of the same truth are almost necessarily impure by comparison (a version of the scripture versus tradition syndrome). Or perhaps the point is to try to prove that philosophical categories, Christian or otherwise, inevitably corrupt the truth since they represent the attempt to speak of the nature and being of God and of Jesus, which it is impossible to do, while it is possible, with the use of biblical imagery, to speak of the way in which God and Jesus function together in our lives.

It seems to the present writer to be quite futile, in any case, to try to plot one's way through the intricacies of the early tradition about Jesus while one is burdened by any of the above presuppositions. 'Nature', for instance, is as functional a word as any used of Jesus in the New Testament, though its reference is more general, and theirs more specific: it means 'the way in which a thing grows and functions'.[12] The simple fact of the matter is that the followers of Jesus, when they faced those whose culture was that of Greece and Rome, found themselves with a similar problem to that which they had in relating to their fellow Jews: in neither case, in Pelikan's words, could they claim a complete monopoly on either the moral or the doctrinal truths whose superiority they were seeking to demonstrate.[13] So they had to present their distinctive faith to people who had partially anticipated their vision and, in the case of both Jews and Greeks, this meant that they had to come to terms sooner or later with the familiar modes of thought, imagery and expression of those who could either become their converts or remain their opponents. There was simply no other way for the followers of Jesus to proceed then, nor has there been any other way for them to proceed down to the present day. The danger was always present of diluting their distinctive truth in the terms they borrowed from Jews and Greeks for the purpose of meaningful dialogue – Paul's epistles constantly advert to that danger in its more Jewish form. In every case, though, the danger is truly an occupational hazard, and the factor which facilitates historians in their attempt to attribute the danger almost solely to Greek thought is mainly the fact that the Jewish nation was virtually destroyed early in the second century and traditional Jewish thought, from that time on, was much less of a living threat to the alleged distinctiveness and the alleged superiority of the vision of truth which inspired the followers of Jesus.

So let us simply pursue our quest for the history and logic of the development of the myth of Jesus through its most formative years, bearing in mind no further distinctions of Jew or Greek, Bible or philosophy, function or nature, bearing only in mind what has already been said in an earlier section on myth (in Chapter 2 above). For myth, which deals in image and symbol, and philosophy, which relies almost exclusively on analysis and synthesis of abstract concept, can in their different ways reach the same depth of reality and can as accurately tell as much truth about it as is given to humans to perceive. Perhaps, though, in the present context, we could add as follows one more difference between myth and conceptual analysis to the differences already noted in the perceptual priorities and the manner in which these appeal to the subject – but this is as far as the present writer would be prepared to go in the direction of the often crudely expressed discriminations indicated above.

Briefly, myth, it seems, can take us to the final depth of possible human experience and particularly to the experience of God, by means of a process perhaps best described as evocation, whereas conceptual analysis can take us to the same depth by means of analytic adjustment. For it is characteristic of abstract concepts that they are meant to be taken literally, and so when one intends that they carry the mind to a level deeper than their first literal reference, one has to make literal, analytic adjustments to their connotation.[14] It is difficult to distinguish between evocation, on the one hand, and analytic adjustment, on the other, between the evocative power which makes an image symbolic and the type of explicit correction which alone fits common concepts for the deeper probes of the human mind. Certainly it is difficult to do this without the use of elaborate examples. But we already have the example of images of illness and cure which apply immediately and literally to the sickness and health of the organism with which the medical profession deals but which become symbols precisely by their power to evoke similar patterns of experience, of 'sickness' and 'wholeness' at levels of our experience much deeper than the organic. It is the similarities in the patterns of experience at different levels of that experience that allow this evocation to take place, and the image can be manipulated according to the canons of literary art, or some other art, so as to produce the evocation. The process is called evocative rather than analytic precisely because the mind is lured away from the literal interpretation as the original image becomes symbol. In this way the mind is directed on a certain line along which deeper and deeper levels of human experience can be plumbed until, at that point at which what is known as the experience of God takes place, the spirit is propelled outward (or inward, depending on your present preference of imagery) into darkness and formless space, where the familiar contours of the symbol no longer apply, and only the conviction is left that the direction is correct and that, along that route, one will somehow, sometimes come in closer contact with the absolute healer or saviour, or whatever the symbol is that, at the moment, stands for the unknown God.

It is characteristic of concepts, on the other hand, that they must be taken literally at every step of their use. Hence, if I wish to use the concept of cause, or substance, or person in order to set my mind on a trajectory that may carry it to the conviction of God, I may have to explain that the concept of cause may apply to an agency which does not itself undergo change when it effects change in something else; that the concept of substance may apply even where there is no possibility of dividing materially; that the concept of person may be made to convey distinctive individuality and nothing else. All of these are brief indications of analytic adjustment of concepts, adjusting their normal range of meaning quite literally and deliberately, because the conviction needs to be expressed that there is being above or within the empirical reality of our world which can be named cause or substance or person, but not as these words are normally understood. Once again, by means of this more pedantic method, the spirit is impelled along a trajectory until it reaches a point at which all recognizable content has been analytically adjusted to the stage of disappearance, and again all that is left is the conviction that the direction is correct and that along these routes, one will somehow, some time, come in closer contact with the 'First' Cause, the 'Real' Substance, or

Being of our empirical world, the Infinite Person who willed it all and knows its goal, or whatever concept it is that, at the moment, stands for the unknown God.

In both cases, it is scarcely necessary to observe, the process may come to a premature halt, and what can only be called idolatry can result, either by yielding to the temptation to take a symbol literally at some point, or by ceasing to adjust a concept and leaving it with still too much empirical content. In either case one reached a 'god' too much delimited on human terms, a god too well understood and too easily manipulated, in short, an idol.

Now it is characteristic of the two terms which we have chosen to plot the development of the myth of Jesus in its formative years – Son of God and Logos – that they can be treated either symbolically or conceptually. And what is characteristic of the post-biblical period is that, due to the tradition's necessary involvement with Greek philosophical thought, conceptual analysis becomes as strong a feature of the development of the confession of Jesus as does myth and symbolism. We shall therefore have to watch the two processes in the development of religious confession, symbolic evocation and analytic adjustment, and note the characteristic pitfalls of both (known, when they occur, as heresies). The ensuing investigation will therefore be somewhat more complicated, but with the same goal as before, namely, to note the history and question the logic of the development of the myth of Jesus. But first, since it is Greek philosophical theology which introduces the newer dimension to our quest at this point, let us make some brief, general remarks about the distinctive contributions of that great ancient tradition of human speculation.

One of the most pervasive problems of the religious quest from the beginning has been the problem of affirming, simultaneously, the transcendence and immanence of the divine; for if divinity did not reach far beyond our empirical world it would perhaps be too much identified with the ambivalent character of this world to hold out much hope for its betterment; but if, on the other hand, divinity were altogether transcendent and in no way immanent, its effects could never be felt within our empirical world and its existence would then be largely a matter of indifference for us. The distant divinity of the eighteenth-century deists is in the end of no more use to the religious quester than is the totally immanent divinity which Feuerbach mistakenly identified with the limitless possibilities of the nature

of the human species. It is no surprise, then, to find the problem
of transcendence and immanence very much in evidence during
that period of the development of classical Greek thought which
coincides with the development of the classical myth of Jesus.

> The dominant philosophy at the time of the first Apologists and the
> beginning of Christian literature was Middle Platonism, i.e. Platon-
> ism much mixed with Pythagorean and Stoic elements. The
> Pythagorean influence, especially the theory of Numbers, had been
> there from the time of Plato himself; the Stoic-Platonic fusion began
> in the Middle Stoa with Panaetius (185-190 BC), but more especially
> Posidonius (130-46 BC), and, on the Platonic side, Antiochus of Asca-
> lon (c. 130-68 BC), who was head of the Academy for about twelve
> years before his death, maintained that Platonism and Stoicism were
> identical. Apart from the writings of Plato himself, we have to
> reckon with the influence of the Academic tradition as represented
> by such people as Plutarch (c. AD 45-125), Gaius, Apuleius, Maximus
> of Tyre, Albinus, and Numenius (all of whom lived in the second
> century AD). It is a fact, apart altogether from our special interest
> here, that these writers concentrated almost exclusively on the
> religious side of Plato, and it is possible that there existed
> anthologies of passages from Plato drawn up with this interest in
> mind.[15]

Monotheism was as much a concern of Greek religious
thought as it has been a concern of any religious thought or
imagination now known to us. In fact, some describe the whole
purpose of Greek philosophy rather airily as the search for the
one behind the many. For monotheism, in one sense, simply
answers to the need felt to protect the transcendence of divinity
in the course of affirming its immanence. The search for the
ensuing balance has taken as many forms as there are distinctive
religious traditions. It may not be too crude a generalization to
say of the Platonic tradition (a tradition which has been subjected to more than its fair share of crude generalizations) that
this tradition tries to satisfy the twin demands of transcendence
and immanence by thinking in terms of emanation, the natural
symbol for which is light from light, light streaming from a
source that would blind the naked eye which tried to look at it
directly, but which becomes visible on its way to illumine distant
objects.

Plato himself wrote that God was 'beyond being' (*Republic* 6,
509B); and there was a tradition amongst Platonists that their
founding-father delivered a lecture or lectures 'On the Good' in
which he set up the One as the first, formal principle and over
against this, as material principle, the Dyad, the divided and

divisible. Xenocrates, Plato's second successor as head of the Academy, constructed a system in which the One, or Monas, or Nous, was the First God, and the Unlimited Dyad was second. The pattern emerges even more clearly in Middle Platonism, with Numenius, for instance, whose Second God, Dyas, looked up to the First God, Monas, and, as Demiourgos, looked after the world. A trinitarian pattern begins to emerge, which is perfected in the third century in the Neo-Platonism of Plotinus. In this system the divine existence and emanation took a threefold form: the One which was beyond being and naming, the Nous or Mind, and the Soul or World-Soul, each of the latter two *hypostaseis* contemplating the one above and thus drawing the power and the pattern to diffuse itself downward in an emanation and extension of the divine, until the limits of matter were reached. (In fact, the word *hypostasis* could be used of each of these three – and one remembers that Christians later evolved the formula of three *hypostaseis*.)

Moderatus, a Pythagorean philosopher of the first century AD, in the course of claiming that the whole Platonic tradition was nothing short of plagiarism, a parasite on the philosophical tree of Pythagoras, gives the following account of the divinity:

> There is a first, a second, and a third One. The first One is beyond all being and *ousia*. The second, i.e. that which is actually being and intelligible, equals ideas. The third One, viz. the psychical, participates in the first One and in the ideas. [16]

Now there is no doubt that the ideas and images of this complicated philosophical tradition make admirable theology. For religious people have always thought of divinity as both transcendent and immanent, beyond the being we can think and talk about and yet effective within it, and effective, furthermore, in two main ways: in one way making things intelligible, and so like Ideas, Thought, Word, or Mind, and in another way providing the power or energy to exist, and so like Spirit or Soul. The image of light from light contains the element of unseeable source, and the elements of both illumination and energy (heat or fire), and it is sometimes helped out by the image of life-giving water streaming from a hidden spring. Furthermore, emanation, which is a central feature of this conceptuality and imagery, gives the impression of a gentle, flowing, continuous, and unbroken process.

When in the first, fresh thoroughness of my youthful researches into the Christian doctrine of the Trinity (three *hypos-*

taseis or 'persons' in one *ousia*, or substance) I first looked up a Greek lexicon to find what *hypostasis* meant, I remember being dismayed to learn that it could mean an overnight camping site or station. There are three overnight camping sites in one God? Well, yes, in a sense there are. After all the formula of the three *hypostaseis* in God could have been derived from Platonic theology even before it became a badge of Christian orthodoxy: it was well suited to a gently emanating divinity within which the 'first', 'second' or 'third' had to be regarded less as distinct individuals or 'persons' of divine rank and more as identifiable stages of the human mind's journey into God, the first two stages named from the power and light which conviction of the divine brings to our experience of the world, before the mind passes beyond to a stage where all possibility of naming simply ceases altogether. Combine the need for transcendence (monotheism) with the two main forms of perceived immanence (the light of intelligibility and the fire of power or energy) and it is indeed difficult to avoid a kind of Plotinian emanational concept of divinity in which the human mind identifies three stations and finds it can name only the first two.

The attraction for the followers of Jesus moving out into the civilized world of such high expressions of religious faith must be very obvious indeed. That powerful impulse toward transcendence which is the source of all monotheism, all emphasis on the uniqueness and oneness of God, who cannot be thought to share being or substance (*ousia*) with any other, and who is ultimately incomprehensible to humans, that impulse, in highly developed form, is common to sophisticated Jew, Jesus-follower and Greek alike. For however different the literary forms may be in the hymn to the unknown creator in Job, on the one hand, and the negative metaphysics of the One in Plotinus' *Enneads*, on the other, the instinct behind both is ultimately the same.[17]

The opposite impulse, to relate to this empirical world of ours the God who is always acknowledged to be wholly other, is also common to all religious quests, and so, naturally, it is common to the Jew and the Greek. In fact many of the terms in which this relationship can be expressed were common to both traditions, as some of the early Christian apologists were anxious to point out in great detail.[18] The key to the understanding of the kind of concept and symbol one finds when religious people yield, as they must, to this second impulse, is this: all talk which seems to proceed from God's side and to explain how the utterly transcendent God relates to our empirical world is really talk which proceeds from the human side and explains how the human spirit can travel toward the utterly transcendent God. So when one hears talk about sons of God, either from Jew or Greek, one must never be tempted to think that the talkers possess any privileged information of any generation-process which took place within the divinity. One must realize, rather, that the talkers are presenting some person, whether real or imaginary, because they think they have reason to believe that this person, more than any other, bears God's image in the world. Similarly, when one hears talk about the word of God, again from either Jew or Greek, one must not imagine some privileged stenographer at the heavenly court, or some privileged recipient on earth of God's whispered confidence. One must realize, rather, that one's attention is being drawn to some feature of nature or history in which something of God can be 'heard'. The movement, as far as the human spirit is concerned, is always from below upward, from human experience in and of this world to intimations of divinity. This is always the case, no matter how much the finished schemata of any theology might tempt us to think otherwise. (The same point was made in the case of myth, in saying that the myth-maker tries to identify those features of existence which favour life and existence, as against those which threaten both, and, on the assumption that God is the ground of being, talks of God in those terms.) In the case of both impulses, then, the movement of the spirit is in the same direction, from below upwards; the impulse to relate God to our world tries to identify the features that lead the spirit to God, whereas the impulse to transcendence harps, in the case of concepts, on continual adjustment until nothing is left of intelligible content, and, in the case of symbol, on evocation, rather than literal description – and all this is common to Jew and Greek.

There may be some very general differences between Jewish and Greek questers for divinity, in that the former may tend to proceed more from the concrete experience which makes up his all too ordinary history, whereas the latter, at least in his more elitist philosophical garb, may prefer to take as his starting point some cosmic features of his empirical world, such as change, for instance, change which blights all prospects of permanence for a beauty that is nevertheless real, and makes each one pray that he or she may

> find under the boughs of love and hate,
> In all poor foolish things that live a day,
> Eternal beauty wandering on her way.[19]

But wherever one begins, one must end with concepts or symbols of cosmic range, unless one's religious faith is for ever to remain localized and temporal.[20] For unless the Word, or Son of God, identified by the believer (or whatever other concept or symbol the believer applies to the chosen candidate), can be shown to have relevance for the destiny of our whole empirical world, it cannot lead us to the one true God. This cosmic emphasis, then, is as essential to the Jew as it is to the Greek, as both knew perfectly well.

And yet there is no doubt about the fact that the adoption of Greek philosophical terms, however necessary for the spread of their good news about the significance of Jesus, proved hazardous enough for the early followers of Jesus. The struggle for orthodoxy, for the correct view of the significance of Jesus, in the early centuries provides ample illustration of that hazard. But what exactly was the hazard, and why did it prove so difficult to avoid for so many people and in so many similar ways?

The general answer to that question, I think, is this: then as now, it proved difficult for the followers of Jesus fully to come to terms with the radical nature of the faith with which he tried to inspire them, and to give it clear and uncompromising expression in all their ways of talking about and dealing with God, Jesus and the world. More particularly, the gentle emanationism of Greek theology proved difficult to handle for Jesus followers whose Jewish tradition had accustomed them to the more abrupt and discontinuous impressions inevitably conveyed by their creation imagery.[21] The Word (Logos) can convey the impression of an inner thought gradually taking shape in outward expression or artifact – like the poet's image maturing into words, or the sculptor's vision slivering away the excess matter until it itself emerges from the stone. Alternatively, though, Word can convey the impression of an expletive, thundering forth a decision of will, making things happen or changing their direction, an instrument producing an effect rather than an inner key to the nature of that which emerges into reality.

In the gentle emanationist theology of the Greeks the names encountered along the way, names like Mind, Soul, Demiurge, were more like stages which the human mind could identify on its journey to the ultimately unknown God than separate entities each with its own claim to its own theology. For example, probably the best explanation of the role of Logos in the theology of Plotinus sees it as a name for the two-way dynamic which forms the binding continuity of the *hypostaseis* (stages, or expressions, or objectifications) by which the ultimately remote God approaches our world and, at the other extreme, by which this race of intelligent and spirited animals gradually approaches God.

Naturally, the more abrupt creationist mentality derived from the Jewish tradition is more inclined to see these same names as names for distinct entities, and, of course, to distinguish is to pose acute questions of relationship which, when raised in an atmosphere of mixed Jewish and Greek traditions, almost inevitably tend to be answered in strongly subordinationist terms. Add one other factor, namely, the native resistance of the human mind to its own attempts sufficiently to adjust its concepts for God, its native resistance to allowing the natural evocative power of its symbols for God to draw it to the ultimate depth, in short, its natural tendency to stop short of the one, true God, its perennial penchant for idolatry, and the hazards of Christian theology in these centuries begin to come clear. As always, the radical faith of Jesus, which alone brings us into contact with the God who is truly Father of all, seeks, but does not always find, the kind of expression which will allow it to be itself. In the present case it seeks such expression in its necessary acknowledgment of Jesus himself, and particularly of his relationship to God.

In spite of these hazards, however, the peoples of Graeco-Roman culture had to be spoken to in their own terms and, in the event, both Son of God and Word proved powerful bridge-terms in Christianity's excursion from its Jewish homeland to the ends of the earth. The symbol Son of God was almost equally at home in both cultures. We have already noticed how central the symbol Word of God was in a religion of the word in which to hear/to obey is a synonym for faith itself. And even though, in the Greek tradition, Word (Logos) was used for divinity mainly by the Stoa, whose philosophy, because of its materialism, was largely unwelcome in Christian theological development, its use as a term for divinity was nevertheless in the air, and other factors in any case were present to recommend it. If *Logos* meant 'word' or 'rational thought', *logikos* meant rational and the temptation of Jesus' followers to call themselves Logos-followers and therefore the rational ones was just too powerful for all kinds of Christian writers to resist, from Justin Martyr to Arius' great opponent, Athanasius. Furthermore, Alexandria at least, one of the great centres of early Christian thought, was aware that the Jewish thinker, Philo, probably a part-contemporary of Jesus, in the course of recommending his Jewish faith to his cultured Greek counterparts, had made use of the symbol and idea of God's Word to explain how the supreme God made the world and made contact with it. This Logos Philo described as the first-begotten Son of the uncreated Father and the 'second God'.[22]

Both Tatian (*Address to the Greeks*, 5) and Athenagoras (*A Plea for the Christians*, 10) emphasize the rule of God's word in creation, a natural opening in any attempt to attract the attention of Greek thinkers; but whereas the former says that the Word was created by the will of the Father, the latter prefers not to say that the Word was created, rather that the Father, being eternal mind, always had his Word within himself. Justin Martyr has the Word of God, the Son, begotten before creation; it became man and was then called Jesus Christ. The Word was inseparable from God in power, he affirms, being in the image and likeness of God; and yet, he says, we hold the Word 'in the second place' after God himself (*First Apology* 5; *Second Apology* 6; *Hortatory Address to the Greeks* 38). Theophilus of Antioch made use of the Stoic distinction between *logos endiathetos* and *logos proforikos*, the internal word or thought and the word expressed, in order to show the relationship of the Word of God to both God and the world. At first God was alone, his Word within him,

> But when God wished to make all that He determined on, He begot His Word, uttered the first-born of all creation, not Himself being emptied of the Word, but having begotten Reason, and always conversing with His Reason (*Ad Autolycum* 2.22).

Theophilus thus provided an important part of the conceptual analysis of the symbol Word of God in the development of the confession of Jesus. Put together with the thought of Justin, for instance, it creates a theory of a God who communes with his own Word or Reason (like Aristotle's self-contemplating Mind), who utters or brings forth his Word in order to create, who further sends his Word in epiphanies and to the prophets, and who finally makes his Word fully incarnate in the man Jesus. The same basic theory underlies Irenaeus' *Adversus Haereses*, though it is clear from comparison with Hippolytus that there was some wavering about the full and precise status of the Word of God at the different stages – before creation, before incarnation, and after incarnation.[23] In any case, it was perfectly possible for Tertullian, using this same kind of conceptual analysis of the symbol Word of God, to express clearly the subordination of the Son to the Father:

> For the Father is the entire substance, but the Son is a derivation and portion[24] of the whole ... Thus the Father is distinct from the Son, being greater than the Son, in as much as He who begets is one and He who is begotten is another (*Against Praxeas* 9).

It was out of this climate of theological thought that Arianism came, the most determinedly subordinationist of all statements about the Word or Son of God incarnate in Jesus. And it was Arius, a priest who preached in Alexandria at the beginning of the fourth century, who finally forced the Christian tradition to clear up this area of the profession of its distinctive faith, the precise area in which it chose its terms to acknowledge the founder of that faith.

There were more immediate precedents for Arius' preaching, of course, and broader factors than those already mentioned to prepare a reception for his cause. One side of the theological thought of the illustrious and influential Origen, who had also taught at Alexandria, had apparently spelled out a subordinationist position in some detail: Origen called the Logos God, for instance, but not 'the God' or 'the true God', and he insisted that whatever attributes were predicated of the Father – like truth, wisdom, etc. – must be asserted of the Son, as image of the Father, in a lesser and relative manner.[25] Indeed the whole problem of the origin of the Word or Son of God from the Father proved to be one of those broad factors which made the Arian case seem at first sight feasible enough. For it does seem obvious that whatever originates is inferior, at the outset at least, to that which gives it origin, though it may later equal or surpass its source. The tradition had always regarded the One God, the Father, as unoriginate. In the fight against Arius his opponents tried to single out one form of origin which they felt implied no inferiority. They chose a begetting from eternity, as opposed to other forms of origin, also mentioned in the earlier tradition, such as creating, making, and so on, which they now claimed did imply inferiority. But it must be confessed that such distinctions depend mainly on the say-so of those who make them. Justin Martyr had long ago realized that even begetting had to be qualified as taking place 'in a peculiar manner' (*First Apology*

22), else it could convey the wrong impression about God and the Word. And the earlier tradition had seemed serenely indifferent, when defining the specific attributes of the divine, as to whether it said 'unbegotten' or 'unoriginate', thereby implying, by its verbal looseness at least, that whatever was either begotten or originate in any way could not be fully or truly God.[26]

Christian history has not been kind to the literary remains of heresiarchs, and a climate in which anything from personal slander to political persecution was too often considered an acceptable form of God's judgment on one's adversaries is not one in which trust in the accuracy of reports offered by the heresiarchs' opponents can easily grow. From the few scraps of authentic Arian literature which we now possess we can see Arius declaring that the Son was constituted by God's will and counsel, before times and before ages, divine, unique, unchangeable; and before he was begotten, or created (*ktisthe*), or ordained, or founded, he was not, for he was not unbegotten. We find Arius complaining that he is persecuted for saying of the Son that 'He is out of things that were not.'[27] It seems clear from these few excerpts that Arius is as convinced that the divine Son comes from the One God as he is hesitant about describing the mode of this origin. This hesitancy comes across positively in the number of apparently interchangeable words used for the mode of origin – constituted, begotten, created, ordained, founded – and it comes across negatively in his insistence that the Son was not fashioned from any pre-existing stuff, either divine or creaturely, and that there is a 'before' (though it may not have been a temporal 'before', since time presumably came into being with the 'times and the ages') in which that which is begotten is not, for it is not, as he reasonably points out, unbegotten. In other words, there is always an antecedent to that which is thought to have origin of whatever kind.

Later on, in a 'confession' addressed to Alexander of Alexandria, Arius and some of his friends wrote: 'Before everlasting ages (the One God) begot his unique Son, through whom he made the ages and all things. He begot him ... a perfect creature (*ktisma*) of God, but not as one of the creatures – an offspring, but not as one of things begotten.'[28] Here, by means of a form of the Platonic *via negativa*[29] Arius seems to be saying that the Son originates from the One God, but not as any other things originates. For, of course, we can all be called creatures and sons or offspring of God, but there was something unique about the origin of the Word.

Finally, some time after his condemnation by the Council of Nicaea in AD 325, Arius offered a creed to the Christian emperor Constantine, as part of a process for his reconciliation with the church (a reconciliation which the death of Arius unfortunately prevented from taking place):

> We believe in One God, the Father Almighty; and in the Lord Jesus Christ, his Son, the God-Logos who was begotten from him before all the ages, through whom all things came into being, things in heaven and things on earth, who came down and took flesh.[30]

There is nothing unorthodox about this creed in itself, although, as has often been pointed out before, its studious omission of any characteristic phrase of those who were victorious at Nicaea – *homoousios to patri* (one in being or substance with the Father), true God of true God, begotten not made – could, and did, make men suspicious that the great heresiarch had not really mended his ways.

But what exactly were his ways? Through the dust and smoke of that ancient battleground it is not easy to see. And even his studied ignoring of characteristic Nicene phrases does not immediately bring the precise pathways of his thought into view. Arius and his party were not the only ones in the course of the fourth century to remain unhappy with the phrase *homoousion to patri*. In fact much of the fourth century debate is taken up with disagreement about that phrase. Writing to his constituents to recommend the decision of Nicaea, Eusebius of Caesarea paraphrases the *homoousion* as follows:

> that the Son of God bears no similarity with the creatures of God that came into being, but in every way is made like only to the Father who begot him, and is not of any other hypostasis or essence, but of the Father.[31]

Now, though Eusebius abjures any use of substance in a crude material sense, he is nevertheless using imagery here which suggests that the Son is of the same stuff as divinity, and not like those Eusebius calls creatures – a sentiment which Arius, also, could express, and did express, though Arius would certainly not use the phrase 'of the same substance as', the *homoousion to patri*, to do so. Only towards the end of that same century, and mainly due to the ingenuity of the Cappadocian Fathers, did the *homoousion* phrase come to mean that the one identical substance or being of the Father was also in the Son, and it is at this stage of its development that we soon have to take that phrase

seriously as the most substantial literal claim ever made in the
conceptual explication of the myth of Jesus. In between these
points, however, the phrase had been interpreted, dropped,
and reinterpreted by so many people that Arius cannot seriously
be blamed for avoiding it.

We have already noticed that Arius could have good reason to
be sceptical of the ability of any one word for a mode or origin to
do better than others when attempts are made to speak of
inner-divine processes. We must notice also that the few writings we have from Arius himself use *ktisthe* (created), not
poiethenta (made), which latter word Nicaea refuses, when it
says of the Son that he was begotten, not made. And that brings
us to 'true God of true God'. Arius' omission of this phrase
could lead to the correct perception of his mind on the subject of
Jesus and God. For apparently his principal fault lay in his penchant for pressing toward systematic expression those suggestions of subordination of the Word or Son of God to the Father
which, though always vague and undeveloped and of uncertain
status, were plentifully present in the tradition which preceded
Arius. As far as Arius was concerned, then, it seems, though the
Son incarnate in Jesus was definitely divine, his was a lesser
divinity than that of the One, the true God who alone was
unoriginate. Arius may have had difficulty in finding suitable
terms for this subordinate divinity of the Son, terms which
would leave the Son divine and still leave no doubt about his
subordination – he tried 'there was when he was not', 'a creature but not as one of the creatures', etc. – just as Arius' opponents had difficulty in finding terms to express the conviction
that the Son was not a lesser divinity; but in the end, through all
the confusion of words, the convictions were contradictory, at
least as long as Arius had his own way, and they were known to
be so.

We can easily suspect that the twin dangers which from the
outset threatened this type of speculation worked their worst
effects in the mind of the great heresiarch. For the mixing of an
abrupt and discontinuous Jewish creation imagery with the
more flowing and continuous emanation conceptuality of the
Greeks obviously contained the hazard of conceiving of the
forms or *hypostaseis* of divinity perceived before or after the One
(depending on the upward or downward direction of the mind's
motion) as separate, and thus subordinate to the point of no
longer sharing with the One in the same idea or 'stuff' of divinity. And this hazard, to the extent that it was not surmounted,

could only increase the incidence of that other hazard, the danger that lurks in the native laziness of the human mind, the danger of stopping somewhere along the path of evocation down which its best religious symbols try to draw it, the danger of tiring of the task of modifying the concepts it uses of divinity before it has modified all recognizable human content out of them and arrived at last at the Platonic *via negativa*. For when the mind stops on its journey to God it takes its symbols literally, and its concepts, which are by nature meant to be taken literally, it leaves with too much of their empirical content still intact. Then the symbol of God's Son begins to be taken as a literal description of a generation-process within the divinity, resulting in a relationship such as one finds on earth – from which the original image was taken – a relationship between any parent and offspring. The symbol of God's word begins to be taken as a literal description of the emergence in the divine consciousness and then the expression of an intelligible thought, resulting in a relationship such as one experiences between oneself and one's own conscious and expressed thoughts. Or, since Son and Word can be conceptualized as well as they can become symbols, one simply fails, in the course of using them to depict the relationship between God and Jesus, to divest them of all remaining vestiges of empirical content drawn from human generation, whether physical or mental. In both cases, one thinks literally in terms of a divine being, Son or Word, coming forth from God the Father and entering the man Jesus, with inevitable implications of separate and subordinate status, and one is Arian whether one likes to admit that or not.

Having said all this, though, it is not normally recognized, the principal question still remains to be asked, namely, what was wrong with Arius' myth of Jesus? What is wrong with being Arian? For it may be all very well to say that the drive of the human spirit to monotheism and transcendence will not brook any stoppages along the way, but all that surely has to do with human attempts to talk about the one, true God, the Father and creator of all. When Jesus spoke his 'I', though, he was clearly indicating one who was other than the one God whom he called Father, and so the question of the divinity of Jesus arises again in spite of all the cautions issued above. For all the cautions issued above surely apply to the mind's journey to the one, true God. Arius wanted to safeguard his monotheism and the consequent total transcendence of God by insisting, on the one hand, that the one God had no equal and, on the other, that the divinity of Jesus was of a separate and totally subordinate kind, the divinity, by some kind of participation, of one who was *par excellence* in the image of God.

Now for anyone who insists that it was not God the Father who suffered on the cross, is any other conclusion possible? Centuries of unreflective acceptance of the victorious side in that ancient dispute as the orthodox ones, and of the Arians, as the heterodox, has blunted the theological minds of the most astute Christians to the still persistent point of that problem. One simply has to accept Maurice Wiles' contention that there is nothing inherently illogical or even unspiritual about the Arian myth of Jesus.[32] If it was felt, as apparently it was felt, that the developing myth of Jesus demanded acknowledgment of the divinity of Jesus, and yet it was felt that Jesus was not God the Father, what was illogical about saying that God the Father was the one, true God, and that the divinity of the Son, the God-Logos, was totally separate and subordinate? What was illogical about attributing to the Son divinity in a relative sense and by some kind of participation as an image of the true God, while adding that, of course, the Son who spoke in Jesus was not true God of true God, not that? And what was unspiritual about the Arian view? If it was accepted, as apparently it was accepted in the Greek milieu of that ancient dispute, that the whole point of Jesus' mission was the divinization of human beings, their restoration to the image of God in so far as that was possible for creatures, how was it in any way impossible that such divinization should be effected by one who participated in the divinity as the image *par excellence* of the one true God? In short, what precisely was wrong with the Arian myth of Jesus, and what exactly was so right about the alternative finally offered by his opponents?

The Arian myth of Jesus was wrong, it seems to me, for one reason – though this was not always the reason given, or at least it was not always given in these terms. People are brought into contact with the living God through the faith of Jesus. And they acknowledge that this faith is theirs because it was the faith of Jesus, because Jesus inspired them to such faith. It is the actuality of such faith in their lives, then, that requires of them an acknowledgment of Jesus, or the construction of a myth about Jesus, and it is the precise nature of the faith he enabled them to have which dictates the precise nature of the acknowledgment required of them.

Now the faith of Jesus has been described as the perception

and evaluation of, and the commitment to, all things great and small as the gift or grace of God to all; alternatively, the faith of Jesus is the sense of the presence of God as Father in life itself and in all its supports, animate and inanimate. It is a living attitude to all things and especially to all people, a life-gesture of receiving as gift, rather than grasping and tearing loose; it is that posture which is indistinguishably one of receiving into the cupped hands and offering up from the chaliced hands, a sense of receiving all as grace which is simultaneously a persistent willingness to give and to give up when that is needed. In short, the faith of Jesus, which is also that of his followers, is a distinctive lived conviction of the immediacy of God in the very contingency of our existence. But, above all, it is primarily a life lived, it is attitude and action which embodies evaluation and commitment. It is not primarily a theory, though it can be theorized in doctrine and confessed in creeds. It is not primarily a set of moral precepts or ritual acts, though it can issue in varying precept and ritual. It is not primarily membership in any institution, though the people who share it will organize in various ways. It is a way of life that exists essentially only in the total life of a person. It is primarily in such a lived faith, and not primarily in any particular institution, ritual, creed or code, that people sense the immediacy of God the Father (though institution, ritual, creed and code all exist in the service of such faith).

Now add the necessary historical dimension to that brief description of the nature of the faith of Jesus. Find a way of expressing the implications of the fact that it is the faith of others because of Jesus' life inspiring and infecting them. And you must expect to hear such people speak of the immediacy of God in Jesus for them. To say that they encounter the one, true God in the faith of Jesus is to say what that faith is, to say simultaneously that it was the very life of the man Jesus, and that it is theirs because it was his; and all of this can be abbreviated in the formula that they meet in Jesus the one, true God.

It would undoubtedly be true to say that, in some abstract anthropology, the distinctive faith of Jesus was always possible, just as any other kind of human faith was always possible at any point of the spectrum into which our human perception and evaluation of our contingency differentiates itself.[33] Certainly within the long Hebrew-Jewish tradition, and in the sacred literature of that tradition from the creation myths that open Genesis, the possibility of this distinctive faith is constantly hinted at and attempts are made upon it both theoretical,

imaginative and practical. That, presumably, is why the main
New Testament writers present Jesus, the Jew, as the fulfilment
of all that ancient promise. Paul, for instance, who claims that
the right relationship to God through this faith has been
revealed in Jesus (Romans 2.17; Galatians 1.12), has no hesitation in claiming Abraham as his precedent (Romans 4). Platonic
theology, too, with its conviction that this empirical world
offered imperfect clues to divinity and its insistence on self-
discipline and detachment in order to set out on the quest for
God, could be seen, and was seen, to be a pointer toward the
unique faith of Jesus.

But it is one thing to say that a possibility is present in some
abstract anthropology, and even to say that it was approached in
various ways, proximate or remote; it is quite a different thing to
say that it was actually and fully made a reality in the actual life
of one who could also empower as many as would allow themselves to be empowered to make it a reality in their own lives.
The latter claim demands the kind of acknowledgment of such a
person which is reserved, amongst others, for the founders of
faiths. And then, as already remarked, the specific nature of the
acknowledgment must in each case depend upon the specific
nature of the faith founded.

If Jesus had put people in possession of a doctrine which
could then be detached from his person, however he himself
had exemplified it in his life; if he had provided them with a set
of precepts which would themselves guarantee their acceptance
by God; if he had offered guide-lines the accuracy of which they
could themselves prove simply by following them to the promised absolute, then it would have been sufficient for these
people to acknowledge Jesus as the bearer of a literal divine
revelation about God and the world, or as a prophet of God's
specific will, or as an enlightened enlightener, a guide, leader,
or guru. But since the faith of Jesus is the life of a man, it can
never be contained in any doctrine (though it can be verbalized,
significantly, in a story, a history), it cannot be confined to any
set of moral or ritual precepts, no matter how extensive, and it
continually seeks new paths through our changing world. His
followers, therefore, have to say that it is in the faith lived by
Jesus that they encounter the one, true God; it is in Jesus the
man of this distinctive faith that they encounter the one, true
God; that Jesus is not simply an enlightener, prophet, or bearer
of formulated divine truth, but the human person in whom God
fully and truly encounters humanity in history.

Hence the followers of Jesus felt entitled, indeed obliged, to say that in Jesus they encountered at last the one, true God; only in Jesus did they really, finally, definitively encounter the one, true God, and yet all they encountered in their historical experience was Jesus, the man of flesh, the man of faith. This is the theology of John in the New Testament: 'No one has ever seen God; the only Son, who is in the bosom of the Father, he has made him known' (John 1.18). But this Son is the Word who has just been declared to have become 'flesh', that is, to have been and to be a human being like any other; and elsewhere in the gospel it is made clear that there is no 'view' of the Father beside or above or independently of the man Jesus: 'He who has seen me has seen the Father' (John 14.9). When Jesus is solemnly produced before his own people by Pilate, as he enters upon the death/resurrection culmination of his career, the formula is 'Here is the man' (John 19.5). Now try saying what any follower of Jesus must sooner or later say, as a result of living the faith of Jesus; try saying that in Jesus one encounters the one, true God (this will indicate the nature of the faith of Jesus), only in Jesus does one encounter the one, true God (this will indicate that the person of Jesus is the historical source of this faith), and yet that one encounters only Jesus (this will indicate that there are no detachable views of God, no detachable doctrines, precepts or guide-lines) – and you must find yourself saying that God is in Jesus reconciling the world to himself. Not a lesser divinity, but very God.

This Arius would not say, and in this he was wrong. It was not Jewish theology which misled him, nor Platonic, nor even necessarily a fusion of the two, though this fusion did contain particular hazards. But, like many before him and many since, he was unaware of the full implications of the faith of Jesus which, when they are fully drawn must make Christians say all that is contained in the last paragraph above, and cannot let them stop short on any of it; and therefore Arius did not avoid the hazards. On the contrary, whatever we may now think of the odd exegetical conclusions of some of Arius' opponents or of the often shaky foundation of their confidence in parts of the earlier tradition, they somehow maintained a true sense of the faith in which alone their human condition was healed; and they knew, however difficult they found agreement on formulations other than his, that Arius was wrong.

If Arius had had his original way, we should now have to conclude that Jesus founded a different faith from the faith he actually founded, from the distinctive faith which his followers try to live. We should have to conclude that the Son of God through the human body of Jesus brought literal revelation about the three *hypostaseis* of divinity, of which he himself was the second, essentially subordinate in nature to the one, true God, and divine by participation, in a relative sense, as image *par excellence* of the one, true God. For if these *hypostaseis* were no longer overnight stations identified along the mind's journey to God, as in the smooth emanationist scheme of the Neo-Platonist, but rather distinct *personae*, one of whom formed the individual Jesus of Nazareth, then how should we know about such divine persons except by literal information or revelation from the divine beings themselves? But then our faith would be a matter of assenting to such truth brought by this Son of God incarnate in Jesus, in addition to other truths, perhaps, concerning our relationship to God, our ritual and moral obligations, our prospects in an after-life, and so on. Our faith would no longer be a life lived in distinctive perception-evaluation-commitment which itself allows us to say all that we need to say about God and Jesus. In short, if Arius had had his way, Jesus would have to have been a very different founder of a very different kind of faith than the founder of the faith he actually founded. Arius' myth of Jesus, then, was historically untrue.[34]

That it was a flaw in his appreciation of the very nature of Christian faith which proved fatal to Arius' effort at orthodoxy is put beyond any doubt by another feature of his doctrinal system. It is reliably reported that Arius allowed no human soul in Jesus; instead he had the God-Logos, as he called it, perform the functions of the soul. Since the denial of a human soul to Jesus is a feature of systems other than his, as we shall shortly see, there is no need to spend any time in proving that Arius in particular was guilty of this omission. A truncated humanity, a soul-less body in Platonic terms, fits only too neatly into Arius' theology and it supports only too obviously the most mistaken implications of his system. For a divine *hypostasis* (Arius uses the phrase later adopted in Trinitarian orthodoxy – three *hypostaseis*) sent by the one, true God to inhabit the soul-less body of a man and in this way to bring God's saving truth to earth, would have to be at once too small to be equal to the One, and too large to be circumscribed in human terms. In effect, then, where Christian orthodoxy insists that in Jesus we meet true God and true man, since the fully human man of faith, Jesus of Nazareth, by inspiring others to live that same life of faith, enables us to encounter the one, true God, Arius had us meet in the end neither true God nor true man. And it therefore represents no misunderstanding of his system to say that because Arius would not allow us to meet true man in Jesus, he could not assure us that we encounter true God either.

It would not be fair, of course, to complain so about Arius, and not to acknowledge that most of us have entertained the idea of a literal generation process in the heavens, giving to God a divine Son who then took flesh as Jesus of Nazareth and brought to the human race literal revelations of the nature of God and of God's detailed will and purpose for human kind. We have consequently thought of the Christian faith primarily as intellectual assent to a set of revealed truths. The fully human nature and life of Jesus was an article of that faith – as a proof of divine condescension, or an alleged requirement of a redemption contract as in Anselm's *Cur Deus Homo*? – but it scarcely belonged to its source and essence: and a lesser divine being could certainly have brought us the truth to which our intellectual assent was demanded. The philosophers and historians whom we met in the earlier quest of the historical Jesus and who insisted that the essence of Christianity consisted, not in the confession of supernatural mysteries, but in a moral life which engendered hope of a happy after-life with God, were closer to the truth, for all the limitations of their rationalist models, than were many of their opponents. For the spirit of Arius did not die with the great heresiarch.

But what of the alternative produced by the opponents of Arius? What exactly did that confession mean, and how can it be seen to be true? It would obviously be impossible here to trace the different meanings which different parties at Nicaea placed upon that key phrase 'one in being with the Father'; much more so to investigate the eventful history of that phrase through the middle decades of the fourth century. It is generally conceded that the so-called Cappadocian Fathers – Basil and the two Gregorys – towards the end of that century managed to give the phrase a precision which it did not often achieve afterwards in East or West, even in official church formularies. It will suffice for our purpose, then, if we take the solution to the problem of the confession of Jesus in his relationship to God precisely as proposed in the formula worked out by the Cappadocians, as one of the best examples of a solution to this problem in the long history of our tradition and ask, in this one case, exactly what is meant and how it could be seen to be true. Of course, the Cappadocian formula covered the relationships between God the Father, Jesus and the Spirit, that is to say, it was a trinitarian formula, but since it was principally the needs of the confession of Jesus in the tradition that brought about the formula, we shall do little damage if we confine our attention to its success in this more restricted area.[35]

As far as the Cappadocian formula went, then, the Son or Word of God which was enfleshed in Jesus was one in substance with the Father, but a different hypostasis from that of God the Father. First, then, what did the terms of that formula mean? Here I follow Prestige. *Ousia*, the noun behind the adjective *homoousion*, may be translated 'substance', as we saw, or it may be translated 'being'. But if it is translated 'substance', it is best to understand it in the way in which Aristotle understood primary substance, rather than the way in which he understood secondary substance. Secondary substance refers to the abstract essence which many individuals may be said to have in common, as when I say that Tom, Dick and Harry have all the same human nature or essence; or it can refer to the material substance (clay, metal) out of which many different objects are fashioned. Primary substance, on the other hand, refers to this substantial, concrete individual thing before us – Tom, Dick, or Harry, or the bust of Napoleon – though my attention is still directed by the word substance used in this sense to the inner structure or make-up or stuff of the individual. If I say, for instance, there is a substance in my tea, I am using the word in the sense of primary substance, and yet the natural question which immediately suggests itself is, what is it? What kind of stuff, or what is its nature or essence?

Hypostasis, then, though it can be translated very literally by the Latin *substantia* or substance, and though it is patient of an even wider range of meaning than is *ousia*, was refined to mean, as part of its considerable range of meaning allows, the same substantial thing or individual as the word *ousia* refers us to, but looked at now from the point of view of its external concrete objectivity in relationship to others. If I should say, 'An object has entered my field of vision,' the most obvious immediate question is, 'Where is it?', or, 'How is it located by reference to objects in relationship to which we situate and perceive ourselves?' To quote Prestige:

'Substance' means an object consisting of some particular stuff; it has an inward reference to the nature of the thing in itself, expressing what logicians call a connotation. 'Object' (so he translates *hypos-*

tasis) means a substance marked off as an individual specimen by reason of its distinction from all other objects; it bears an outward reference to a reality independent of other individuals, and expresses what logicians call a denotation.[36]

In the Cappadocian formula, then, if we confine our attention to the statement about the relationship between Jesus and God, what exactly is being said? First, that the Son or Word of God encountered in the historic presence of Jesus (the Word made flesh) is in substance the same as the Father. Here the necessary conceptual adjustment is made which prevents us from taking Son or Word too literally and, consequently, from introducing plurality and subordination into the divinity. Second, it is said that, nevertheless, the Father himself does not become an object to us. The hypostasis we see, or what is objectified for us, is the Word-in-Jesus, or Jesus as Word or Son of God, that is, Jesus as the one in whom we encounter the one, true God.

As already remarked, if Son of God or Word of God were used consistently as images and symbols are used, then, in speaking of Jesus as Son or Word of God the natural, evocative power of symbol would itself draw us to the conviction that in Jesus we encountered the one, true God. But concepts are by nature taken literally and, therefore, when used to talk about God, must be literally adjusted so that at least they convey no false impressions. So, since Son and Word of God, taken literally as concepts, imply differentiation in divinity and subordination, it must be added that it is the one, true God in substance which we encounter, none other, and yet the one, true God is not an object of our experience immediately as other objects are; rather, the 'object' in which the 'substance' of the one, true God is encountered is Jesus. Here is the distinction between *ousia* and *hypostasis* of which the formula makes use.

How is such a formula justified? It is often said that it has to be seen as a faith statement, and that is undoubtedly the truth of the matter. But that is also quite often misunderstood. For if a faith statement here is taken to imply that the statement or formula was revealed by God and as such has to be accepted on faith, that is undoubtedly false. Anyone who is at all familiar with the theological debates of the fourth century knows perfectly well where this formula, and others like it, came from. It comes from the minds and pens of men who were attempting to establish as best they could the intellectual outposts to their distinctive faith. It is therefore a faith-statement in the sense that it seeks to describe at once the distinctive nature and the source of that faith. It is a terse expression for a complex conviction, a conviction which contains at least the following constitutive elements: the conviction that the faith of Jesus, so often and still so inadequately described above, when it becomes ours, alone provides our encounter with the one, true God, whom we cannot directly 'see' or 'hear'; a conviction that the historic person of Jesus, himself a man of such faith, is for us the source of this faith, the one person in our history who inspires and empowers us to such faith; the one, therefore, in whom we encounter the one, true God.

The Fourth Gospel declared: 'no one has ever seen God'. The God whom Jesus called Father and who, indeed, had been called Father by Jews and others both before and after Jesus, was always there, always existed, and in internal structure or nature (*ousia*) was always the same. It matters little in this context whether the internal 'sameness' of God is expressed in Greek essentialist immutability terms or in Hebrew relational terms of constant fidelity and untiring favour. It might even be maintained that God, precisely as Father, was always 'objectified' (*hypostasis*) in our world; not, surely, as an object of our experience over against other objects, but precisely in the contingent character of all the objects of our immediate experience. Paul's accusing finger is pointed at everyone when he says: 'Ever since the creation of the world (God's) invisible nature, namely, his eternal power and deity, has been clearly perceived in the things that have been made' (Romans 1.20). For all life and existence always carries within itself its character as grace or gift to us, its index of the power that gives existence to all things, and gives, and gives, and gives.

And yet, once this is said, one realizes that a number of substantial qualifiers must immediately be added. For the thing about human possibilities is that one never knows that they exist until they are actualized. The possibility of 'hearing' the word of God in creation, the possibility of 'seeing' the giver in the gift, the possibility of seeing the Father in all this life-giving world, the possibility, in short, not of God's own *ousia*, or substance, or being, but of his *hypostasis*, or objectification as Father, that possibility, though it may always be a possibility in some theoretical sense of the word, and though its practical prospects may undoubtedly have been hinted, particularly in the long Jewish tradition, that was not really a practical possibility for us until someone fully realized and actualized it. Then it was a practical possibility for us all, and then also it was known to be a possibility at all times.

Add here something that the study of Jesus' mission has already revealed and this point becomes even clearer and more cogent still. To know God in our world in the *hypostasis* of Father is not and never has been a purely theoretical affair. To know in this case, as a Hebrew would well understand, is to experience in one's life in the most concrete manner conceivable, it is to hold a conviction that shapes one's life because it develops from one's most concrete experience of life. Or, to put the matter in a slightly different way, the truth in question here is not truth that can be satisfied with purely mental existence, and with the quiet contemplation which this suggests; it is rather, in the terminology of the Fourth Gospel, a truth which must be done. For this reason, as we already noticed, the experience of the reign of God the Father could be conveyed by Jesus in his healing and serving, his practice of table-fellowship and his shared life of prayer as much as, if not more than, its conveyance in parable and preaching. And that priority still holds for those who wish to transmit the experience to others. For this reason, too, it is often said, and quite truly, that it was soteriological considerations, and not purely speculative ones, which saw the victory of orthodoxy over impending heterodoxy in the course of the Arian controversy. For, once again, the truth that heals is no theoretical system to be accepted in some single act of intellectual assent; it is the lived experience of all life and existence as God's good gift, an experience which makes us gracious to others, and which is normally available to each of us only through the actual grace of others to us. It is this inspiring and enabling experience that saves or heals us and holds out hope for our common humanity otherwise threatened to death by envy and hubris, division and hostility.

Therefore, though the being (*ousia*) of God may not have been in question at many points in the history of the race, the *hypostasis* of God as Father in the radically gracious sense of Jesus' lived conviction was not available directly and immediately as such. *Hypostasis*, after all, refers to an object, something somehow objectified. And this invites perception. In fact, as we have just argued, it invites a very practical relationship. But this distinctive practical relationship to one's world, and through it to God, apart from hints and approximations (which many early Christian apologists were happy to acknowledge in both Judaism and beyond), was not a real possibility for us until the distinctive *hypostasis* or objectification of God in the person and life of Jesus took place. Jesus' life objectified for us definitively the true Fatherhood of God. That is why we say that Jesus as *hypostasis*, as substantial object, now very much an 'object' in the world's history beside other objects, is the *hypostasis* or objectification which makes the *hypostasis* of God as Father a reality in our lives. That is what is meant by explaining in terms of *hypostasis* the confession of Jesus as Son or Word of God the Father.

In the faith of Jesus we truly encounter God as Father. In Jesus the man of faith we truly encounter God as Father. In God the Father, as Scholastic theology pointed out, the being of God and his *hypostasis* as Father are identical. Further, we have said, God the Father could in theory be encountered independently of Jesus. But we are followers of Jesus because the *hypostasis* of God the Father was not encountered by us in the world at large or through history in general, but rather in the distinctive mode of existence of the concrete existential person of Jesus. In Jesus, then, is a distinct *hypostasis* of God, distinct from God's hidden *hypostasis* in nature and history, a *hypostasis* which we name Son or Word, because through it we encounter the Father. One divine being, two *hypostaseis*. Add that the experience of the power or spirit of God, now encountered by us also as the power or spirit of Jesus, is our encounter with both Jesus and God, and the third *hypostasis* completes what has become known as the trinitarian formula in what is perhaps its most polished form at the end of the fourth Christian century.

These further reaches of trinitarian theology do not concern us here. All that it is necessary for us to see – and what I hope I have shown – is that it is still the same distinctive faith of Jesus which justifies, indeed requires, the fullest development of the myth or confession of Jesus which our tradition has produced.

The anti-climax: diminished humanity

The trouble with formulae is that with the passage of time they become too familiar, and familiarity breeds contempt. The difficult and subtle thought behind the formula is soon forgotten, the meaning is gradually simplified and crudified, and something which at first represented a pinnacle of the human spirit's intellectual achievement all too shortly comes to be regarded as a simple logical stepping-stone to other more comprehensive conclusions. Therein lies the contempt.

Nowhere, perhaps, in Christian doctrine has this contempt

been more manifest over the course of Christian history than in the case of the trinitarian formula we have just examined. It has tempted Christians to think that they had some direct vision of the inner being of God, that they could see three 'somethings' in there, 'three little mannikins', in Calvin's acid phrase. It has tempted otherwise worthy Christian theologians to build theologies of the church or moral theologies on the trinitarian formula; ambitious projects indeed, except that too often the Trinity comes out of it looking like a second holy family in heaven, a somewhat superfluous parallel to the holy family of Jesus, Mary and Joseph on earth, a very talented and co-operative, happy and harmonious group.

Of more concern to us here however, is the fact that an unsubtle use of the trinitarian formula tempts people to think rather crudely of the divinity of Jesus, as if it were some 'person' or 'thing' lodged within the man, Jesus. These crude impressions do double damage to christology. They either lessen our appreciation of the full humanity of Jesus – though it is necessary to his full significance for us that he have fully shared the human condition – or, if insistence is still placed upon his full humanity, they make virtually impossible any intelligible statement of the unity of Jesus' person. We shall see something of this particular damage in the course of the necessarily brief survey of that further development of christology which makes up the content of the present section.

Apollinarius was one of the staunchest allies of Athanasius in the defence of that particular statement of Jesus' relationship to God which has come down to us as Nicene orthodoxy and which is known in Christian shorthand as the divinity of Jesus. But the task of being true to the specific nature of Christian faith in working out the confession of its founder is not easily accomplished: as evidence of this there is the fact that Apollinarius, though he assured us that in Jesus we meet the one, true God, had no more place in his system for the full humanity of Jesus than had his opponent, Arius. There is dispute as to whether Apollinarius denied to Jesus all 'parts' of the soul, or denied him just the rational, self-determining centre of the human spirit. In either case, Apollinarius apparently failed to see how Jesus, if his human nature had its full psychic complement, could have been one concrete individual instead of two (a divine subject and a human one),[37] or how, if his human nature had its own will, we could ever be sure of his sinlessness. Apollinarius' solution was to have the human soul of Jesus, or at least its most

personal parts and functions, entirely replaced by the divine
Logos or Word. Apollinarius is thus the classic example of this
sad feature of the quest for orthodoxy, that even if enthusiastic
profession of what we call the divinity of Jesus does not injure
our appreciation of the true nature of Christian faith, it does not
guarantee it either.

The main achievement of the Council of Chalcedon in AD 451,
as it had been of Nestorius earlier in that century, was to stress
the full, unaltered and undiluted humanity of the man, Jesus.
This it did in terms of the doctrine of two natures already so ably
proposed and defended by Nestorius. The council wished to
state that Jesus was fully human. It said that our Lord Jesus
Christ had a rational soul and a body (thereby choosing Platonic
anthropology in which to embody this conviction),[38] and that he
was 'one in being' with us in his human nature, as much as he
was 'one in being' with the Father in his divinity. This use of the
Nicene *homoousios* already deprived it of much of the accuracy it
had achieved by the end of the fourth century. For if Jesus is said
to have the same substance as us, then substance is being used
in the sense of secondary substance, a generic nature shared by
distinct individuals, and the word cannot be used in that way in
speaking of the relationship of Jesus to the Father; if it were, it
would lead to polytheism. But if we take it that Chalcedon, by
means of this use of the Nicene phrase, is simply saying that just
as in Jesus we encounter the one, true God, so we as surely
encounter a human being fully and completely of our own
species, then the council is stating an essential conviction of the
Christian tradition. For it is in the human life of Jesus, and
particularly, we have argued, in his radical faith, perhaps the
most human condition of all, that we encounter the one, true
God.[39]

Yet many people seem to have great difficulty with Chalcedon
at the present time – for that century or so, from Nicaea to
Chalcedon, did indeed dictate down to the present day the main
catechetical terms on which the confession of Jesus was made
and the myth of Jesus cast.[40] The difficulty seems to centre
mainly upon the theory of the two natures in the Lord Jesus
Christ which Chalcedon used to express the central Christian
conviction we have just outlined. The Council explained that:

> One and the same Christ, Son, Lord, only-begotten (was) made
> known in two natures without confusion, without change, without
> division, without separation; the difference of the natures having
> been in no way taken away by reason of the union, but rather the

properties of each nature being preserved, and both concurring in one person (*prosopon*) and one *hypostasis*.[41]

People come away from this conciliar definition with the impression that there are two distinct and complete natures in Jesus, the divine nature and a human nature (though the document confesses Christ manifest in two natures, not two natures in Christ), and to the extent that they avoid Apollinarius and confess the full humanity of Jesus, to that precise extent they seem to encounter the difficulty for which the name of Nestorius, despite all his just protests, has been used to this day, the difficulty, namely, of perceiving and expressing the unity of the individual, Jesus the Christ. Correspondingly, to the extent that people proved adamant about the unity, to that same extent they tended to fall back into some form of Apollinarianism, however refined and however disguised.

It seems to me that the major mistake made in the reading of Chalcedon is the mistake of taking these words *physis* (nature), *hypostasis*, and *prosopon* (a more 'popular' word than *hypostasis* for an individual person), as words which name different things, or at least different elements, which then have to be combined in block-building fashion, so that they will somehow result in one, credible individual whom we call the Lord Jesus. The fact of the matter is that the word *physis* has a range of meaning almost as extensive as that of the word *hypostasis*.

> Physis means the way in which a thing grows and functions, hence its 'nature'; applied to the universe at large it means 'natural law'. But it is also frequently applied to the actual thing that grows or functions – such as Nature, in the concrete sense of 'the natural world', or some particular creature or subject, regarded always from the standpoint of its function or behaviour, as an individual embodiment of some specific character. Hence in connection with personal beings physis can mean either their constitution and behaviour, or a concrete 'personality'.[42]

Nature, in short, is a functional term. To say that there are two natures, divine and human, in Jesus, or more accurately that one and the same Christ is manifest in two natures, is simply tantamount to saying, what the followers of Jesus realized they must say, that Jesus functions as man and as God, since in Jesus they encounter one like themselves in all things, except that he was no sinner, and they also encounter the one, true God. In actual fact the same term, *physis*, could be used to affirm that in Jesus his followers encounter but one, single personality; and the word was so used by Cyril of Alexandria, when he wrote of the one *physis* (concrete personality) of the Word of God incarnate.[43] So it was, and still is, perfectly possible to remain orthodox while saying that the Christ is manifest in two natures, or manifest as one nature – if one is using the meanings of the Greek word *physis* current in the century in which this definition was hammered out. Chalcedon preferred Nestorius' formula 'one *prosopon*', to which it added 'one *hypostasis*', to express the personal unity of this one in whose human existence we encounter the one, true God. And from what we already know of the meaning of *hypostasis*, that too was perfectly feasible, and probably a good deal clearer.[44]

There were two main ways in which the orthodoxy of this confession of Jesus, in itself capable of such diverse expression, could decline. First, and on an apparently reified understanding of nature, that is, on the implicit understanding that the 'natures' in Jesus were distinct things or elements, questions began to be asked, and unfortunately answered, about the complement or make-up of these natures. For instance, did Jesus have two wills, or just one? Did he have two principles of action (*energeia*), or just one? The Third General Council of Constantinople of AD 680 declared that in Jesus there were two natural wills and two natural active principles inseparably, unchangeably, undividedly and unconfusedly.[45] The intention of such dogmatic definitions is orthodox enough: it is still to protect the full humanity of Jesus in whom we meet the 'will' and the 'activity' of the one, true God. Yet this much must be said: if such questions and answers had gone any further (two intellects? two ...?), it would soon have become quite impossible to conceive of Jesus as one single individual.

But, secondly, the enthusiastic pursuit of affirmations of unity did not of itself guarantee success in orthodoxy any more than did inventories of the 'content' of the 'natures'. Chalcedon saw 'the properties of each nature being preserved, and both concurring into one *prosopon* and one *hypostasis* – not parted or divided into two *prosopa*, but one and the same Son and only-begotten, the divine Word, the Lord Jesus Christ'. Now this is a very simple statement of the individual unity of the Founder, formulated in what were, for that time, very obvious terms. 'One *prosopon*' says in more popular terms what 'one *hypostasis*' can say somewhat more eruditely, namely, that the one in question comes across to others or objectifies himself to others as one, single individual, or 'object', or 'character'. It is all assertion, and no explanation. Now 'one *prosopon*' was a formula for unity adopted by Nestorius. So, when we see Grillmeier make the following assessment of Nestorius, we realize that something more elaborate has attached itself to this formula in the tradition, something more than the simple point of the preceding paragraph above would lead one to suspect. 'Nestorius,' Grillmeier claims, 'does not fully see the metaphysical structure of this word "Christ". He does not show by it that the Logos is subject as the bearer of both the divinity and the humanity.'[46] What Grillmeier here suggests, and what is in fact assumed by much of the Christian tradition, is that the one *prosopon*, the one *hypostasis*, the one 'subject' in question in Chalcedonian orthodoxy is that of the Word of God.

All that can be said here is that it is quite possible to conclude as much; though it is scarcely possible to prove beyond any doubt that the Chalcedonian formula itself requires that we should so conclude. The one *prosopon* or *hypostasis* of Chalcedon is indeed named Son and Word, but the same *prosopon* or *hypostasis* also bears the composite name of Lord Jesus Christ. In any case, it would seem quite orthodox to say that the one *hypostasis* is that of the Word or Son of God. One is then simply saying that in Jesus the Word or Son of God objectifies itself to us and we encounter it. Then also, of course, one should be allowed to say that the one *hypostasis* we meet in Jesus is the *hypostasis* of the man, Jesus,[47] for that is the other side of the coin of our confession, that, if we encounter the Word of God in Jesus, we still encounter only Jesus, the man of faith.

The occupational hazard of such exclusive location of the one *hypostasis*, and it is a hazard only too easy to illustrate from the tradition, is the block-building hazard, that is, the tendency to reify, the tendency to see natures and *hypostaseis* as things (the numbers one and two facilitate this deadly move even more), things like blocks which have to be put together, so that the more there are of them, the more problematic becomes the unity of the ensuing structure. It is generally true of our theological tradition, when, as it generally did, it identified the one *hypostasis* of Chalcedon with the Word, with the divine rather than the human nature, that it immediately began to drift once more, quite unconsciously, toward the attractive sirens of Apollinarius. For this identification resulted, to the block-building mentality at least, in the denial to Jesus of a human *prosopon*, or *persona*, or *hypostasis*.

The trick, then (I hope I do not speak too facetiously of my theological tradition), was this: so to redefine the idea of person or *hypostasis* that its absence to the humanity of Jesus would not take from that humanity in the least. It would not do to deny to the humanity of Jesus, as Apollinarius did, the spirit or rational centre of the personality. But suppose person were defined, as the sixth-century philosopher Boethius defined it, as 'the individual substance of a rational nature'; that was close enough to the Greek word *hypostasis*, stressing as it did substantiality and individuality over against others; and suppose *hypostasis* were further refined in meaning, as it was by the Eastern theologian, Leontius of Byzantium, to refer to independent existence, to the subsistence proper to things which exist in their own right and not as parts of qualities of other things.[48] At this point it seems easy and obvious to say that the human nature of Jesus simply lacked its own independent existence or subsistence, that it was retained in existence by the Word of God, and so it is not a *hypostasis* in itself; the one *hypostasis* is that of the Word of God.

This has become known as the Thomistic solution. Though in this, as in many other matters, it is difficult to define exactly the position of Aquinas himself. At one point Aquinas is simply saying that whatever is contained in or belongs to a person is made one 'in *persona*', and so that must hold also for the humanity of Jesus (*Summa Theologiae* 3, q.2, a.2); one could also say 'made one in *hypostasis*', since this word is equivalent to person where rational natures are concerned (*Summa Theologiae* 3, q.2, a.3). But he does then say that the person in question is the person of the Son of God, so that a human person is not believed to have been assumed in the incarnation (*Summa Theologiae* 3, q.4, a.2, ad 1), and he does also say that the word 'person' implies existence *per se* or subsistence (*Summa Theologiae* 3, q.2, a.2, ad 2); so that those theorists had a good case who interpreted Aquinas to mean that person is defined most strictly by the concept of subsistence, that the human nature of Christ does not have its own subsistence but subsists by the subsistence of the Word, and that the one person in Jesus is therefore purely and simply identical with the Word.

This solution, in my view, represents the least possible form of Apollinarianism,[49] or the most tolerable, whichever expression is preferred. Whether it means anything very much is, of course, another question. For what it could mean to a nature which is complete of its kind to exist but not by its own proper existence is something of a conundrum to the shrewdest metaphysical mind – especially since Christians have traditionally said that God supports all created natures in existence.

Perhaps in the end the only course open to us is one which avoids reifying and block-building altogether. We are once again making faith-statements. And once again that means, not that we have revealed propositions on the subject of the structure of Jesus' personality to which we must give intellectual consent, but rather that the experience of our faith, which is ours because it was Jesus', demands that we say certain things about Jesus, namely, that in Jesus' human existence we encounter God, and yet we encounter only Jesus. We can say this, as Chalcedon said it, by affirming that the one we call Christ the Lord was made known to us in two natures, that is, that he functioned for us as God and as man, and that he was as yet only one, distinct, unique individual. That latter point, that we are dealing with one individual, could have been put in terms of *persona*, *prosopon*, *hypostasis*, or even *physis*; but if one wished to express simultaneously the two sides to Jesus (his total humanity in which we encounter divinity) and his individual unity, it would always be more natural, because of the characteristic range of meanings of the words in question, to say that he was known in two natures concurring in one *hypostasis*, rather than that he was two *hypostaseis*.

In any case, it is the faith of Jesus which is still determinative of how we acknowledge him. It is that distinctive faith of his which, when we catch it from him, allows us to come in contact with the God he called Father, and which then demands that we acknowledge his role between us and God in all the ways in which the orthodox tradition did this. It is still the conviction, the spirit of this lived faith which is important, and these many confessions are important in linking us still to its one historical source, Jesus of Nazareth, and, further, in forming what someone called its intellectual outposts, its notice of intent to remain what it is, its defence against the possible vandalism of those who do not really understand and appreciate it.

7

Christian Faith and Human History

*The perennial value of the modern quest: emphasis on
the human and the historical*

Despite the academic waywardness of some of the early questers, and the dead ends so often encountered in the course of the
quest of the historical Jesus, the main driving instinct behind
that quest, the intent to discover the actual historical character
and to uncover the human Jesus, has lost none of its vitality in
our time. That intent closely corresponded to the dominant
mentality of the age in which the modern quest began. It is still
fed from that obsession with humanity in its historical dimension which dominates the mentality of the West to this day. And
the quest of the historical Jesus, pursued with that intent
uppermost in mind, has never finally proved either to be misconceived in its nature or to have failed in its results. There is no
reason to doubt that the quest of the historical Jesus, pursued
with our particular interests, cannot yet provide the best version
of the faith of Jesus to speak to our age, if only to challenge the
limits we seem to have placed on human prospects in our very
enthusiasm for their discovery.

Strauss was quite correct in his insistence on the presence of
myth everywhere in the New Testament, but he was wrong in
concluding that the historical truth about Jesus and his faith
could only be found after the New Testament had been
demythologized. On the contrary, myth provides us with one of
our most powerful means of probing the deepest significance for
our human existence of some person, or event, or feature of our
world; and it can deal with the real just as easily as it can deal in
the purely fictional. For those who understand its nature and
can work on its terms, myth places no obstacles before the quest
of the historical Jesus.

Bruno Bauer was equally correct in his insistence on the artistic creativity of the New Testament writers. The gospels in particular are the creations of literary artists, with all the freedom in dealing with the available material which this implies. But he was wrong in forcing such a dichotomy between artistic creation and historical veracity that the figure of Jesus finally disappeared altogether from view. Everything depends here on what precisely the artist wishes to convey. If it is the spirit given flesh and form in a man's mature life, a spirit which has inspired the lives of others and which is now to be communicated in word and image, then arguably the artist can do more justice to this than can the more pedantic biographer. It is a commonplace of the visual arts that a portrait by a good painter can do more justice to my person than the most realistic of photographs.

Albert Schweitzer was also correct in his insistence that so many of the questers who preceded him had actually succeeded only in fashioning one Jesus after another, each in turn in the image and likeness of the quester concerned. For it is a notorious feature of the dominant mentality of a time that it can colour the conclusions reached much more than the people of the time are aware. And it is obvious that there can be quite a variation in views about the best historical prospects for humanity. So Kant and Reimarus could only see Jesus as the first exponent of their ideal morality and of the basic religious beliefs which they thought were attached to this. And even the elaborate categories in which Hegel tried to capture the essence of spirit in its historical evolution, however revelatory of the nature of our world, proved incapable in the end of doing justice to the historic founder of the Christian faith. Much less adequate, of course, and even more restricting, were the alleged laws of human psychology which a literary man like Emile Zola was happy to lay down as the basis of the modern realistic novel (Zola's practice, fortunately was better than his psychological theory), and with which Renan approached the character of the historical Jesus. Schweitzer was undoubtedly correct in insisting that those who truly discover the historical Jesus will meet, not an endorsement of their own views of ideal morality, or religion, or humanity, but the most radical challenge to those views they are ever likely to encounter.

But was Schweitzer correct in describing – or, rather, in refusing to describe – the manner in which that challenge comes to us? Is his distinction between spiritual and natural truth itself too absolute? Recall that Schweitzer presented the historical

Jesus as a literal-minded apocalyptic visionary; then said that
the spirit of Jesus would come to us 'as one unknown'. Does it
not seem that at this point the spirit in question was not embodied
in the historical Jesus at all, or was embodied in him only in a
most bizarre and unexemplary way? The question here is an important one, and will bear some unhurried concluding reflections.
It concerns, at one and the same time, the validity of the quest of
the historical Jesus and the true nature of the Christian faith.

Recall Kähler's contention, more recently developed and
made popular by Bultmann, that little could be known with
certainty about Jesus, but that this fact was not of any
significance, since it was the biblical Christ, the Christ of faith,
that was important, not the historical Jesus. By the time Bultmann has finished developing Kähler's thesis, it is clear, the
embargo on the quest of the historical Jesus is no longer based
primarily upon the alleged inability of historical method working on the sources at our disposal to paint a substantial picture
of the historical Jesus. It is the nature of Christian faith, rather,
which is invoked in order to deter Christians from continuing
with the quest of the historical Jesus. The point is made with
mainly theological intent by Bultmann, as in his oft-quoted sentence: 'Faith, being personal decision, cannot be dependent
upon a historian's labours'.[1] It is made with more philosophical
intent by Van Harvey when he describes the difference of quality in the judgments made by believers and historians: the
believer's judgment is expressed with utter conviction, the historian's must always be qualified appropriately by the present
state of the evidence for it.[2] Clearly enough, the suggestion in
both cases is that Christian faith should not require the support
of critical history.

Now there is no doubt that the New Testament is comprised
of faith documents, written by men of faith in order to arouse a
similar faith in others. There is no doubt that these writers
would prefer me to be a saved ignoramus, saved by this faith,
than a damned, good historian. There is no doubt that they
would prefer me to take Jesus as God's anointed, as my Lord,
than to see me demonstrate my ability to write his definitive
biography. But does any of this imply that the Christian faith is
essentially independent of history? I do not think so.

My personal suspicion is that people who try to force upon me
a too dichotomous choice between Christian faith and critical
history are hiding from me, and perhaps from themselves, a
very definite, and a very questionable, presumption about the

Christian faith. This need not necessarily be a questionable presumption about the content of Christian faith, about the answer
to the question: what do you believe? Bultmann, as one might
expect from so great an exegete, is as accurate an advocate for
the meaning of Christian faith as the faith could desire. In a
sermon which he preached during the summer of the year I was
born, he portrayed in a masterly fashion, devoid of the ruinous
jargon of German theology, the faith we can learn from the
crucifixion, that all things are from God and are nothing without
God.[3] His professional exegesis of the faith-documents which
make up the New Testament, and particularly his magisterial
expose of the theology of *The Gospel of John*[4] is as valuable a
presentation as one could wish of the real message of these
documents. But when the question concerns the source of this
faith in our lives, the manner in which we can contract this faith,
then Bultmann's presumptions begin to show, and then they are
questionable.

Of course, no man or woman of Christian faith would deny
that God is the original source of faith, as God is the original
source of everything, nor would any question the fact that God
works in mysterious ways. But those who take the incarnation at
all seriously[5] must agree that it is possible also to point to the
ways in our world through which we may believe God works.
Otherwise incarnation, whether as myth or theory, is a simple
falsehood, an inexcusable error.

The object of our faith, according to Bultmann, is the Christ of
the kerygma (the Christ of Christian preaching or proclamation)
and not the person of the historical Jesus,[6] and 'the Christ of the
kerygma is not a historical figure which could enjoy continuity
with the historical Jesus'.[7] The Christ of Christian preaching is
the risen Lord, not the historical Jesus. Bultmann would not
want us to think that the faith by which our lives are quite
literally saved is 'mere knowledge' or intellectual acceptance of a
'theoretical world view' that refers all existence back to a creator
God.[8] Rather, there is 'an individual man like us in whose action
God acts, in whose destiny God is at work, in whose word God
speaks'.[9] And to have faith in this one is to let God rule our lives
and not let them be ruled by any human power or plan or any
worldly possession. 'What we are to learn from the cross of
Christ is to go so far as to believe precisely this; and it is for this
reason that Christ is our Lord, through whom are all things and
through whom we exist.'[10]

But, of course, 'in the kerygma the mythical form of the Son of

God has appeared in place of the historical person of Jesus'. [11]
This means, in effect, that in Bultmann's system the specific
content of the Christian faith, the obedience of faith which we
already described in this book and which coincides with Bultmann's descriptions, the lesson we learn from the cross, comes
to us from the risen Lord presented in the preaching and not from
the historical Jesus. The man in whose action God acts, in whose
destiny God is at work, in whose word God speaks, is the Son of
God, not the historical Jesus. 'The obedience and self-emptying
of Christ of which he (i.e., Paul) speaks (Phil. 2.6–9; Rom. 15.3;
II Cor. 8.9) are attitudes of the pre-existent and not of the historical Jesus,' 'and the cross is not regarded from a biographical
standpoint but as saving event.'[12] What can one say to this?

That the Christian preaching brings us into contact with
Christ, Son of God, Lord, a crucified and risen saviour, coincides with some principal conclusions of this present work. That
the acceptance of Jesus as Lord, Son of God, Christ, and the
living of the kind of faith already so often described, are one and
the same thing: to this we have already agreed. But that our
acceptance of Lord and faith is due (under God) in no way to the
historical Jesus, his words, deeds, and destiny, but is due, under
God, only to the kerygma – to that it seems impossible to agree.

Since we are here in the presence of the most determined
challenge to any quest of the historical Jesus as in any way
relevant to the future of Christian belief, a challenge that is
offered now, not on behalf of historical method and historical
sources, but on behalf of the alleged source of Christian faith
itself, it seems necessary to meet that challenge in some detail.

Just because Bultmann insists that the object of our Christian
faith is the Christ of the proclamation, the risen Lord rather than
the historical Jesus, we are not entitled to conclude that he is
totally sceptical about the prospect of discovering the historical
Jesus. His particular challenge to the historical quest, as we have
just remarked, is based on considerations concerning the Christian faith, not on distrust of the historical sources. So, with due
respect for the qualifications with which all historical judgments
must be accompanied, he agrees with a good deal of what the
so-called post-Bultmannians discovered in the course of the new
quest of the historical Jesus, a venture of some of his own pupils
which took its name from the very fact that the quest began
again after Bultmann had declared its irrelevance to Christian
faith. In fact, in an essay of his on 'Jesus and Paul', Bultmann
provides a masterly interpretation of Jesus' own preaching and

he concludes that 'what one encounters in Jesus is the same God who is encountered in Paul – the God who is Creator and Judge, who claims man completely for himself, and who freely gives his grace to him who becomes nothing before him.'[13] So there is no basic difference, in Bultmann's view, between the preaching of Jesus and that of his followers. Our conclusions, in Chapter 5, about the basic possibility of repeating Jesus' teaching in different forms, follow Bultmann, and indeed were much indebted to him.

Bultmann was even prepared to admit (again in duly qualified historical judgment) that though Jesus may not have claimed for himself any of the titles in which his followers later confessed his religious significance to them, some christology may well have been implicit in 'Jesus' own claim that man's destiny is decided with reference to his person'.[14] So neither could Bultmann object in principle to our conclusions on this point which closed Chapter 4.

Where, then, exactly does Bultmann's challenge to the quest of the historical Jesus lie? The answer, in terms of the table of contents of this book, is this: just at that point where we tried to discover and validate the logic by which the myth about Jesus developed from Jesus' own myth of the reign of God. It is just at this point, where we tried to see the connections of a living logic of faith, that Bultmann insists on an unbridgeable gap. For, he asks, if the simple repetition of Jesus' own proclamation could give us the new life of faith, where is the need for the demand that we confess Jesus as Christ, Son of God, Lord? In Bultmann's view, there would then be no need for the latter confession. History, by recovering the preaching of Jesus, could bring to us the challenge of Jesus' own proclamation, could face us with it, and we could by God's grace accept it. The fact that Jesus is our Lord precisely because he, the historical Jesus, inserts into our history the challenge and the possibility of new faith and new life, by his preaching which is continued in various forms, by the prayer he introduces to our lives, by the ritual he invites us still to celebrate and the service to which he inspires us – this Bultmann is not prepared to admit. He would object to our use of the present tense in the verbs of that last sentence, and with that objection we shall have to deal in our very next section, for it is potentially damaging to our understanding of the resurrection as the first myth of the man Jesus. He would continue to insist that what we really mean is that history can bring us back to 'then', to the preaching of the historical Jesus, and can face us with the challenge of faith, by simply repeating the preaching it has recovered. He would add that such repetition, on the basis of historical research or historical memory, does not make Jesus present 'now' as our Lord, as the Christian faith confesses.[15]

His alternative suggestion is this: it is the proclamation of the Christian community, not the repetition of the alleged preaching of Jesus or of the implications of his ministry, that can enable us, by God's grace, to confess Jesus as our present Lord, the crucified and risen saviour, in the confession of whose name we contract that faith in God as the creator and giver of all life and existence by which we must then live. Only the Christian preaching demands our faith in the fact that this once crucified man is Lord of the world, and thus faces us with the awful paradox that the least likely of events is God's saving action in the world. It is not our acceptance of the faith by which we know he lived, and for which we know he died (a faith that reverses our natural tendencies to idolize human plans and mundane powers) that makes us confess him our Lord. Rather the preaching demands that we accept him in faith as our Lord and then the proclamation of his crucifixion clearly indicates that, as part of the content of this faith, 'it is demanded of man that he subject himself to God's judgment, i.e. to the judgment that all of man's desires and strivings and standards of value are nothing before God, that they are all subject to death'.[16]

It is not clear how the proclamation reads that lesson into an ancient execution the details of which are no longer relevant; unless it be that the sheer unlikelihood of declaring Lord and Christ a man executed as a common criminal is thought to imply such a general judgment on all human wisdom. Or perhaps, since we are dealing with a proclamation which simply demands faith, we are not supposed to ask such logical questions. In any case, the corollary of the proclamation of the crucified Lord is the proclamation of the risen Lord. For if faith in the crucified Lord which the proclamation demands implies that we cease to idolize created things, faith in the risen Lord in the same proclamation means that we entrust our lives to God, and that the God of the living will give us true life. Just as the actual historical details of the death of Jesus are irrelevant to the faith demanded by the Christian proclamation when it presents the crucified Lord, so naturally stories of empty tombs and of appearances, if taken literally, are 'a concession to the weakness of man' and 'of no consequence' to the faith contained in the preaching of the risen Lord and to the belief that God alone is the giver and guarantor of life.[17]

There is no doubt about the fact that Bultmann truly understands the heart, the essence, the basic content of the Christian faith. But some very puzzling questions about its source and origin remain. Where does the Christian proclamation come from and where did it get this specific content, if not from the actual, historical life and death of Jesus of Nazareth? It came from God. Of course. So, according to itself, does everything. But from whom, or from what, or from where, under God, does it come? From Paul, or from the last preacher you heard, or from the last Christian you met whose life really gave witness to it? But where did they get it?

Clearly Bultmann does not want such' questions asked or answered. All attempts to raise and resolve such questions represent to him an illicit procedure, an attempt to 'legitimate' our preaching and our responding faith, an attempt to give ourselves 'a good conscience' about it.[18] We are faced purely and simply with the proclamation which Bultmann has outlined and with the challenge contained in it to respond with radical faith in the one, true God. It makes no difference from what human words or deeds it came to us (oddly enough the only one from whom we can be quite sure this proclamation did not come is the historical Jesus). We are to make no attempt to get behind the proclamation to look for source and origin. We are to respond in faith, and that is all. There speaks a true representative of the *sola fide* position of the Protestant Reformation.[19] There also is the final indication that it is considerations concerning faith, and not disappointment with the historical sources, that motivate Bultmann to insist on the irrelevance of the quest of the historical Jesus.

Very well. But we should at least note that a high price may have to be paid for such success in keeping Christian faith pure and uncontaminated by the contingencies of human history.

For, on Bultmann's account of it, and no matter how much Bultmann himself may insist that it is not just another theoretical world view but a kind of life to be lived, the Christian faith is bound to look, first and foremost, like a message telling us how life is to be lived, and coded in these strange old symbols of divine persons being crucified and raised again: a gospel, origin unknown, which makes the world of our ordinary human history its object, but to the source and content of which that same world of humanity and its history is originally as irrelevant as is the human life and tragic human death of Jesus of Nazareth; a

proclamation which, even when decoded according to Bultmann's demythologizing programme (shades of Strauss),
speaks to or at humanity and its history rather than from
humanity and its history, and yet supposedly speaks of the
deepest springs and most distant goals of our empirical existence; a faith that bears all the marks of being adventitious,
however insistently it proposes that we shape our historical lives
by means of it.

Although this theory of the Christian faith does not lower the
world of our historical experience quite as much as do literal
theories of special divine revelatory interventions, on the one
hand, or absolute theories of fallen nature, on the other, it
nevertheless refuses adamantly to admit that that world of our
historical experience could itself be the very source of our faith
in the God who created it and gave it to us – if only through the
mediation of the man Jesus. It refuses utterly the possibility that
our Christian faith, which is the appreciative sense of our historical existence as itself a grace of God which urges us to make all
our historical existence gracious, has its source in that same
historical existence. It refuses, in the end, the great and obvious
strength of knowing that the treasure we seek is in and of our
world, belongs there and always did belong, however long we
may have trampled over it uncaring, and that there is thus as
much hope for our world as we could ever want. Those who
force a dichotomy between faith and history are really the last of
a long line of human beings who have given up on history.

Humanity and its history: such is the preferred perspective of
the modern quest for meaning. We may be led beyond it, but we
will not be led away from it. And there is every prospect that we
may be led much further beyond the conditions of our present
existence, at least in hope, if our world and its history is itself the
source of our faith in God and not some proclamation into the
origin of which we may not even inquire.

The great advantage of the quest of the historical Jesus is that
it directs us to the mundane source of our faith within our world
and our history. The problem is not, as some think, that the quest
has gone on too long or gone too far; the problem is that it has not
yet been pursued with that combination of unqualified enthusiasm and unprejudiced professionalism which it deserves.

The lasting nature of Christian faith: seeking God in human history

'As far as faith is concerned,' wrote Unamuno, 'it is not a question of whether a spiritual, or historical, force existed once, but of whether it exists now.'[20] If history is to be understood as an academic exercise with its resulting array of scholarly argument, then Bultmann was correct in his insistence that faith does not depend upon a historian's labours. For even the most learned product of historical research, should it succeed in bringing us back to the time of Jesus, face-to-face with the challenge of his own words and deeds, would be as unlikely to arouse in us the distinctive Christian faith as would a verbal kerygma of the Lordship of the Crucified which refused to allow its credentials to be in any way questioned.

It is history the reality of our world, not history the science of the past, which provides the intra-mundane source for that distinctive Christian faith by which some people today still try to live. History the reality is not something discovered or revived by raising it with scholarly incantation from an ancient sepulchre of dry and fragile manuscripts; history the thing is a spiritual, or historical, force that exists now. History the science has its subsidiary role to play in maintaining the identity and vitality of history the reality, and we shall acknowledge that role later. But for the moment we are concerned to understand how persons and events from our past can be for us a spiritual, and a religious, force in the present, and that means returning briefly, for one last time, to the myth about the man Jesus.

The myth about Jesus ranged from the resurrection preaching to the statement at Nicaea that the Word of God enfleshed in Jesus was 'one in being' with the one God whom Jesus called Father. It has been our conviction that myth can tell the truth about the deepest human significance of historical characters and events just as well as it can convey such significance by the use of the fabulous. It has also been our conviction that once myth has been allowed to exercise upon us that powerful evocative force which can bring us to our deepest appreciation of the conditions of human existence, we can then express that appreciation in more literal ways. Finally, it has been our conviction that when myth speaks of God, it does so by taking its symbols from the facts and features of our mundane existence which seemed most significant to the mind of the myth-maker; for, as the Fourth Gospel put it rather peremptorily, 'no one has ever seen God'. The very fact that a myth attached itself at all to the man Jesus means that some people think him significant still for our lives. Our question here is: how does the myth convey the present spiritual or historical force of Jesus? It is in answering that question, if we can do it, that we discover the lasting nature of the Christian faith.

The myth began, let us recall briefly, by conveying to us, in the central element of resurrection preaching, the conviction of an act of God on and through Jesus, the origin of which was not detectable (as is the case with acts of God), but the effect of which was, or could be, contemporary with anyone who heard the myth proclaimed in any acceptable form at any time. The myth, therefore, had many ways of asserting the identity of the Jesus we could meet at any time with the Jesus who once walked with Peter and James and John – the myth talked of seeing, hearing, touching, eating with. The myth, finally, made its most explicit claim that in this same Jesus, as Son or Word of God, we truly encounter the one, true God; that Jesus, as Son or Word, is 'one in being with the Father'. Is it possible to say in more literal, conceptual terms how all this could be? It is, and let the following few paragraphs stand as an example of how this can be done.

The attempt might well be built round the answers to two very obvious questions. First, in what exactly is thought to consist this alleged identity which the myth in its way claims between Jesus of Nazareth and the one Christians say they still encounter as Lord in their lives? Second, how is it at all conceivable that, in Unamuno's words, one who was a spiritual, or historical, force once should be a spiritual and historical force now? Another way of putting the second question: what on earth allows us to juggle tenses as we have done? Instead of saying 'Jesus once inspired people to live thus', we say 'Jesus inspires people to live thus', and in many similar linguistic constructions we show similar disregard for the distinction between past and present tenses. How is such apparent grammatical indiscriminacy justified?

The first question is undoubtedly the simpler of the two. The identity of Jesus which is recognized by his followers and which can be discovered by historical research is the identity forged by the major thrust of his life. That is the kind of answer which must be given in the case of people who turn out to be of some significance to others. Most of us prove to be of little or no significance for others principally because our own identities are dispersed and fluctuating. They are due more to accident than to design: accident of birth, accident of job availability, accident of personal encounter, and even death turns out to be the last unexpected accident of life. On the contrary, there are those who gradually forge for themselves out of all they do and all they meet such a strong identity for themselves that even death seals their identity with its own awful finality. The identity of Jesus which makes him of supreme significance for others was forged by what the New Testament writers call his obedience, and what we understand as his faith, that distinctive faith of his which has been so often, and yet so inadequately, described in the course of this book. The life he lived was to him a gift from God, in itself and in all its supports, and as precious to God as only a gift can be which one truly desires to give. It would have been achievement enough had he lived his life as a carpenter or fisherman in such faith. But he made it his life's work, as his public mission attests, to convey in word and attitude and action such faith conviction to others. For, to quote Unamuno again, from a book called *Our Lord Don Quixote* (in which Don Quixote bears more than a passing resemblance to Jesus):

> Faith is contagious, and Don Quixote's is so robust and fiery that it redounds upon those who love him, and they share it without loss to Don Quixote, whose faith instead increases. And such is the condition of living faith: it increases by spending itself and grows upon being parcelled out – since, if it is true and alive, it is nothing else than love.[21]

So much was this faith his own personal identity that those who caught it from him in the brief contagion of his public ministry could only call themselves slaves of this one master; and those who rejected it could see no other option than to rid their world of his person. How wrong they were in thinking that death could put an end to him we shall have to try to explain in answer to our second question. For the moment it is necessary only to notice that the personal identity of Jesus was forged and is still recognized by the distinctive, powerful and contagious spirit of his life and mission.

But how does a spiritual, or historical, force which existed once, exist now? Our century has less excuse for failure clearly and cogently to answer that question than had any century which preceded ours. For we are more and more aware of the evolutionary, historical nature of our world. We are more and more convinced that the way we are, and the way our world is, is itself in every way the result of those dominant mutations which make up the evolution of our world and our history. How a spiritual force which once existed could still be effectively present today must be less a mystery to us than it may have been to any of our predecessors. In other words, we have more than one way of understanding transcendence, the process of passing beyond the boundaries of any place and time.

Sartre distinguished the two kinds of transcendence toward the end of his essay on *Existentialism*: the transcendence which is a constituent element of man in the existential conditions of our empirical world, and the transcendence of God. (Camus also describes, toward the end of *The Rebel*, a transcendence of which beauty holds the key and the artist is mediator.) By the latter Sartre meant a region of reality and truth which is itself above and beyond our world, but which in its own unmistakable form enters our world by select divine interventions in our history. Now it may be that previous centuries were of necessity more prone than we are to understand transcendence in this latter way: and that they were therefore more prone to take literally the symbolism of the myth about Jesus. When they repeated the story of the eternal generation of God's Son, of his incarnation on a particular day, of his 'revelation' of the mysteries of God's own being and mind and will, of his return to his former state and place, then of his further returns to earth, first in physical form, then in the consecrated bread and wine of the eucharist, and finally in still more 'spiritual' and indefinable ways, they may have been prone to think that they were actually issuing literal descriptions of personal processes which took place in another world and of the periodic commerce of persons in that world with ours. Though, of course, there was no Christian century which did not understand that the spirit of Jesus was transmitted through the lives of Christian people, their words and attitudes, and their deeds, both moral and ritual.

However that may be, we have no excuse if we fail to give a more defensible account of that transcendence of Jesus which we confess when we call him our risen Lord, the one in whom we still encounter today the one, true God.

There came a man to rule over the world, wrote Schweitzer; he ruled it for good or ill, as history testifies; he destroyed the world into which he was born and the spiritual life of our own time seems like to perish at his hands. The spirit of Jesus, by which his very person is identified, shaped and still shapes the world of our common experience. For there is no neutral reality out there which our efforts at knowing are simple attempts to record. There is only the reality that has made us what we are and that we have made what it is in that long and inextricably woven process of perception, evaluation and interaction which we can call either history or faith. The faith of Jesus, in so far as the world would allow it, has given us the world that we know.

The same faith of Jesus is the centre of his historical and historic identity, and he is therefore present in our world (though it is still far from his full stature). This is the kind of transcendence which Sartre described as a constituent element of our human existence. It is a passing beyond the boundaries of particular people, places, and times which is due to the free creativity of human beings in our historical world.

How, though, is it a transcendence which carries us to religious heights? How does it involve God? Not because of the nature of this transcendent process, but because of its content; for the process of human transcendence is present and palpable in any area of human creativity, whether it be political, economic, military, artistic, or religious.

But Jesus was neither statesman nor economist, neither general nor renowned author, though he was certainly a story-teller and probably something of a poet. He was a man who lived a faith in God, who lived the significant years of his life, and died, for that same faith in God. Jesus saw the presence of God as Father in all things and particularly in all people: he responded to the invitation issued in every existence and event. Because he did so and gave his life to this faith, anyone can see the Father God, as Jesus knew him, in Jesus. The same stuff of existence is still all around us, land and sea, cattle and fowl and fruit-trees, bread and wine, oil and energy, and people. And the spirit which Jesus breathed into a dying world is still present in books and buildings, in lectures and rituals, and above all in patterns of living and in people; still pointing to the invitation issued in every existing thing and event, and enabling us to respond.

No one has ever seen God. But in this spirit, which we identify as Jesus of Nazareth, we encounter God. By this faith, which is the personal identity of the man Jesus, we are acquitted of our complicity in evil, knowing that the price of our complicity has been paid (someone always pays for lost innocence), we are healed of our self-destructive tendencies, freed from our fatal enslavement to fear, in touch, to put it positively, with the ultimate power of life which we call God. So when we talk of Jesus we naturally talk of an act of God by which Jesus is the Lord who is victorious over the powers of death and destruction. We are not referring to any publicly verifiable act of God which took place after Jesus' death, much less at his baptism, birth or conception.[22] No, we are referring rather to the fact that we sense ourselves in touch with the power of life through the distinctive spirit, the distinctive faith of Jesus, a spirit which is as alive today as it was when the man of flesh and blood, Jesus of Nazareth, set out to summon people to prepare for the reign of God the Father. What happened to the man of flesh and blood, Jesus of Nazareth, after his death, what happened to the body and mind which first housed and breathed that spirit into the world (without which that body and mind would be to us those of a stranger), we have no reliable historical evidence, specifically bearing on that point, to enable us to decide. The personal resurrection of that individual casing for the spirit we still know is an article of faith for us, based on everything we know and believe about that individual; it is not a preamble to that faith.[23]

The distinctive faith of Jesus, the distinctive spirit of Jesus, is history. This means *both* that we can discover it by historical method, and that it is woven into the very texture of our historical experience. If, then, as would-be followers of Jesus, we would seek the presence of the living God, we are directed, without alternative, to that human history in which it is both hidden and revealed. We are directed to the unevenness of our human world, to its loyalties and betrayals, there to find the spirit of Jesus which is present in the sheer gratuity of things, and in the spirit of Jesus we are enabled to accept all as God's good grace, even those who, like ourselves, have betrayed the spirit of Jesus. In this way we are required to be embodiments of Jesus' spirit in the world.

The Lord of history

Jesus is Lord. That is the most basic confession of our faith, and one of the oldest. Jesus is Lord of history. That is to say: he reaches and effects us through the ordinary stuff of which history is made, our eating and drinking, work and play, marrying and procreating and dying. He is no colonial Lord, however; he is a native leader. He does not descend into our spatio-temporal continuum from another world. Born of a woman, like everyone else, he is like us in every way, though not like us in sin.

For every colonial Lord who might come from eternity to our temporal shores would carry with him the implicit claim that he is of superior nature to ours. All colonial overlords have exercised their coercive power over their subject peoples, and have collected their exorbitant fees, in the name of such innate superiority. And they always will. Even when they do not deliberately set out to destroy it altogether, their very presence is a commentary upon the inferiority of native life. And even their attempts to foster the native arts are seldom more than haphazard instances of enlightened and benign condescension. Colonialism corrodes the native substance and devalues it. Now we Christians believe that we are not colonial subjects of God, ruled by his lieutenant on earth and his lieutenant's lieutenants; we are sons and daughters of God. And Jesus, correspondingly, invites his followers; he does not coerce inferiors. We may, of course, be mistaken about all this. But then the mistake we have made is the mistake of trying to be Christian.

The truest and deepest evaluation of our world, of all things great and small, and all people, good, bad, and indifferent, is not conveyed to us by a decree issued to us by someone outside our world. That would be as anomalous as the prospect of one human person being given his or her human rights by another (for if you have to be given rights, they are not, and will never be your rights); or as anomalous as a long conceptual explanation which has to be attached to a symbol every time it is used (for if a symbol has to be explained, it is not symbolizing; it is not a symbol any more). In the same way, to give something value by decree is as artificial as sticking a price-tag on it, and just as arbitrary. Even the value which something has as a gift cannot be decreed, not even by the giver. The value of all life and existence as gift of God could not be decreed, not even by God, and not by Jesus as literal bearer of God's decree to our world. The act of valuing issues from the living centre of personal freedom. The giving of value to a gift is not done by decree of the giver, not even if the gift is life itself and the giver is the creator God. The giving of value to a gift is the joint act of the giver in giving, and of the receiver in free and appreciative reception. (The Giver places the treasure at our feet where we can walk on it or take it up in appreciation, and issues an invitation to the feast of life, which we can refuse.)

All human perception has an evaluation at its core, and all genuine evaluation issues in attitude and action. Jesus dared to perceive and value his own life, to accept it, as the cherished gift of God. He held it in the chalice of his allotted span, in that Janus-like attitude of letting go and yet anticipating, of reception and offering. He dared to accept also as gift of God all that he met on the face of this lean earth, especially all the people, and to treat them as such in open acceptance of their persons and service to their human needs. That was his perception-evaluation-action, his faith. In no other way, then, than the living of such a human life, could Jesus have conveyed the value of all life and existence, of all the stuff of which all ordinary human history is made, as the gift of God by which we are bound to and for our Father. He could not do so by being the other-wordly bearer of a decree of literal divine revelation. The faith of Jesus is utterly inseparable from the life of Jesus which fashioned his historic personality. It is the Jesus of history who is the Lord of history; the man Jesus who is in and of our history, who leads history from within, and does not try to govern it as a drop-in.

This faith lived by the man Jesus, and conveyed by him to his true followers in the living contagion of which Unamuno spoke, is our healing experience of the presence and power of God – if we are open to it. Hence we say that in Jesus we meet the one, true God; only in Jesus do we meet the one, true God; and yet we meet in our present historical world only Jesus. If there were another divine being, other than the one, true God whom Jesus called Father, or if another divine person had come (as we understand and apply the word 'person' in our culture), then Arius would have been correct. For there would then have been no way of refuting his logic that the one who takes origin (and orders) is inferior to the one who has no origin. And we should be facing in Jesus no real man, but a supernatural being who, by taking human form, faced us with some divine dispensation. Our historical existence would then be as devalued as would be our appreciation of the utter uniqueness of God. Consequently, the 'one in being' of Nicaea saved us not only from an inadequate understanding of the Christian God, but it saved us simultaneously from a depreciated sense of the value of our historical existence, in which, through the medium of Jesus' historical presence, we encounter the one, true God. The first letter to Timothy put the point of the Nicene definition when it said: 'There is one God, and one mediator between God and man, a man, Jesus the Christ' (2.5).

For those who say the Nicene creed to this day it is the ordinary history of their world, as shaped by the historical Jesus, that puts them in the presence of God. For them there is no significant difference between the Jesus of history and the Christ of faith, because there is no impenetrable mystery about the way in which the historical Jesus becomes Lord of history. For them, too, just as there are no supernatural beings who bring to their world good news which could not be humanly experienced in and through it, so there are for them no especially sacred people

or places, times or actions. It is the world or our ordinary history
that is valued as the gift of God and the path to his presence.

The eucharistic meal is sacrament and sacrifice to Christian
people precisely because it focuses attention on the sacrament
and sacrifice of all human meals, and especially on the universal, on-going meal which invites all God's family to the round
table of the earth to share in festive mood the abundance of the
sustenance for life. Sunday is a holiday only because it reminds
people through rest and recreation that all days, including working days, are holy, all just units of the total gift of life which
comes to us from God alone and which no work can give or
guarantee. The sabbath is for man, man is not for the sabbath.
Churches gather people under their roofs on occasion only to let
them know that wherever and whenever two or three people
who follow Jesus are gathered together, Jesus is present in the
midst of them. And some men and women can be accepted as
leaders in the Christian community only because their example
of service is an inspiration to their peers and never because they
try to lord it over any of the followers of Jesus. For one is lord
and master, and we are all brethren. No human beings are, by
virtue of office or state in life, holier or more sacred in their
persons or closer to God than others; and whatever sense we
may now make of priesthood in the Christian community, we
may never again think of priests as 'other Christs' in a sense in
which all Christian people cannot be called other Christs, nor
can we see them as standing between God and others,
mediators between God and humanity. One is the mediator,
Jesus, and through him all have equally immediate access to
God. Neither cult nor creed, neither code nor institution, can
ever again be allowed to rob people of the conviction conveyed
in the mission of Jesus that God is Father to all, present to all in
the gift of life and world which he gives to all without distinction, and accessible to all through the lives they live in the world
they know.

The final flowering of this faith which nourishes itself from all
ordinary history and then makes history in its turn is hope without limit, hope that even the last enemy will be defeated, the
death we must all of us one day die. Only those who receive life
as a precious gift and cherish it as such can yield it up in hope;
those who treat it as a conquest can only in despair see it torn
from their grasp.

Of course, just as there are those who are disappointed to
hear that there is no coercive evidence for the personal resurrec-

tion of the man Jesus, that instead our belief in his personal destiny is part and parcel of the faith we have from and in him, there are also those who regret having to entrust their own prospects of after-life to mere hope. They would far prefer to believe that we *know* about the after-life, that we had some verbal promises of its future reality, and some fairly literal descriptions of its content. They do not realize that even if we had such verbal promises, we should have as much trouble verifying their true origin and their possible reliability as we would have in believing in an after-life without them; nor do they realize that literal descriptions of an after-life would only serve to make it so much like this one that the whole project of trying to see it as the culmination of our human existence is threatened. But, most of all, people who express this kind of disappointment have failed to understand the nature of hope and to feel its power.

They are not altogether to blame for this. Just as in Western theology the Holy Spirit has been the neglected member of the Holy Trinity, so in Western philosophy hope has been the neglected member of the trinity of virtue: faith, hope and charity. Much has been written on faith and love, little or nothing, until quite recently, on hope. Yet hope is as important to human life as is faith or love. If human beings are stunted for want of love, and atrophy because of loss of faith, they literally wither away if they are deprived of hope. Hope, in fact, anchors faith as a perception of our world to our world; it strengthens love as an evaluation of our world; and it sustains active commitment to the causes we adopt.

Hope cannot be confused with knowledge; it is not a kind of prescience, since it is characteristically unable to describe in any literal way the lengths or depths or heights to which it moves us. But neither can it be reduced to mere wishing; and it has nothing whatever to do with idle calculation. Hope, quite literally, is the future of faith and love and active commitment. It is a rare plant which on certain soil grown sturdy and, in the end, indestructible. The soil on which it grows is the soil of active commitment in and to our world, an active commitment which itself is compounded of a certain perception and evaluation, of faith and love. (Before we get involved there is no hope for us.) On this soil, and only on this soil, hope grows. It binds this soil and takes it up into itself to reach for heaven. Amongst the acts of the human spirit it is to hope, which has its roots in the historic faith of Jesus, that the prospect of life beyond death may be most securely entrusted. So that here, even in the farthest reaches of the Christian faith, people are not dealing with known worlds that are alternatives to their own world; it is only through their perception and evaluation of this world and their commitment to it that they can hope to go beyond its known limits. The substance of Christian faith and the substance of human history is still the same substance.

Finally, even the writing of books such as this one (and perhaps the reading of them) is an act of faith and hope, besides being sometimes also a labour of love. Van Harvey, who was quoted some time back in favour of the distinction between faith and history, was quite correct of course in saying that historical studies can evoke only qualified assent. Books like this one, even if they were ten times as adequate to their subjects, cannot yield of themselves the Christian faith commitment. It is history, the reality of our world, the bearer still of the spirit of Jesus, that inspires faith. Books like this one suffer the same incapacity as history the science, which it is their business to research and record. But they play a contributory role, nevertheless, in that on-going process of reflection which is one of the least of the dues we can pay to the Christian faith.

And there is, in any case, an instructive analogy between the probabilities in which books such as this one deal and the type of commitment which is known as Christian faith. On one level the probabilities of history are part and parcel of all empirical attempts to see our world, past or present, as it really is, to give it its true value, and to make of it all that it can yet be. They thus correspond to faith, in that faith also operates, not with static realities which literally reveal God's nature and will (like deposits of revealed truths or immutable laws of nature), but with rich hints full of promise for those who can risk commitment. Faith's certainty is not the certainty of a clear and distinct idea which corresponds to a definitive objective reality, God and God's mind (a Cartesian ideal of knowledge never actually achieved in any area of the human quest for truth). Faith's certainty takes the form of fidelity, fidelity to a hint of promise contained in the gift of life and carried to us by the spirit of Jesus, and the ensuing task of unflinching commitment to the quest for God in the world, and unwavering hope. One does not need logically or empirically certain knowledge – even if such a thing is ever available in any area of human research – in order to support one's distinctive faith. The probabilities of history and the decisive commitment of evaluation and involvement which we call faith are complementary; they are not mutually exclusive or contradictory. The act of faith can take many forms; even the forms of researching, writing and reading books.

Appendix

The Baptism and Birth of Jesus

Sufficient notice has already been given to the penchant of some people for postulating a historical 'event' which enjoys the unquestioned status of a divine revelation and which takes the form of the personal resurrection of Jesus himself. This 'event', Martin Dibelius's 'x', is required to explain the origin and motivation of the full Christian faith, faith in Jesus as the Christ.

We have by now sufficient reason for thinking that when we follow the exegetes in search of this 'event', which will show us the first revelation of the distinct Christian faith, we finally arrive at an uncertain and highly inconclusive empty tomb, and at some 'non-hallucinatory' visions enjoyed by an uncertain number of individuals about which no reliable details can be given.

It seems obvious by now that the first historically verifiable event of the life and destiny of Jesus himself which the historian finds is the death of Jesus, not his personal resurrection. But the death of Jesus was such a scandal! How could anybody see in the execution of this man as a criminal the definitive revelation of God in human history? No, we could not seriously be expected to do so. There must have been another event which would remove the scandal of the first, which would show us a truly glorified Son of God, so that we could reasonably be expected to believe that this is indeed the Son of God.

Such is still the reaction of so many of us. No matter how minute the 'event' of the personal resurrection of Jesus left to us by the critical scholars, we still want it to do all that we demand of it. Dibelius's 'x' is still back there, whatever it was, and it founded the full Christian faith in Jesus. Above all, the 'x' excused us from going back to the place where we did not want to go, to the definitive revelation of God on Calvary.

I suspect that in this all too common attitude to the death/

resurrection of Jesus there is a pattern which applies also to our understanding of New Testament material on his birth and baptism, both, once again, very human historical events to which revelatory acts of special divine intervention, we like to believe, are attached. The pattern, I believe, could be expressed somewhat as follows: we are for ever looking for some well-documented divine intervention, some unquestionably divine words or acts, some clear signs from the heavens, from which we can derive the substance of our faith and its motivation. We do not wish to find the substance of our faith in the ordinary, the insignificant, the unpalatable, the weakness of this world which was to confound its strength; and we do not wish to find its motivation in the spirit of a man who tried to convey to all people and especially to outcasts and sinners, in his words, his prayer, his ritual meals, and above all in his service to them, that they were the cherished children of God. So when we find in the New Testament an unpalatable event together with a statement of the true significance of the one who underwent it, we try as best we can to divide it into two dimensions at least, if not two events, so that one part of the now double event will be human, all too human, but the other will clearly be of divine origin. (This is what we do with the event we sometimes call death-resurrection.) We thus impose our own system, in particular our own understanding of revelation, on the source of Christianity, and then, most tragically of all, we mistake the true nature of the faith of Jesus.

The baptism

The baptism of Jesus was not, of course, nearly as scandalous for his would-be followers as was his death. But it must have been quite scandalous nonetheless. It seems as if the movement begun by John the Baptizer was strong and widespread in the years that saw the birth of Christianity (Acts 19. 1-7), and, of course, to followers of John a man baptized by John would not automatically qualify for any office, except perhaps that of disciple of John (see the question posed by John's disciples in Luke 7. 18-25).

The baptism of John was, as our synoptics all agree, a baptism of repentance for the forgiveness of sins, a ritual of conversion which prepared one for the coming of God's reign. So those who came to John, the same accounts tell us, were baptized in the Jordan, confessing their sins. It was a cleansing, purifying, preparational ritual (Matthew 3.2,6,16; Luke 3.3; Mark 1.4f.). And Jesus, his followers can neither forget nor deny, underwent it. So perhaps the disciples of John were correct after all in considering Jesus' movement questionable, at least in so far as it tried to be distinct. Jesus pursued the reign of God as a convert of John the Baptizer; Jesus was not even original; he needed conversion before he could convert. Something of an upstart, perhaps, a parvenu.

In the New Testament the accounts of the baptism of Jesus and the references to it, it is by now well recognized, are mixtures of polemics and christology and, of course, a rather uncomfortable historical memory. The polemical interest is satisfied by having John renounce titles, some of which at least were applied to Jesus (this happens mainly in John 19-24), by making John protest at Jesus being baptized by him, and by putting on the lips of John words of personal subordination and recognition of the one who really had God's spirit and who really was God's Son. The christological interest, already obvious in that last point above, is clarified in the descent of the Spirit and the heavenly word of the baptismal scene itself.

Probably because the baptism of Jesus is not quite so scandalous as his death, the historical investigation of this incident in his life does not get quite so much attention and may not meet with quite the same resistance. In the patristic period, and indeed in most uncritical views of the matter, the description of the baptism of Jesus in the synoptics is taken to be factual through and through. It is therefore the source and paradigm for Christian baptism. Indeed impressions of a certain similarity with the death/resurrection are unavoidable. Just as resurrection is deemed to be the historical source of Christian faith itself, so the special divine 'extras' in John the Baptizer's baptism of Jesus – mainly the descent of the Spirit – provide the historical source for specifically Christian baptism, the initial ritual experience of the Christian faith.

But it is just these similarities which should alert the critical historian to the question: is there, in addition to Jesus' rather embarrassing baptism at the hands of John the Baptizer, some special divine intervention of a revelatory nature which took place on this occasion, and which would remove the scandal for those would-be followers of Jesus who either witnessed or heard of this act of public repentance?

The coming of the Spirit, it is hardly necessary to remark, is not a public revelatory event – one can hardly take the dove literally. The presence of the Spirit is palpable, if at all, in the quality of a life, in the deeds that are done, in the trials undergone and overcome. Nothing that was visible at the moment of Jesus' baptism in the Jordan could have told the participants that the Spirit was descending in an unprecedented way. But what of the voice from heaven? It is here that the similarity with the resurrection kerygma is most striking. God is made to declare that Jesus is his beloved son. Luke, in fact, has 'you are my beloved son' (not 'this is my beloved son') and some ancient manuscripts of Luke have, instead of the usual following words 'with thee I am well pleased', the words 'this day I have begotten you' (see the RSV note to Luke 3.22). Now this is the very theme of the earliest resurrection kerygma we know: Romans 1.4 talks of the resurrection in terms of Jesus being designated Son of God; Luke himself in Acts 13.33 has Paul's resurrection kerygma use that very quotation from the old enthronement psalm (2.7): 'You are my son, today I have begotten you.' Again the familiar themes from that old enthronement ritual of Judaic kings.

One can scarcely avoid the impression that we are here in the presence of a kerygmatic construction similar to that which Jesus' followers produced after his death. The primary theme of the old Davidic enthronement texts is being used once again to say that the one we meet in this event (baptism now, not death this time) is indeed God's Son. So, once again, if the historian does his job well enough, he will not come upon two events, or even a double event, one event or part of the event scandalous, but the other of such a divinely revelational character that it reverses the implications of the first and successfully removes its scandal (for then our conclusion would have to read: yes, Jesus was Son of God *in spite of* the fact that John the Baptizer baptized him, that is, to say, in spite of what history left to itself could tell us). No, the historian will find just one event, Jesus' baptism by John the Baptizer, and he knows already what that baptism was, and he will then be told in the same context, by use of the old enthronement theme and by reference to the coming of the Spirit of God, that the one who is here baptized is Son of God.

There is no 'in spite of' in evidence here. We are told quite plainly that this one who cleanses and purifies himself in preparation for the coming of God's reign is God's Son and bearer *par excellence* of the Spirit of God, just as later on in the resurrection kerygma we are told that this one who was judged a threat to the secure power of both ecclesiastical and civic leaders and was condemned and executed on such a charge, is God's Son and breather of God's Spirit. Apparently, in both cases, because of, not in spite of, what happened. We may prefer a different kind of Son of God. We normally do. We may be secretly quite disappointed with the one we got. We usually are. Well, that's just too bad.

On the other hand, we should resist the temptation to think that because our New Testament preachers and writers are using the 'you are my Son, this day I have begotten you' theme for both baptism and resurrection, we are entitled to conclude that they think and are telling us that on these days – of his baptism and his death – he was actually made Son of God, as the king was made king only on his enthronement day. In the first place, such a conclusion would imply that the authors revised previous views – for if they thought that he was made Son of God at his death, they could not later think, without explicit revision, that he was made Son of God earlier at his baptism. But we have no evidence whatever for such revision. And, in the second place, the whole hypothesis is quite unwarranted. The preachers and writers were clearly borrowing a messianic theme from the enthronement ceremony of the ancient Davidic kings, and they are applying that theme to what is clearly – to put the matter very mildly – an entirely different type of situation. It is obvious, then, that they feel the theme applies because they believe Jesus fulfils all their messianic hopes, though in a very unexpected way; not because the details of the enthronement ceremony (for instance, that the king was actually declared Son only when he actually became king) are applicable in any literal way.

In no way, then, should we try to evade the point which is made in the New Testament about baptism and death, namely, that the one who was baptized by John's baptism and died as a criminal is God's Son, and for these reasons rather than in spite of them. If we insist that these early Christians thought that they were describing, in addition to the scandalous events of death and baptism, special divine interventions which were either constitutive of Jesus' sonship or literally revelatory of it, we are carrying our own presuppositions to their texts, and coming away from the texts with our presuppositions still intact.

The birth

We never really give up, though. We may not be able to find in our normative scriptures any well-evidenced revelatory event accompanying baptism or death which would take away the scandal. But we will discover an extraordinary birth! We will have our Son of God with his divine credentials intact in historical records, however difficult it may be, and however ingenious we may have to be, to find them.

The infancy gospels appear only in Matthew and Luke. They have not drawn to themselves nearly as much real scholarly attention as they deserve. They are the source of convictions concerning Mary and Jesus about which many Christians, and particularly Roman Catholics, prove to be very touchy. I shall therefore confine my attention, in dealing with them, to the basic question of this appendix: what do they tell the critical historian? And what do they then say to Christian faith?

It has long been recognized that the infancy gospels are first and foremost christologies. That is to say, their primary purpose is to express the messianic significance for us of the one whose conception, birth, infancy (and, in Luke's case, youth) they pass in review. Hence they are woven, as are the passion narratives, from Old Testament themes; in their case, for instance, from narratives about Abraham and Moses. And, as in the case of the resurrection kerygma and the baptism pericopes, the theme of the Spirit of God coming and the theme of the Son of God (reminiscent once again of the enthronement ceremony of Davidic kings) both appear with the obvious purpose, once more, of conveying the significance for our relationship with God of this Jesus who was crucified, whom John baptized, and who was born of a Jewish woman called Miriam. 'The Holy Spirit will come upon you, and the power of the Most High will overshadow you; therefore the child to be born will be called holy, the Son of God' (Luke 1.35). Matthew simply has 'that which is conceived in her is of the Holy Spirit' (1.20); but later in the scene of the return from Egypt the 'son' theme appears in a quotation he uses: 'out of Egypt have I called my son' (2.15).

The infancy gospels also contain their quota of polemics; as did the narratives of Jesus' baptism at the hands of John the Baptizer. The polemical strain is perhaps most obvious in Matthew – as one might almost expect if one remembered Matthew's resurrection kerygma with its own heavy polemic against Jewish stories about a stolen corpse (Matthew 27.62 – 28.15). Matthew clearly does not intend to let his Jewish opponents get away with very much!

It is almost as difficult to decide what actual memories, if any, underlie the present infancy gospels, as it is to discover by what means of transmission these could have reached such relatively late documents as Matthew and Luke. But the most likely content of such a memory, if there was one, is that Jesus was conceived between the time that Mary was betrothed (married) to Joseph and the time at which he took her to his house, the latter being the time at which legitimate marital relations could have taken place. There is certainly evidence of early Jewish polemic to the effect that Jesus was illegitimate – the 'natural' conclusion one would come to if the memory just recorded above had actually been preserved and had been in any way widespread. Think of the way in which people's eyes still click shut on mental conclusions as soon as the word gets out of a birth within eight months, let us say, of the honeymoon night. Hence the need for answering Christian polemic.

Perhaps the most intriguing part of Matthew's counter-polemic is found in the genealogy of Jesus, the son of David, the son of Abraham, with which he opens his gospel. He includes in his gospel genealogy the names of women, as Luke does not; four women in fact, and what a selection of women! Judah begot Perez by Tamar, his daughter-in-law, who disguised herself as a prostitute in order to become pregnant by him (Matthew 1.3; cf. Genesis 38. 12-30). Salmon, next, was the father of Boaz by Rahab, and the only Rahab we know from the Old Testament is the famous prostitute of Jericho (Matthew 1.5; cf. Joshua 2; 6). We know that Rahab was 'rehabilitated' in the course of the Rabbinic traditions of the inter-testamental period (cf. Megilloth 14b – 15a); at least to the extent that her chosen profession was no longer mentioned! And she then appeared as ancestress of prophets, of Huldah the instigator of the reform of Josiah (II Kings 22), and even of Jeremiah. She appears on two other occasions in the New Testament: in Hebrews 11.31 as one of the heroines of faith, and in James 2.25 as an example of salvation by works; so whether you are Protestant or Roman Catholic, justified by faith or works, this versatile lady will serve your interests! The point, though, is not so much what she became in the course of later traditions – some of the other ladies in this group may have been 'rehabilitated' also – the point is to notice just what kind of person could and did become such a paragon of virtue.

Boaz begot Obed (for Naomi) of a Moabitess called Ruth, as an act of pure gratuity, for he was not even the nearest of kin, and she, as a foreigner, had no rights to him or to his lineage (Matthew 1.5; cf. the Book of Ruth). David, finally, begot Solomon of the wife of Uriah, in an adulterous act which David, when he failed to disguise his own paternity, further aggravated by the murder of Uriah (Matthew 1.6; cf. II Samuel 11).

Why, one wonders, are we reminded of this winsome foursome in the course of Jesus' genealogy – one who played the prostitute, one professional prostitute, one foreigner who bowed her way into favour and royal lineage, and one adulteress? Why are we faced with an opening and closing reminder of adulterous conception, with one irregular marriage situation and the ubiquitous Rahab thrown in between for good measure? Obviously the intent is to say that God does not necessarily elect those of unimpeachable pedigree to do his work in this world. For those who knew their Jewish history, it was a powerful piece of polemic indeed. But what does it say to us?

In the case of those who circulated a story that his followers stole Jesus' body Matthew could simply circulate another story to the effect that these people were lying in their teeth and that it paid them well to do so – and in this contention he was undoubtedly correct. But he could not apparently as easily say that those who called Jesus illegitimate were lying in their teeth, and so his polemic here has to be much more complex. We shall return to this point shortly.

A second part of Matthew's polemic has Joseph perform the naming ceremony for the child, thus legally making him his son, and giving him his Davidic lineage (Matthew 1.25).

But it is a third part of the polemic which most interests us at the moment: the part at which it joins the themes of Spirit and Son, themes in which we have already seen christology expressed at the moments of baptism and death. Here in the infancy gospels, by means of the twin themes, polemics and christology are interwoven in a very complex way. Spirit is one of the most ancient symbols in these near Eastern cultures for God and particularly for God's active presence in our world; son is one of the most powerful natural symbols known by which to express the extension of one's favour to a person who is the very continuation of one's effective presence in the world. Naturally, then, as one can quite easily see both from the description of Jesus' baptism and from the resurrection kerygma in the New Testament, the primary result of saying that the Spirit comes on, or is with, or (even more so) is breathed by, Jesus, as of saying that Jesus is God's Son, is to convey the conviction that God acts in Jesus. But the infancy gospels, once they go beyond the first two forms of polemic outlined above, apparently intend also to convey that the coming of the Spirit at Jesus' conception makes that a virginal conception and makes the conceived God's Son. At least that seems to be the literal impact of the Lukan text already quoted above (Luke 1.35). It is precisely at this point, where the themes of Spirit and Son are used in a dual role, to describe the person's conception in addition to describing God's relationship to that person, that we have difficulty in understanding what exactly is being conveyed. Or, to be more precise, though we can well understand the meaning of the Spirit and Son themes in the latter role, we have great difficulty in understanding them in the former. Why?

Well, we do not wish to think of the Holy Spirit acting as the male principle in the conception of Jesus. That would make the birth of Jesus too much like that of some semi-divine beings who were conceived, in other mythologies, of the mating of a god with a human female. But then we ask ourselves: just what do we understand by the role of the Spirit in the conception of Jesus and of Jesus' subsequent divine sonship? I don't really know the answer to this question. I don't know what Luke in particular had in mind. I can only hazard a guess that the Spirit of God, if it did not act as the male principle, and yet Jesus was born from the body of Mary in an otherwise natural way, must have supplied what was necessary to the embryonic Jesus by an act such as creation out of nothing. Jesus' being God's son *as a result of this act* (see Luke's 'therefore') could then mean only what Luke meant when he calls Adam 'the son of God' in his genealogy of Jesus (Luke 3.38) – for to call Adam God's son there presumably refers to the belief that Adam was created by God (out of nothing, or out of 'dust') and not derived in the normal way from parents. This explanation would mean, of course, that Son of God had as little in common with its real meaning in the other christological contexts, where it refers to God's salvific activity in Jesus, as the coming of the Spirit for conception has in common with the coming of the Spirit in the other christological contexts. We should simply find ourselves in the presence of two well understood symbols now put to some unique usage. And to what purpose? Apparently to inform us that Jesus was conceived of one who nonetheless remained a virgin.

Now we are undoubtedly correct in seeing the infancy gospels as, first and foremost, christologies, statements of the function and significance of Jesus as he was known from his public life and even more public death. Therefore we are undoubtedly correct also in concluding that the principal function of the themes of Spirit and Son in the infancy gospels is identical with that of those same themes when we meet them in other parts of the gospels and in the rest of the New Testament: namely, the christological function, the functional description of Jesus as the one in whom God acted in the world. The function of these same themes in explaining the mode of Jesus' conception must then be a subsidiary one – and I think we must confess that it introduces as much obscurity to our inquiring minds as it throws light on the subject. For if we ask such questions as, 'How did Mary know that the Holy Spirit somehow formed the embryonic Jesus in her womb?', we either have her guessing this from the enormous improbability of 'natural' virginal conception, or we have her informed of this by a literal revelation from God (since creative acts of God are not naturally detectable). Then if we ask how Matthew and Luke knew of this action of the Holy Spirit (not just of Jesus' conception before Joseph took Mary to his house – there is no mystery in understanding how people could know about that!) we have to suppose, in the absence of any real evidence for this, a tradition which was carried from Mary herself right down to the very different formulations of it in Matthew and Luke (Matthew has the virginal conception announced to Joseph only; Luke has it announced only to Mary). In the end, I think it safe to say, we have to believe on the word of these two evangelists, if that is our decision, that the Holy Spirit somehow formed the embryonic Jesus in his mother's womb; or we may believe this because the church to which we belong makes this part of its authoritative teaching.

But – and here at last is the point of this long section – if we act, as we are also entitled to do, as critical historians, what shall we find we can say about the birth of Jesus?

That it was obscure, to a point of unusual vulnerability.

Obscure? Yes, absolutely unimpressively obscure. It is hard to say where he was born. Matthew gives the impression that his folks were native to Bethlehem, but had to move to Nazareth out of fear of Herod's son when they came back from Egypt. Luke, who has not heard that they were in Egypt, regards them as a Nazareth family who had to go to Bethlehem just when Jesus was born, for a census which Matthew has not heard of. His native town uncertain, his parents are people of no significance whatsoever. The genealogies are obviously late and discordant attempts to give them royal lineage.

And vulnerable? The very circumstances of his conception are clouded in suspicion which no naturally available evidence can disperse (well, just imagine yourself trying to tell someone that your son, whom they know to have been born seven months after your wedding, and whom they consider with good cause to be a threat to both civil and ecclesiastical law and order, was conceived of the Holy Spirit!). No wonder Matthew's triple polemic tries to cover all the bases.

And this is God's Son, in whom God's Holy Spirit comes, and on whom he remains?

Yes.

The pattern holds.

A man of obscure and, from the natural point of view, questionable birth, a man baptized by John the Baptizer's baptism of repentance for the forgiveness of sins, a man executed as a threat to ecclesiastical and civil law and order after due legal trial before the highest courts of the land – this is God's Son? Yes. And because of all this; not in spite of it. For there are no well-evidenced events of a divinely revelationary character to remove the offence of birth, baptism and death. The scandal for the Jews and the folly for us Gentiles always remains intact in spite of all our misguided half-theological, half-historical attempts to get rid of it and to have our Son of God and God's Spirit, not in weakness but in strength, on our terms rather than his.

We have most of us been led to presuppose that the origin and indeed much of the substance of our Christian faith lies in one or more acts of divine revelation adequately witnessed and indisputably emerging as such: acts of God, events on the historical record so far above anything our poor world is capable of that their divine source and their divine intent could not for one moment be mistaken by people of even minimal good-will. The fact that our contemporary theology of revelation, when it did finally settle for a theory of divine revelation in the form of historical events, immediately fell foul of all the doubts and difficulties for which modern historical scholarship is renowned – this fact did not remove our presupposition about the incidence and nature of divine revelation, nor even seriously damage it. Dibelius's 'x', together with other smaller 'x's, at least baptism and birth, stood their ground in the unconscious depths of our theological minds from which our presupposed ideas wield their indomitable influence.

Somewhere at the back of our conscious minds we knew, of course (or, if we did not, the historical scholars could quickly remind us), that his death was scandalous, his baptism odd, and the respectability of his human origins not easy to prove to the sceptical. But, then, our faith had its source and substance, had it not, in incidents of indisputable divine origin which accompanied these events, and not in the events themselves? Our presuppositions not only remained intact, they muscled the New Testament material unwillingly into a supportive role.

That the source of our faith could be in a man whose birth was obscure and therefore vulnerable to suspicion, whose baptism advertised him as a convert, and who died the death of a condemned criminal; that the substance of our faith should consist in the deep conviction that obscure and despised illegitimates, sinners and convicted criminals, can say Abba to God, and that the prostitutes can enter into God's kingdom before the religiously respectable – that is not a vision which we find easily compatible with the vision of our faith which we normally presuppose. But it is one we had better soon consider, or reconsider.

The substance of this distinctive faith which Jesus inspired in his followers, and of which he is therefore the source in our history, could not of course be gleaned simply from an analysis of birth, baptism and death alone. Only a careful study of his public ministry, and particularly of his experience and understanding of the reign of God which it was his mission to introduce, could fully yield the substance of that distinctive faith. In the light of this, then, the full significance of his death would appear, and also the justification for the use of the Spirit and Son symbolism in the resurrection kerygma and in connection with birth and baptism. It was because he inspired and enabled those who could take it to experience themselves, no matter who or what they were, as equally cherished children of the one Father, and above all to treat each other as such across all destructive human barriers, that this Jesus, born of Mary, baptized by John, and crucified under Pontius Pilate, is God's very Son to his followers, and the very embodiment of the Spirit of God in human history.

Christian faith and critical history, we may be permitted to conclude once more in this brief appendix on baptism and birth, are natural allies, not natural enemies. The dichotomy which the critical period introduced between faith and history was due to a misunderstanding of one (faith) and a failure to press the other (history) to its fullest possibilities and its final results. The faith of Jesus, radical as it is, is not outside the human historian's range. A mixture of confusion and fear it was that put it outside our intellectual grasp. Confusion about the nature of faith due to preconceptions. And fear of pressing our investigations sufficiently far, perhaps because we did not wish to disturb religious authorities (as Jesus did in his time), perhaps because, more honest now, we were afraid of the awful challenge of what we might find. Glorious sons of God, odd as it might seem, are much easier to manage than the one who was finally sent, and glorious representatives of glorious sons of God, resplendent in title and raimant, are much easier to placate, than those who truly serve and thus lay upon us the claim that we should be servants in turn. But it is never too late for scholarship to play its admittedly contributory role. And it is never too soon. The world is still ridden by the quest for dominating power and envious prestige, in churches as well as states, and service to genuine human needs is still available only at prohibitive prices.

Notes

1. The Problem of the Quest of the Historical Jesus

1. G. W. F. Hegel, *Lectures in the Philosophy of Religion*, London: Routledge and Kegan Paul 1895, Vol. 1, pp. 28f.

2. I. Kant, *Critique of Pure Reason*, New York: Doubleday 1966, p.xxiv.

3. I. Kant, *Philosophical Correspondence 1759-99*, University of Chicago Press 1967, n.642.

4. I. Kant, *Religion within the Limits of Reason Alone*, New York: Harper and Row 1961, p. 11.

5. Kant, *Religion*, pp. 79f.

6. H. S. Reimarus, *Fragments*, Philadelphia: Fortress Press and London: SCM Press 1970, p. 230.

7. Reimarus, *Fragments*, p. 234.

8. N. Perrin, *What is Redaction Criticism?*, Philadelphia: Fortress Press and London: SPCK 1969, p. 4.

9. G. W. F. Hegel, *Early Theological Writings*, Chicago University Press 1948, p. 79.

10. Ibid.

11. G. W. F. Hegel, *The Phenomenology of Mind*, London: Allen and Unwin 1949, pp. 84ff.

12. Hegel, *Early Theological Writings*, p. 273.

13. Hegel, *Lectures on the Philosophy of Religion*, Vol. 1, p. 50.

14. Hegel, *Lectures on the Philosophy of Religion*, Vol. 1, p. 30.

15. See the chapter on Hegel in Franz Grégoire, *Aux Sources de la Pensée de Marx, Hegel, Feuerbach*, Publications Universitaires de Louvain 1947.

16. F. C. Baur, *On the Writing of Church History*, New York: Oxford University Press 1968, pp. 275f.

17. For additional texts on Hegel's disinterest in the historical Jesus see his *Lectures on the Philosophy of Religion*, Vol. 2, p. 345; Vol. 3, pp. 110-20.

18. James M. Robinson *A New Quest of the Historical Jesus*, London: SCM Press 1959, pp. 66ff.; R. Brown, 'After Bultmann, What?', *Catholic Biblical Quarterly* 26, 1964, pp. 7f.

19. Van A. Harvey, *The Historian and the Believer*, New York: Macmillan and London: SCM Press 1969, pp. 187ff.

20. D. F. Strauss, *The Life of Jesus Critically Examined*, reprinted Philadelphia: Fortress Press and London: SCM Press 1972, p. 80.

21. Strauss, *Life of Jesus*, p. 86.

22. Strauss, *Life of Jesus*, p. 74.

23. K. Marx and F. Engels, *On Religion*, Moscow: Foreign Languages Publishing House 1955, p. 194.

24. Albert Schweitzer, *The Quest of the Historical Jesus*, London: A. & C. Black 1954, p. 159.

25. Ernest Renan, *The Life of Jesus*, New York: Modern Library 1955, p. 54.

26. Renan, *The Life of Jesus*, p. 374.

27. Renan, *The Life of Jesus*, p. 64.

28. J. D. Crossan, *In Parables*, New York: Harper and Row 1973, pp. 24ff.

29. Schweitzer, *The Quest*, p. 2.

30. Schweitzer, *The Quest*, pp. 368f.

31. Renan, *The Life of Jesus*, p. 65.

32. Schweitzer, *The Quest*, p. 399.

33. Schweitzer, *The Quest*, p. 401.

34. M. Kähler, *The So-Called Historical Jesus and the Historic, Biblical Christ*, Philadelphia: Fortress Press 1964, p. 56.

35. Kähler, *The So-called Historical Jesus*, pp. 63ff., 77.

36. Kähler, *The So-called Historical Jesus,* p. 89.

2. The Death of Jesus

1. The tendency is noticeable in recent christology to start with the resurrection of Jesus, principally on the grounds that the New Testament, our most authoritative source for Jesus, is written 'backwards' from the writers' and the communities' experience of the Risen Lord. This tendency is illustrated, for instance in Peter de Rosa's *Jesus Who Became Christ*, Denville: Dimension Books 1974 and London: Collins 1975, a book which provides an admirable example of clear understanding and presentation of what is meant by saying that the gospels in particular are written in the light of the resurrection of Jesus. In choosing a starting point, I have opted to follow, rather, John Reumann's plan of campaign in *Jesus in the Church's Gospels*, Philadelphia: Fortress Press and London: SPCK 1968. Some of my reasons for this option take the form of reflections on the centrality of Jesus' death, just outlined above, and coincide with Reumann's. Other reasons, and perhaps the most substantial of them, can be gleaned only from the argument of the book as a whole. Briefly, I am convinced that the historical events of Jesus' life on earth culminating in his death explain (according to the kind of explanation admissible in such a context as this) the resurrection kerygma and the rest of the Jesus myth in the New Testament, rather than vice versa – though I should not wish this too dichotomous im-

pression, inevitable in such a brief statement of the argument of the book, to remain long in the reader's mind.

2. Books which can profitably be consulted on background information for the life of Jesus include: J. Jeremias, *Jerusalem in the Time of Jesus*, London; SCM Press and Philadelphia: Fortress Press 1969; W. L. Foerster, *From the Exile to Christ*, Philadelphia: Fortress Press 1964; Bo Reicke, *The New Testament Era*, London: A. & C. Black and Philadelphia: Fortress Press 1969; R. Bultmann, *Primitive Christianity in its Contemporary Setting*, London: Thames and Hudson 1956 and New York: Meridian Books 1957; S. Benko and J. J. O'Rourke, *The Catacombs and the Colosseum*, Valley Forge: Judson Press 1971; M. Hengel, *Judaism and Hellenism*, London: SCM Press 1974 and Philadelphia: Fortress Press 1975.

3. On the question of the violence or pacifism of Jesus see the difference of viewpoint between, on the one hand, M. Hengel, *Was Jesus a Revolutionist?*, Philadelphia: Fortress Press 1971, and *Victory over Violence: Jesus and the Revolutionists,* Philadelphia: Fortress Press 1973 and London: SPCK 1975; J. H. Yoder, *The Politics of Jesus*, Grand Rapids: Eerdmans 1972; and, on the other hand, S. G. F. Brandon, *Jesus and the Zealots*, Manchester University Press 1967, and *The Trial of Jesus of Nazareth*, London: Batsford and New York: Stein and Day 1968. B. Lindars, *New Testament Apologetic*, London: SCM Press and Philadelphia: Westminster Press 1961.

5. Reumann, *Jesus in the Church's Gospels*, p. 63; see also Reumann's introduction to G. Sloyan, *Jesus on Trial*, Philadelphia: Fortress Press 1973.

6. Paul Winter, *On the Trial of Jesus*, Berlin: de Gruyter 1961.

7. D. R. Catchpole, *The Trial of Jesus: A Study in the Gospels and Jewish Historiography from 1770 to the Present Day*, Leiden: Brill 1971.

8. G. Sloyan, *Jesus on Trial*, pp. 127ff.

9. Gospel accounts of the Jewish trial are found in Matthew 26; Mark 14; Luke 22 and John 18.

10. I am assuming in all this that the Jewish authorities before whom Jesus was arraigned were acting in function of their constituted offices and according to the Law, and not as self-interested murderers. The latter assumption is not only quite gratuitous at this stage of the inquiry – we are, after all, dealing with the duly constituted political and religious leaders of the nation – but likely to contribute to that antisemitism which has marred Christian attitudes to Jews from the very beginning.

11. Frances Young, 'Temple, Cult and Law in Early Christianity', *New Testament Studies* 19, 1973, pp. 325-38.

12. Accounts of the Roman trial are found in Matthew 27; Mark 15; Luke 23 and John 18-19.

13. Martin Hengel, one of the most determined opponents of the claim to Jesus by modern revolutionaries, wrote about Jesus' alleged statement on taxes to Caesar: 'This whole complex of "what belongs to Caesar" is, however, unessential in view of the nearness of God', and: 'World power is neither justified nor condemned; it is deprived of its power, however, through the word "but" (but to God the things that are God's), which points to God's side' (*Was Jesus a Revolutionist?*, pp.

33f.; the parenthesis is mine). If I were Caesar, I would not fear the man who fought me over taxes – for he at least recognized who I was – half as much as the man who, if Hengel is correct, went about telling people that I really didn't matter after all.

14. Albert Camus, *The Fall*, London: Hamish Hamilton and New York: Knopf 1957, p. 83, translated by Justin O'Brien from *La Chute*, Paris: Éditions Gallimard 1956.

15. Maud Bodkin, *Archetypal Patterns in Poetry*, Oxford University Press 1963, pp. 16f.

16. Not according to G. S. Kirk in *Myth: Its Meaning and Function*, Cambridge University Press 1970.

17. It was Hegel who pointed out that knowledge of the immediate, of what is, seems first to be the richest kind, the truest, the most authentic, 'for it has not yet dropped anything from the object'. 'This bare fact of certainty, however,' he added, 'is really and admittedly the abstractest and poorest kind of truth.' One pure 'this' facing another pure 'this' need have neither depth nor universality of significance. G. W. F. Hegel, *Phenomenology of Mind*, London: Allen and Unwin 1931, reprinted New York: Humanities Press 1966, p. 149.

18. See G. Watson, *Plato's Unwritten Teaching*, Dublin: Talbot Press 1973, pp. 81-97.

19. J. Campbell (ed.), *The Portable Jung*, New York: Viking Press 1971, p. xxxi.

20. Marie-Louise von Franz, a disciple of Jung's, sometimes conveys this impression (*Patterns of Creativity Mirrored in Creation Myths*, Zurich: Spring Publication 1972, pp. 10ff.). On the other Hand, Maud Bodkin's *Archetypal Patterns in Poetry* takes Jungian psychology more as a suggestive hypothesis than a restrictive dogma and, as a result, provides an enlightening account of a wide variety of the most resonant images and powerful themes in poetry.

21. See, for instance, Paul Ricoeur, *The Symbolism of Evil*, Boston: Beacon Press 1967, pp. 15f. The same point is central to F. W. Dillistone, *Christianity and Symbolism*, London: Collins and Philadelphia: Westminster Press 1955.

22. Ricoeur, *The Symbolism of Evil*, p. 18.

23. This is very much the view taken in J. A. Stewart, *The Myths of Plato*, Southern Illinois University Press 1960, esp. p. 74.

24. Kirk, *Myth: Its Meaning and Function*, p. 259.

25. This attitude, if I understand him correctly, is admirably argued in Watson's *Plato's Unwritten Teaching*.

26. Paul Tillich appeared to prefer an affirmative answer here, despite his own abstract conceptualization of Christianity (*Dynamics of Faith*, New York: Harper 1956, p. 53). So does Thomas Fawcett, *The Symbolic Language of Religion*, London: SCM Press and Minneapolis: Augsburg 1971. Karl Jaspers thinks, on the contrary, that all forms of thought and perception can become equally transparent to transcendence (*Truth and Symbol*, New York: Twane Publishers 1959). Finally Rudolf Bultmann, whose famous demythologizing process implies a clear distinction on his part between myth and other forms of religious language, comes

under heavy critical fire from Ronald Hepburn precisely for his inability to maintain such a distinction in his own theological writings ('Demythologizing and the Problem of Validity', in A. Flew and A. MacIntyre, *New Essays in Philosophical Theology*, London: SCM Press and New York: Macmillan 1955, pp. 227-42).

27. See Jaspers, *Truth and Symbol*, passim.

28. Bodkin, *Archetypal Patterns in Poetry*, pp. 77ff.

29. The images we associate more readily with myth, perhaps, are those of sun and storm and sea, sun-gods and storm-gods and sea-gods, but these and many, many others fit our formula just as well. Sun, wind (air) and sea provide powerful natural images of our dependent existence, our contingency, as sickness/health, bondage/freedom, guilt/innocence provide moral or personal ones, and kings or war-lords provide social ones.

30. As already remarked, only the cultural chauvinism of a so-called age of enlightenment, of science or of history, could consider myth archaic and dispensable. But, unfortunately, such chauvinism is still too widespread. Even some Jungians seem at times to refer to myths as illusions, though illusions apparently necessary in the lives of the majority (see J. Campbell, *Myths to Live By*, New York: Viking Press 1972, pp. 11f.). Jung himself, in fact, could sometimes be reasonably suspect of not appreciating the full stature of myth. He writes of symbol, for example, as the expression of an intuitive idea which cannot *yet* be formulated in any other or better way (Campbell, *The Portable Jung*, p. 30). Even of myth he requires translation into conceptual language, so that we should have 'an abstract, scientific understanding of the unconscious processes that lie at the roots of the primordial images' (Campbell, *The Portable Jung*, p. 320). Myth here seems dispensable indeed and it is difficult to disagree with Mircea Eliade's criticism of Jung, that he tended to reduce myth to what may undoubtedly be one of its functions as an intra-psychic regulator. That is like regarding *Madame Bovary* as a sociological treatment of adultery (Mircea Eliade, *Myths, Dreams and Mysteries*, London: Collins and New York: Harper and Row 1960, p. 14).

31. R. H. Fuller, *The Formation of the Resurrection Narratives*, London SPCK and New York: Macmillan 1972, p. 2.

32. W. Pannenberg, *Jesus – God and Man*, Philadelphia: Westminster Press and London: SCM Press 1968, p. 67. See also John B. Cobb, *Christ in a Pluralistic Age*, Philadelphia: Westminster Press 1975, p. 137, where Cobb supports the view of Pannenberg and his circle that a verifiable event of resurrection was necessary to vindicate the claims of Jesus in the minds of his followers, and then tries to help out with Whiteheadian categories Pannenberg's halting description of a vision which was nevertheless clearly objective.

33. Luke 24.21.

3. *The Resurrection*

1. Lindars, *New Testament Apologetic*, p. 72.

2. The claim is found everywhere. One example: Reumann, *Jesus in the Church's Gospels*, chapter on the resurrection, claims that 'glory', which is God's physical environment, is gradually moved back to the earthly life of Jesus from its first application to his risen status, that 'Lord', too, a title of the risen Jesus, is transferred to his days before Calvary.

3. R. E. Brown, 'After Bultmann, What?', *Catholic Biblical Quarterly* 26, 1968, pp. 22f.

4. B. Vawter, *This Man Jesus: An Essay Toward A New Testament Christology*, New York: Doubleday 1973 and London: Geoffrey Chapman 1975, pp. 144f.

5. This view is widely attributed to Bultmann. It is also suspected to be the view of many Bultmannians and even post-Bultmannians (that is, Bultmannians who have entered some disagreement with their teacher on the necessity and prospects of the quest of the historical Jesus). G. Ebeling, for instance, writes: 'The appearance of Jesus and the coming to faith of the man who is granted an appearance, or his becoming a witness to faith, are one and the same thing' (*World and Faith*, Philadelphia: Fortress Press and London: SCM Press 1963, p. 30). W. Marxsen, too, makes a distinction between the fundamental meaning or intent of a statement and the conceptuality in which it is couched. (This I take to imply that the same meaning or intent can be conveyed in symbol or concept, or in different symbols or different concepts.) Applying this distinction to the resurrection-preaching, he maintains that historical research can get us back only to Peter's faith in Jesus or Paul's, and to their conceptualizations of Jesus as risen and appearing. But we cannot get behind their faith and its conceptualization to any historical evidence of an event such as the individual revival of Jesus, or what we will call the personal resurrection of Jesus himself. We can therefore emulate the faith of Peter and Paul, and we should do this. But we can never prove that their conceptualizations should be taken literally. (*The Resurrection of Jesus of Nazareth*, London: SCM: Press and Philadelphia: Fortress Press 1970.)

It is important to understand here that Marxsen is not denying that Jesus personally experienced something called resurrection, nor is he denying that Jesus' followers have early and late believed that Jesus experienced resurrection, nor that they have hoped and do hope that God will overcome for them also even the last enemy, death. What he is saying is that the New Testament writers have many quite different ways of depicting what they call also the resurrection of Jesus, none of which we can take literally; and that, consequently, we have in the New Testament no evidence offered us which was ever of an objectively verifiable kind and which could prove the personal resurrection of Jesus. It is to this last point that Cobb objects (*Christ in a Pluralistic Age*, pp. 239ff.; see also U. Wilckens, *God's Revelation: A Way Through the New Testament*, Philadelphia: Westminster Press 1970, pp. 44f.).

We shall be involved in this debate as we proceed. The only point of importance at the moment is this: we should be careful not to attribute too hastily to too many authors who talk of the resurrection preaching as the myth of Jesus a denial that God overcame death for Jesus as, we may hope, he will do for us. Peter de Rosa, for instance, writes: 'Their faith was this meeting (with the Risen Lord)' (*Jesus Who Became Christ*, p. 309). But those who would, on the strength of this, suspect him of holding that resurrection preaching was merely a way of saying that Jesus-faith survived, would then be puzzled to see him also write: 'The Christian holds not that Jesus lives by his faith but that his faith lives by Jesus. And Jesus lives by the power of God. It was the God whom Jesus preached, not the faith of the disciples, that raised Jesus from the dead' (*Jesus Who Became Christ*, p. 310). In short, the type of view of the resurrection preaching which concerns us here is the type that takes this preaching merely as a way of saying that the faith of Jesus survived, *to the exclusion* of any statement at all about Jesus himself or about our own survival beyond death.

6. This summarizes a question prepared in C. F. D. Moule's introduction to a collection of essays on resurrection: *The Significance of the Message of the Resurrection for Faith in Jesus Christ*, London: SCM Press 1970.

7. I once heard an old pastor in San Francisco misread the lines of the Easter Preface: 'Dying he destroyed our death, rising he restored our life.' 'Dying,' he announced sonorously to a rather indifferent congregation, 'he destroyed our faith.' The old man's eyesight may have failed, but his sense of some contemporary resurrection theology was still quite acute.

8. See Reumann's chapter on resurrection in *Jesus in the Church's Gospels*. R. H. Fuller, in *The Formation of the Resurrection Narratives*, p. 21, refers to Jesus' resurrection as 'the eschatological breakthrough'. Since the word eschatological is probably the most abused word in contemporary theology, a kind of pseudo-verbal escape mechanism from all kinds of conceptual difficulty, it is not easy to say what this means. To say that it means that Jesus' resurrection was 'an event which occurs precisely at the end of history' (*The Formation of the Resurrection Narratives*, p. 22), presumably in some anticipatory fashion, is probably the very plainest of plain nonsense. But if it means that the personal resurrection of Jesus could only be described in apocalyptic imagery (a particular type of eschatology), which cannot be taken literally, and therefore that 'event' is 'not accessible to witnesses' (ibid.), then it makes sense.

9. Sentences obscured in heavy theological jargon like Cobb's, 'The vision of Jesus as the centre of God's eschatological reality vindicated the claim of Jesus to be announcing that reality' (*Christ in a Pluralistic Age*, p. 237; he is summarizing Wilckens with obvious approval here), can only prompt the question, What do the words 'as the centre of God's eschatological reality' add to the vision of Jesus after his death? Is

the reference to something he wore? Looked like? did? said? what? And
there's that word eschatological again, trailing its usual confusion in its
wake. Cobb is right in criticizing a hope that is supposed to rise out of
the structure of faith, if faith itself cannot be tied to anything that ever
happened. But it might be better to consider tying our faith to something that happened during the life of Jesus, than to tie it to some
problematic 'non-hallucinatory' vision of Jesus after his death.

10. John Reumann, in his chapter on the resurrection in *Jesus in the
Church's Gospels*, p. 132, has illustrated diagramatically essentially as
follows the different tableaux which form, we might say, the physical
framework of the different authors' symbolic presentation of the
resurrection of Jesus. The tableaux clearly differ one from another, but
the differences do not matter in the way differences between literal
descriptions of an event would. We are dealing here with part of the
symbolic or mythic presentation of the resurrection, and we dare not
take its details literally.

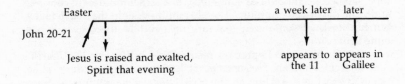

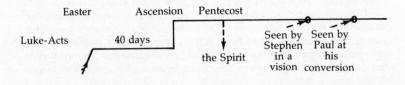

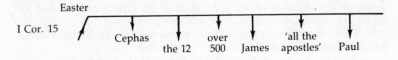

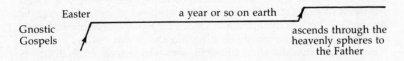

Unbroken lines represent 'resurrection', 'ascension' and 'appearances', broken lines 'visions' and descending dots the sending of the Spirit.

11. It is perhaps necessary to say here that this is not meant as a criticism of Fuller's book, so much as a criticism of those who would read or wish for no other kind of book on the resurrection of Jesus. Fuller, after all, called the book *The Formation of the Resurrection Narratives*, not *The Resurrection of Jesus according to the New Testament*. So, apart from Fuller's reference to the resurrection of Jesus as an eschatological event, 'which occurs precisely at the end of history', references which have already drawn some caustic comment and which remain undeveloped, to say the least, in the book, Fuller gives no hint of a different priority in dealing with the resurrection of Jesus.

12. The words I use to make this point may not be too happily chosen, though I can think of no better at this moment. But what I have in mind is this: a little reflection will show that hope of victory over death is an enormous achievement and an almost incredible blessing, and that nothing ordinary, nothing which comes easily within our grasp could for very long sustain it. Picture yourself at the burial of a deceased friend, feel the moist clay close in with heavy finality. Look around for something to support hope that this utter destruction could ever be reversed. You will not find it, I think, in reports, however credible, that once upon a time a man, however unique, was seen alive after he was known to have died. Nor in any verbal promises issued at any time in history. But a deep faith in God, and a consequent love that can serve all, attempt all and endure all – on such soil this enormous and blessed hope could conceivably grow. But this is the faith of Jesus-followers. And from thoughts such as these we can glean what Paul means by saying that the risen Jesus is first-fruits of those who die. Paul's immediate readers, we may confidently believe, were no different from us when it came to assessing the grounds for hope.

13. In selecting the explicit texts on resurrection from the Pauline corpus, I am following D. M. Stanley, *Christ's Resurrection in Pauline Soteriology*, Rome: Analecta Biblica 1961, though I do not necessarily follow his theological interpretation of these texts.

14. Ingo Hermann, *Kyrios und Pneuma*, Munich: Kösel 1961.

15. Hermann, particularly in his concluding chapter, is careful to point out that this functional, experiential identity between the risen Lord and the Spirit of God, since it makes a statement only about our experience, counts neither in favour of later trinitarian dogma (which was finally formulated more than three centuries after Paul), nor against it.

16. Fuller, who agrees that the 'original' Mark ended at 16.8, still believes that there is at least a reference to an appearance to Peter in 16.7 (other scholars like Lightfoot and Marxsen think this a reference to the *parousia*); and there may be other scenes which were originally resurrection scenes, now transposed to the life of Jesus in the body of the gospels – the transfiguration scene, for instance, of Mark 9 (see Fuller, *The Formation of the Resurrection Narratives*, pp. 62ff.).

17. Contrast, for instance, Lampe's contribution to G. W. H. Lampe

and D. M. MacKinnon, *The Resurrection*, London: Mowbray 1966, for he thinks the empty tomb stories devoid of historical reliability, with U. Wilckens, *Auferstehung: das biblische Auferstehungszeugnis historisch untersucht und erklärt*, Stuttgart: Kreuz 1970.

18. John 20.15, see also Luke 24.11, 24. Wilckens, with many others who believe empty tomb stories to be early and independent, does not think they establish the resurrection of Jesus (*Auferstehung*, p. 151). That attitude seems preferable to Vawter who, though he admits an empty tomb was at best ambiguous, still thinks that 'a tomb that was not empty would not be ambiguous at all' (*This Man Jesus*, p. 44). It is doubtful if the finding of a tomb empty was or is even that necessary to belief in resurrection.

19. See, for instance, Fuller, *The Formation of the Resurrection Narratives*, p. 109.

20. Hans Conzelmann, whose work on *The Theology of Luke*, London: Faber and Faber and New York: Harper and Bros 1960, is already something of a classic, points out how the eucharist in Luke carries the abiding benefits of Jesus' ministry and keeps the fellowship in being (pp. 206, 218). Once Jesus has gone, his followers have the Spirit, the message from appointed witnesses, and the sacrament, and with these the work of the ascended Jesus continues in the world to the end of time. In other words, Jesus is present in these, redeeming the time.

21. 'The Exaltation of Jesus could be an alternative way of speaking of the Resurrection, throwing the emphasis on the place at God's right hand. This in turn was inseparable from the thought of the Messiah's function. The two testimonies which convey these ideas in the substratum of Acts 2.33 are each deeply involved in the evolution of dogmatic formulation, and are at the foundation of the two theologumena of the Session at the Right Hand and the Gift of the Spirit' (Lindars, *New Testament Apologetic*, pp. 44f.).

22. There is one classic story in the gospels themselves which seems specifically designed to teach the lesson that if faith is absent or moribund, it cannot be given or recovered by someone appearing back from the grave. It is the story of Dives and Lazarus, and its punch-line reads: 'If they do not hear Moses and the prophets, neither will they be convinced if someone should rise from the dead' (Luke 16.31). The line is tailor-made for transposition to Jesus, who alone interested Luke: 'If they do not hear Jesus, then neither will they be convinced if he should rise from the dead.'

23. Norman Perrin, in his last published work, *The Resurrection according to Matthew, Mark and Luke*, Philadelphia: Fortress Press 1977 (published in England as *The Resurrection Narratives*, London: SCM Press 1977), treats the resurrection preaching as myth, while explaining to victims of the scientific age the unobjectionable sense in which the word myth should be used. I have not thought it necessary, as Perrin did, to distinguish primordial myth from foundation myth, though that distinction can be illuminating in its way.

24. See, for instance, Paul's catechesis on baptism in Romans 6.4-11.

4. The Life of Jesus

1. Renan, as already noted in the first chapter, believed that one who set out on the quest of the historical Jesus should have once believed, but no longer. The bias he then betrayed, that belief hinders objectivity in a way that apostasy does not, is a bias so general as to be deep and practically indetectable. The only bias, in fact, which cannot hinder objectivity, is not the one which is hidden, but the one which is openly acknowledged and allowed for by the quester.

2. The infancy narratives have produced a literature of their own, and it would be impossible here even to summarize the main themes of the debate. Some think these narratives have some actual memories behind them. See R. Brown, *The Virginal Conception and Bodily Resurrection of Jesus*, New York: Paulist Press and London: Geoffrey Chapman 1973; *The Birth of the Messiah*, New York: Doubleday and London: Geoffrey Chapman 1977. Bruce Vawter also, towards the end of *This Man Jesus*, regards the narratives as legend which may, therefore, contain a nucleus of historical fact, but he says that they are still of secondary importance to the great myths where christology is concerned. Others think these narratives to be 'christology in picture form' (Reumann, *Jesus in the Church's Gospels*, p. 141). Lindars, once again, in his chapters on 'The Pre-existent Messiah' and 'Out of Nazareth' in *New Testament Apologetic*, throws a good deal of light on the way in which Old Testament details first used to show Jesus as Messiah (e.g. born in David's city of Bethlehem) were later taken biographically. See the appendix, pp. 272ff.

3. Peter de Rosa in the first chapter of *Jesus Who Became Christ* gives a very persuasive account of the way in which the nativity narratives depict the Jesus who died and triumphed; and he is especially good on Jewish attitudes to virginity.

4. Contrast Conzelmann's chapter on John the Baptist in his *Theology of Luke* with W. Marxsen's 'study' of John the Baptist in *Mark the Evangelist*, Nashville: Abingdon Press 1969, to see how two 'redactors' make such different use of, presumably, the same traditional material.

5. One of the most powerful historical novels on the life of Jesus, though one based on the author's own particular dualism of spirit and flesh, is Nikos Kazantzakis, *The Last Temptation of Christ*, New York: Simon and Schuster 1960 and Oxford: Cassirer 1961.

6. See W. Manson, et al., *Eschatology*, Edinburgh: Oliver and Boyd 1953, pp. 1f., where eschatology is described as 'the religious determination of mind by which in the Bible men are impelled to think of all history and all life by reference to an ultimate transcendent Event, an End towards which, under the judgment and the mercy of God, the world is hastening'. On the other hand, 'Jewish apocalyptic thinking about the last things, from the year 100 BC onwards, took a direction definitely away from this world towards a transcendent heavenly order of existence ... Jewish phantasy about a purely heavenly world, like

certain forms of Jewish millenarianism, represents essentially an eva-
sion of the historical question.' It is probably to this tendency to take
apocalyptic imagery too literally that the attractive facility of D. Crossan's distinction applies, when he says that prophetic eschatology deals
with the ending of world (the ending of any absolute claims on us by
the empirical dimensions of reality), while apocalyptic eschatology
deals with the ending of this world (*In Parables*, New York: Harper and
Row 1973, p. 25).

7. For a more detailed treatment of the theme of the reign of God, see
N. Perrin, *The Kingdom of God in the Teaching of Jesus*, London: SCM
Press and Philadelphia: Westminster Press 1963; R. Schnackenburg,
God's Rule and Kingdom, New York: Herder and Herder and London:
Search Press 1968.

8. The first view was propounded, as we already saw, by
Schweitzer; the second was proposed, against Schweitzer, by C. H.
Dodd in his book, *The Parables of the Kingdom*, London: Nisbet 1935. In
1954 the question still had high priority in R. H. Fuller's *The Mission and
Achievement of Jesus*, London: SCM Press. See again the attractive facility of Crossan's suggestion that Jesus did not deal in linear time, the
common assumption of the consistent and realized eschatology debate
(*In Parables*, p. 25). That, once again, is probably as good a way as any of
saying that we have to do here with images and symbols for some deep
human experience, and not with the literal categories of clocks and
calendars which can measure more superficial events.

9. See Stewart, *The Myths of Plato*, p. 25.

10. See Crossan, *In Parables*, pp. 8-10; also Bodkin, *Archetypal Patterns
in Poetry*, a book in which the deep and peculiar power of a wide variety
of poetic images is analysed and described.

11. In addition to works on the parables already mentioned, two
other works which have influenced the present writer also contain differing categorization of the parables: J. Jeremias, *The Parables of Jesus*,
London: SCM Press and New York: Scribner 1963, and N. Perrin, *Rediscovering the Teaching of Jesus*, London: SCM Press and New York: Harper
and Row 1967.

12. Perrin, *Rediscovering the Teaching of Jesus*, pp. 93ff.

13. There are implicit references here to some sections of the Sermon
on the Mount in Matthew 5-7. The Sermon is Matthew's composition,
but it undoubtedly contains traditional material. Though it would be
difficult to detect actual words of Jesus, there is no doubt that his spirit
breathes through the different sections of this sermon, and even his
style is imitated in its concrete imagery. Note especially the classic
passages on loving one's enemies in order to be like God, on the sense
of being enriched and provided for like the birds of the air and the lilies
of the field. This is no romantic posturing. The same serious point is
being made here as was made in the parables. Instead of being anxious
and care-ridden, grasping and soon, consequently, dividing the world
between our friends and our enemies, we are to be open and generous
to all as we have all been so generously provided for.

14. There are deliberate echoes here of the Genesis creation myths,

an implicit reference which I hope to make explicit later on.

15. One sometimes hears it said of a person who literally slaves for wealth or status that he or she has no life, has never really lived at all.

16. Ever get the feeling as you struggle to pay off a mortgage on a large home that you come home each night to your owner?

17. For a broader discussion of these issues, see my *The Problems of Religious Faith*, Chicago: Franciscan Herald Press 1972, also my 'Faith: A Bibliographical Survey', *Horizons* 2, 1975, pp. 207-38.

18. For a classical statement of atheism in contemporary Western culture, see J. P. Sartre, *Being and Nothingness*, New York: Washington Square Press 1966 and London: Methuen 1969.

19. This kind of inflated humanism had its hey-day in the nineteenth century with writers like L. Feuerbach, *The Essence of Christianity*, reprinted New York: Harper 1957. Two world wars and the prospect of nuclear holocaust have considerably dampened its spirit in this century and driven its defenders to academia and to some select salons on Park Avenue.

20. See S. Runciman, *The Mediaeval Manichee*, Cambridge University Press 1947.

21. See Nikhilananda, *Self-Knowledge*, New York: Ramakrishna-Vivekenanda Center 1946, on the different degrees of 'reality' accorded to this empirical existence in different Hindu systems. It is difficult to know where to place Buddhism in the scheme outlined above. Which just goes to show that the scheme is no substitute for the study of comparative religion, but rather a crude way of indicating how the same sense of contingency, because of its own possible range of perception and evaluation, is at the source of atheism, different kinds of religious faith, and idolatry. The necessity for brevity in the context will, I hope, excuse the crudity of the scheme.

22. See J. A. Burns, *The Phenomenology of the Holy Spirit*, Ann Arbor: University Microfilms 1970.

23. See J. B. Pritchard (ed.), *The Ancient Near East*, Princeton University Press 1958, pp. 31ff.

24. Most developed mythologies also contain analyses of the sources of those life-negating forces which in our empirical experience make up the ambivalence or contingency of life, and against which we are asked to take sides. These sources can be either an evil divinity, some lesser but still powerful spirit, or a fall by such a spirit or by humans, the evil effects of which snowballed down the hill of history. We do not have the space to enter into this aspect of religious myth here. We should only remember that it follows the same logic as the rest of myth and should be taken no more literally. In any case, though Jesus may well have shared the common belief of some of his contemporaries in Satan and demons, his own myth obviously preferred to see the source of evil in human greed and pride and their consequences.

25. Neither is this the place to raise the vast question as to how one can justify adopting one myth rather than another, or, to put the matter another way, how one can decide between an atheist (who can use myth as well as abstract thought), an idolator, or the various religious

faiths which history has to offer. It is probable that epistemology, though the most dominant concern of philosophy since Descartes, simply has not grown sufficiently even to tackle this question in a professional manner. The dominant epistemology of the West has suggested that a view of reality could be considered true if it could be shown to correspond to some supposedly objective facts in the world, neutrally given for comparison to some judge or other. More recent epistemologies, like the American Pragmatist or the Marxist, have suggested in their different ways that truth is vindicated, in part at least, also by action. Certainly some epistemology more elaborate than the classical Western one seems necessary to do justice to the Johannine insistence that we should *do* the truth, and that we can know it when it is done or as it is done.

26. Ernst Bloch, the Marxist philosopher, captured the true texture of the experience of the reign of God which Jesus wished to convey when he spoke of 'the saint who succeeds with the kiss of love, ignoring evil creatively' (*Man On His Own*, New York: Herder and Herder 1971, p. 36).

27. See Ephesians 4.32, 'be kind to one another, tender-hearted, forgiving one another, as God in Christ forgave you'. Or the story of Zacchaeus in Luke 19, which is a perfect illustration, without one hint of moralizing, of the way in which acceptance inspires generosity.

28. Perrin, *Rediscovering the Teaching of Jesus*, p. 104.

29. The reference here is to Hans Lietzmann's famous thesis in *Mass and the Lord's Supper*, Leiden: Brill 1953, that there were two kinds of eucharist in the earliest years of the Jesus movement: 1. a simple breaking of bread, attested by Luke-Acts (Luke 22.19; 24.30; 24.35; Acts 2.42; 20.11, etc.), which continued the common table-fellowship of Jesus' ministry and was a sacramental or ritual means, then as before, of reconciling sinners; 2. a solemn and elaborate ritual of the interpreted symbols of bread broken for body and wine poured for blood, a ritual memorial of Jesus' covenant death, going back to an authentic memory of a last meal held with some of his close disciples.

30. J. Jeremias, *The Eucharistic Words of Jesus*, London: SCM Press and New York: Scribner 1966.

31. Perrin, *Rediscovering the Teaching of Jesus*, pp. 102ff.

32. For a near approach to this middle road, see E. Lohmeyer, *Lord of the Temple*, Edinburgh: Oliver and Boyd 1961.

33. See also Luke 5.30; the story of Zacchaeus, already referred to, in Luke 19; and Perrin's exegesis of Matthew 11.16-19 in *Rediscovering the Teaching of Jesus*, p. 105.

34. As we are not interested in the fine details of exegetical controversy about the accounts of the 'institution' of the eucharist at the Last Supper, we are even less interested in the recent controversies about transubstantiation and other theologumena for the real presence of Jesus, controversies which also have much to say about the 'words of institution'. It is sufficient for us that the so-called words of institution – this is my body which will be given, my blood which will be shed – stamp the ritual of the meal with explicit sacrificial symbolism. Further,

what we have already said about symbol and ritual is sufficient to explain the effects of this particular ritual on the lives and experience of those who take part in it. We seek only a full understanding of the experience of the reign of God in the ministry of Jesus, and have no intention of providing a complete sacramental theology in a couple of pages.

35. Reimarus, *Fragments*, p. 230.

36. An example of historical prejudice is this: one can only deal with alleged events on the principle of analogy, that is to say, if something quite similar is not part of present possible experience, I have no way of dealing with allegations concerning its occurrence in the past. An example of philosophical prejudice is the view that the great scientific project of the race could not get off the ground at all if there was interference with irrefragible laws of nature. For further discussion of these points, see my *Problems of Religious Faith*, pp. 126ff.

37. This is not to say that events which could reasonably be called miracles do not happen; but it does considerably restrict their role.

38. C. H. Dodd, *The Founder of Christianity*, London: Collins and New York: Macmillan 1970, p. 32.

39. See C. Cuénot, et al., *Evolution, Marxism and Christianity*, London: Garnstone Press 1967, p. 67.

40. See, for instance, Luke 11.29; Matthew 12.39.

41. See N. Perrin, *The New Testament: An Introduction*, New York: Harcourt Brace Jovanovich 1974, p. 49, where the cures of the Gerasene demoniac, the daughter of Jairus, the woman with the haemorrhage, of Mark 5 and 7, are seen by this scholar as depicting the fluid divine power emanating through Jesus, so that he comes across as a kind of Greek 'divine man'. And all these are healing miracles.

42. How conventional this function is can be seen from the life of Gautama Siddhātha, who was virginally conceived, already as an infant seen by a wise old man in his future role, etc. (H. C. Warren, *Buddhism*, New York: Athenaeum Press 1969, pp. 43ff.).

43. See the opening chapters of Perrin's *Rediscovering the Teaching of Jesus* for a discussion of these criteria.

44. See the catechesis of Jesus which followed the wrangling among his disciples over who should have first place: 'You know that those who are supposed to rule over the Gentiles lord it over them, and their great men exercise authority over them. But it shall not be so among you; but whoever would be great among you must be your servant, and whoever would be first among you must be slave of all' (Mark 10.42-44). See also the criteria on which people will be judged in the great judgment scene of Matthew 25.31-46.

45. The foregoing has some deliberate echoes of the Sermon on the Mount, Matthew's masterly presentation of the experience of the reign of God in the teaching of Jesus (Matthew 5-7).

46. Perrin, *Rediscovering the Teaching of Jesus*, pp. 130ff. (section on 'Faith in the Teaching of Jesus'); also G. Ebeling, *Word and Faith*, Philadelphia: Fortress Press and London: SCM Press 1963, especially p. 232.

47. The RSV translation here reads 'we ... who know that a man is not justified by works of the law but by faith in Jesus Christ, even we have believed in Jesus Christ, in order to be justified by faith in Christ' – which sounds very repetitive, to say the least. 'I who know that vegetables, not animal fats, are beneficial, eat vegetables, in order to benefit from vegetables.' For other such texts and a defence of the view that it is the personal faith of Jesus, not faith in Jesus (subjective, not objective genitive), that is referred to, see G. Ebeling, *Word and Faith*, p. 303. Interestingly enough, the old King James Version sometimes prefers to translate *dia* or *ek pisteos iesou* as 'by the faith of Jesus'.

48. Thomas Aquinas, *Summa Theologiae*, Madrid: La Editorial Catolica 1952, Part III, Question 7, article 3: '*Christus autem in primo instanti suae conceptionis plene vidit Deum per essentiam ... unde fides in eo esse non potuit.*'

49. C. E. Braaten and R. Harrisville (eds.), *The Historical Jesus and the Kerygmatic Christ*, Nashville: Abingdon Press 1974, p. 34.

50. Bultmann himself had no hesitation in describing the faith of Jesus, at least in an early book of his, *Jesus and the Word* (1926), New York: Scribner and London: Fontana Books 1958, p. 136, and at least the faith which Jesus recommended, if not his own personal faith: 'Faith is for him the power, in particular moments in life, to take seriously the conviction of the omnipotence of God; it is the certainty that in such particular moments God's activity is really experienced; it is the conviction that the distant God is really the God near at hand, if man will only relinquish his usual attitude and be ready to see the nearness of God.' But faith in Jesus as our Lord, he was convinced, should never depend on the uncertainty of such historical findings. We shall have something to say later on this separation of faith and history, à la Bultmann.

51. Though much recent theological literature on Jesus from Karl Rahner, Raymond Brown, Peter de Rosa, etc., has tried to persuade us to make this move.

52. Some Roman Catholic writers have begun to suggest tentatively that we should speak of the personal faith of Jesus. P. Schoonenberg, *The Christ*, New York: Herder and Herder 1971 and London: Sheed and Ward 1974, pp. 146-52, does so, but then he seems to me to suggest that Jesus was 'object' of his own faith also, and that point might be difficult to establish. Gabriel Moran offers solid defence of the attribution of personal faith to Jesus in his *Theology of Revelation*, New York: Herder and Herder 1966 and London: Search Press 1967, pp. 63-71. But the most substantial investigations along these lines are those of Ebeling, in *Word and Faith*, and E. Fuchs, *Studies of the Historical Jesus*, London: SCM Press 1964, though one has to make adjustments to the argument depending on one's view of the general description of faith offered by Fuchs and Ebeling.

53. See, for instance, G. Kittel (ed.), *Theological Dictionary of the New Testament I*, Grand Rapids: Eerdman's 1964, p. 218.

54. T. S. Eliot, 'Ash Wednesday', in *Collected Poems 1909-1962*, London: Faber and Faber and New York: Harcourt, Brace Jovanovich Inc. 1963, p. 102.

55. There is no original sin in the creation myths of Genesis: certainly not in the Priestly creation myth (1.2-4a); but no more than that in the Judaean creation myth (2.4b-3). In the latter myth, the serpent is one of God's creatures, the wisest of these. The only 'temptation' which comes from this creature of God is to seek knowledge or experience without limit (a union of all finite contraries: 'good and evil'). Such a quest brings first the experience of struggle, of suffering, of death. But we learn faith, as Hebrews will later inform us, from what we suffer. And though the tree of life is not available just now, God who sent us forth (3.23) on this hazardous odyssey also placed cherubim to keep for us the way to the tree of life. Eternal life is now at the end of our fateful freedom, not at the beginning of what Kiekergaard called our dreaming innocence.

56. The Greek need not be read 'although he was Son' here, for that goes against the logic of the argument: it was precisely by learning faith/obedience through suffering that he became the Son/high priest of the Hebrews myth. Incidentally, we have here an example of a New Testament text basing the development of the myth of the man Jesus precisely on his personal faith.

57. Philippians 2.6-11 obviously provides a parallel to the thought of Hebrews. Becoming obedient unto death cannot mean obeying (in the moral sense of that word) an explicit command to die. It means having a faith so radical and true that it is triumphant through death itself, the last enemy. I Timothy 6.11-16 compares the Christian's confession to Jesus' confession. I Peter is almost the equal of Hebrews in its insistence on Jesus' likeness to his followers, and holds up his trust during persecution in particular (2.23), as an example.

58. On food Jesus said: 'Not what goes into the mouth defiles a man, but what comes out of the mouth' (Matthew 15.11); on the subject of religious leaders, he said that men should listen to the teaching of Moses which they transmitted, that is, the traditional wording of their faith, but not imitate their oppressive search for power and honour and ostentation (Matthew 23.1-12). We have already seen his word on service and his word against the Temple. It does not matter whether these things were actually said in these words or not by the historical Jesus. They are clear and immediate implications of the religious faith he inspired in people, as the more perspicacious of his disciples saw.

59. See the relevant section of G. Bornkamm's *Jesus of Nazareth*, London: Hodder & Stoughton and New York: Harper and Bros 1960.

60. Vawter, *This Man Jesus*, p. 140.

5. The Myth that Jesus developed and the Myth that developed about Jesus

1. See Robert M. Grant's lucid discussion of Paul's attitude(s) to tradition in R. M. Grant et al., *Perspectives on Scripture and Tradition*, Notre Dame: Fides 1976, pp. 3-11.

2. See R. Bultmann, 'Paul' and 'Jesus and Paul', in *Existence and*

Faith, London: Fontana Books 1964, pp. 130-72, 217-39. 'Paul's theology is not dependent on Jesus' proclamation ... Paul was not Jesus' disciple, either directly or through the mediation of the original disciples. Indeed, he himself sharply rejects such mediation (Gal. 1.1) and affirms that he has received his gospel directly by revelation (Gal. 1.11f.). Naturally, he was acquainted with the kerygma of the church, else he could hardly have persecuted it. But what was the kerygma with which he was acquainted? In a word, it was the message that God had raised the crucified Jesus of Nazareth and had made him the Messiah' (pp. 219f.).

3. The so-called conflict stories in the gospels have their setting either in Galilee, where his opponents are usually described as scribes and Pharisees (Mark 2.1-3.6; Matthew 9.1-12.14; Luke 5.17-6.11), or in Jerusalem, where these are said to be joined by Sadducees and Herodians, priests and elders (Mark 11.27-12.44; Matthew 21.33-23.36; Luke 20.1-21.4). The former conflicts concern the forgiveness of sins, the calling of tax-collectors, eating with sinners, not fasting, plucking and eating and healing on the Sabbath. The latter conflicts concern the question of his authority, the parable of the wicked husbandmen, the tribute to Caesar, the resurrection, the great commandment, the Messiah as David's son, and the widow's mite.

4. For an account of Paul's life, see G. Bornkamm, *Paul*, London: Hodder & Stoughton and New York: Harper and Row 1971.

5. See, for instance, R. Bultmann, *Theology of the New Testament*, Vol. 1, New York: Scribner and London: SCM Press 1952, pp. 192ff.

6. A few perceptive Christian scholars and a number of indignant Jewish scholars – like Samuel Sandmel, *We Jews and Jesus*, New York: Oxford University Press 1965, p. 80 – have rightly protested against the Christian penchant to mistake, amongst other texts, Paul's point in Romans and Galatians, and to depict the Jewish law as dry and sterile, a burden and a yoke, from which Jesus was understood to liberate one *tout simple*. For though legalism exists where there is law – and where is there not? – what the Jew knew as a privilege he could not consider a burden, and whatever Jesus is thought to have done about law, he certainly did not leave his followers lawless.

7. In these main contexts from which this material is drawn Paul has, in fact, provided an analysis of the nature and destiny of law which is applicable far beyond the boundaries of rabbinic Judaism. He has illustrated here – Romans 1-8 and Galatians – from the formulations of his own tradition, some of the classic bonds between morality and religious faith. See my *Problems of Religious Faith*, Part Four and especially p. 265, for an analysis and a summary of these bonds between morality and faith, and particularly for some notes on the way in which the moral quest, so central to every human consciousness, can bring us to a keen sense of our contingency and so introduce us to the possibility of religious faith, or, as it has been put in these pages, can carry to us the claim of the Absolute.

8. See above p. 163.

9. No. 57 in *Poems of Gerard Manley Hopkins*, ed. Robert Bridges and

W. H. Gardner, London: Oxford University Press [3]1948, p. 96.

10. Although it does seem to the present writer that Herbert Braun's notorious formula – the christologies change, the anthropology remains the same – is a little too simple. For though he recognized the variations in the development of christology, he treats in far too cavalier a fashion the logical connection between these and the self-understanding of people in the world brought about by Jesus. H. Braun, 'The Meaning of New Testament Christology', in *God and Christ*, ed. R. W. Funk, New York: Harper 1968, pp. 89-127.

11. Uncertain as to where I should place Paul's major terms on that spectrum of human perception and expression which ranges from the most concrete image to the most abstract concept, I am using here a Hegelian-type term for something which Hegel thought characteristic of religious discourse, the intellectual symbol or inadequate concept, somewhere between the 'sensible symbol' of the artist and the perfect concept of the philosopher, containing and evoking some analysis of reality but with major appeal to sentiment and imagination. See the section on moral values in F. Grégoire, *Aux Sources de la Pensée de Marx, Hegel, Feuerbach*, Presses Universitaires de Louvain 1947.

12. See my *Life and Grace*, Dublin: Gill and Chicago: Pflaum 1966, and also 'Grace', *The Furrow* 24, 1973, pp. 338-52.

13. See above p. 94ff.

14. See Hans Küng, *On Being a Christian*, New York: Doubleday 1976 and London: Collins 1977, pp. 424-6. We have already noted that when the death of Jesus is explicitly mentioned in the myth about Jesus, the images of overcoming the negative features of existence tend to predominate. Presumably because of this negative leaning, the myth of the man who died also attracted to itself images and symbols drawn from the cultic practices of sacrificial immolations (see in particular the Epistle to the Hebrews), rituals which are no longer a feature of contemporary civilizations and whose symbolic or mythic power of communication is therefore largely lost on us.

15. Walter Kasper, *Jesus the Christ*, New York: Paulist Press and London: Burns and Oates 1976, pp.100ff.; Oscar Cullmann, *The Christology of the New Testament*, London: SCM Press and Philadelphia: Westminster 1959, pp. 137ff.; R. H. Fuller, *The Foundations of New Testament Christology*, London: Lutterworth Press 1965, p. 130; H. E. Tödt, *The Son of Man in the Synoptic Tradition*, London: SCM Press and Philadelphia: Westminster 1965.

16. Perrin, *Rediscovering the Teaching of Jesus*, pp. 164-98.

17. Conzelmann, *The Theology of Luke*, pp. 190ff.

18. See Norman Perrin's *The New Testament: An Introduction*, New York: Harcourt Brace Jovanovich 1974, for a brief but up-to-date redaction criticism of the gospels.

19. Küng, *On Being a Christian*, pp. 348-89, is correct in suggesting that since the titles are used to alert different peoples to the real importance of Jesus, it is the achievement of Jesus which should be investigated rather than the titles. But to convey the impression that the titles are therefore simply interchangeable is to ignore the development of

the myth of Jesus, the variety of New Testament christologies and, hence, the distinctive contribution of each individual title.

20. W. F. Albright, *From the Stone Age to Christianity*, New York: Doubleday 1957, p. 195.

6. *Faith in the Founder: the Question of Divinity in Human Form*

1. Faiths do not exist in sacred books or buildings, in sacred objects or acts, but only in the spirits of those who write and read such books, who build and frequent such buildings, and who use such objects and perform such acts.

2. W. Rahula, *What the Buddha Taught*, New York: Grove Press 1959.

3. The word 'sraosha' is like the Hebrew and Greek for hear/obey.

4. R. C. Zaehner, *The Dawn and Twilight of Zoroastrianism*,London: Weidenfeld and Nicolson and New York: Putnam's Sons 1961, pp. 43f.

5. See H. A. R. Gibb, 'Islam', in R. C. Zaehner, *The Concise Encyclopedia of Living Faiths*, London: Hutchinson 1971 and New York: McGraw-Hill 1975, pp. 453ff.

6. Raymond Brown is one proponent of this thesis – see his *Jesus, God and Man*, Milwaukee: Bruce and London: Geoffrey Chapman 1968 – since he thinks that Jesus is certainly called God in three places in the New Testament (Hebrews 1.8f.; John 1.1; John 20.28), and probably in more. But even in the three cases Brown finds that there are difficulties to be overcome before the desired exegesis is obtained.

7. Norman Pittenger, *Christology Reconsidered*, London: SCM Press 1970, p. 42. The Fathers of the church, Pittenger correctly points out, nowhere make an absolute identification of Jesus and God.

8. See the section on Hellenistic-Jewish titles of Jesus in Fuller's *The Foundations of New Testament Christology*; also Perrin, *The New Testament: An Introduction*, pp. 51ff.; also Bruce Vawter, *This Man Jesus*, pp. 169ff. The converse of the statement in the text above is that there is something of God in creation, and something Godlike especially about man.

9. See the conclusion to Hermann's *Kyrios und Pneuma*.

10. See the introduction to Cullmann's *Christology of the New Testament*.

11. This discrimination is sometimes expressed as crudely as by saying that Greek divinities were but basic forms of cosmic reality – see K. Rahner, following Kittel's *Theological Dictionary of the New Testament* (theos), *Theological Investigations*, Vol. 1, London: Darton, Longman and Todd 1961, p. 90 – a grudgingly qualified slander on the best of Greek theology and a partisan ignoring of the anthropomorphism and indeed the polytheism of much popular Jewish and Christian thought.

12. G. L. Prestige, *Fathers and Heretics*, London: SPCK 1940, p. 345.

13. J. Pelikan, *The Christian Tradition*, University of Chicago Press 1975, p. 37.

14. Elaborate formal schemes, explaining how such adjustment is made, were worked out in the Platonic tradition as the doctrine of the three ways, the *via affirmativa*, the *via eminentiae*, and the *via negationis*, and in the high Scholastic tradition in the doctrine of analogy

developed by the great commentators on Aquinas. On the contrary, it appears to be a thematic denial of the possibility of such analytic adjustments, at least beyond a certain point, that allows M. Durant to argue the ultimate unintelligibility of the Christian doctrine of the Trinity, the final theological flowering of the developed myth of Jesus (see Durant's *Theology and Intelligibility*, London and Boston: Routledge and Kegan Paul 1973).

15. Quoted from some notes of Gerard Watson on the influence of Greek thought on early Christian thinkers.

16. A. H. Armstrong (ed.), *The Cambridge History of Later Greek and Early Medieval Philosophy*, Cambridge University Press 1967, p. 93. Stoicism contributed little or nothing directly to Christian thought about God in the development of the acknowledgment. The basic materialism of Stoic philosophy made it mostly unpalatable to Christian thinkers. Cicero, who transmitted Stoic influence to Christian moral thought in particular, himself wondered how the totally immanent Logos divinity of the Stoics could be thought to be a living being (*De Natura Deorum* 1, 36). But he is aware of the Platonic tradition about a God who cannot be named, so transcendent is he (*De Natura Deorum* 1, 12), and in any case, as Watson says, Cicero found references to divinity a good rhetorical weapon in his fight for law and order (G. Watson, 'Pagan Philosophy and Christian Ethics', in J. P. Mackey (ed.), *Morals, Law and Authority*, Chicago: Pflaum 1969, p. 69).

17. J. N. D. Kelly lists absolute transcendence and uniqueness, unicity of God and his absolutely incommunicable *ousia* as features of Arianism – see his sections on Arianism in both *Early Christian Doctrines*, London: A & C. Black 1958, and *Early Christian Creeds*, London: Longmans ²1960. Does he mean that all this was distinctive of Arians and so somehow constitutive or originative of the heresy? If so, he can hardly be correct, since it is a common heritage and a prize achievement of the religious spirit.

18. Justin Martyr's *First Apology* presents a list of 'sons of God' from the Greek religious tradition and instances Hermes (Mercury) as 'the angelic word (logos) of God'.

19. W. B. Yeats, 'To the Rose upon the Rood of Time', *Collected Poems*, London: Macmillan 1950, p. 35.

20. R. V. Sellers, *Two Ancient Christologies*, London: SPCK 1954, p. 245, has seen very well that an emphasis on the cosmic Christ is essential if Christianity is not to die. This insight is much to be preferred to that other attitude so often found which traces the roots of Arianism to an emphasis on the cosmic functions of the Word of God. T. E. Pollard, whose *Johannine Christology and the Early Church*, Cambridge University Press 1970, is a very valuable survey of our two titles during the relevant centuries, too easily concludes that Son must always predominate over Word, and especially over the cosmic functions of the latter, if heresy is to be long avoided, and, further, he too easily uses this contention as a kind of criterion which, it seems to me at least, he then forces on his evidence in order to separate the good writers from the bad.

21. From Theophilus and the second century onward some Christian writers are developing the doctrine of *creatio ex nihilo* in conscious contrast to Neo-Platonists (amongst others), partly, I presume, because they cannot see the real possibilities for the affirmation of transcendence in the Platonic tradition.

22. See Henry Chadwick's chapter on Philo in Armstrong's *The Cambridge History of Later Greek and Early Medieval Philosophy*, esp. p. 143.

23. See Pollard, *Johannine Christology and the Early Church*, pp. 56f.

24. Pollard translates this: 'The outflow and assignment of the whole', but he still cannot deny the overall subordinationist impression of the passage. He does, however, somehow maintain that the passage does not imply 'an inferior . . . God'. See op. cit., pp. 68f.

25. Maurice Wiles, 'In Defence of Arius', *Working Papers in Doctrine*, London: SCM Press 1976, pp. 28-37.

26. G. L. Prestige, *God in Patristic Thought*, pp. 37ff.

27. For the text of this letter of Arius to Eusebius of Nicomedia, written *c.* 318, see G. Bardy, *Recherches sur Saint Lucien d'Antioche et son Ecole*, Paris: Beauchesne 1936, pp. 226ff.

28. See Bardy, op. cit., pp. 235ff.

29. In Platonic theology, in the affirmative way one said what one thought one could say about God, e.g. that he is good; in the way of eminence one emended one's statement to add that God was eminently good, and, finally, faced with the thought that one did not know just how eminently good he was, that is, how far above human goodness is divine goodness, then, in the way of negation, the *via negativa*, one denied that God was good, as one understood that term in one's human way.

30. Bardy, *Recherches*, p. 275.

31. For an English translation of this letter see E. R. Hardy, *Christology of the Later Fathers*, London: SCM Press and Philadelphia: Westminster Press 1954, p. 339.

32. 'In Defence of Arius'.

33. See above pp. 135-42.

34. See my 'The Faith of the Historical Jesus', *Horizons* 3, 1976, pp. 155-74, for further details of the argument here.

35. There are many fine works on the Trinity which may be consulted by those who wish to investigate the fullest extent of the application of the trinitarian formula, e.g. K. Rahner, *The Trinity*, London: Burns and Oates and New York: Herder and Herder 1970, and many fine historical studies are available to those who wish to trace further the development of these trinitarian theologies, amongst them the works of Kelly and Prestige quoted in this chapter.

36. Prestige, *Fathers and Heretics*, p. 88; *God in Patristic Thought*, p. 168.

37. John McIntyre, *The Shape of Christology*, London: SCM Press 1966, p. 98.

38. It need hardly be stated that the philosophical anthropologies in which orthodoxy is stated are largely a matter of cultural preference, though J. Liébaert, for instance, behaves in his history of early christol-

ogy as if a Platonic anthropology were *de rigueur* (*Christologie von der Apostolischen Zeit bis zum Konzil von Chalcedon*, Freiburg: Herder 1965).

39. See my 'The Faith of the Historical Jesus' for details on the small extent of modern christological literature which discusses Jesus as himself a man of faith, in comparison with the literature which has recently been inviting us to think of Jesus as sharing our human condition in every other way (ignorance of the future, etc.), and despite Rahner's oft-repeated insistence that openness to the address of God, to which faith is the response, is almost the definition of the human condition.

40. The most trenchant criticism of Chalcedon's christology, at least as a vehicle for modern preaching, is carried through in P. Schoonenberg's *The Christ*, pp. 54ff.

41. See J. M. Carmody and T. E. Clarke (eds), *Word and Redeemer: Christology in the Fathers*, New Jersey: Paulist Press 1966, pp. 104f.

42. Prestige, *Fathers and Heretics*, p. 167.

43. Carmody and Clarke, *Word and Redeemer*, pp. 52, 93 – the phrase was Apollonarius', though Cyril did not know that, and it did not matter.

44. The corresponding Western formula, two natures, one person, goes back at least to Tertullian. See Liébaert, *Christologie*, pp. 43-6.

45. H. Denzinger, A. Schönmetzer, *Enchiridion Symbolorum*, Rome: Herder 1965, nn. 556f.

46. A. Grillmeier, *Christ in Christian Tradition*, London: Mowbray and New York: Sheed and Ward 1965, p. 377.

47. Schoonenberg, *The Christ*, pp. 67ff.

48. Leontius worked out this definition at the beginning of a work entitled, significantly, *Against the Nestorians and Eutychians*.

49. Other and more subtle forms of Apollinarianism appeared in the course of the Christian tradition, in the form of conferring, out of reverence no doubt, on the humanity of Jesus such privileges as the enjoyment of the beatific vision from the moment of his conception, full knowledge of all things, past, present and future, and immeasurable sanctifying grace. This all had the effect, of course, of making his share in the actual human condition scarcely credible, but since it has been adequately dealt with in modern christology by the Rahners, the Browns, the de Rosas, and many, many others, there is no need to deal with it again here.

7. Christian Faith and Human History

1. Bultmann, *The Theology of the New Testament* I, p. 26.

2. The historian 'does not solicit mere assent but a quality of assent' (Van A. Harvey, *The Historian and the Believer* p. 121).

3. R. Bultmann, *Existence and Faith*, pp. 202-16.

4. Oxford: Basil Blackwell and Philadelphia: Westminster Press 1971.

5. To Bultmann, of course, incarnation is a myth, but myth, whether Bultmann realized it or not, is a way of telling the truth which has perennial value. For an extensive discussion of the mythic nature of

incarnation theology, see the over-publicized John Hick (ed.), *The Myth of God Incarnate*, London: SCM Press and Philadelphia: Westminster Press 1977.

6. R. Bultmann, 'The Primitive Christian Kerygma and the Historical Jesus', in Carl E. Braaten and Roy A. Harrisville, *The Historical Jesus and the Kerygmatic Christ*, Nashville: Abingdon Press 1964, p. 17.

7. Bultmann, 'The Primitive Christian Kerygma', p. 18.

8. Bultmann, *Existence and Faith*, pp. 209, 208.

9. Bultmann, *Existence and Faith*, p. 212.

10. Bultmann, *Existence and Faith*, p. 214.

11. Bultmann, 'The Primitive Christian Kerygma', p. 16.

12. Bultmann, 'The Primitive Christian Kerygma', p. 20.

13. Bultmann, *Existence and Faith*, p. 239.

14. Bultmann, *Existence and Faith*, p. 232.

15. See section VI of Bultmann's essay 'The Primitive Christian Kerygma and the Historical Jesus'.

16. Bultmann, *Existence and Faith*, p. 234.

17. See, for instance, Bultmann's treatment of the appearances stories in his commentary on *The Gospel of John*, pp. 683-99.

18. Bultmann, 'The Primitive Christian Kerygma', p. 25.

19. Notice how Bultmann *contrasts* legitimizing with faith, so that one rules out the other: 'Faith does not at all arise from the acceptance of historical facts. That would only lead to legitimizing, whereas the kerygma really calls for faith' ('The Primitive Christian Kerygma', p. 25).

20. Miguel de Unamuno, *Our Lord Don Quixote*, Princeton University Press 1976, p. 439.

21. Unamuno, *Our Lord Don Quixote*, p. 56.

22. See the Appendix for the birth and baptism of Jesus.

23. It would be simply malicious to suggest that those who make the personal resurrection of Jesus himself – as we have termed it – an article of faith rather than an item of historically probable knowledge, are denying it.

Index of Names

Index of Subjects